Ph

The Future of Events and Festivals

The growth of events and festivals has been significant over the last decade, and a wide range of skills is essential to ensure those events are successful. This requirement has been instrumental in stimulating the creation of more tertiary education opportunities to develop events management knowledge. As the discipline develops, knowledge requires direction in order to understand the changing advances in society.

This is the first book to take a futures approach to understanding event management. A systematic and pattern-based understanding is used to determine the likelihood of future events and trends. Using blue skies scenarios to provide a vision of the future of events, capturing not only how the events industry is changing but also important issues that will affect events now as well as in the future. Chapters include analysis of sustainability, security, impacts of social media and design at both mega event and community level, and review a good range of different types of events from varying geographical regions. A final section captures the contributions of each chapter through the formation of a conceptual map for a future research agenda.

Written by leading academics in the field, this groundbreaking book will be a valuable reference point for educators, researchers and industry professionals.

Ian Yeoman is a specialist tourism futurologist who believes in *Star Trek*, an eternal optimist, is Sunderland AFC mad and studying towards a higher doctorate.

Martin Robertson is a Lecturer in Event Management at Victoria University, Melbourne (Australia). His research and publications focus on festivals and destination image, socio-cultural impact, development and evaluation, and event leadership and professionalism. He has co-edited several books and special issue peer-reviewed journals. He is passionate about tourism and events.

Una McMahon-Beattie is Head of the Department for Hospitality and Tourism Management in the University of Ulster (United Kingdom). Her research interests include tourism and event marketing, revenue management and tourism futures. She is an editor/author of a number of books, book chapters and journals articles in these areas.

Elisa Backer is a Senior Lecturer in tourism at Federation University, Australia (formerly called University of Ballarat). She previously lectured at Southern Cross University and prior to academia worked in industry. Elisa is considered a leading world expert in the field of Visiting Friends and Relatives (VFR) travel.

Karen A. Smith is Associate Professor in tourism management at Victoria University of Wellington, New Zealand. Her research areas include event and tourism volunteering, event ticketing and distribution and the future of events and festivals. Karen has also co-edited *Event Volunteering* in the Routledge Advances in Event Research Series.

Routledge Advances in Event Research Series
Edited by Warwick Frost and Jennifer Laing
Department of Marketing, Tourism and Hospitality,
La Trobe University, Australia

Events, Society and Sustainability
Edited by Tomas Pernecky and Michael Lück

Exploring the Social Impacts of Events
Edited by Greg Richards, Maria deBrito and Linda Wilks

Commemorative Events
Warwick Frost and Jennifer Laing

Power, Politics and International Events
Edited by Udo Merkel

Event Audiences and Expectations
Jo Mackellar

Event Portfolio Planning and Management
A holistic approach
Vassilios Ziakas

Conferences and Conventions
 A research perspective
Judith Mair

Fashion, Design and Events
Edited by Kim M. Williams, Jennifer Laing and Warwick Frost

Food and Wine Events in Europe
Edited by Alessio Cavicchi and Cristina Santini

Event Volunteering
*Edited by Karen Smith, Leonie Lockstone-Binney, Kirsten Holmes and
Tom Baum*

The Future of Events and Festivals

Edited by Ian Yeoman, Martin Robertson, Una McMahon-Beattie, Elisa Backer and Karen A. Smith

Routledge
Taylor & Francis Group

LONDON AND NEW YORK

First published 2015
by Routledge
2 Park Square, Milton Park, Abingdon, Oxon OX14 4RN

and by Routledge
711 Third Avenue, New York, NY 10017

Routledge is an imprint of the Taylor & Francis Group, an informa business

British Library Cataloguing-in-Publication Data
A catalogue record for this book is available from the British Library

Library of Congress Cataloging-in-Publication Data
The future of events & festivals / edited by Ian Yeoman, Martin Robertson, Una McMahon-Beattie, Elisa Backer and Karen A. Smith.
   pages cm. — (Routledge advances in event research series)
  1. Special events—Planning.   2. Special events—Management.
3. Festivals—Planning.   4. Festivals—Management.   I. Yeoman, Ian.
  GT3405.F88 2014
  394.2—dc23
  2014007930

ISBN: 978-0-415-82462-0 (hbk)
ISBN: 978-0-203-37039-1 (ebk)

Typeset in Times
by Apex CoVantage, LLC

To the best redhead in New Zealand who often accompanied me to the ballet, comedy festivals and other music events whilst researching this book but who insists that I have no sense of comedy timing or a future in karaoke. I. Yeoman

To Ishbel, my current and future special event. M. Robertson

To Graham, James and Lucy who make every day a great event. U. McMahon-Beattie

To my husband Edward, and to my four children, James, Chantelle, Jonathan and Sebastian, whose futures I hope are filled with many wonderful festivals and events. E. Backer

To Simon, Sam and Ben and many happy event experiences. K. A. Smith

Contents

x   *Contents*

Figures

Tables

Editors

Ian Yeoman, PhD, is a specialist tourism futurologist who believes in *Star Trek*, an eternal optimist, is Sunderland AFC mad and enjoys cooking. Ian is a Trainee Professor at Victoria University of Wellington (New Zealand) who is studying towards a higher doctorate. For further details visit www.tomorrowstourist. com.

Martin Robertson is a Lecturer in Event Management at Victoria University, Melbourne (Australia). His research and publications focus on festivals and destination image, socio-cultural impact, development and evaluation, and event leadership and professionalism. He has co-edited several books and special issue peer-reviewed journals. He is a passionate about tourism and events.

Una McMahon-Beattie, PhD, is Head of Department for Hospitality and Tourism Management in the University of Ulster (United Kingdom). Her research interests include tourism and event marketing, revenue management and tourism futures. She is an editor/author of a number of books, book chapters and journals articles in these areas.

Elisa Backer, PhD, is a Senior Lecturer in tourism at Federation University, Australia (formerly called University of Ballarat). She previously lectured at Southern Cross University and prior to academia worked in industry. Elisa is considered a leading world expert in the field of Visiting Friends and Relatives (VFR) travel.

Karen A. Smith, PhD, is Associate Professor in tourism management at Victoria University of Wellington, New Zealand. Her research areas include event and tourism volunteering, event ticketing and distribution and the future of events and festivals. Karen has also co-edited *Event Volunteering* in the Routledge Advances in Event Research Series.

Notes on contributors

Vida Bajc, PhD, is Assistant Professor of Sociology at Methodist University, United States, and a 2013/14 Fulbright Fellow at Adam Mickiewicz University, Poland. Her research is focused on surveillance and security in collective public life, global events, Christian pilgrimage and inter-church relations in Jerusalem, and the ethnographic method.

Tom Baum is Professor of International Tourism and Hospitality Management, University of Strathclyde, Scotland. Tom's research focuses on the social construction of work in the low-skills economy, contextualised to the tourism and hospitality sector. Over 30 years, Tom has published more than ten books and 200 scholarly papers.

Peter Bolan is Director of International Travel and Tourism Management at the University of Ulster in Northern Ireland. He holds a master's degree in eTourism and a PhD in Film-Induced Tourism. His research interests and specialisms include film- and media-induced tourism, eBusiness, social media and mobile apps in tourism.

Steve Brown, PhD, is Head of Tourism and the Event Design and Management programs at Flinders University (Australia) and is internationally recognised in the field of event design. He consults for organisations, festivals and events and has written chapters for a number of event texts and published a book on event design.

Barbara A. Carmichael, PhD, is a Professor in the Department of Geography and Environmental Studies and the Director of the Laurier Centre for Research in Entrepreneurship in the School of Business and Economics at Wilfrid Laurier University, Waterloo, Ontario, Canada. Her research interests are in tourism entrepreneurship, quality tourism experiences, special events and resident attitudes towards tourism.

Clare Carruthers, PhD, is a Lecturer in tourism and marketing in the Ulster Business School, University of Ulster, Northern Ireland. Her research interests include the role of cultural festivals and events in culture-led regeneration, the role of the European City of Culture in urban tourism development and urban tourism destination marketing.

Alan Clarke is Professor at the University of Pannonia in Veszprém, Hungary. He has published widely on culture, tourism, hospitality, festivals and events, with his research currently focused on communities and meanings in the experience economy. He is still a Sheffield Wednesday supporter, so he has firsthand experience of the creation of local meaning!

Adrian Devine, PhD, is a Lecturer in the Ulster Business School at the University of Ulster, Northern Ireland. He is also the course director for the BSc (Hons) Leisure and Events Management. His current research interests include the impact of the recession on sports events and the lessons event organisers can learn from history.

Larry Dwyer is Professor of Travel and Tourism Economics in the School of Marketing, Australian School of Business, University of New South Wales. He publishes widely in the areas of tourism economics, management, planning and policy, with over 200 publications in international journals.

Matt Frew, PhD, is a Senior Lecturer in Event Management within the School of Tourism at Bournemouth University (United Kingdom). With over 15 years of industrial experience gleaned across the cultural industries his current interest centres on the impact of new media technologies in the production and consumption of cultures of co-created convergence.

Warwick Frost, PhD, is Associate Professor in the Department of Marketing, Tourism and Hospitality at La Trobe University (Australia). His research interests include events, heritage tourism, national parks, and tourism and the media. He is currently working on a book examining the imagining of the American West through film and tourism.

Donald Getz retired in July 2009 from his full-time academic position at the University of Calgary, Canada, where he remains Professor Emeritus. He held a pro rata appointment as a Professor in the School of Tourism, The University of Queensland (Australia) until March 2014, and he is a Visiting Professor at several other universities.

Kirsten Holmes, PhD, is Senior Lecturer in tourism at Curtin University (Australia). She has 15 years' experience of researching volunteerism and has presented her work at international conferences and published in leading journals. Her book *Managing Volunteers in Tourism* (with Karen Smith) was published by Elsevier Butterworth-Heinemann in 2009.

Leo Jago, PhD, is Professor of Hospitality and Events at the University of Surrey. He was formerly the Chief Economist for tourism and General Manager of Tourism Research Australia. Prior to this he spent 15 years as a Research Professor and Director of university research centres in Australia and the United Kingdom. His personal research activities have focused on event management and evaluation.

Allan Stewart Jepson, PhD, is Senior Academic in Event Studies, and a researcher within the Marketing Insight Research Unit (MIRU), University of Hertfordshire

(United Kingdom). He has developed undergraduate and postgraduate degree programmes in Tourism, Hospitality and Event Management. He has extensive experience in community festival and events praxis and research.

Jennifer Laing, PhD, is a Senior Lecturer in the Department of Marketing, Tourism and Hospitality at La Trobe University (Australia). Her research interests include travel narratives, the societal role of events and adventure travel. With Warwick Frost, Jennifer has co-written books on commemorative events and links between books and travel.

Gavin Lees, PhD, is a Lecturer in marketing at Victoria University (Australia). His research interests include consumer behaviour, marketing management, empirical generalisationalist research methods and behaviourist theories. He has published articles on radio listening, radio research, financial services, market research and concept testing.

Leonie Lockstone-Binney, PhD, is Associate Professor in Event Management at Victoria University (Australia). Leonie's main area of research expertise relates to volunteering, specifically in event and tourism settings. Leonie has published in several top-tier journals including *Leisure Sciences*, *Tourism Analysis* and *International Journal of Hospitality Management*.

Kelley A. McClinchey has a PhD in Geography and is a part-time Lecturer in the Department of Geography and Environmental Studies at Wilfrid Laurier University, Waterloo, Ontario, Canada. Her research interests include sense of place and tourist experiences, cultural festivals, mobility and migration, and place representation and place marketing.

David McGillivray holds a Chair in Event and Digital Cultures at University of the West of Scotland. His research interests focus on the contemporary significance of events and festivals as markers of identity. His current research focuses on the value of digital media within the saturated media landscape.

Andrew McLoughlin is Director of Postgraduate Programmes at Hollings Faculty, Manchester Metropolitan University (United Kingdom) and Senior Lecturer in International Events Management. Andrew has worked in the event industry for over 25 years. He is currently a doctoral candidate, and his research interests include event marketing, event design and experiential activity within events.

Gayle McPherson holds a Chair in Events and Cultural Policy at University of the West of Scotland. Her research interests revolve around the interventions of the local and national state in events and festivity of all types and the social and cultural impacts of events on communities.

Judith Mair, PhD, is a Senior Lecturer in Event Management at the University of Queensland, Australia. She is joint Editor-in-Chief of the *International Journal of Event and Festival Management*. Her research interests include climate change, sustainable tourism and events, and the social and environmental impacts of festivals and events.

Nyasha Musarurwa grew up in Harare, Zimbabwe. She was awarded her bachelor's degree in Tourism Management from Victoria University of Wellington (New Zealand) in 2012, and was awarded the 2011–2012 Summer Scholarship for research in the area of music events. She enjoys cooking, swimming and taking long nature walks.

Debbie Sadd lectures on the BA and MSc Event Management programmes at Bournemouth University in the United Kingdom. She focuses on marketing and strategic management. Her research interests include the social impacts of mega-events, stakeholder management, evaluating the impacts of cultural events, and frameworks for assessing the impacts of major events.

Louise Todd, PhD, is a Lecturer in Festival and Event Management at Edinburgh Napier University, United Kingdom. Her background is in visual art, communications, and marketing of festivals and events. Louise's research interests include the arts, festivals and events, brand image and relationships, event design and experience, and qualitative and visual methods.

Hans Wessblad has a PhD from Lund University in the area of High Reliability Organizations and is a Senior Lecturer at Linnaeus School of Business and Economics, Linnaeus University, Sweden. His research interests include events management, culinary tourism, tourism consumption dynamics, general destination development and cultural economy.

Carol Wheatley has a BSc (Hons) in Pharmaceutical Chemistry (UK) and a MBA (New Zealand). Her background includes self-employment within the Pharmaceutical and Veterinary industries. She is currently freelancing in editing, proofreading, publishing, research, and writing, with a focus on academic publications.

Foreword

Events and festivals: preparations, successes and the future

Brendan McClements
Chief Executive Officer, Victorian Major Event
Company Limited, Australia

As the world changes – and as countries, cities and regions change – so too do our major public events. Here in Victoria, Australia, we are immensely proud of the way in which our portfolio of major events speaks to its recipients. But we cannot be complacent. We know that we need to engage, enthral and amaze. This is true for everyone, whether they are spectator, viewer, performer, competitor, organiser or simply someone who has been standing by and enjoying the spectacle. This requires painstaking research, painstaking planning and – very often – courage. We need to be sure that what we plan now will be a success in the future when the event is held.

It is not surprising then – when so much is at stake – that the capacity to look into the future, to determine trends and to make preparations to offer the best events for that future is crucial. Whether it is one year, two years, five years, ten years, 15 years or 20 years, the more we know the better we are able to make dreams come alive. We know that thinking about, understanding and preparing for the future has to happen now – as much as it does in the future!

I, and many other people like me, and those involved at every other level of major event and festival provision, have looked forward to a book such as this one.

Part 1
Setting the scene
Past, present and future

Part 1

Setting the scene

Past, present and future

1 An introduction to the future

*Ian Yeoman, Martin Robertson,
Una McMahon-Beattie, Elisa Backer
and Karen A. Smith*

Future points

- The first book to discuss the future of events and festivals.
- Each chapter begins with a series of points as indicators to the future.
- Each chapter concludes with a discussion on the implications of the future on the present.

What is the present state of events and festivals research?

The growth of the events industry and the provision of events, in all its many forms, is documented often, and by many. However, there has been far less said about the growth of its content, of its research base and the progress of this research in the future. Lockstone-Binney, Robertson and Junek (2013: 176) comment that core areas of event management knowledge will 'need to be rebalanced with new knowledge areas to ensure that the events industry is ready to adapt to global competition, the rapidly changing business environment and possible global crisis'. For some time, Professor Don Getz has charted the evolution of events as an area of study and research, its capacity to progress in new directions, and the opportunity to create new discourses (Getz, 2007, 2008, 2012). He suggests events can be considered as an area of study, and that it can develop with – as well as go beyond – the management disciplines, and, accordingly, build interdisciplinary theory. Currently, while there are many researchers representing an array of disciplines involved in the discussion of festivals and events, they rarely work together.

Similarly, while there is some agreement that professionalisation of the events industry should go hand-in-hand with increased academic credibility for it as an area of studies (Robertson, Junek and Lockstone-Binney 2014), it is often inhibited in doing so. Hamstrung by the pragmatic approach of event organisers and the preponderance of research related to the economics of events (Davies, Coleman and Ramchandani 2013), there may now be a paradigm shift in research related to festivals and events. This is indicated in the diverse range of methodologies applied in current work (Mair and Whitford

2013). Nonetheless, at a time when there is great opportunity to surge forward, there continues to be much critical introspection by event (studies) researchers and educators (Baum, Lockstone-Binney and Robertson 2013). One vital area that has received remarkably little coverage – and may be indicative of that introspection – is future studies. It is for this reason that this book is an important one.

Making explanatory claims

Prediction is a statement about the way things will happen in the future (Bergman, Karlsson and Axelsson 2010), in which the outcome is expected from an ontological perspective. Therefore, the future is informed upon expertise as inductively valid. An inductively valid future is a premise of strong evidence: probable, explained and truthful; thus the arguments presented are based on what will happen rather than what could happen. Some would say in the field of future studies that prediction is a naive scientific activity in which a single view is too precise and narrow and cannot be achieved (Hojer and Mattsson 2006; Strand 1999). However, if a prediction is based upon causal layers (Slaughter 1996) in which arguments are captured, linked and analysed, a prediction does have a conclusion, which is important for business. What Blackman (1994) and Slaughter (1996) argue is not whether a prediction is right or wrong but whether it is robust enough, based upon a process of getting to the future and conclusions that are drawn in order to make a prediction.

Events and festivals futures, as presented in this collection of writing, make explanatory claims about the future. Some are truthful, some less truthful and some are fantasy (or very uncertain). Explanatory claim presumes an argumentation of explanation which Habermas (1984) proposes as representatively (i.e. distinguishes between what is and what seems to be said), expressively (i.e. distinguishes between what the individual is and what he or she pretends to be) and to develop common values (i.e. distinguishes between what and what ought to be); thus the contributors explain the future phenomena of events and festivals. What the contributors do with different degree is truthfulness. Truthfulness in its absolute format is an exact and precise future – something that is clinical. Contributors in the volume who follow this high degree of certainty include Bajc in chapter fourteen looking at security and surveillance, and Wessblad, with a focus on sustainability in chapter ten.

From quite a different perspective, some other contributors speculate about the future and draw upon what might seem to be science fiction to demonstrate the future, using the important futures question, *What if?* This is evidenced in the work by Yeoman *et al.* (chapter four) and McLoughlin (chapter eighteen). Importantly, combined, the collection of all the contribution represents a spectrum of knowledge that draws from leading minds in events and festivals academia. This will assist industry, community and academia to make sense of the future – in recognition that this is, ultimately, the place where everyone will be.

Contributors

Setting the scene: past, present and future

Devine and Carruthers in chapter two, *Back to the future: analysing history to plan for tomorrow*, reflect upon the past as a representation of the future, thus allowing futurists to create a framework for response and preparedness. Getz leads the debate about the fundamental role of events from a social, symbolic and economic exchange perspective in chapter three. *The forms and functions of planned events: past and future* embroils readers in the drivers of change focused around present legitimacy and political discourse predicting that the future will have larger public events, citing that this is because of their capacity to meet multiple goals and to attract wide audiences for special-interest tourist segments. Yeoman and colleagues in chapter four, *Scenarios for the future of events and festivals: Mick Jagger at 107 and Edinburgh Fringe*, consider two scenarios as demonstrations of future possibilities. First, *Heritage rock: Mick Jagger plays Woodstock at 107* portrays an ageing and ageless society from a music festival perspective. Second, *Edinburgh Fringe 2050* demonstrates how technology *is* changing and *could* change the comedy festival experience. The chapter identifies a number of themes that are significant for the future of events and festivals including the contribution to life and well-being, liminal experiences, nostalgia and collection of cultural capital. Yeoman and colleagues make explanatory claims on the future, but leave readers pondering, *What if* this were to happen?

Contested issues, thoughts and solutions

In chapter five, *Scotland in 2025: dependent or independent event nation?*, Frew and colleagues discuss Scotland as example of a nation vexed by questions about independence and the role of events and culture while also defining distinction in an age of acceleration. Drawing upon two scenarios, they present Scotland as a nation where events and cultural policy are deployed in a dynamic discourse of identity. Events and culture are positioned as key players in a global game in which the formulaic demands of the corporate agenda clash with the vibrancy of local community culture. The chapter concludes that a power and policy shift is emerging as communities connect and digitally disrupt the neo-liberal approach to events. Jepson and Clarke in chapter six, *The future of power decision making in community festivals*, reveal the existence of a multitude of stakeholder relationships, connected and enforced in different ways. In chapter seven, *Industry perceptions of events futures*, Backer discusses the perceptions amongst event managers concerning the future of tourism events. She indicates a belief that in the future large events may be more professionally run, suggesting that technology will enable spectators to benefit from improved transit routes and virtual experiences. Improvements to health and an ageing population may also extend the age bracket of event staff and event attendees. In chapter eight, *Economic evaluation of special events: challenges for the future*, Dwyer and Jago demonstrate the importance of evaluating the economic contribution that special events make – but only as one contribution to communities. The chapter gives an overview of the techniques that have been used to assess the economic impact of special events, arguing that computable general equilibrium modelling is the most credible approach. However, economic impact assessments can give contradictory results to a cost-benefit analysis, highlighting the need to integrate the two methods to give more consistent outcomes. The chapter concludes that there is a need to broaden the base of special event evaluations. In so doing events will be more able to demonstrate their true potential and secure a more sustainable future.

Chapter nine, *The greening of events: exploring future trends and issues*, by Frost and colleagues, considers the growing trend towards environmentally sustainable or *green* events – with a high degree of truth claim. Using a scenario planning approach focused on 2050 they highlight eight key drivers, which in the future are likely to affect future levels of sustainability. These are economic and demographic inequities; increasing urbanisation; existential authenticity; levels of environmental consciousness; the regulatory paradigm; green communities; the growth in corporate social responsibility; and technological developments. Four scenarios are developed, which each represent alternative possible futures, based on analysis of the impacts of the identified drivers. Continuing the theme of sustainability, in chapter ten, *The future is green: a case study of Malmoe, Sweden*, Wessbald offers a visionary future in which Malmoe has an ambition of becoming more sustainable – environmentally and socially. This chapter describes the launching of a sustainable 'hospitality and events' city project and identifies the developing process into essential 'pieces' for progress. The Malmoe case indicates that patience and persistence in changing people's minds is the road to a sustainable hospitality and event city.

In chapter eleven, *The future of local community festivals and meanings of place in an increasingly mobile world*, McClinchey and Carmichael focus on the implications of increasing cultural mobilities, uneven power struggles and the lack of connection with place for the future of festivals. They suggest the future of urban festivals lies in their ability to conceptualise space differently and ground place and its meaning through locals' conceptualisations of culture, place and identity. Todd in chapter twelve, *Developing brand relationships theory for festivals*, illustrates the significance of the interpersonal relationship paradigm to consumers and brands in a future festivalscape scenario. Here, primary generators of change are technological advancement, channel fragmentation, and a power shift from brand owners to consumers. Further shaping the future festivalscape are provision and consumption modes; consumers; and increased substitutability fuelled by digital connectivity. To survive, future festivals must develop positive, reciprocal and enduring consumer brand relationships. In chapter fourteen, *The future of surveillance and security in global events*, Bajc ponders over a security meta-ritual framework as advice to understand surveillance and security, thus providing readers with a prognosis of likely future outcomes. In chapter thirteen, *Exploring future forms of event volunteering*, Lockstone-Binney and colleagues conceptualize a typology of future forms of event volunteers based upon the trends and reasons, thus providing event organizers and human resource professionals with future profiles. Bolan, in chapter fifteen, *A perspective on the near future: mobilizing events and social media*, examines how digital media is influencing and impacting upon events and the field of event management. Bolan focuses on the application and importance of social media and the evolving nature of mobile apps to the event industry, identifying a number of key areas and themes that warrant attention.

In chapter sixteen, *The future is virtual*, Sadd critically discusses the how technology has shaped event production and attempts to provide future prediction, as to what events in the next few years may become. Sadd proposes that a virtual world of events based on innovative concepts and designs could take the event experience into new realms, yet the need for physical belonging and togetherness are aspects that can never be replicated. In chapter seventeen, *Leadership and visionary futures: future proofing festivals*, Robertson and Brown state that an event's audience is the primary factor in the success of the event, now and in the future. Proposing a rise of the practitioner academic will, they suggest, have significant implications for the direction of future event research. Co-creativity and the demand for bespoke experiences will increase, while the impact of new technologies will, controversially, decrease.

In chapter eighteen, *The future of event design and experience*, McLoughlin approaches the topic of event design from a futuristic perspective – delivering into the space between an operational and experiential perspective, which considers the mutuality of co-creation and the importance of the event practitioner. Robertson and Lees in chapter nineteen, *eScaping in the city: retailvents in socio-spacially managed futures*, use an exploratory trend impact analysis to explain the core drivers associated with retail and events futures with shaped city spaces, immigration, ageing and generational gaps intertwined with technological consumption.

What does this all mean?

In conclusion, in chapter twenty, Yeoman and colleagues present *Cognitive map(s) of events and festivals futures*. These draw on three viewpoints as where the debate and change will be focused on using the process of cognitive mapping that brings together the collective contributions of this book. Those viewpoints – *new consumer values and identity, political reasons and power, and the future role of technology* – should be viewed as emergent agents.

Conclusions

According to Getz (2008), the proliferation of new events and festivals has been immense and rapid and has created an extremely competitive environment. But it is also suggested that events management – and more recently, event studies – are relatively new. Research may be viewed as embryonic. The growth and interest in festivals and events does then mirror the growth of the experience economy (Yeoman *et al.* 2012). The future – a continuation of exponential growth or not – is untold. The contributors to the book have set out to provide explanations of how the future could be drawing upon a range of stages or degrees of truthfulness or certainty. Thus, unless readers can become time travellers and travel back in time, the only place they can be is the future. Hence, the contributors and editors of this publication will be of assistance on those journeys into the future.

References

Baum, T., Lockstone-Binney, L. and Robertson, M. (2013) 'Event studies: finding fool's gold at the rainbow's end?', *International Journal of Event and Festival Management*, 4(3): 179–85.

Bergman, A., Karlsson, J.C. and Axelsson, J. (2010) 'Truth claims and explanatory claims: an ontological typology of futures studies', *Futures*, 42(8): 857–65.

Blackman, C. (1994) 'From forecasting to informed choices', *Futures*, 26(1): 3.

Davies, L., Coleman, R. and Ramchandani, G. (2013) 'Evaluating event economic impact: rigour versus reality?', *International Journal of Event and Festival Management*, 4(1): 31–42.

Getz, D. (2007) *Event studies: theory, research and policy for planned events.* Amsterdam, London: Elsevier Butterworth-Heinemann.

Getz, D. (2008) 'Event tourism: definition, evolution, and research', *Tourism Management*, 29(3): 403–28.

Getz, D. (2012) 'Event studies: discourses and future directions', *Event Management*, 16(2): 171–87.

Habermas, J. (1984) *The theory of communicative action.* Cambridge: Polity.

Hojer, M. and Mattsson, L. (2006) 'Determinism and backcasting in future studies', *Futures*, 32(3): 613–34.

Lockstone-Binney, L., Robertson, M. and Junek, O. (2013) 'Guest editorial: emerging knowledge and innovation in event management', *International Journal of Event and Festival Management*, 4(3): 176–78.

Mair, J. and Whitford, M. (2013) 'An exploration of events research: event topics, themes and emerging trends', *International Journal of Event and Festival Management*, 4(1): 6–30.

Robertson, M., Junek, O. and Lockstone-Binney, L. (2014) 'Introduction: professionalization and event management', *Event Management*, 18(1): 1–3.

Slaughter, R. (1996) *New thinking for a new millennium: the knowledge base of futures studies*. London: Routledge.

Strand, S. (1999) 'Forecasting the future: pitfalls in controlling for uncertainty', *Futures*, 31(3): 333–50.

Yeoman, I., Robertson, M. and Smith, K. (2012) 'A futurist's view on the future of events', in S. Page and J. Connell (eds.) *The Routledge handbook of events*. London: Routledge, pp. 526–34.

2   Back to the future

Analysing history to plan for tomorrow

Adrian Devine and Clare Carruthers

Future points

- Increased regulation will require event organisers to strike a balance between risk and creativity.
- Event organisers need to influence policy makers and to achieve this industry must speak with a united voice.
- Event organisers need to treat the media as potential partners and supply it with good news stories, which highlight the positive impacts of events.
- Event evaluation should be a high priority for all event managers, and the findings should be disseminated to all stakeholders including government agencies.

Introduction

Today events are an integral part of our lives. Allen *et al.* (2011) discuss how an increase in leisure time and discretionary spending has led to a proliferation of public events and celebrations. However, this is not a new phenomenon, as history is littered with examples of human beings organising events to celebrate and mark important occasions in their lives and culture. Indeed, valuable lessons can be learnt from past events, and this chapter will discuss how history can help those currently involved in the events industry plan for the future.

According to Clark (1992), our ability to look backwards, to view the present as the outcome of the past and at the same time as a platform for planning new developments in the future is one of the principal ways in which human beings display their identity as members of a distinct species of primate. There are, however, different views on how history can be used to plan for the future; for example, Howe and Strauss (1997) support the cyclical view of time, whilst Tosh (1999) is an advocate of the linear view of time. Staley (2010) in his examination of the relationship between history and the future recommends that futurists should consider the scenario method when thinking forward, and this will be the approach the authors use in this chapter.

It is important to note from the outset that a scenario is not a prediction. Both the designer and user of a prediction assume that a prediction is a certainty: predictions often contain the word 'will'. A prediction is relatively rigid and inflexible. A scenario, by contrast, is a statement that assumes uncertainty. It describes not a certain world but only a possible world: scenarios are often written in the subjunctive or future conditional tense. A scenario is flexible because its designers and users assume there are credible alternatives, and that the scenario can change as new information is received.

In order to use history to make statements about the future, scenarists study the past and draw inferences from it with the aim of identifying the 'driving forces' that will determine the shape of the future. Staley (2010) is keen to stress, however, that scenarists do not simply extend trend lines from the past into the future; the scenarist will dissect the past, identify patterns and from it draw conclusions. The resulting scenario will then be presented in the form of a written narrative.

For those involved in a turbulent industry such as events, the scenario method can help deal with uncertainty. Like all managers, the organisers of events require some tool to guide their decisions about the future, and scenarios based on historical evidence can help them plan for the future and react to change. The future is by definition unknown and unpredictable so managers must think in terms of possibilities rather than definite predictions. Scenarios are flexible and as they provide event organisers with a mental map of the future, this will encourage them to think 'outside the box', which can make them more robust and adaptive – capable of dealing with unintended surprises.

In this chapter the authors will present and defend the following scenario: 'Government intervention will increase over the next decade and beyond as governments rely more heavily on events to stimulate local and national economies. This will mean increased public funding for events but the operating environment will be more controlled and regulated'. To introduce this scenario the authors will look to the past, and in particular Elias's (1982) theory of the 'civilising process', before focusing on the present and how history is currently repeating itself. The final section of this chapter will discuss the implications this scenario will have for event organisers in the future.

The civilising process

Elias's (1982) theory of the 'civilising process' describes a trend in which the level of acceptable violence in society has gradually declined through the centuries. Elias (1982) uses sport to illustrate his theory that society has become more civilised and that it demands greater personal self-control and restraint. He discusses how compared to the days of the ancient Greeks the 'threshold of repugnance' has gradually decreased and men and women no longer enjoy but in fact are disgusted at the sight of excessive damage being inflicted on human beings and animals in the name of sport.

Elias does stress that the actual changes appear gradual to those who live through them, and only when we look back at history do we realise the extent to which violence has been reduced at sports events. For instance, much of what the ancients would have regarded as expressions of civilisation would now be seen as barbarous from the standpoint of the twenty-first century. Gouging, biting, breaking and the use of spite thongs were all permissible in Greek combat events. For Romans, part of the appeal of sport lay in the climax of killing, and they had preparatory schools exclusively for gladiators, who would sooner or later be publicly feted or slaughtered. Coakley (2003) discusses how the Romans were motivated by 'blood lust' and would joyously witness the death of one human being by either another or a beast. During the Middle Ages, violent blood sports continued to enjoy popularity. For example, Cashmore (2000) describes how large crowds would celebrate as they watched tethered bears being prodded by sticks before being set upon by fierce dogs. Getz (2012) builds on this argument and discusses how hooliganism was also a problem during this period, with parochial rivalries among spectators often resulting in riots.

Although Elias's theory purports that the 'civilising process' was gradual and spread over centuries, he does make reference to what he called a 'civilising spurt' during the nineteenth century, during which the most dramatic changes took place in society. According to Elias (1982), this period had a profound effect on the public's sensitivity to, and acceptance of, violence. Once again he used sport to illustrate his theory and discussed how by the end of nineteenth century most sports took on a much more orderly character. In fact, the changes that were introduced heralded the birth of what we now regard as modern-day sport, as both participants and spectators came to recognise the legitimacy of governing organisations, the standards of conduct they laid down and the structures of rules they observed. From an event management perspective it is important to note that the effects of this 'civilising spurt' were not confined to sport and sports events. Edensor (1998) sums this up when he compares the chaotic, unruly and often violent fairs and festivals of the seventeenth and eighteenth centuries to the more structured, ordered, controlled and self-disciplined events of the late nineteenth century.

Drivers of change

The basis of Elias's theory is that society is now more civilised. Indeed, even the brief snapshot of history provided in this chapter illustrates how, compared to our ancestors, we are more sensitive to, and less tolerant of, violence and disorderly behaviour. However, although interesting, this overview lacks substance and on its own does not provide the authors with enough information to develop or defend a scenario for the future. The American Historical Association (cited by Getz 2012) argues that the true value of history is that it helps us understand the complex process of social change. Within this context, in order to be able to draw lessons from the past the authors must therefore go beyond description and establish why the changes associated with the civilising process actually occurred.

Since the most dramatic changes associated with the 'civilising process' took place during the nineteenth century, it is only logical to focus on this period. If we use Britain as a case study and dissect this period of British history it is apparent that there were two main drivers of change: the Industrial Revolution and the insecurity of the ruling classes. Both contributed to the acceleration of the civilising process and thus had a major impact on events.

According to Thompson (1963), industrialisation and urbanisation generated a volatile demography, which the ruling classes feared would provide a breeding ground for political militancy and working class revolt. The introduction of the factory system brought together, often in brutish and insanitary conditions, large masses of people in numbers that had never before been experienced. Given the fear of instability, discipline for the new urban masses was seen as crucial, and it was often in their recreational lives that such groups illustrated the least control. Cunningham (1980) discusses how the gathering of large crowds for spectator events such as prize fighting, racing, public executions, fairs and wakes, animal baiting and the like were simply not only brutish and unruly, they were also occasions of considerable damage and potential disorder.

Henry (2001) discusses how concern with recreational behaviour was not only related to worries about social disorder, but it was also a matter of concern to industrial interests, which regarded the instilling of work discipline as essential to the obtaining of a reasonable return on investment. While agrarian production had relied on seasonal patterns of work with extended periods of effort, particularly at harvest time, followed by traditional feasts and holiday periods, industrial production was ruled by the twenty-four-hour clock. In order to maximise production machines had to be in operation around the clock, and this meant that workers had to be available for labour at the appointed hour. Absenteeism and drunkenness at work were seen as the result of uncontrolled revelry and resulted in loss of profits in factories that depended on a workforce to be regularly available, compliant and alert. Thus, control of recreation was regarded as essential to maintain of levels of production.

From the mid-nineteenth century onwards, like many other European countries and the US, the British state intervened in free-time activity so as to establish a greater sense of social integration, social control and community bonding, which it deemed necessary in a politically stable industrial society (Foley, McGillivary and McPherson 2011). This had a major impact on what events were held and how they were organised. For instance, Hobsbawn (1983) discusses how during the nineteenth century many events were banished from the calendar in the name of civilisation and new ones were 'invented' to fulfil a more meaningful social function. Harcup (2000) described it as a period of history strewn with examples of governments shutting down urban festivals and events because of moral panics regarding their effects. According to Smith (2012), the most blatant example of this was the UK's 1871 Act of Parliament. This particular piece of legislation allowed central government to suppress fairs in England and was ultimately responsible for the closure of 700 events over the next decade.

Thus, in the nineteenth century Britain experienced rapid industrialisation and unplanned urbanisation, and this had a significant impact on events. The state took on a more interventionist role in the policy and provision of leisure and events in an attempt to maintain order and improve productivity. Popular activities, including festivals, fairs and wakes, were suppressed by the recently legitimated public authorities of the nineteenth century out of concern for public order and to ensure adherence to the new work discipline required by the owners of production (Henry 2001). This is in line with Smith's argument that (2012) traditionally governments acted to regulate events in order to stimulate productivity and promote their values.

Lessons from the present

According to Allen *et al.* (2011), we now live in a more civilised society. During the twentieth century a technological revolution changed work practices and transformed economies, whilst the growth of the voluntary and commercial sectors has allowed governments to adopt a more lassiez-faire approach to events. However, in recent years we have seen a policy shift and increased government activity within the industry. For instance, Foley, McGillivary and McPherson (2011) discuss how governments are now using policy levers to govern and plan events (and their outcomes) in a manner unheard of a decade ago. Thus, it seems history is repeating itself, and this raises two important questions: why are governments adopting an increasingly interventionist approach to events in the twenty-first century and what implications will this have for event organisers in the future?

Earlier in this chapter the authors discussed how events have been part of human civilisations since ancient times. They have marked changing seasons, heralded the appointment of new leaders, celebrated religious rites and rituals and also signified births and deaths. In the twenty-first century they continue to serve these functions, but they have become significantly more complex and elaborate and their audiences have grown exponentially. Ferdinand and Kitchin (2012) refer to the inauguration of the 44th American President, Barack Obama, which set records for being the most popular presidential inauguration by attracting a live viewing audience of over 2 million and an online audience of over 45.5 million viewers. In 2012, the opening ceremony of the Summer Olympic Games in London attracted a global TV audience of 900 million people (Reuters 2012). According to Ferdinand and Kitchin (2012), these two examples demonstrate how drastically the roles of events in societies have changed and how integral they have become to daily life in the twenty-first century. Governments in both developed and developing countries have recognised this, which helps to explain their shift up the political agenda.

According to Getz (2012), there are many political reasons why governments often try to influence how events are managed and marketed. For instance, Hall (1992) discusses how ideological reasons lie behind many mega events, wherein the dominant power in society seeks to demonstrate and reinforce its value, or to win support. However, Foley, McGillivary and McPherson (2011) believe that when it comes to event policy, economic and political systems are inseparable. They discuss how events are deemed unsupportable unless they achieve economic goals.

Roberts (2004) described mega-events as the leisure industries supernovas. He discussed how every town, city and country wants to bid for and host events primarily because they attract visitors and their money. In fact, Roberts (2004) goes as far as to state that the economy of most cities and holiday resorts would stutter without a stream of major and minor events. The economic potential of events is summed in the following quote by Foley, McGillivary and McPherson (2011: 48):

> throughout the world, events and mega-events have been recognized for their potential to change perceptions of host cities and nations, generate significant economic value, catalyse physical and social regeneration, reposition a destination and provide opportunities for the celebration of local and national identities.

From an event management perspective it is encouraging that the economic and political value of events has been recognised by central and local governments, which in turn has led to an increase in the number of government agencies offering subsidies or absorbing the costs associated with events. Unfortunately for event organisers as their industry moves up the political agenda their events have and will continue to come under increased scrutiny. Politicians and public officials must be mindful of the fact that they are spending tax payers' money and are ultimately accountable for their actions. Shaw (2003) highlights this when he discusses how the unintended socio-economic and fiscal consequences of events have triggered political dissent and regime change when outcomes fail to meet expectations, or when adverse impacts on particular communities outweigh the promised benefits. Politicians and their officials are also aware that the hosting of large-scale events has also left countries facing substantial long-term debt due to cost overruns or losing face internationally due to poor organisation and planning (Ferdinand and Kitchin 2012). Consequently, as more governments include events in their economic strategies the events industry has become more regulated and controlled. For instance, Smith (2012) discuses how more public authorities are 'clamping down' on events that they perceive to be unruly or unsafe. Moreover, as governments want a return on their investment, they are reluctant to support or grant permission to events that they deem unsuitable or controversial.

In order to portray a positive image of the country (and the government) public authorities in some instances have also interfered with the actual content of some events. For example, Foley, McGillivary and McPherson (2011) discuss how government policy, driven by economic motives, has affected cultural events such as New Year celebrations. These cultural events are increasingly choreographed, as towns and cities look to boost their international profiles from media exposure. According to Foley, McGillivary and McPherson (2011), these events now essentially colonise civic space and then proceed to make this space feel like a gated community where barriers are erected, security guards are employed and CCTV cameras are ubiquitous. They use Edinburgh's Hogmanay celebration to illustrate how commercial and political intervention has helped to reshape an event. This event, which is the highlight of the city's events calendar, has moved from being a relatively organic celebration to an increasingly managed and mediatised cultural experience for the consumption of a watching audience across the globe. The 'public culture' expressed is controlled and contained rather than being spontaneous and negotiated.

Another area of the events industry that has been subject to increased intervention from government in recent years is the carnival. Carnivals have existed for centuries and were historically defined by their rituals, symbols and localised 'meanings'. However, with the onset of post-industrialisation and the associated global economic restructuring that accompanied it, the authorities in cities such as New Orleans and Rio de Janeiro have tried to control the content of these extravagances in order to maximise their economic return (Foley, McGillivary and McPherson 2011). To illustrate this point Smith (2012) discusses the New Orleans Mardi Gras Carnival and how its growth has inevitably led to changes both in the meaning of the festivities and the actual organisation of the parades. He describes how barricades now separate spectators from the processions, which in recent years have been have become more confined to the city centre. According to Foley, McGillivary and McPherson (2011), however, this is only one example of what they refer to as creeping regulation. Public officials and politicians in New Orleans slowly but surely have attempted to grasp control over the event from the local communities and have developed a tighter permit system through which each and every parade must be processed. This approach allows the local state to guide and frame the sort of parades it judges as acceptable and, conversely, the ones it views as inappropriate.

There are numerous other examples of governments intervening in events to maximise economic returns. For instance, Ravenscroft and Matteucci (2002) discuss the San Fermin Fiesta (also known at the Pamplona Bull Run), which is held annually in Spain and has become popularised in the media for its uniqueness and apparent authenticity. Because the city's tourism industry is reliant on this event, the local authorities have intervened to ensure the event is safe and secure by adopting a zero-tolerance approach to anti-social behaviour. Although this will help protect the reputation of the city, it could be argued that this event is in danger of losing its 'unique selling point'– the excitement generated from a high-risk free-flowing activity.

Concluding remarks: the implications for the future of the events industry

Staley (2010) argues that history is an excellent way to think about and plan for the future, as it can help futurologists devise scenarios. So what can we learn from the two periods in history that were discussed in this chapter? Admittedly these were very different periods, yet from an event management perspective a common theme emerged: increased government intervention. During the nineteenth century the government controlled events to ensure political stability and promote productivity, whilst during the first decade of the twenty-first century increased government involvement was driven primarily by economic gain.

According to Staley (2010) the goal of scenario planning is not to predict the one path the future will follow but to discern the possible states towards which the future might be attracted. To this end the authors of this chapter would like to present the following scenario:

'Government intervention will increase over the next decade and beyond as governments rely more heavily on events to stimulate local and national economies. This will mean increased public funding for events but the operating environment will be more controlled and regulated.'

Based on this scenario, the authors would urge event managers to be strategic and consider the following four areas when planning events in the future. To begin with, it is important that event organisers keep abreast of the laws and regulation that govern the industry. Goldblatt (2011: 379) suggests four primary reasons for complying with laws and regulations: 'to protect your legal interests, to abide by ethical practices, to ensure the safety and security of your event stakeholders and to protect your financial investment'. At present event organisers have to contend with laws and regulations covering issues as wide ranging as corporate manslaughter to waste disposal. They must obey all laws to avoid adverse legal consequences such as being sued for negligence or losing premises and licenses that allow them to operate in the industry.

If the events industry becomes even more regulated in the future, the issue of liability and the fear of ligation is going to create a dilemma for event organisers who will be reluctant to take risks, yet must be creative in order to differentiate their event and give it a Unique Selling Point (USP). Increased regulation should not be allowed to stifle creativity. Bladen *et al.* (2012) make reference to the WOW factor, and this should remain the guiding principle of event managers during the twenty-first century. Increased competition will mean customers will expect and demand more from an event. Thus, event organisers need to be innovative if their event is to 'stand out from the crowd' and compete for the 'leisure dollar'. To achieve this they must work within the law and strike a balance between risk and creativity; otherwise the events industry will suffer from what Foley, McGillivary and McPherson (2012) referred to as 'sameness'.

Linked to the issue of creativity is the need for event organisers to 'stand up' to government. However, if event organisers want to influence policy makers, a more proactive approach is required. If they feel that proposed laws and regulations are unjust, then the industry must speak with a united voice and the trade bodies/associations that represent the industry must do more to lobby government. It is equally important that local communities have a voice and are involved in the planning process. Researchers such as Getz (2012) and Smith (2012) have recognised the importance of the host community being involved in and owning the event. Event managers must work with the host community because, at the local level in particular, politicians seeking reelection will be more reluctant to tamper with an event that has the support of the local electorate.

On a similar note, event organisers should also forge closer links with the media. For many people, the media fills a large part of their social and leisure time, so the stories and images it relays can be highly influential. While the media is not always seen as a positive force in advanced societies, and it is often considered too powerful, it cannot be ignored (Bladen *et al.* 2012). It communicates with millions of people and has the potential to change an individual's attitude towards specific events including politicians. According to Allen *et al.* (2011), once event organisers treat the media as potential partners they have much more to offer the event. Event organisers must be proactive and supply the media with good news stories and highlight the positive impact their event has on the host destination. There should also be a plan to deal with any stories that might damage the reputation and quality of their event, with crisis management built into the overall planning process.

Finally, as the industry becomes more regulated it is vital that all event organisers recognise the importance of event evaluation. According to Masterman (2009), although the majority of event planning theory recommends the use of post-event evaluation in practice event managers are all too quick to move on and not commit funds or time to this important undertaking. Yet Hall (1992) and Bowdin *et al.* (2011) describe event evaluation as a strategic necessity that will help professionalise the industry. This is in line with Ferdinand and Kitchin's (2012) argument that one of the best means for the industry to gain credibility as an industry is for events to be evaluated honestly and critically, so their outcomes are known, their benefits acknowledged and their limitations accepted.

Building on this argument Allen *et al.* (2011) discuss how event evaluation serves a much deeper purpose than just 'blowing the trumpet' for events. It is at the very heart of the process where insights are gained, lessons are learnt and events are perfected. Event evaluation, if properly utilised and applied, is the key to the continuous improvement of events and to the standing and reputation of the events industry. Therefore, it should be a high priority for all event managers to conduct an evaluation of their event and to disseminate this evaluation to their stakeholders and the relevant government agencies. A detailed evaluation will not only enhance the reputation of the event, but also that of the event organiser and the industry in general. In the long term this will help to convince government that the industry is a responsible profession that can be trusted to self-regulate.

References

Allen, J., O'Toole, W., McDonnell, I. and Harris, R. (2011) *Festival and Special Event Management*. 5th ed. Chichester: Wiley.

Bladen, C., Kennell, J., Abson, E. and Wilde, N. (2012) *Events Management: An Introduction*. London: Routledge.

Bowdin, G., McDonnell, I., Allen, J. and O'Toole, W. (2011) *Events Management*. 3rd ed. London: Butterworth Heinemann.

Cashmore, E. (2000) *Making Sense of Sport*. London: Routledge.

Clark, G. (1992) *Space, Time and Man: A Prehistorian's View*. Cambridge: University Press.

Coakley, J. (2003) *Sport in Society: Issues and Controversies*. Boston: McGraw-Hill.

Cunningham, H. (1980) *Leisure in the Industrial Revolution.* London: Croom Helm.

Edensor, T. (1998) 'The culture of the Indian street' in N. Fyfe (ed.) *Images of the Street: Planning, Identity and Control in Public Space.* London: Routledge, pp. 46–67.

Elias, N. (1982) *The Civilising Process.* New York: Pantheon.

Ferdinand, N. and Kitchin, P. (2012) *Events Management and International Approach.* London: Sage.

Foley, M., McGillivary, D. and McPherson, G. (2011) *Event Policy – from Theory to Strategy.* London: Routledge.

Getz, D. (2012) *Event Studies: Theory, Research and Policy for Planned Events.* 2nd ed. London: Elsevier.

Goldblatt, J. (2011) *Special Events: A New Generation and the Next Frontier.* 6th ed. Chichester: Wiley.

Hall, M. (1992) *Hallmark Tourist Events: Impacts, Management and Planning.* London: Belhaven Press.

Harcup, T. (2000) 'Re-imaging a post-industrial city: the Leeds St Valentine's Fair as a civic spectacle', *City,* 4(2): 215–31.

Henry, I. (2001) *The Politics of Leisure Policy.* 2nd ed. Hampshire: Palgrave.

Hobsbawm, E. (1983) 'Mass producing traditions: Europe 1870–1914', in E. Hobsbawn and T. Ranger (eds) *The Invention of Tradition.* New York: Cambridge University Press, pp. 104–29.

Howe, N. and Strauss, W. (1997) *The Fourth Turning; an American Prophecy.* New York: Broadway Press.

Masterman, G. (2009) *Strategic Sports Event Management: An International Approach.* 2nd ed. Oxford: Elsevier.

Quinn, B. (2013) *Key Concepts in Event Management.* London: Sage

Ravenscroft, N. and Mateucci, X. (2002) 'The festival as carnivalesque: social governance and control at Pamplona's San Fermin Fiesta', *Tourism Culture and Communication,* 4(1): 1–15.

Reuters (2012) London 2012 TV Viewing Figures. Online. Available: <uk.reuters.com> Accessed: 1 July 2014

Roberts, K. (2004) *The Leisure Industries.* China: Palgrave MacMillan.

Shaw, S. (2003) 'The Canadian world city and sustainable downtown revitalisation: messages from Montreal 1962–2002', *British Journal of Canadian Studies,* 16(2): 363–77.

Smith, A. (2012) *Events and Urban Regeneration; the Strategic Use of Events to Revitalise Cities.* London: Routledge.

Staley, D. (2010) *Future and History; Using Historical Thinking to Imagine the Future.* New York: Lexington Books.

Thompson, E. (1963) *The Making of the English Working Class.* London: Gollancz.

Tosh, J. (1999) *The Pursuit of History.* London: Longman.

3 The forms and functions of planned events

Past and future

Donald Getz

Future points

- Convergence of functions magnifies the power of planned events and will result in new forms that cannot yet be anticipated; the potential for creativity in event design will be unlimited.
- The synergies arising from convergence will generate many new permanent hallmark events as brand symbols, creators and preservers of valued traditions, outlets for group/community identity building and personal fulfilment, and as tourist attractions and facilitators of business and trade.
- Divergence will continue to generate more growth, and variety in the form of events, with unlimited potential in the realm of design, participation (active and passive), setting, and social interaction.
- Symbolic value is on the ascendency in terms of propelling growth, compared to events as tourist attractions (within the economic dimension). Heightening the symbolic value of events requires either focusing on particular interest groups, or on obtaining wider, potentially global, exposure. Therefore symbolic value will be increasingly evident in the realm of iconic events that are created for, and often by social worlds.

Introduction

The fundamental functions of planned events do not change; they have remained the same since civilization began. One cannot imagine a world without events that facilitate social and economic exchanges, promise highly desired experiences, embody cultural differences, communicate symbolic meanings, and nourish both individual and group identity. Forces of globalization have heightened these roles and accelerated changes within the events sector.

As events continue to grow in importance, reflecting increased legitimation as instruments of diverse public policy fields and corporate strategies, often within a global marketplace, we can expect growth in numbers and increased attention given to managed, overlapping portfolios. Increases in the size and impacts of events are also inherent in this evolutionary process.

Within this context there are two clear trends that will shape the future, namely divergence and convergence. On the one hand events are becoming more alike, with forms and functions blending, and on the other hand there is increasing divergence in terms of forms or styles of events. These are not opposing forces; both reflect underlying functions.

The first section of this chapter discusses four fundamental roles of planned events, or their functions, in terms of why they are inherent in all civilizations and consequently why people and societies need them. Then the convergence and divergence trends are addressed, with emphasis on Hallmark and iconic events. In the third and final section future implications are drawn, both as forecasts (expressed as general trends) and with regard to research needs.

To position this chapter within future studies, reference is made first to Yeoman, Robertson and Smith (2012: 509) who noted, 'Futurists understand the change, can see beyond the horizon. They have the ability to layer patterns of trends and to draw conclusions in order to make predictions'. Accordingly, the approach taken in this paper can be termed 'prediction', as defined by Bergman, Karlsson and Axelsson (2010). Predictions claim future knowledge, or make ontological 'truth statements', and these are expressed in the conclusions of this chapter in the form of propositions. While a simple trend extrapolation would result in a 'prognosis' of how things will be in the future (Bergman, Karlsson and Axelsson 2010), this chapter also provides explanatory power by examining the underlying forces shaping change in the planned-events sector.

There is no normative component to this chapter. That is, the trends and predictions are not being represented as good or desirable, but as trends that will likely gain strength in the future. Planners and policy makers can thereby test the propositions (employing them as hypotheses) and employ the predictions singly or jointly as scenarios to test alternative policies and strategies. No dates are assigned to the forecasts, but the main consequences – both convergence and divergence – are already evident and growing in significance.

The fundamental functions of planned events

Planned events have been important elements in all societies throughout recorded history, and we can therefore conclude they meet a number of fundamental needs: economic, social, cultural/symbolic, and personal. At a societal level, exchange theories can be applied to gain a fuller understanding of the roles of planned events. Marshall (1998) explained that 'rational-choice' exchange theory pertains to the advantages people gain by co-operating, whereas:

> Anthropological-exchange theory claims that both order and the pursuit of individual advantage are effects of the underlying ritual and symbolic nature of the thing exchanged. In both versions social conflict (or disorder) is simply the consequence of the breakdown of the exchange process.

In the ensuing discussion of the four broad dimensions these rational versus symbolic views of exchange and social order are evident, but there are additional considerations related to a hierarchy of needs/meanings from the individual level through higher-order abstraction like place marketing.

Economic exchange

The basic meaning of 'to exchange' is the act of giving and receiving, which can either be direct and reciprocal or mediated by a third party. In complex modern economies there exist elaborate, and often impersonal, electronic systems of exchange. The value of things exchanged has to be determined in some way, and in economic systems this is normally a monetary value. The value attached to any exchange might also be subjective, even irrational, or formed through social representations such as media reports that might or might not be accurate or impartial. Value is sometimes negotiated face to face, and sometimes with imperfect knowledge on the part of one or another party in the exchange. There are hidden costs in many exchanges, notably the transaction costs of participating in a market, seeking and utilizing information, negotiation and contracting, and enforcement (Klaes 2008).

Planned events facilitate direct exchanges of goods and services (i.e., purchases in the marketplace) as well as meeting the need to meet in person in order to seek information and learn, to arrange for ensuing trade, and to promote, all of which gives rise to fairs and exhibitions, meetings, and conventions. Throughout history these forums of economic exchange have frequently been combined with entertainment, feasting, and ritual, even to the point of becoming, or being integrated with holy days (Waters 1939; IAFE n.d.). Even though business is the underlying purpose of these types of events, they are of necessity social in nature and those involved generally want them to be personally and socially rewarding as well as being good business. Business can nowadays be conducted virtually, yet people still frequently prefer to meet in person. Many experts (e.g. Duffy and McEuen 2010) agree that virtual events cannot ever fully replace social events, and it can even be suggested that the more communications occur between people, governments, and companies, the more live events will result. This is clearly true in social worlds, which mediate participation and event-tourism both by encouraging interactions (such as through blogs, information websites, e-zines, and social media) and by offering more event-tourism options (i.e., through the intervention of event producers, destination marketing organizations, tour companies, or travel agents) (Getz and Patterson 2013).

According to the service-dominant logic that has reshaped the entire philosophy of marketing (Lusch and Vargo 2006), all marketing is about service. Whether a tangible or intangible product is being sold, the value it provides is in serving the needs of clients and purchasers. The benefits or value of all goods and services is defined by the users, not the manufacturers or providers. And, this is well known to event designers, all service experiences are co-created. What this means is that business events are experiences built around service, and not what they once were – the actual exchange of goods and money. Service incudes learning, communicating, problem solving, and relationship building. Live events do this better than any other mode.

At a higher level of abstraction, the meanings assigned to events must be considered. Within the economic frame we have to measure the importance of events to place marketing, the reimaging and repositioning of cities, to destination branding, and urban development or renewal (see, for example, Richards and Palmer 2010). Events are often conceived as catalysts for these higher-order economic and developmental goals, or as necessary accompaniments, so much so that the term 'festivalization' has been used to describe the process by which cities exploit events (Richards 2007). To realize these benefits inevitably requires infrastructural investments, with the trend being bigger and better in order to compete in the global event-tourism marketplace. Cities cannot do without their convention and exhibition centres, arenas and stadia, festival places, and cultural/ arts venues. Much of this tourism-oriented infrastructure exceeds the needs of residents, raising questions about where the 'public good' lies, especially when huge facilities are built for one-time mega events. As well, considerable debate rages over demands for public subsidies by private sport companies and resultant public-private deals (Rosentraub 2009).

Differences exist between the public and private-sector perspectives on planned events. The economic value of events to corporations and industries (i.e. tourism, hospitality) has accelerated through emphasis on branding, in which events constitute 'live communications' (Wuensch 2008) as well as media for sales and business-to-business actions. Corporations, industries, and the public sector increasingly combine their efforts, and while some of these are legitimate public-private partnerships creating 'public good', others seem to be a conspiracy of elites in society – especially with regard to bidding on and producing unaffordable mega events, which result in gains for a few and enduring debt for the remainder. Alarm has been growing over the trend to 'gigantism' in events (Preuss 2009), while more and more critical attention is being given to the provable costs and benefits of mega events and their opportunity costs (Preuss 2009), and to the imputed value of bidding on mega events (Pomfret, Wilson and Lobmayr 2012).

Social exchange

Superficially, the social nature of planned events is clearly about people interacting, which can be as casual as people watching or taking one's family on a pleasant outing. But planned events facilitate, and indeed are dependent upon, direct and indirect exchanges of many kinds: hosts meeting guests, providing hospitality, tourists interacting with residents (sometimes socially but also commercially), or subculture bonding. Perhaps the most significant exchanges (or meanings) have been termed *communitas* by Victor Turner (1969), based on belonging and sharing, and a sense of equality. As well, many authors believe that planned events generate 'social capital', attributable to the networks that are built, and the goodwill generated for communities (Arcodia and Whitford 2006; Finkel 2010; Schulenkorf, Thomson and Schlenker 2011).

Social exchange theory (Homans 1958) deals with immediate, event-specific exchanges as well as broader issues of how residents perceive impacts and the attitudes they develop about events. Essentially the theory says that the perceived costs and benefits associated with a particular behaviour predict intent to engage, or remain engaged, in that behaviour. This would clearly apply to why people volunteer for events or attend them repeatedly – the benefits outweigh the costs.

The events literature contains a number of examples of how social exchange theory has been utilized for more indirect exchanges, primarily in the examination of perceived impacts (e.g., Deccio and Baloglu 2002; Boo, Wang and Yu 2011). As with tourism in general, the findings of various studies confirm that impacts are perceived more positively and positive attitudes are formed more by those who believe they benefit from tourism and events (Fredline and Faulkner 2002). When asking residents about perceived benefits, it is usually framed in terms of employment or direct financial gain, or in terms of engagement with events by means of attendance or participation of another kind. Those who attend or participate in some way enjoy 'use benefits' that can be measured through questions on expenditure and willingness to pay (or contingent valuation), as described by Dwyer, Forsyth and Dwyer (2010).

There are, however, 'nonuse values' to consider. Andersson, Armbrecht and Lundberg (2012) asked residents of Gothenburg, Sweden, if they valued a specific event enough to help pay for its survival through increased taxes, and if so what were their reasons: existence value (its good for the city), option value (I could attend in the future), or bequest value (it should continue for the youth of the city). Indeed, one can think of a range of specific reasons why support would exist for events that people have not attended, most of which indicate a perceived benefit or value such as preservation of traditions, but also including mere acceptance of the fact that in modern societies many things are subsidized that individuals do not necessarily agree with.

The special case of social integration

Rituals, festivals, and other cultural or religious celebrations hold many deep meanings, and spring organically from the cultural and social needs of individuals and communities (see, for example, Van Gennep 1909; Manning 1983; Falassi 1987; Turner 1969, 1974). One school of thought purports that rituals and events bind people together (Durkheim 1978), and this belief is driving major investment in festivals and celebrations, particularly in divided and troubled communities. The opposing position is that through the carnival (or carnivalesque behaviour) people express their opposition or even rebellion to authority. In the modern world we see these disruptive elements in planned protests and riots, or more modestly in pillow fights and other relatively tame flash mobs.

An underlying tension remains and cannot be eliminated: the constraining forces of regulation and establishment versus a fundamental desire for liberating experiences – if not rebellion. Ehrenrich (2006) refers to 'collective ecstasy' in describing how carnival and festivity liberate people, yet event producers and civic authorities constantly seek to constrain behaviour, if only to prevent disasters. It can be hypothesized that the more constraints are imposed, the more people (or subcultures) will express themselves through anti-social behaviour. In an ever more densely populated world, social exchange has to become more regulated and peaceful, with the aim of achieving social integration goals, otherwise the centrifugal (disintegrating) forces will grow. Events as tools of constraint will therefore likely become more popular among policy makers, in direct response and proportion to increasing social problems.

Symbolic exchange

Events are themselves symbols, and their programming always incorporates symbolic meanings. Symbolism is expressed in many ways by and within events, so that to sociologists the festival is a text to be read about the host community and culture (e.g., Manning 1983). Myths and legends are expressed through festivals (Quinn 2003), and this is either an explicit or hidden part of the text. Now storytelling has become accepted in retailing and destination marketing, so that events have an additional role to play in communicating stories about places (see Moscardo 2010).

'Iconic events' are themselves symbols – of the biggest, best, most prestigious – for people with special interests. Highly involved people, engaging in serious leisure, often develop event-tourist careers that incorporate a hierarchy or progression of desirable events to attend (Green and Jones 2005; Getz and Andersson 2010; Getz and McConnell 2011). This even applies to business and professional travellers, including academics, who 'must attend' conventions and exhibitions. In the same vein, 'hallmark events' are co-branded with, and are therefore symbols of, the destination (Getz 2013). In this context, the notion of secular pilgrimage applies, usually with some blending of appeal from both place and event (Hall 2002). Sacred sites have pilgrimages (Nolan and Nolan 1992), while iconic sport venues hold appeal through major competitions and as places with meaning.

The symbolic value of events has merged with the branding, both of places and corporations or their products. Sponsors seek goodwill through association with events and the causes or values they represent; cities co-brand with events that gain exposure, convey positive images, and communicate city-brand values such as cosmopolitan, exciting, sophisticated, or fun. Repositioning of post-industrial cities is as much about symbolism, in which events figure prominently, as it is about attracting tourists and generating jobs in the 'creative industries'.

Personal development

Personal development is the most recent fundamental need to emerge, as it is largely dependent on having freedom of choice and variety in leisure opportunities. If leisure is voluntary action, as posited by Rojek (2004), it can be can manifested in all forms of planned events through intrinsically motivated forms of participation (such as volunteering). Leisure is also increasingly giving rise to participation events aimed at the particular needs of specialized leisure and, at the group level, myriad communities of interest and social worlds. Leisure and self-development opportunities are also possible in all forms of business events, or packaged around them, so the distinction between intrinsically and extrinsically motivated event attendance is being reduced.

What do people want from their event experiences? The personal benefits and meanings can include any of the following (from Getz 2012) and partially derived from Diller, Shedroff and Rea (2006: 320):

- communitas (as a result of belonging and sharing, from reaffirmation of roots or of connections and values)
- esteem: validation of oneself in the opinions of others; self-worth; prestige and reputation (such as may be realized though competitive or intellectual accomplishments)
- learning, enlightenment (for example, from new cultural experiences or a connoisseur's appreciation of food, art, or music
- self discovery, self actualization, understanding, wonder
- transformation (religious, spiritual, personality or character, renewed, motivated)
- redemption and atonement (from failure or sins)
- mastery (from skills, physical triumph)
- accomplishment or success (from business, trade, commerce, networking, creativity, artistic expression)
- creativity or innovation (making a lasting contribution)
- fulfilment of responsibility (professionalism, or as a dedicated sport fan, or from getting involved as a volunteer)
- health and well-being (through physical activity, learning)
- security (living without fear)
- duty (military or civic) fulfilled; patriotism and loyalty to a cause
- truth, honesty, integrity (a meaning given to relationships and to one's own behaviour)
- beauty or aesthetic appreciation
- freedom (acting without constraint; intrinsically rewarding pursuits)
- harmony (with nature or others) and oneness (belonging, unity)
- justice (fairness and equality; democratic expression)

Analysis of trends suggests that people who are involved want more engagement, while many prefer to sit and watch passively. These contradictions are important for event design and marketing! Researchers have also observed the following:

- increasing social-world participation, giving rise to more events that are aimed at specific interests and facilitate identity building and communitas among adherents (Stebbins 1992, 2006; Unruh 1980); use of social media and the Internet are accelerating this phenomenon (Getz and Patterson 2013)
- more participation events that physically challenge people through competitive events (Getz and Andersson 2010); new sport variations arise all the time
- search for fulfilment through volunteering and organizing events (Stebbins 2004)
- more emphasis on events that challenge participants and build fitness and healthy lifestyles, from yoga to ironman (Getz and Patterson 2013).

Moscardo (2010) suggested that the search for cultural and existential authenticity remains a driving force for personal engagement in events, while others have argued that more people seek interactive and co-created experiences (Gilmore and Pine 2007). Because it's getting harder to find unique events, engaging patrons with surprise has become a theme. Total immersion, learning, sensory, and emotional stimulation are elements of design that promise to engage and fulfil individuals.

The personal and social dimensions clearly overlap, especially with regard to identity. Here, a great deal of theory can be applied, starting with serious leisure (Stebbins 1992, 2006), social worlds (Unruh 1980), and ego-involvement (Havitz and Dimanche 1997, 1999). It has been demonstrated repeatedly that personal identity can be nurtured through being a fan (Chen 2006) and participation in various leisure and work pursuits that give rise to event attendance and event-tourism (Funk 2008; Shipway and Jones, 2007, 2008). And since all events are social in nature, group identity building of some kind will usually also be applicable. This can be at the level of travelling with fans of the same sport club (Fairley 2009), participating in events with members of one's subculture (Green and Chalip 1998), or sharing a feeling of pride and communitas with residents of the same city.

Convergence and divergence

Within this environment of legitimation and growth are two nonopposing trends – divergence and convergence. Both trends are rooted in the underlying, fundamental roles that events play. On the one hand, we see convergence of form and function, and on the other, increasing diversity of types and styles. Figure 3.1 illustrates how convergence and divergence works, with convergence leading to more events that combine form and function to meet multiple goals, while divergence leads to more unique events, especially in terms of iconic events that hold special meaning for communities of interest or social worlds. Such events include challenging running and mountain-biking events like those produced by TransRockies Inc. for highly involved, amateur athletes (Getz and McConnell 2011; Getz 2013). A related trend is for amateur athletes to challenge themselves by developing a portfolio of activities and competitions, and subsequent event-travel careers.

Convergence is particularly evident in public events that are created and produced for multiple stakeholder goals, and that are intended to attract the most attention and generate the highest possible tourism or economic value. So-called community festivals that are permanent institutions in their host communities are indicative of convergence, as they seek to satisfy every interest. An example is that of the annual Kentucky Derby Festival in Louisville, Kentucky. This city was winner of the IFEA award as top North American Festival City, population over 1 million, in 2010. What was once a simple horse race (now iconic in the world of Thoroughbred racing) is now something much more. Its mission is:

> 'Bringing the community together in celebration. The Derby Festival represents the spirit and pride of the community and showcases Louisville at its best. To provide creative and unique entertainment and community service

for the people of Greater Louisville, that directly contributes to the aesthetic, cultural, educational, charitable and economic development of the area.

The Kentucky Derby Festival's schedule includes over 70 events, most of them occurring in the two weeks leading up to the Kentucky Derby horse race.' (http://derbyfestival.org)

The Olympics is ostensibly a celebration of amateur sport, but they are also mandated by the IOC to include an arts festival. Host cities add conventions, exhibitions, and many other functions designed to leverage these and other mega events. Television turns the whole thing into entertainment and spectacle, packaged in such a way as to maximize advertising revenue. As an example, look at London's 2012 Summer Olympic games (source: www.london2012.com). Preceding the Games were four years of Cultural Olympiad, called 'the largest cultural celebration in the history of the modern Olympic and Paralympic Games'. It culminated in the London 2012 Festival: 'a chance for everyone to celebrate London 2012 through dance, music, theatre, the visual arts, film and digital innovation and leave a lasting legacy for the arts in the UK'.

The emergence of so-called 'world parties' (Dakota 2002) also signifies a tendency toward convergence, even standardization, with events that are aimed at global audiences (and with a global media reach) yet based on some local cultural theme. Issues of cultural authenticity are raised by this trend, as they are by all event-tourism phenomena. Because authenticity is a subjective concept, and open to debate, there cannot be any projections about more or less of it in the future. What can be certain is that opinions on authenticity will keep evolving. In particular, scholars should be examining how exploitation of events for tourism, or any other strategic or policy purpose, by its very nature changes meanings and values assigned to events.

The Hallmark Event, defined here as being a permanent institution and co-branded with the city or destination for marketing purposes, is a special case of convergence. Most hallmark events are old, embody valued traditions, and have diverse programming to attract both residents and tourists. Being Iconic or a Hallmark event is not dependent upon the form or style; it is a matter of function.

Divergence is occurring mostly within the realm of leisure events, including sports, in response to potentially unlimited demand from special-interest groups and the needs of social worlds. It occurs within sport, the arts, hobbies, and lifestyle pursuits. Facilitated by the Internet and social media, spurred by globalization and increasing disposable income, new forms of events are springing up continuously. This innovation is in part entrepreneurship and in part the voluntary action of countless interest groups. There really is no predicting what types of events will arise, as defined by their content and elements of style, so the potential for uniqueness is expanding dramatically. Within this exploding domain of leisure events (with unlimited potential for event-tourism) are iconic events that hold symbolic meaning for members of social worlds and communities of interest. Iconic events, like hallmark events, possess real power to generate travel, but perhaps less potential to generate global media coverage.

(Events in the inner ring hold maximum value in all four dimensions)

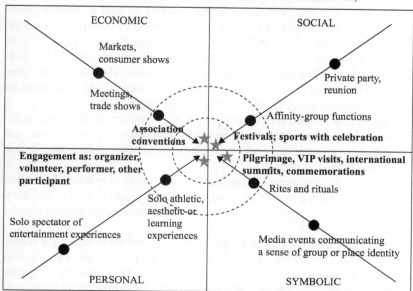

Figure 3.1 A model of convergence

In Figure 3.1, at the innermost zone of convergence, planned events of all forms can possess high value on social, economic, personal, and symbolic dimensions. This reflects, in part, their scale and related attractiveness to residents, tourists, and the media – they generate substantial economic exchanges even if that is not their goal. Individuals will find ample scope for meeting their self-development needs through volunteering and direct participation. These events – often called mega, iconic, hallmark or signature – are symbols for their host communities/nations and foster pride, identity, and cohesion. By their nature, permanent events in this zone tend to become institutions, supported by powerful stakeholders because they perform all these necessary functions. As well, they tend to converge in terms of form, with a high degree of blending of all the elements of style.

At the outermost range of the *economic dimension* are events, like attending a market to shop, or a consumer show to look around and learn, that are low in social exchange (i.e. group experiences are not facilitated), symbolic value, and personal development. But a trade show, while ostensibly all about business for particular industry groups, does also embody social and symbolic dimensions. Although meetings and conventions are often conducted for business reasons, they can also be positioned (alternatively or equally) in the social exchange dimension for purposes of group identity building and cohesion. Those attending events targeted at specific groups generally experience a sense of communitas.

When events meet more than one of these core needs, they become more powerful. At individual events the convergence of form and function generates additional and broader appeal, or drawing power, as well as value to more stakeholders. For example, sports are at once symbolic of cultural differences, reflections of civilized tribal conflict, and entertainment; they offer possibilities for personal and group identity building, not to mention the meeting of physical challenges. Add other forms of consumption, entertainment, elements of the carnivalesque, and you easily build a festival around a sport competition. This produces a vastly more appealing and symbolically powerful event.

Hallmark events that have become permanent institutions in their communities demonstrate this power of convergence through diverse programming and multi-stakeholder involvement – all of the elements of place and community are engaged.

Those desiring the creation of a Hallmark Event, or development of an existing event into one more powerful in generating desired impacts, will of necessity bring together the four, fundamental forces and the resulting synergy will elevate the event.

Governments, industries, corporations, and myriad interest groups have recognized the power of convergence for some time, with the process being accelerated by the forces of globalization. In this context, events have become primarily instruments of policy and strategy, place marketing and brand communications. Planned events are now of central, strategic value to politicians, development agencies, and social marketing.

The *social dimension* emphasizes the importance of events as both reflections and facilitators of essential social exchanges, the kinds that form and reinforce group identity, from the level of friends and family, through all kinds of affinity groups and subcultures, all the way to city and national identity. Private parties are at the outer range, while public festivals/celebrations are within the inner zone. The largest and most public events also generate economic activity by attracting sponsors, grants, and tourists; they are typically high in symbolic value, with the event being iconic within some groups and important to places, as in hallmark events. These planned events typically combine elements, such as sports, with festivals and exhibitions, or conventions with gala banquets and tours. And they offer many opportunities for personal engagement and growth.

Along the continuum representing the *personal dimension*, the individual displays a range of levels of involvement or engagement, beginning with being a solo spectator at a sport competition or concert in which entertainment/spectacle prevails. Solo experiences in social events are frequent, such as running in a race or going to an event as a learning or aesthetic opportunity (e.g. art exhibitions). Within the inner zone the individual experiences a high level of engagement (or involvement), such as in team sports, as a volunteer or performer, and these experiences are associated with both personal development (or self-actualization) and socializing.

All events can hold *symbolic* value to persons and groups, but many fall primarily within this dimension. Events broadcast to the community or world are often intended to foster a positive image, community pride, and group identity; they may be any type of event, or expressly produced as media events with small numbers of direct participants or guests. A panoply of rites and rituals exist that are more social in nature, clearly engaging individuals and groups in symbolic activities: from birthdays and anniversaries to bar mitzvahs and religious processions. Parades, read as social texts, can easily fit into this category. Within the inner zone of convergence are large-scale, social events that also have economic significance such as pilgrimages, VIP visits, international summits, and heritage commemorations. Individuals can experience these events as being spiritually, culturally, or intellectually rewarding, and even transforming.

Perhaps the most neglected power concept is that of deliberately augmenting the symbolic value of events. Many organizers appear to be reluctant to do this, perhaps fearing the alienation of one group when dominant-group symbols are utilized. This can be dealt with in several ways, starting with the planned inclusion of obvious stakeholders and many communities. But symbolism can also be neutral, accepted by most groups through constant media exposure, and universal in meaning.

Future perspectives

Fundamental forces such as globalization and economic development are propelling growth in the planned-events sector, while the basic roles of events in society and the economy remain constant. While the forms of events might change, the functions (i.e. meeting needs) will not. Within this context, both convergence and divergence of forms and functions are acting upon event design and meanings. We can therefore gaze into the future with some certainty that planned events will continue to occupy an essential place in all societies, but we will have to settle for speculation and uncertainty when it comes to specific forms of events and how they will be planned, managed, and marketed.

Emphasis is first placed on convergence, then divergence, leading to these propositions:

P1) Convergence of functions magnifies the power of planned events and will result in new forms that cannot yet be anticipated; the potential for creativity in event design will be unlimited.
P2) In deliberately designing events to meet multiple needs, the programming of events is of less consequence than functionality. Therefore many planned events will take their form from function, not from tradition, artistic considerations, or preconceived notions about what events should look like.
P3) The synergies arising from convergence will generate many new permanent Hallmark events as brand symbols, creators and preservers of valued traditions, outlets for group/community identity building and personal fulfilment, and as tourist attractions and facilitators of business and trade.
P4) Mega events will all be conceived as meeting diverse goals, in all four dimensions, meaning that it will be incorrect to label them as sport, celebration, or business events – they will be merged in form and function.

P5) Divergence will continue to generate more growth, and variety in the form of events, with unlimited potential in the realm of design, participation (active and passive), setting, and social interaction.

P6) Symbolic value is on the ascendency in terms of propelling growth, compared to events as tourist attractions (within the economic dimension). Heightening the symbolic value of events requires either focusing on particular interest groups, or on obtaining wider, potentially global, exposure. Therefore symbolic value will be increasingly evident in the realm of iconic events that are crated for, and often by, social worlds.

P7) Although the ways in which business is conducted are evolving, including more virtual exchanges, the social value of meeting in person will not diminish. It is therefore likely that the social value of in-person meeting will remain essential. Individuals will increasingly pursue personal development, identity, and social networking through planned events.

Concluding remarks

The implications for the future of the event industry based upon the present are contained in the aforementioned set of propositions. It seems clear that convergence of forms and functions will be increasingly employed to increase the symbolic and marketing power of events, generating more Hallmark events that are co-branded with cities and destinations. At the same time, destinations along with interest groups and private companies will add more and more iconic events to the mix, each one highly targeted in both form and function. Given the basic needs met by planned events, growth is assured – at least until major forces such as climate change or energy costs act to constrain the ongoing expansion of this sector.

The fundamental roles or functions of planned events will continue to grow in importance in all societies. Events facilitate, and are essential to, economic, social, and symbolic exchanges, and to personal development. Two nonopposed trends have been discussed in this context, namely the convergence of forms and functions, especially in mega and Hallmark events, and divergence of forms reflecting the explosion of special leisure, lifestyle, art, hobby, and sport interests, which generates iconic events with high symbolic value for social worlds and subcultures.

While continued growth of the events sector can easily be predicted (unless underlying forces propelling globalization and travel decline), along with rising importance of events as instruments of many diverse policy fields and corporate strategy, predicting the form of future events is not as simple. Form will follow from function and combinations of functions, alongside diversification in special interests and social worlds or subcultures. Plurality in society and cultural diversity gives rise to unpredictability in the events sector, and therefore pleasant and strange surprises will follow.

Trend spotters can detect divergence and new forms of events through passive net-nography, and by actually getting involved in social-world interactions such as blogging. Researchers need to make such work systematic and help generate theory, including the testing of various hypotheses that arise from the convergence-divergence model presented in this chapter.

Perhaps the biggest theoretical challenge will be to frame event studies within broader and more diverse disciplinary perspectives pertaining to the fundamental roles and particularly the exchange processes described herein.

References

Andersson, T., Armbrecht, J. and Lundberg, E. (2012) 'Estimating use and non-use values of a music festival', *Scandinavian Journal of Hospitality and Tourism*, 12(3): 215–31.

Arcodia, C. and Whitford, M. (2007) 'Festival attendance and the development of social capital', *Journal of Convention & Event Tourism*, 8(2): 1–18.

Bergman, A., Karlsson, J. and Axelsson, J. (2010) 'Truth claims and explanatory claims: an ontological typology of futures studies', *Futures*, 42: 857–65.

Boo, S., Wang, Q. and Yu, L. (2011) 'Residents' support of mega-events: a reexamination', *Event Management*, 15(3): 215–32.

Chen, P. (2006) 'The attributes, consequences, and values associated with event sport tourists' behaviour: a means-end chain approach', *Event Management*, 10(1): 1–22.

Dakota, D. (ed.) (2002) *World Party*. London: Big Cat Press.

Deccio, C. and Baloglu, S. (2002) 'Nonhost community resident reactions to the 2002 Winter Olympics: the spillover impacts', *Journal of Travel Research*, 41: 46–56.

Diller, S., Shedroff, N. and Rhea, D. (2006) *Making Meaning*. Upper Saddle River, NJ: Pearson.

Duffy, C. and McEuen, M. (2010) 'The future of meetings: the case for face-to-face', *Cornell Hospitality Industry Perspectives*. Cornell University.

Durkheim, E. (1978) 'Sociology and the social sciences', in, M. Traugott (ed.) *Emile Durkheim on Institutional Analysis*. Chicago: University of Chicago Press.

Dwyer, L., Forsyth, P. and Dwyer, W. (2010) *Tourism Economics and Policy*. Bristol: Channel View.

Ehrenreich, B. (2006) *Dancing in the Streets: A History of Collective Joy*. New York: Metropolitan Books.

Fairley, S. (2009) 'The role of the mode of transport in the identity maintenance of sport fan travel groups', *Journal of Sport and Tourism*, 14(2/3): 205–22.

Falassi, A. (ed.) (1987) *Time Out of Time: Essays on the Festival*. Albuquerque: University of New Mexico Press.

Finkel, R. (2010) 'Dancing around the ring of fire: social capital, tourism resistance, and gender dichotomies at Up Helly Aa in Lerwick, Shetland', *Event Management*, 14: 275–85.

Fredline, E. and Faulkner, B. (2002) 'Variations in residents' reactions to major motorsport events: why residents perceive the impacts of events differently', *Event Management*, 7(2): 115–25.

Funk, D. (2008) *Consumer Behaviour in Sport and Events*. Oxford: Elsevier.

Getz, D. (2012) *Event Studies: Theory, Research and Policy for Planned Events*. 2nd edition. London: Routledge.

Getz, D. (2013) *Event Tourism*. New York: Cognizant Communications.

Getz, D. and Andersson, T., (2010) 'The event-tourist career trajectory: a study of high-involvement amateur distance runners', *Scandinavian Journal of Tourism and Hospitality*, 19(4): 468–91.

Getz, D. and McConnell, A. (2011) 'Event tourist careers and mountain biking', *Journal of Sport Management*, 25(4): 326–38.

Getz, D. and Patterson, I. (2013) 'Social worlds as a framework for examining event and travel careers', *Tourism Analysis*, 85(5): 485–501.

Gilmore, J. and Pine, J. (2007) *Authenticity: What Consumers Really Want.* Boston: Harvard Business School Press.

Green, B. and Chalip, L. (1998) 'Sport tourism as the celebration of subculture', *Annals of Tourism Research*, 25(2): 275–91.

Green, C. and Jones, I. (2005) 'Serious leisure, social identity and sport tourism', *Sport in Society*, 8: 164–81.

Hall, C.M. (2002) 'ANZAC Day and secular pilgrimage', *Tourism Recreation Research*, 27(2): 83–7.

Havitz, M. and Dimanche, F. (1997) 'Leisure involvement revisited: conceptual conundrums and measurement advances', *Journal of Leisure Research*, 29(3): 245–78.

Havitz, M. and Dimanche, F. (1999) 'Leisure involvement revisited: drive properties and paradoxes', *Journal of Leisure Research*, 31(2): 122–49.

Homans, G.C. (1958) 'Social behavior as exchange', *American Journal of Sociology*, 63(6): 597–606.

International Association of Fairs and Expositions (IAFE) (www.fairsandexpos.com)

Klaes, M. (2008) 'Transaction costs, history of', in J. Eatwell, M. Milgate and P. Newman (eds.) (1987) *The New Palgrave: A Dictionary of Economics.* London and New York: Macmillan and Stockton.

Lusch, R. and Vargo, S. (2006) 'Service dominant logic: reactions, reflections, and refinements', *Marketing Theory*, 6(3): 281–88.

Manning, F. (ed.) (1983) *The Celebration of Society: Perspectives on Contemporary Cultural Performance.* Bowling Green, OH: Bowling Green University Popular Press.

Marshall, G. (1998) 'Exchange theory', in *A Dictionary of Sociology.* Online. Available: <www.encyclopedia.com/doc/1O88-exchangetheory.html> (accessed 24 December 2009).

Moscardo, G. (2010) 'The shaping of tourist experience: the importance of stories and themes', in, M. Morgan, P. Lugosi and B. Ritchie (eds.) *The Tourism and Leisure Experience: Consumer and Managerial Perspectives.* Bristol: Channel View, pp. 43–58.

Nolan, M. and Nolan, S. (1992) 'Religious sites as tourism attractions in Europe', *Annals of Tourism Research*, 19(1): 68–78.

Pomfret, R., Wilson, J. and Lobmayr, B. (2012) *Bidding for Sport Mega-Events.* The University of Adelaide School of Economics. Research Paper No. 2009–30.

Preuss, H. (2009) 'Opportunity costs and efficiency of investments in mega sport events', *Journal of Policy Research in Tourism, Leisure and Events*, 1(2): 131–40.

Quinn, B. (2003) 'Symbols, practices and myth-making: cultural perspectives on the Wexford Opera Festival', *Tourism Geographies*, 5(3): 329–49.

Richards, G. (2007) 'The festivalization of society or the socialization of festivals? The case of Catalunya', in G. Richards (ed.) *Cultural Tourism: Global and Local perspectives.* New York: Haworth, pp. 257–69.

Richards, G. and Palmer, R. (2010) *Eventful Cities: Cultural Management and Urban Revitalisation.* Oxford: Butterworth Heinemann.

Rojek, C. (2005) *Leisure Theory: Principles and Practice.* Basingstoke, England: Palgrave Macmillan.

Rostenraub, M. (2009) *Major League Winners: Using Sports and Cultural Centers as Tools for Economic Development.* New York: Basic Books.

Schulenkorf, N., Thomson, A. and Schlenker, K. (2011) 'Intercommunity sport events: vehicles and catalysts for social capital in divided societies', *Event Management*, 15: 105–19.

Shipway, R. and Jones, I. (2007) 'Running away from home: understanding visitor experiences and behaviour at sport tourism events', *International Journal of Tourism Research*, 9(5): 373–83.

Shipway, R. and Jones, I. (2008) 'The great suburban Everest: an 'insiders' perspective on experiences at the 2007 Flora London Marathon', *Journal of Sport and Tourism*, 13(1): 61–77.

Stebbins, R. (1992) *Amateurs, Professionals, and Serious Leisure*. Montreal: McGill-Queen's University Press.

Stebbins, R. (2004) 'Serious leisure, volunteerism and quality of life', in J. Haworth and A. Veal (eds.) *Work and Leisure*. London: Routledge, pp. 162–85.

Stebbins, R. (2006) *Serious Leisure: A Perspective for Our Time*. Somerset, NJ: Aldine Transaction Publications.

Turner, V. (1969) *The Ritual Process: Structure and Anti-Structure*. New York: Aldine de Gruyter.

Turner, V. (1974) 'Liminal to liminoid, in play, flow and ritual: an essay in comparative symbology', in E. Norbeck (ed.) *The Anthropological Study of Human Play*. Rice University Studies, 60: 53–92.

Unruh, D. (1980) 'The nature of social worlds', *Pacific Sociological Review*, 23: 271–96.

Van Gennep, A. (1909) *The Rites of Passage* (1960 translation by M. Vizedom and G. Coffee). London: Routledge and Kegan Paul.

Waters, H. (1939) *History of Fairs and Expositions*. London, Canada: Reid Brothers.

Wuensch, U. (2008): *Facets of Contemporary Event Communication: Theory and Practice for Event Success*. Bad Honnef, Germany: K.H. Bock.

Yeoman, I., Robertson, M. and Smith, K. (2012) 'A futurist's view on the future of events', in S. Page and J. Connell (eds.) *The Routledge Handbook of Events*. London: Routledge, pp. 507–25.

4 Scenarios for the future of events and festivals

Mick Jagger at 107 and Edinburgh Fringe

Ian Yeoman, Martin Robertson,
Una McMahon-Beattie and Nyasha Musarurwa

Future points

- The future of experiences is not new but elasticated, as festival and events will be revisited.
- Whilst world economic growth will be driven by Asia, the United States will still be the world's No. 1 consumer of events and festivals.
- Society will be ageing and ageless in the near future.
- Technology will be part of the festival and event experience and a facilitator of future festivals and events.

Introduction: a tipping point

The power of festivals and events is multifarious. As both historic artefacts and barometers of current beliefs, opinions and the state of society, events and festivals can be inordinately useful tools. Festivals have always had a social function. They are for people and, in large, celebrations of those people. The celebration may be of people's creation or their creativity, their work or their play. Sport, artistic performances, traditions, culture and religion are all possible foci of a festival. Getz (2012a) notes that there is consensus in research that festivals and other leisure events are a convergence of activities at a defined time and place and that they are shared experiences. As such cultural celebrations, business events, arts and entertainment, sports and recreation, and political functions are all typologies of planned events (Getz 2012b). The number, type and frequency of them may be indicative of wealth, cultural stability and local and national identity. Many of the current expectations of planned events and festivals have emerged from their socio-political environment. They have strong links with politics and policy (Dredge and Whitford 2011).

In this chapter the authors explore whether festivals and events have reached a tipping point, that is, the stage at which the driving forces of change in relation to events and festivals cannot be reversed. These forces may include the emergence of global experiences, or how climate change is changing tourism products, or the scarcity of oil for international travel (Yeoman 2012; Gladwell 2003). From a festival and event perspective, the survival of festivals will not only have much to do with the shift of economic power from the western world (predominantly Europe and the United States) to the east (Asia and Pacific-Asia), but also their capacity to make an adjustment in lieu of cultural taste and lifestyle changes. In a world of change, people will share a desire for new experiences (Yeoman 2008, 2012, 2013) and will want those experiences to be unique and demonstrate a degree of individuality (Yeoman 2013; Future Foundation 2013). As such festivals and events will live and die by their capacity to ensure these two elements. Similarly, their propensity to involve festival and event visitors in such a way as to ensure co-creative activity is important if a higher level of meaning is sought from the attendee (Ryan 2012). Even now this desire for sharing and co-creation is highly evident in festivals as attendees use their smart phones to photograph, tag and share their experiences via Facebook or Twitter (Yeoman 2012). There was once a clear delineation between our online and offline worlds; one had a clear sense of 'using the Internet' or 'going online'. The explosion of smart phone capabilities is now transforming the way in which people access the Internet. Boundaries between the online and offline are becoming increasingly blurred as consumers embrace a culture of constant connectivity.

Being older does not stop consumers from being interested in looking good or following fashion (Future Foundation 2013). Many cultural tastes overlap and are being shared in what is increasingly becoming an ageless society (Yeoman *et al.* 2011). More people who were once labelled 'old' do not see themselves that they way (see Figure 4.1). Indeed there has been less of a shift to a maturity in cultural consumption. For example, whilst the classical arts are enjoyed now by a largely older segment, these are not being followed in the same numbers by the next generation. It is suggested therefore that the range of choice offered to all ages has given festival and event activity a common platform for this shared activity, and, concomitantly, has made competition for that provision more profound.

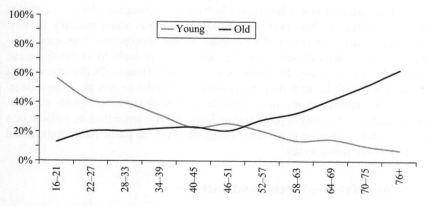

Figure 4.1 Self-Perceptions of Age

Why study the future?

The future is the indefinite time period after the present (Hasting, Selbie and Gray 1908). Whether it is less than a millisecond or a billion years away, its arrival is considered inevitable due to the existence of time and the laws of physics. Due to the nature of the reality and the unavoidability of the *future*, everything that currently exists and will exist is temporary and will come to an end. The *future* and the concept of eternity have been major subjects of philosophy, religion and science, and defining them noncontroversially has consistently eluded the greatest of minds. Future studies, or futurology, is the science, art and practice of postulating possible futures, or more basically, the study of the future seeks to understand what is likely to continue, what is likely to change, and what is novel. If the field of events and festivals are at a point of tipping, understanding how changes will occur is of absolute importance of the communities, businesses and researchers involved in events and festivals. One way to understand how the future could unfold is the use of scenarios. The history of scenario planning lies in two worlds (Lindgren 2009). The first was future studies, where scenario analysis became an important method for generating futures thinking and scenarios became an effective presentation format. The second was strategy, where strategists and managers since the 1970s have searched for new and more relevant tools to work with complex issues. Modern scenario planning is attributed to Herman Kahn (van der Heijden 2002) and the RAND Corporation. Kahn developed a technique called 'future-now' thinking. The scenarios he developed were part of military strategy research conducted for the US government, and he coined the term 'thinking the unthinkable'. Walton places scenario planning in the paradigm *constructivist interpretation* based on the underpinning criteria of emergent construction, development of alternatives, internalization, localism and plausibility (Walton 2008). However, Walton's arguments are undermined by the notion of plausibility in which he argues that any scenario should be possible, credible and relevant. Fahey and Randall also use the argument as (1998: 9): 'Plausible evidence should indicate that the projected narrative could take place (it is possible), demonstrate how it could take place (it is credible) and illustrate its implications for the organizations (it is relevant)'. However, as scenario planning is about multiple futures, a spectrum of different forms of knowledge is also appropriate, otherwise audiences will never think of new ideas. Fundamentally plausibility is the discourse of rationality and certainty. Bergman, Karlsson and Axelsson (2010) have argued rationality needs to be stretched and disordered in order to find new knowledge. Hence future studies can or cannot claim the truth or can or cannot claim explanation. Sometimes, the story is just a future drawn from science fiction, a vision or a prognosis, but as Yeoman *et al.* (2012) suggest, it is how participants engage and act out possible future states.

Scenarios of future of events and festivals

In this section two scenarios are presented and considered. First, *Heritage rock: Mick Jagger plays Woodstock at 107* portrays an ageing and ageless society from a music festival perspective. Second *Edinburgh Fringe 2050* demonstrates how technology *is* changing and *could* change the comedy festival experience. Each scenario has been constructed using three driving forces that are considered to be near or at a point of tipping. These drivers are the basis of the story portrayed in each scenario to demonstrate how change could occur (Yeoman 2012).

Scenario 1: Heritage rock: Mick Jagger plays Woodstock at 107

James and Melanie live in New York, where James has recently retired from a long career as a teacher. Melanie gave up work when their first child was born, and since the kids have left home she has focused on creative pursuits, particularly music. They are revisiting Woodstock to celebrate retirement and rekindle fond memories. Mick Jagger and the Rolling Stones are the headline act along with the New York Philharmonic, Phish Juniors and Led Zeppelin II. The visit is also a chance to holiday in Sullivan County, which will allow them to trek in the local mountains, go boating on nearby lakes, play the odd round of golf and see the Experimental Theatre Troup at Highland Lake. James and Melanie are not roughing it at Woodstock as they did in 2012 but rather taking the glam camping option and staying in the yurt luxury tents, which are an alternative to a hotel in reality. The tents or yurts are wooden frameworks covered in canvas that come with spa, infinity pool, ensuite facilities, a king-size bed with the finest Egyptian cotton and butler service. All in all, James and Melanie are enjoying their festival holiday: a real five-star experience.

Driver 1: US wealth

The accumulation of personal and national wealth represents a primary socio-economic trend, with wealth improvement (or the *promise* of wealth improvement) forming the basis for the lifestyle preferences, behaviours and expectations of the US consumer. Just as affluence boosts effective demand in an economy, it also creates a *culture of expectation* among consumers, as wealth gains empower millions to demand, for instance, ever-expanding choice from companies and brands, efficient and personalized customer service (at no extra cost), premium quality innovation, visible corporate commitment to tackling environmental, ethical problems and so on. For all of the economic tumult felt during the Global Financial Crisis (GFC), US citizens remain among the most wealthy in the world and are forecasted to continue to be the leaders in 2050 (Yeoman 2012), with per capita incomes exceeding those in many other developed markets and dwarfing those in the emerging nations of China, Brazil and India. Meanwhile, as a home to the super-wealthy, the United States remains a considerable global force: by 2012 almost 4 in 10 of the world's dollar millionaires resided in the United States (Credit Suisse 2012). Affluence breeds the *upgrade culture* in so many consumer sectors today, energizing propositions such as super-luxury products, personalized communication, special club memberships, exclusive events, sophisticated concierge services or a behind the scenes tour at a festival. The definition of luxury is changing in the United States, according to the Future Foundation (2013), with a clear shift to experiential forms of consumption.

Driver 2: Elasticated experience

Millions of lives are now no longer marked by defining *things will never be the same after this* moments. Fewer individuals will face only one wedding ceremony or cohabit with the same person forever. Fewer will achieve only one major but unitary ambition (climbing Everest, attending Woodstock, witnessing an eclipse, etc.). As consumers accumulate wealth they search for self-esteem and self-actualization because they perceive that they have all the material goods they need and their basic requirements have been met. This trend has been coined as the *Desire for New Experiences* (Yeoman 2008). The consumer focuses his or her expenditure on goods and services, which will improve his or her quality of life and enhance his or her sense of life. Therefore, as the experience economy grows, consumers devote their wealth to travel, events and other experiences.

The tourism sector has long had to address the issues of long distance and big spending, that is, how to persuade consumers to take expensive vacations in far-flung destinations. This has led to promotions that emphasize a *once in a lifetime* dimension or a *do this before you die* aspect. But as life expectancy extends, affluence stabilizes and (even extreme) experiences multiply, is there now a generation of over 65s who will have to make more than one bucket list? Why should a young Californian backpacker assume that she will visit Macchu Picchu or attend Woodstock only once? Many consumers will survive life-endangering illnesses only to face others some time later and then, in due course, survive them too. Many too will have multiple careers when once a single one was more than enough. Such *elasticated* experience will bring the widespread realization that no moment, no choice and no state of affairs is unique and irreversible: they can all be revisited (Future Foundation 2013).

Driver 3: Ageless society

As society develops and solves many of the riddles of disease, people will live longer. Futurist Ray Kurzweil (Kurzweil and Grossman 2010) is a pioneer of such a cause, where the human body integrates with technological advancement; when body parts wear out or are no longer functional, they are simply replaced with technological substitutes. DePinho and colleagues (Jaskelioff *et al.* 2010) at Harvard Medical School have brought this proposition to reality through partially reversing age-related degeneration in mice, resulting in new growth of the brain and testes, improved fertility, and the return of a lost cognitive function. The research achieved a milestone in ageing science by engineering mice with a controllable telomerase gene. The telomerase enzyme maintains the protective caps called telomeres that shield the ends of chromosomes. As humans age, low levels of telomerase are associated with progressive erosion of telomeres, which may then contribute to tissue degeneration and functional decline in the elderly.

By creating mice with a telomerase switch, the researchers were able to generate prematurely aged mice. The switch allowed the scientists to find out whether reactivating telomerase in the animals would restore telomeres and mitigate the signs and symptoms of ageing. So, have DePinho and colleagues discovered the secret to the fountain of youth? If so, Mick Jagger may well live beyond 107 as portrayed in the scenario.

The research of DePinho in the wider context facilitates a discussion of the demographic trend of populations living longer and the redefinition of age stereotypes. As the present generation of Baby Boomers enters retirement, they have little sense that their attitudes and behaviours are evolving exactly in line with those traditionally associated with 'old age'. Attitudes to the ageing process are evolving, and the relevance of age-specific marketing messages is falling under scrutiny. Increasingly, it is argued that there is less support for the idea that reaching one's 60s or 70s need imply an automatic rejection of concerns about appearance, well-being or physical activity. Nor do many millions of older consumers believe that certain leisure activities or interests should be the exclusive preserve of younger generations. The result is the emergence of what we might call *ageless attitudes*, that is, the idea that age should be less of a determining factor in how the typical person defines him/herself (Yeoman *et al.* 2011). While increases in longevity are clearly important here, perhaps the most transformative factor is that Americans, for example, are remaining healthier for longer. Indeed, many can now expect to enjoy the later stages of their lives not just in relative good health but in material comfort too. Society is witnessing the rise of a healthy, wealthy older generation for which the classic associations of old age may seem simply irrelevant. In the twenty-first century, the emphasis on perma-beauty grows stronger; expectations surrounding aesthetic perfection are pronounced, and age is less and less of a valid excuse for not maintaining one's appearance, especially as a wide range of older celebrities show how one can remain perpetually glamorous, fashionable and youthful in attitude. The arrival of the Baby Boomers at the retirement stage is creating a greater demand for activities that allow them to stay active and involved.

Scenario 2: Edinburgh Fringe 2050

Zhang Ming is 28 years old and lives in London but is originally from Shanghai. Some would describe her as a no-brow cultural vulture, that is, a person who loves both comedy and the opera. She has just completed a PhD on Thought Technologies and the Experience Economy. She admits she is a technology geekess. With the blink of an eyelid she can access the semantic web via her contact lens and play the latest interactive games using Google's Thought Cap. She loves comedy and has developed an interest in real, blended and virtual comedians. Over 3,000 acts are playing at Edinburgh Fringe Festival in 2050 including Norman Wisdom VIII, the Cambridge Footlights, Beijing University Liberals and Tony 'the Political Comedian' Abbott. The comedy festival, which is spread over 21 days during the month of August, is the world's largest gathering of funny people, from clowns to ex-political leaders seeking a new career to vintage performers. Zhang was in Edinburgh for the weekend, having arrived on the Friday evening and bunking with some old university friends who live in the city. Highlights of the weekend included the Norman Wisdom VIII's performance with the virtual but dead Norman Wisdom in a series of Mr Grimsdale sketches. Zhang was able to capture the performance using the video facility attached to her contact lens retina and share with friends worldwide. It was as if she was saying 'I'm here; where are you'? At the city's Comedy Club Zhang and friends laughed at ex-Australian Prime Minister Tony Abbot's routine of political satire to the point that Zhang's clothes created a happy sensation feeling for her. Zhang even bumped into old friends who were performing at the club; her facial recognition software provided all the information she needed for conversation's included milestones, careers paths and favourite laughs. All in all, a fantastic weekend at the world's greatest comedy festival.

Driver 1: Creative consumption

Driven by the Digital Revolution and the rise of co-creation as a more mainstream proposition, consumers are better positioned than ever before to design, customize and influence the products and services they buy (Yeoman *et al.* 2012). This is reflected in Zhang sharing her experiences at the comedy club. In turn, the concept of creativity has been elevated in importance and, as an activity, can now deliver high levels of social capital. For the consumer of the 2010s, opportunities to express one's creativity and artistry have become widespread through the rise of sophisticated home technologies and online platforms brought about by a digital society, the clamour for greater corporate transparency and the move towards establishing more intimate dialogues between consumers and experiences. Against this background co-creation has grown rapidly and, in the YouTube era, anyone can now submit their ideas for consideration by a potentially global audience. Creative consumption is about using *smart* and *social* technology to showcase one's views as experiences unfold; no more do consumers delay broadcasting their thoughts on a visit to a trendy restaurant or holiday destination. Live streams of updates allow consumers to seize the social zeitgeist, and the strategic 'tweet' has become key to status enhancement in real time. Yeoman (2012) identifies this trend as one of the motivations for travel through which travellers immerse and share experiences through visualization, hence gaining forms of capital.

As noted above, new technology platforms such as the smart phone have enabled these changes in consumer behaviour. Axelsson (2010) has observed how young, Swedish adults are posting real experiences through social media, and Hollenbeck and Kaikati (2012) have noted how consumers use Facebook in real time to accumulate social capital. Within Asian culture Ito and Crutcher (2014) have highlighted how creative forms of play have emerged into a liminal state in which reality and virtual experiences cannot be separated. Yeoman and colleagues (2012) have also noted how events and festivals have become increasingly important narrations of creativity. They envisage that as a result of globalization, digitalization, the rise of the knowledge worker, the boom in intellectual property, changes to leisure consumption and social networks, the festival and event goer from China and other emerging economies will be like those from the west in the terms of creative consumption. In China, the attraction of being a media producer, an artist, or a designer has never been so enticing. Here, consumption of cultural goods and services has increased, and creative workers from Europe, North America and Asia are moving to Chinese cities; thus culture is increasingly positioned as a pillar industry (Keane 2013).

Driver 2: Catwalk computing

The concept of wearable technology is gaining acceptance, as smart watches, glasses and other accessories are offered in the marketplace (in the scenario thought caps, contact lenses and clothing are types of wearable technologies). Technology has been impatient to break free from clunky interfaces and unportable devices. It is no longer confined to mysterious aluminium boxes or trapped behind glass screens; it is coming out of people's pockets and onto their clothes, skin and surroundings. In the last two to three years there has been an explosion of networked devices that talk to each other, made possible by new industry developments such as Bluetooth. Just as the consumer has seen the migration of tasks from desktop computer to smartphone, the possibility exists that there will be a migration of activities from smartphone to wearable technologies. The most profiled of the wearable technologies is Google Glass, which allows owners to use hands-free voice-technology to reply to messages, search the Internet, record video and images, view traffic directions and even translate their voice. Its developers claim the technology offers a more human means of interacting with the outside world, without devices interrupting the flow of everyday life (Thad 2013; Olsson *et al.* 2013). Additionally, a contact lens with simple built-in electronics is already within reach at the University of Washington. The project is known as 'A Twinkle in the Eye' (Parviz 2009). This new display technology creates visual images as laser light is scanned directly on to the viewer's retina to create a perception of a virtual image. A very small spot is focused onto the retina and is swept over in a raster pattern. Today, consumers may not be using contact lenses but Google Glass delivers many of those features (Thad 2013; Olsson *et al.* 2013) looking like a pair of glasses with a head-mounted display with augmented reality and ubiquitous computing.

Driver 3: Virtual experiences

The experience economy is today, whereas tomorrow's technology will focus on enhancing the consumer experience though virtual encounters. For example, holograms are slowly becoming a reality today and appearing in festival experiences (Harris 2013). A hologram is a three-dimensional photograph made with the aid of a laser, which can serve multiple functions, e.g. as a combined lens, aspheric corrector, beam combiner and narrow filter (Yeoman 2012; Taylor 2013). This technology is moving to television in the form of 3D holographic sets, which could potentially be projected on a table for people to watch. Holographic telepresence allows for the recording of a three-dimensional image in one location to show it in another location, in near real time, anywhere in the world. Illustrating this Japan has promised in its 2022 World Cup bid to beam live matches directly onto pitches in stadiums throughout the world. This will be made possible by placing 200 8K Ultra-HD TV cameras around the stadium. The images will then be shown on massive flatbed screens laid on the pitch of the 400 stadiums across 208 countries (Tanimoto 2012). The match will then be viewed as a live 360 degree hologram and there will be no need for 3D glasses. In relation to music festivals, auto stereoscopic and volumetric displays will be used to provide three-dimensional images that can be viewed without additional apparatus like glasses. This technology currently exists but as yet the displays are not suitable for large-screen theatres, making the expense not justifiable for small audience (Yi-Pai, Chen and Yi-Chang 2012). In the home, it will become a thing of the past to have television sets in the living room, as television will become part of the house infrastructure, with technological appliances as thin as wallpaper being fitted to the walls, projecting pictures. Since holograms are essentially a thin film, they are not sensitive to the shape of the substrate to which they are attached, hence full wall television screens are possible. The key to this invention is through photorefractive polymer, a plastic material that allows 3D images to be recorded and updated every two seconds (Blanche *et al.* 2010). Virtual experiences will also be combined with haptic technology, which is tactical feedback technology based on the science of applying the sense of touch in human-computer interaction. There are a number of distinct subtypes here including proprioceptive (general sensory information about the body), vestibular (the perception of head motion), kinaesthetic (the feeling of motion in the body) and cutaneous (sensory information from the skin). These haptic sensations are created by actuators or motors, which create vibrations that are managed and controlled by embedded software (Saddick *et al.* 2011). Haptic technologies create fulfilling multimodal experiences that improve usability by engaging touch, sight and sound. They also inject a sense of realism into user experiences by exciting the senses and allowing the user to feel the action. Finally they allow for restoration of mechanical feel by creating a more confident user experience, and they improve safety by overcoming distractions. So, haptic technologies will allow tactile feedback by applying forces and vibrations creating a sense of place.

What is the significance?

In order to consider the significance of the scenarios and drivers from a futures perspective, a number of questions and statements are propositioned and answered in this section. They include the meaning of life, liminal state, celebrity status and accumulation of cultural capital.

The role of events and festivals and the meaning of life

Events and festivals have entered the psyche of the population. There are a myriad of events, with many forms and functions (Getz 2008, 2012a, 2012b), and they appear in government policy at all levels of application (social, economic and cultural) (Dredge and Whitford 2011; Hall and Rusher 2004). As economic responsibility is increasingly decentralized, the political and policy significance of festivals and events places them as ever more important in socio-spatial strategies (Benneworth and Dauncey 2010; Robertson and Wardrop 2012). Similarly organized events are either applied to, or else associated with, the private sector at many levels (e.g. training, advertising, communication strategy component, community involvement, brand communication and celebration). As such they are wrapped up in the future of both public and private sector enterprises. Importantly, aside from their organizational function, festivals and events have a very long-standing significance for individuals and groupings in every country. Historically and socially, they are a thoroughly human manifestation. As such, as humankind goes forward, festivals and events will remain an important feature of society.

In the past, the trend of the mega-event has been a western society manifestation but now, and into the future, it will be a truly global one. Weber and Ali-Knight (2012) note that Asia, the Middle East and North America are currently truly global players in this respect. Jones (2012a, 2012b) notes that staging such events is not without its problems, particularly for emerging economies. Nonetheless, projecting into the future, it is clear that mega-events and festivals will be part of the global narrative of change.

How events, festivals and play have become liminal

Contemporary consumer societies have become serious about the act of being at play. Nobody thinks that fun is frivolous any more. Usage of play *technologies*, from Internet-enabled consoles in the home to social games played on social networking profiles has become widespread, with significant proportions of global consumers claiming to play video games on a regular basis. Meanwhile, as mobile devices become increasingly sophisticated, tactile and game-friendly, *gaming-on-the-go* is evolving into a popular leisure activity, enabling consumers to cleverly fill moments of otherwise unproductive downtime with digital fun. However, gaming as it is traditionally known is changing. Leisure and play are undergoing a real-time revolution, one in which acquiring social capital has become an instant, *on-the-go* affair. Play is now constant and technology has being the enabler of an experience economy that is right here, right now. What is liminality? It was Victor Turner who called play 'liminal', meaning that it occupies a threshold between reality and unreality, as play is difficult to define and separate from the behaviours of everyday life (Turner 1977). He goes on to define liminality as an ambiguous state of being, a transition, period or space 'betwixt and between' normal states or conditions that is present in many rituals, both sacred and secular. From an events perspective liminal spaces are well documented in the literature (Andrews and Roberts 2012), with technology acting as the bridge between reality and science fiction. Central to the dimension of liminality is an understanding of how technology has changed experiences. Technology allows the personalization of experiences in a real-time environment, whether it is video streaming, sharing or tagging. But events and festivals are *real* experiences, and it is important for event and festival organizers to realize how technological advancement can enhance those experiences.

The desire for celebrity and magic nostalgia

The past represents an important element of a modern world, one through which festivals and events can establish an emotional connection with certain groups of consumers by leveraging feelings of nostalgia, warmth and familiarity. Yeoman (2008) has identified that there is a feel amongst consumers that the past was a happier and better place than today. They refer to real or imaginary worlds in which community and family ties were stronger, neighbourhoods were safer and the pleasures in life were generally simpler and healthier. These consumers have a desire for authentic heritage, places, moments or experiences that have a real *history* and *story*, that have weathered difficult times and that can be relied upon to do their best for them (Holyfield *et al.* 2013). Particularly in periods of social or economic volatility and uncertainty, consumers experience a heightened fascination for the past and are drawn to the symbols, smells, sounds, language and brands that are associated with it. Although many remain willing to embrace the convenience and cost benefits offered by mass-produced goods and services, this authentic-seeking trend references the search undertaken by some for real and original experiences or products (Carnegie and McCabe 2008; Chambers 2009). In turn, this can influence purchasing decisions across a wide range of sectors including food, leisure and travel. In summary, this sense of the past drives the authentic-seeking individual who enjoys finding experiences that have clear links to a place, time or culture. That individual prefers experiences that are produced in a traditional way, that are unique and that have a genuine story behind them. Such authenticity is perceived as adding value, of offering premium lustre and as a component of self-actualization (Pearce and Moscardo 1986).

Buoyed by the public's near-constant and ever-more intimate levels of access to the lives of the rich and famous, it is possible to talk of a 'cult of the celebrity'. This cult is able to influence and mould some consumers in their everyday decisions and attitudes. In many cases, knowledge of celebrities (concerning the brands of clothes they wear, their favourite perfume, the names of their pets, the restaurants and bars they regularly visit) could rival the knowledge that consumers have of a family member or close friend. Indeed for some, celebrities are seen as public property, with access to their personal information being viewed more as a right than a privilege. This has been enhanced by the social media and seemingly limitless content sharing. Consumers can follow a celebrity's thoughts as they are *tweeted* (typed and sent in to the social media environment using Twitter, the social-media/microblogging site). A Google alert can keep the public informed of the celebrity's latest comings and goings. The use of a Twitter hashtag can create such a global swirl of gossip that a story can become almost unstoppable and unpreventable (as the failure of several high-profile super-injunctions demonstrates all too clearly). Although few may choose to admit it, consumers are now more receptive to the opinions of celebrities than ever before. In this sense, famous figures have benefited from what social commentators describe as the death of deference, i.e. the erosion of the respect that was traditionally held for established institutions and the formal political classes. Celebrities often operate as a social honey pot, providing a shared focal point for everyday conversations and social media exchanges. The details of their glamorous lives serve as a powerful source of inspiration for the way consumers behave and what they consume. Celebrities showcase luxury, the latest fashion trends and beauty products, cutting edge diets or gastronomy and, as such, can provide inspiration or stimulate copycat behaviour. So much of what celebrities have, consumers want. This leads them to mimic aspects of celebrities' lives and even take advice from them. As such consumers buy products or identify with ideas because they think the celebrity in question is beautiful, successful, fashionable, politically sound, and shares their values. Although consumers may claim not to be influenced by celebrities' opinions or endorsements, countless success stories of brand-celebrity partnerships or products launched under the name of famous figures tell a quite different story.

How event goers accumulate cultural capital

The essence of this trend is that as consumers grow wealthier and better educated they like to display twenty-first-century sophistications through boasting about what they have done and where they have been. This is not about conspicuous consumption and materialism but rather a desire to accumulate social and cultural capital. Indeed, in an eco- and price-sensitive, post-recession landscape, ostentation and/or excessive consumption has, for so many millions of consumers, long since lost much of the appeal it may once have held. Consumers accumulate cultural capital by acquiring knowledge and skills, by realizing personal accomplishments and partaking in fulfilling experiences. It can be found in any number of ways from critiquing the latest nominated comedian to watching the Bolshoi ballet. This is an age in which it is seriously unimpressive not to be able to show some accomplishment or some private knowledge accumulation. As such future festival and events attendees are likely to be more cultured, knowledgeable, have a desire for experiences (whether new or revisited) and want to experience local culture. Indeed in terms of festival patronage, comedy and creativity are one of the key drivers, as event goers place more emphasis on live cultural experiences than on traditional physical heritage attractions (Bartie 2013).

Research has also dwelt on the significance of events in the terms of image, which is increasingly being viewed as part of cultural capital. Richards and Palmer (2012: 2) go as far as to state that cities either 'develop to meet the challenges created by the pace of global change, or they resist the impulse of transformation and stagnate'; thus cultural capital has become the defining factor for cities.

As noted in the *Edinburgh Fringe 2050* scenario, mobility is an important feature of a modern world – the change for openness and desire for escape (Picard and Robinson 2006) – as events and festivals offer an opportunity to create experiences that are distinct and formed around 'place' through history, difference and authenticity. The Edinburgh Fringe Festival (Prentice and Anderson 2003) positions Edinburgh as a creative city and this compliments the traditional image of Scotland as the home of dramatic landscapes and bagpipes. The Fringe is also part of the night-time economy (Evans 2012), as the festival is focused around live performances and social gatherings in clubs, bars, restaurants and other venues. The night economy is about creative expression, facilitated through social exchange, alcohol and feeling good, which can be categorized as hedonism.

Concluding remarks

The implications for the future of the events industry based on the present are significant, as for some time now the marketing of festivals and events has moved away from product consumption to experience engagement. As the *Edinburgh Fringe* scenario highlights, the interaction of technology and play in the enhancement of experiences is a trend that is affecting all demographic groups. The use of smart phones to share experiences is now commonplace, and innovation, personalization and interactivity are set to become even more important. The adoption of technology by audiences also allows festival and event organizers to segment and target attendees more effectively, since the profiling of consumer behaviour and socio-demographics becomes easier. Furthermore, as the scenario portrays, the interaction of play and technology allows the consumer to be part of the co-creation process, and this can only enhance the Edinburgh Fringe experience. Technology becomes part of the entertainment (a virtual Norman Wisdom) and facilitates greater immersion in the experience. This results in the enhancement of Zhang's cultural capital and identity.

The *Mick Jagger plays Woodstock at 107* scenario highlights that festivals and events are no longer the preserve of the young. A highly educated generation of Baby Boomers, who are in better health and have more disposable income than previous generations, will exit the workforce en masse during the next decade. Many of this generation profited from the housing boom of the last decade and represent a financially potent, demanding, still aspirational and ever more technologically aware market-segment (Yeoman *et al.* 2011). Older generations are often seen as more traditional, conservative and less enamoured by the idea of embracing modern technology to its full extent. But the ageless society is a trend with a long trajectory and, progressively, it will lead to a weakening of such age-determined distinctions (especially as the middle-aged grow older but remain youthful in their attitudes). Event experiences designed explicitly for 'old' people will become less common and any older consumers who feel patronized will vote with their feet. The ageless society mind-set will also be engendered by the impact of high-profile, high-achieving older celebrities such as Elton John and Mick Jagger. 'Ageing rockers' such as these are and will be role models who influence attitudes, appearance and fashions.

Marketers of twenty-first-century festivals and events are engaging attendees as storytellers, facilitators and co-creators who provide high quality, exciting and interactive content that enhance the experience. Entertainers and performers are the advertisers and the draw of the 'celebrity' becomes an important feature of festivals and events. When *Mick Jagger plays Woodstock* he is the central feature of the appeal for attending; he and the Rolling Stones are the headline act. A 107-year-old Mick Jagger is still a celebrity who exudes good health, glamour, and an active lifestyle. That said the hype surrounding 'traditional' types of celebrities will not diminish. Film stars, singers, and actors will continue to be central to marketing activities of festivals and events. Roll on Woodstock 2050!

References

Andrews, H. and Roberts, L. (2012) *Liminal Landscapes: travel, experience and space in-between*. London: Routledge.

Axelsson, A. (2010) 'Perceptual and personal: Swedish young adults and their use of mobile phones', *New Media and Society*, 12(1): 35–54.

Bartie, A. (2013) *The Edinburgh Festivals: culture and society in post-war Britain*. Edinburgh: Edinburgh University Press.

Benneworth, P. and Dauncey, H. (2010) 'International urban festivals as a catalyst for governance capacity building', *Environment and Planning C: Government and Policy*, 28(6): 1083–100.

Bergman, A.K., Karlsson, J.C. and Axelsson, J. (2010) 'Truth claims and explanatory claims: an ontological typology of future studies', *Futures*, 42(8): 857–65.

Blanche, P., Bablumian, A., Voorakaraam, R., Christenson, C., Lemieux, D., Thomas, J., Norwood, R., Yamamoto, M. and Peyghambarian, N. (2010) 'Future of photorefractive based holographic 3D display', *Proc. SPIE* 7619, Practical Holography XXIV: Materials and Applications, 76190L. Online. Available: <http://proceedings.spiedigitallibrary.org/proceeding.aspx?articleid=1339701> (accessed 10 August 2013).

Carnegie, E. and McCabe, S. (2008) 'Re-enactment events and tourism: meaning, authenticity and identity', *Current Issues in Tourism*, 11(4): 349–68.

Chambers, E. (2009) 'From authenticity to significance: tourism on the frontier of culture and place', *Futures*, 41(6): 353–59.

Credit Suisse (2012) *Global Wealth Report*. Online. Available: <https://publications.credit-suisse.com/tasks/render/file/index.cfm?fileid=88EE6EC8–83E8-EB92–9D5F39D5F5CD01F4> (accessed 1 December 2013).

Dredge, D. and Whitford, M. (2011) 'Event tourism governance and the public sphere', *Journal of Sustainable Tourism*, 19(4–5): 479–99.

Evans, G. (2012) 'Events, cities and the night-time economy', in S. Page and J. Connell (eds.) *The Handbook of Events*. London: Routledge, pp. 415–30.

Getz, D. (2008) 'Event studies: definition, scope and development', *Link*, 20: 2–3. Online. Available: <http://www.heacademy.ac.uk/hlst> (accessed 31 January 2014).

Getz, D. (2012a) 'Event studies: discourses and future directions', *Event Management*, 16(2): 171–87.

Getz, D. (2012b) 'Events studies', in S. Page and J. Connell (eds.) *The Handbook of Events*. London: Routledge, pp. 489–506.

Gladwell, M. (2003) *Tipping Point: how little things can make a big difference*. London: Back Bay Books.

Fahey, L. and Randall, R.M. (1998) 'What is scenario learning?' in L. Fahey and R.M. Randall (eds.) *Learning from the Future: competitive foresight scenarios*. New York: Wiley.

Future Foundation (2013) *Global Citizen*. Online. Available: <http://nvision.futurefoundation.net> (accessed 1 December 2013).

Hall, C. and Rusher, K. (eds.) (2004) *Politics, Public Policy and the Destination*. Oxford: Butterworth-Heinemann.

Harris, M. (2013) 'The hologram of Tupac at Coachella and Saints: the value of relics for devotees', *Celebrity Studies*, 4(2): 238–40.

Hastings, J., Selbie, J.A. and Gray, L.H. (eds.) (1908) *Encyclopedia of Religion and Ethics*. Edinburgh: T. & T. Clark.

Hollenbeck, C. and Kaikati, A. (2012) 'Consumers' use of brands to reflect their actual and ideal selves on Facebook', *International Journal of Research in Marketing*, 29(4): 395–405.

Holyfield, L., Cobb, M., Murray, K. and McKinzie, A. (2013) 'Musical ties that bind: nostalgia, affect, and heritage in festival narratives', *Symbolic Interaction*, 36(4): 457–77.

Ito, K. and Crutcher, P. (2014) 'Popular mass entertainment in Japan: Mango, Pachinko and Cosplay', *Society*, 51(1): 44–8.

Jaskelioff, M., Muller, F., Thomas, E., Jiang, S., Sahin, E., Kost-Alimova, M., Protopopov, P., Horner, J., Maratos-Flier, E. and DePinho, R. (2010) 'Telomerase reactivation reverses tissue degeneration in aged telomerase-deficient mice', *Nature*, 469: 102–06.

Jones, C. (2012a) 'Events and festivals: fit for the future?', *Event Management*, 16(2): 107–18.

Jones, C. (2012b) 'Festivals and events in emergent economies: a sea change, and for whom?', *International Journal of Event and Festival Management*, 3(1): 9–11.

Keane, M. (2013) *Creative Industries in China: art, design and media*. London: Polity.

Kurzweil, R. and Grossman, T. (2010) *Transcend: nine steps to living well forever*. Rodale: Emmaus.

Lindgren, M.B.H. (ed.). (2009) *Scenario Planning: the link between future and strategy*. Basingstoke: Palgrave Macmillan.

Olsson, M., Heinrich, M., Kelly, D. and Lapetina, J. (2013) Wearable device with input and output structures. US Patent and Trademark Office. Online. Available: <www.google.com/patents/US20130044042> (accessed 28 May 2014).

Parviz, B.A. (2009) *Augmented Reality in a Contact Lens*. Online. Available: <http://spectrum.ieee.org/biomedical/bionics/augmented-reality-in-a-contact-lens/0> (accessed 31st August 2013).

Pearce, P.L. and Moscardo, G.M. (1986) 'The concept of authenticity in tourist experiences', *Journal of Sociology*, 22(1): 121–32.

Picard, D. and Robinson, M. (2006) *Festivals, Tourism and Social Change*. Bristol: Channelview.

Prentice, R. and Anderson, V. (2003) 'Festival as creative destination', *Annals of Tourism Research*, 30(1): 7–30.

Richards, G. and Palmer, R. (2012) *Eventful Cities*. Oxford: Elsevier.

Robertson, M. and Wardrop, K. (2012) 'Festival and events, government and spatial governance', in S. Page and J. Connell (eds.) *The Handbook of Events*. London: Routledge, pp. 489–506.

Ryan, C. (2012) 'The experience of events', in S.J. Page and J. Connel (eds.) *The Routledge Handbook of Events*. London: Routledge, pp. 248–59.

Saddick, A., Orozco, M., Eid, M. and Cha, J. (2011) 'Touching the future: HAVE challenges and trends', in A. Saddick, M. Orozco, M. Eid, and J. Cha (eds.) *Haptic Technologies: bringing touch to multimedia*. Berlin: Springer, pp. 183–94.

Tanimoto, M. (2012) 'FTV: Free-viewpoint television', *Signal Processing: Image Communication*, 27(6): 555–70.

Taylor, R. (2013) 'A curious conundrum: the state of holographic portraiture in the 21st century', *Journal of Physics: Conference Service*, 415(1): 1–15.

Thad, S. (2013) 'Project Glass: an extension of the self', *Pervasive Computing IEEE*, 12(2): 14–16.

Turner, V. (1977) 'Variations on a theme of liminality', in S.F. Moore and B.G. Myerhoff (eds.) *Secular Ritual*. Assen: Van Gorcum Ltd, pp. 36–52.

van der Heijden, K.A. (2002) *Sixth Sense: accelerating organizational learning with scenarios*. Chichester: Wiley.

Walton, J. (2008) 'Scanning beyond the horizon: exploring the ontological and epistemological basis for scenario planning', *Advances in Developing Human Resources*, 10(2): 147–65.

Weber, K. and Ali-Knight, J. (2012) 'Events and festivals in Asia and the Middle East/North Africa (MENA) region: opportunities and challenges', *International Journal of Event and Festival Management*, 3(1): 4–8.

Yeoman, I. (2008) *Tomorrow's Tourist*. Oxford: Routledge.

Yeoman, I. (2012) *2050: Tomorrow's Tourism*. Bristol: Channel View.

Yeoman, I. (2013) 'A futurist's thoughts on consumer trends shaping future festivals and events', *International Journal of Event and Festival Management*, 4(3): 249–60.

Yeoman, I., Hsu, C., Smith, K. and Watson, S. (2011) *Demography and Tourism*. Oxford: Goodfellows.

Yeoman, I., Robertson, M. and Smith, K. (2012) 'A futurist's view on the future of festivals', in S. Page and J. Connell (eds.) *The Handbook of Events*. London: Routledge, pp. 507–25.

Yi-Pai, H., Chen, C. and Yi-Chang, H. (2012) 'Superzone Fresnel Crystal Lens for temporal scanning auto-stereoscopic display', *Journal of Display Technology*, 8(11): 650–55.

Part 2

Contested issues, thoughts and solutions

Part 2

Contested issues, thoughts
and solutions

5 Scotland in 2025

Dependent or independent event nation?

*Matt Frew, David McGillivray and
Gayle McPherson*

Future points

- Scotland, as a nation wrestling with the possibility of political independence, provides an exemplar of a nation in transition, which in building towards 2025 will see events and culture deployed as the symbolic weapons of warfare in the politics of national and community identity.
- Events and cultural policy is framed within the backdrop of neoliberalism and current network of national agencies and destination marketing organizations strategically positioning and promoting Scotland as a Festive Nation.
- Future scenario one sees the triumph of the neoliberal drivers of events, and future scenario two pictures an independent Scotland where events and culture promote a future focused, progressive and culturally vibrant Scotland.
- The chapter concludes by asserting that Scotland of 2025 will have undergone a discursive shift in events policy and practice.

Introduction

The trajectory of human civilization can be marked by the development, depth and value that nation states place on the cultural content of their citizenry. Whether perusing the ancient artifacts of museums or art galleries, participating in community fetes or fairs, consuming classical or pop music, attending football matches or fashion shows, or performing in local theatre group or national arts festivals, culture is central to personal, community and national identity. Yet, culture is also always a contested terrain, as its symbolic meanings are deployed in the semiotic warfare of identity politics (Kidd 2002) and increasingly subject to the vagaries of capital. As a prominent expression of a nation's cultural soul, events (sporting, cultural and business) provide a useful context through which to consider important political, economic, social, cultural and technological futures (Raich 2013) and their implications looking forward to the global landscape of 2025.

Scotland represents an ideal canvas upon which to sketch out the future of events in 2025. It has arrived at an historical crossroads (Carrell 2013), culminating in a series of 'events' that could have fundamental implications for the economy and polity of this nation in 2025. For example, in 2014 Scotland's citizens will vote on national self-determination via a referendum on independence. In the same year, Scotland will host the Commonwealth Games and Ryder Cup – two events with international (some would argue, global) resonance and repercussions. In 2014 it will also wrestle with its own self-image via a second Year of Homecoming, where (re)invented traditions and symbols of national identity will be played out in a series of staged events that call upon a rich and influential cultural heritage that (it is said) is the envy of the world. In 2014, Scotland will, at one and the same time, be presenting itself at the vanguard of the future (major sporting events, internationally leading cultural events) and as a leader in preserving and celebrating a commonly promoted past (inventor of golf, mythical historical figures, land of whisky and shortbread).

This chapter, whilst placing current event policy and practice under a critical gaze, advances a future focused or reshaped Scotland of 2025. In an age of acceleration where technological connectivity and sociability are prominent influences on identity production, the role and impact of events and culture are of central importance. Although events and culture have always been seen as markers of being, providing a rootedness to place, self, citizenship and nationhood (Getz 2013; Kidd 2002), this chapter examines contemporary forces that challenge this continuing role. The chapter opens by framing Scotland's present position within the wider global events circuit before examining future forces that will see events and culture take centre stage in the contestation of postmodern identity. Informed by a series of socio-cultural analyses and taking cognizance of the powerful political, economic, social, cultural and technological forces that will collide in 2014, the chapter proposes two alternative event futures for Scotland in 2025. The first places the development of modern events and culture under a critical gaze that sees neoliberal ideology and the preeminence of the market as an insipid given. Left unchecked or challenged, scenario one sees this accentuated in 2025, as Scotland is the subject of, and in subjection to, the brandscaping (Klingmann 2007) tendencies of corporate power. Scenario two presents a resistance to corporatism and a rebalancing of identity through a digitally literate and globally connected localism. Here, in an independent Scotland of 2025, events and culture are symbolic weapons of identity deployed to defend against the corporate puppeteering of the Scottish stereotype whilst celebrating an externally facing, globally engaged and vibrant cultural identity. Finally, in acknowledging the limitations of projecting the trajectory of future forces the chapter concludes with a reflexive discussion of these two ideal type scenarios and the place of events and culture in Scotland 2025.

Locating Scotland in the global events circuit

In Scotland, over the last decade, there is evidence of a step change in the importance given over to events within the corridors of government at local, regional and national level. The national events agency, EventScotland, was established in 2003 as a joint venture between the Scottish Executive (now renamed the Scottish Government) and VisitScotland (the national tourism organization) with the aim of strengthening and promoting Scotland's events industry. It was established as a response to a perception that Scotland was not making the most of its rich and diverse sporting and cultural assets. With an annual budget of £5 million from the Scottish Government, EventScotland is charged with the responsibility to further establish Scotland as a world-leading event destination through its national events strategy, *Scotland: The Perfect Stage*. Functionally, EventScotland influences, leads, coordinates and supports people and organizations to help deliver on the event strategy (Getz 2013). They fund events that meet the criteria of having national and international significance, defined by their ability to deliver impacts including tourism, business, image and identity as a nation, media and profile, participation and development, environment and social and cultural benefits (Getz 2013). The local state can apply for funding and support, but investment will only be forthcoming on the satisfaction of these key criteria. The private sector can also apply, but again, publicly accountable outcomes must be delivered.

To complete this outline sketch of Scotland's event infrastructure, it is necessary to discuss the emergence of destination marketing organizations (DMOs) in the country's major cities. These agencies are relatively autonomous from local government structures, enabling them to operate in a more entrepreneurial fashion. In Scotland's two largest cities, Glasgow City Marketing Bureau (GCMB) and Marketing Edinburgh Ltd operate as companies targeting event business globally in tandem with EventScotland and the private sector. Both agencies have major events strategies for their cities (e.g. *Glasgow's Sport Event Strategy to 2018*), which lays out national and international positioning ambitions and is at the forefront of the 'refashioning of urban governance in the context of the neoliberalized state' (Foley, McGillivray and McPherson 2011: 66). The association of events with accelerating regimes of accumulation and city and/or nation branding in Scotland 2025 is the first of our future focused scenarios to which we now turn.

Scenario 1: Scotland the (brave) brand

Picture Scotland 2025 – Glasgow's Gazprom George Square is hosting the Brit Awards. Under a lazer-coloured sky, an animatronic set cuts through the audience and converges where a host of holographic and live celebrities, actors and artists perform an opening medley. Buildings come alive with augmented reality visualizations as sponsor-profiled products are personalized and beamed to the audience at home and abroad. Cut to the Exxon Edinburgh Military Tattoo where a crescendo of bagpipes and drums herald the entrance of the Scots Guards bands as traditional kilts, sporrans and Saltires mingle with Exxon logos and cutaway promotional ads.

Scotland, like most of the United Kingdom and many other western democracies, owes much of the assimilation and centrality of events into its economy to transformations wrought from the late 1970s onwards, which initiated the sustained march of neoliberalism and an unfaltering belief in the power of the free market with its associated celebration of individualism and consumerism (Henry 2001).

Envisioning the trajectory of Scotland towards 2025 is inseparable from the ideological triumph of the past. Scotland's industrial base, so central to the nation's economic, social and cultural identity, was decimated in the 1980s and 1990s through processes of deindustrialization. Manufacturing industries in Scotland's urban centres were replaced with new service- and consumer-focused policies for urban revitalization (Johnson 2011). In this new ideology, market relations are preeminent, and the role of the local and national state is to incentivize entrepreneurial behaviours on behalf the nations' citizenry (Lees and Melhuish 2013). In Scotland's largest city, Glasgow, events and festivals played a significant role in setting the groundwork for a leisure economy based on consumption rather than production and consumers in place of citizens. Where once arguments reigned over the worth of promotion and positioning a city or nation using events, festivals and entertainment (Richards 2013), this is no longer the case. Civic boosters of the future can now get on with the task of securing more 'business', exploiting a city or nation's *assets*, *products* or *portfolios* without having to make the case to government that state investment will result in economic return. As Paul Bush, Chief Executive of EventScotland has suggested, there is no longer a debate amongst political leaders that major international events (sporting and cultural) should be attracted to Scotland – the only question is over the extent of public investment to make it happen (Getz 2013). The neoliberal modality of government is normalized, bringing activities previously outside of the realm of commodity under its gaze. In Scotland, this is clear in the establishment, since 2009, of Years of Focus where the nation's assets have been 'spotlighted' and made open to commodification. Scotland's diaspora were targeted in 2009 (Year of Homecoming), its local produce in 2010 (Year of Food and Drink), its creative and cultural activities in 2012 (Year of Creative Scotland), its landscape and environment in 2013 (Year of Natural Scotland) and the second Year of Homecoming in 2014.

These commodification processes, enshrined in events, are a product of the active mobilization of state power in the naturalization of market relations. Institutional arrangements (DMOs, national event and tourism agencies and government departments) enable the vigorous pursuit of strategies of event bidding and delivery. Notions of community and citizenship are reworked in this redefinition of political and economic imagination (Brenner and Theodore 2005) to produce the conditions through which cities and nations become brands and events facilitate the process of brandscaping (Klingmann 2007). For Pavoni (2010) brandscaping refers to the 'institutional engineering of material and immaterial, visible and invisible spaces' (9), which rely on the utilization of 'affective strategies . . . producing, managing and securing atmospherically enriched experiences'.

In Scotland's largest cities in particular, the triad of quasi-autonomous national event agency (e.g. EventScotland), city promotional unit (the DMO) and entrepreneurial local state comes together to create the most amenable business conditions to attract the world's major event products. International sporting federations, business conventions and spectacular entertainment events are targeted – in return, sponsors are offered free rein to dress the city as they feel fit, accessing valuable urban real estate to advertize their products and services, whilst having their assets protected by the local legislative and regulatory system. As Foley, McGillivray and McPherson (2011: 73) argue elsewhere, 'the local state is increasingly required to dance to the tune of major sponsors in bidding for and delivering events . . . local objectives and interests can be sidelined as sponsor agreements exclude these in favour of the pursuit of their global corporate objectives'. The transmission of urban symbolism and the pursuit of influential opinion formers (e.g. travel magazines) take precedence over any concern with being faithful to recorded historical facts. Place identities become elastic, open to reinterpretation and reimagination. Historical buildings, landscapes and public spaces, though inanimate, can be draped to fit whatever look and feel is required.

The direction of travel towards Scotland the Brand in 2025 is already compelling. Scotland's principal cultural agency, Creative Scotland, refers to Scotland as the 'Festival Nation' (Creative Scotland, Corporate Plan 2010). As Glasgow and Edinburgh, Scotland's major cities, compete with Barcelona, Madrid and Milan for events, there is an acceptance of international competition and demands to do more to ensure greater (economic) success. Creativity and forms of cultural expression are framed by a language of commerce and market relations. Value is accorded to activities that make a contribution to place promotion, attracting international media interest – justified using market ready impact evaluation tools (e.g. AVE). In order to compete, internationally, Scotland has had to participate in the competitive process of bringing in already-branded events (Foley, McGillivray and McPherson 2011). Though aware of the value of tartan, heather, shortbread, hills, and Braveheart to an international audience, Scotland is concerned at not being able to compete if its cultural cryostasis continues.

Looking forward to 2025, Scotland could be a nation that trades its authenticity and meaning of its very soul for the rewards of capital and commodification. Building on its success (in economic terms) in offering itself as a film set for Disney's *Brave* in 2012, Scotland's First Minister (or perhaps President) makes regular visits to Hollywood as a promotional agent working on behalf of Scotland PLC. Taking advantage of new fiscal powers as an outcome of political and economic independence from the United Kingdom, the First Minister offers attractive tax incentives to cement this most fruitful relationship. Elements of self-determination, fought so hard for over many years, are conceded in the name of attracting non-taxpaying transnational corporations. In 2025, global corporate brands will be ever present, sponsoring new arenas, creating new venues and commodifying the natural, the authentic and the historical. These will be synonymous with experiences and lifestyles aspired to by the affluent middle class, spending their money on consumption experiences enabled (and encouraged) by those in political office.

Whilst in 2013 the importance of greater environmental compliance for events was at the forefront of strategic rhetoric, by 2025, the economic impact of adherence has placed Scotland in an uncompetitive position *vis-à-vis* their main event bidding rivals in the Middle East, Southeast Asia and South America. The decision is taken that such is the importance, economically, of securing Scotland's place on the world stage, that it needs to reduce the importance of its environmental impact assessment processes. The Scottish Government now has the power to overrule local government decision to ensure that major business opportunities are not lost on the basis of possible negative environmental consequences.

In this brand-infused scenario, the resident citizen becomes of secondary concern to the (apparently) endless inflows of capital promised by the global market and tourist gaze (Urry 1990). The local state becomes an entrepreneurial unit, operating commercially to exploit business opportunities. But, fears are growing that the strategy of accumulating event trophies (world championships, MOBO awards, comedy festivals, food and drink showcases) lead to diminishing returns, whereby Scotland's positioning and stated uniqueness places it in a nonplace shared by many other aspiring event nations.

And what of technology? By 2025 the technologically mediated consumer experience will be firmly established as part of the events experience economy. The (social) digital revolution of the early 2000s promised much – greater collaboration, creativity, co-creation and the generation of stronger communities (Solis 2012). However, based on the logic of brandscaping, in 2025 the emancipatory and liberatory possibilities of digital tools and technologies have not materialized. Transnational (stateless) global brands use their vast corporate resources to flood digital media platforms, eliminating the last vestiges of open, collaborative and free communication online (Lanier 2013). Channels of hope established to contest the commercialization of the web and imagined as way of facilitating greater public interaction and sharing are now nothing more than sophisticated vehicles for greater revenue generation. Social media is social business (Qualman 2012) – where the value of events and their ability to secure attention is reduced to new market penetration strategies. Expressions of protest and dissent online are extinguished as quickly as they ignite. Police and security bodies intervene to suppress resistance using the legislative powers secured in the name of protecting citizens from (unidentified) global threats. In 2025, as previously emergent economies (e.g. Brazil and Russia) reach the saturation point for market exploitation (e.g. Twitter and Facebook), so technological start-ups target Africa – the location of the next growth economies. By 2025 tourist and citizens alike will walk through Scotland's largest cities where civic space literally speaks as apps, social media and geolocation integrate (Schmidt and Cohen 2013) to offer advice on attractions, recommend entertainment and events, offer deals and so intensify dwell time of the overall consumer experience. Here the investment of Glasgow 2013 Smart City is exploited to leverage consumer spending and greater urban revenue generation. Agencies of place promotion (DMOs) mobilize the interface of advanced technological infrastructure and digital convergence of consumers to mine the bid data (Mayer-Shonberger and Cukier 2013) of individual spending patterns and consumption behaviours. In the brandscaped Scotland of 2025 event audiences passively accept the reality of personalized augmented reality and the bombardment of social business. Events and festivity are instrumentalized spectacles where the 'whispering dream' of brand is 'burned into the deepest recesses of the brain' (Frew 2013: 25). Scotland the Brave becomes Scotland the Brand, where the policy approach is one that sees consciousness as a cathedral of consumption that can be aggressively tapped through an event portfolio that sees brandscaping as a given – the only alternative.

Scenario 2: Made in Scotland

Picture Scotland 2025 – An independent, non-nuclear, environmentally aware and digitally advanced nation that finds its cultural policy, national to local events and festival calendar networked nationally and globally. From Edinburgh Hogmanay, Red Bull Glasgow Adventure, Shetland's Up Helly Aa, Irvine Marymass, Largs Viking Festival, Google's Music Experience, Tomintoul's 174th Highland Games to community carnival, local galas and games the cultural content and identity of new Scotland is an open conversation between policy makers, strategic practitioners and a multicultural active citizenship.

Whereas scenario one traces a past Scotland towards a future of amplified hyper-capitalism and brandscaping, where the value of events is reduced to economic considerations, scenario two sets Scotland in a very different political, economic, social and cultural context. In this scenario, Scotland is positioned as an independent nation wrestling externally with its place in the world and internally with its sense of itself, its prevailing culture and future direction (Carrell 2013). In an events context, its governmental and nongovernmental agencies are managing the difficult balancing act between old and new events – a Scotland of the mythical past and a confident, creative, distinctive Scotland of the future.

Future scenarios are, by definition, always counterfactual, but debates about an independent Scotland foreground critical debate about identity, connectedness and culture that will influence the shape of the event sector come 2025. Political and economic independence would have considerable ramifications for the institutional arrangements of governance and civic culture in Scotland, the wider United Kingdom and internationally. These debates demand reflexivity on the nature of being and becoming: who we are and what we shall, or want, to become. The Scottish independence debate, regardless of its outcome, compels politicians, business leaders and the wider public to soul search and the realm of events plays a fundamental part in negotiating the version of nationhood that will emerge (Raich 2013).

In the event of the annulment of the union between Scotland, England, Wales and Northern Ireland, Scotland would no longer automatically be invited to be part of UK-wide bids for major sporting events. Whereas in 2012 Scotland hosted several events as part of the London 2012 Olympic Games, there would be no political, cultural or economic imperative for Scotland to be included in any major event bidding process or consideration between the national cultural and events agencies of England, Wales or Northern Ireland. Moreover, cross border bureaucracies resulting from an acrimonious divorce from the Union could make Scotland a less attractive destination to visit for (previously) domestic visitors. On the other hand, as an individual member of the United Nations, NATO and the European Union, Scotland could have a more pronounced profile that enabled new alliances to be forged. Interestingly the seismic fallout from the break-up of the Union offers a platform of international promotion for the new Scotland, a reshaped political geography and new strategic alliances with its Scandinavian cousins (Massie 2013). With its social democratic political system, commitment to social justice, good quality social welfare provision and a strong historical cultural connection, the Scandinavian model resonates with the instincts of many Scots and further distances them from their UK neighbours.

Most importantly, while an independent Scotland brings significant challenges, it also opens possibilities for re-envisioning and reimagining cityscapes, communities and citizens. Political and economic independence allows the cultural canvas of Scotland to be repainted if not replaced. Scotland in 2025 sits in a global environment where shifting labour and knowledge capital are enticed by the comfort and cultural commodities that target the embodied digital lifestyles of techno-capitalism (Kellner 2003). Scottish political and economic policies must balance the territorializing desire of the market with the demand for rootedness, community and civic responsibility. The Scotland of 2025 reflects the being and becoming of postmodern identity as the local is nourished alongside the global, externally facing spectacles of national pride, growth, recognition and cultural autonomy. *Being* echoes tradition, is local, grounded in community, secure and always present. *Becoming* is globalizing, collective, technologically convergent, ever seeking and always absent. Internal social and cultural identity plays alongside the need to engage in international competitions for distinctiveness. Scotland in 2025 has understood the importance of building a sustainable festival and event infrastructure that retains a past heritage while being one that reflects a dynamic, vibrant and future focused nation.

In 2025, the detached, abstract reimagining of place identity that dominated in 2013 has been revised and more importance has been given to providing support for local distinctiveness to flourish. Small-scale festivals and events are viewed as crucial not only to cement an internal sense of (re)new(ed) Scottish identity. Whereas the legacy of 2013 and impact of policies of austerity saw the reductions in local community culture and focus on market spectacles, 2025 reanimates the local. Traditional fairs, galas and Highland Games sit alongside critically acclaimed art and cultural events to produce a multicultural mashup that reflects the diverse Scotland of 2025. These local spectacles provide a rich cultural tapestry, reflecting and attracting an international labour force essential to a Scotland that depends on immigrant inflows to avoid population drift. Building on its own migrant past in welcoming the Irish, the Italians, Eastern Europe and further afield, Scottish identity again morphs to embrace new identities.

Rather than bankroll expensive bids for nomadic international events (see scenario one), in 2025 Scotland promotes from within, exploiting the rewards of its decade-long incubator investments. Rather than feed the major event Leviathans of corporate capitalism, localism is celebrated and self-sustainingly mediated. Whereas the era of 2013 saw the McDonaldization (Ritzer 1993) of culture, the Scotland of 2025 challenges McEvents with its commitment to a rooted localism that promotes, digitally and personally engages and builds reputation through recommendation. This reflects the shift beyond the glocalization (Robertson 1995) and experience economy (Pine and Gilmore 1999) popularized in the early part of the twentieth century. Here, rather than the cherry picking of 'saleable' event assets apparent in 2013, the convergence between local ownership and global promotion is more meaningful as it is networked and engaged sociability (Solis 2012).

To address the acknowledged postindependence dangers associated with isolation and marginality, Scotland has not only invested in political affiliation (with Scandinavia) but also in the creation the conditions for virtual connectivity (McQuivey 2013). By 2025 Scotland is a digitally connected and convergent nation, priding itself on its population's levels of digital literacy. In an event setting, the merging of diasporic community and complex online environments has enabled Scotland to take its messages across the world, illustrated in the hugely successful KILTR social media platform that 'exemplifies the values of interdependence, heritage, organization and bonds . . . and embodies all that is best from Scottish people when the join together' (KILTR 2013). KILTR takes the concept of clan and reimagines it for a contemporary Scotland, exploiting the international outlook of the Scottish people and diaspora to create economic, cultural and social value. It overcomes geographical peripherality to form an international community of connectivity, an essential element for any nation seeking a larger audience for its future events. This uniquely Scottish 'community' provides the digital heartbeat that tells a story, which builds and binds community at home and abroad.

Globally, in 2025, mega, hallmark and major events have become cultural earthquakes where digital tremors and aftershocks feed off as much as sustain the epicentre event itself. With the growing sophistication, mobility and ubiquity of digital and social technologies, the spectacle of events make them ideal for self-promotion. Most importantly, while this marriage of technologies and events contributes to the current propulsion of events and empowerment of the citizen and the local, such self-mediation has, ironically, become central to capturing consumer consciousness for brand extension (Frew 2013). Glasgow's Smart City provided one technological future, within which digitally enabled citizens utilize gesture and speech recognition with embodied audio-visual interfaces to access free citywide wifi and integrate real-time travel information, work, shop, video call or post online (Dourish and Bell 2011). However, as a nation defined by its concern with social justice and a rejection of unfettered hypercapitalism, in the Scotland of 2025 there exists deep concern from civil liberty groups about the misuse of personal data generated as an outcome of the Smart City initiative.

Debates over big data, which were in their infancy in 2013, are now a major issue in Scotland 2025. Big data and the sophisticated algorithms that allow the amalgamation of all digital behaviours, profiling and preference patterns (Mayer-Schonberger and Cukier 2013) are welcomed by DMOs, but subject to critique by others for their exploitation of the consumer. Campaigners urge those creating the Smart City to reflect and retain the values of social justice and the co-created democracy of its digital citizenship whilst resisting the creep of neoliberalism and the inequity of unfettered capitalism. Scotland of 2025 is for the affluent and the aspirational, for those who struggle as much as those who strive, the poor as much as the privileged. Of course commerce is essential and the Smart City targets markets with high purchasing power. However, this does not need to be at the expense of addressing the complex and systemic inequalities that continue to blight the birth and growth of the new Scotland of 2025. Instead, the socially responsible (and responsive) Scotland of 2025 is held to account in governance terms by a civic gaze that is dynamically mobile and mediated. The barriers of the boardroom, class, gender or elite phrase regimes are broken under the cacophony of techno-voices of an actively engaged, participative citizenship.

Concluding remarks: the implications for the future of the event industry based on the present

In keeping with the focus of the book, this chapter has explored the place of events and festivity in the future. Scotland's story is a valuable addition to this text because it brings into sharp focus the delicate balancing act that many nations face in building an event portfolio that respects the past whilst planning for the future. The impact of the neoliberal revolution, promulgated by the twin forces of Thatcherism and Reaganomics, not only shifted the political spectrum to the right, especially in western Europe in the 1980s and early 1990s, but also enshrined the mantra of free market in the provision of cultural content for future generations. Even in times of austerity, when accusations of global economic downturn are placed at the door of the free market pioneers, the power of neoliberalism continues to resonate. While in 2013 Scotland finds itself dealing with the fallout of an ideological (neoliberal) heritage, it is also facing an even more important question relating to the political future that will lead the nation towards 2025.

Independence, it is stressed here, is a question for Scotland, the United Kingdom and the wider world. Presently the global environment is volatile, uncertain and insecure, as worldviews compete and clash over possible futures. Warring worldviews, coupled with the global economic crisis, fears over migrant labour, jobs and standard of living, have brought questions of nation, community and individual ontological anchors into critical relief. Scottish independence accentuates the logic of identity and in asking who are we, what are we, where are we going and what defines us, places the cultural content of events and festivity firmly in the mix of identity politics.

In light of this, two scenarios were presented for a Scotland of 2025. Firstly, we outlined a Scotland where the ideological grip of market forces is intensified and hypercapitalism reigned supreme. Here, events are externally focused on global competition and tourist markets. Scotland, its cities and civic spaces are prostrate and prostituted before the market. Events are circuses of consumption where spectacle is a dazzling vehicle of promotion for brand partners and sponsors. Scotland in 2025 becomes the blank canvas for extreme brandscaping, and major events are the spectacular baubles that burn brand into the deepest recesses of the brain. Citizenship is marked by a consumptive logic that privileges the absent global tourist market over the indigenous, present population. Interestingly, citizens play a relatively passive role, perpetuating the brandscaping of their nation and civic spaces, where commerce and consumption preside over citizenship and community.

In the second scenario an alternative vision of Scotland in 2025 was advanced. Against the backdrop of independence and an intensifying digital age, events are part of an open conversation with citizens. The Scotland of 2025 reanimates its revolutionary heritage of educational, scientific and technological innovation by advancing a digital democracy where the use of advanced technologies are integrated into institutional mechanisms of governance. No longer is the political elite able to dictate event and cultural policy or commodify civic space without the input of the electorate. Political apathy is replaced by an active citizenship whose gaze of governance is ever present. The Scotland of 2025 reflects the paradox of postmodern identity as the stereotypical Scotland of tartan, kilts, bagpipes, whisky and golf sits alongside the dynamic mix of multicultural local community content. The strategic balancing act is to produce sporting and cultural spectacles that speak to a Scottish diaspora and global market whilst avoiding cultural cryostasis by supporting and celebrating the live and lived local. In a digital world of co-created convergence the vision is one where the spectacles of national and community events and festivity engage in a local to global interplay of preservation and promotion.

Whilst neither ideal type scenario is likely to exist materially, the weight of evidence to date would suggest that the Scotland the Brand narrative will be even more aggressively marketed as the only future for events come 2025. Should Scotland's population vote to remain part of a political union with the rest of the United Kingdom, then brandscaping, based on a continuing commitment to a neoliberal modality of governance, will be extended rather than rolled back. However, were Scotland to become an independent nation in 2014, then the content of its event portfolio could be reshaped with greater concentration on locally produced events rather than corporately produced ones: events that dynamically shape Scotland the story rather than Scotland the stereotypical brand. This is a future that capitalizes on, and has a conversation with, a digitally literate and connected global diasporic Scots community whilst building international alliances: Scotland with a story to tell, future to build and cultural identity that no longer sits on the periphery of a UK union but aspires to be a protagonist on a global stage.

References

Brenner, N. and Theodore, N. (2005) 'Neoliberalism and the urban condition', *City*, 9(1): 101–07.

Carrell, S. (2013) 'Scottish independence: the essential guide', *The Guardian*. Online. Available: <www.guardian.co.uk/politics/scottish-independence-essential-guide> (accessed 15 May 2013).

Creative Scotland (2010) *Corporate Plan 2010* Edinburgh: Creative Scotland.

Dourish, P. and Bell, G. (2011) *Divining a Digital Future: mess and mythology in ubiquitous computing*. Cambridge, MA: MIT Press.

Foley, M., McGillivray, D. and McPherson, G. (2011) *Events Policy: from theory to strategy.* London: Routledge.

Frew, M. (2013) 'Events and media spectacle', in R. Finkel, D. McGillivray, G. McPherson and P. Robinson (eds.) *Research Themes for Events.* Wallingford: CABI.

Getz, D. (2013) *Event Tourism: concepts, international case studies and research.* New York: Cognizant.

Henry, I. P. (2001) *The Politics of Leisure Policy.* London: MacMillan.

Johnson, A. (2011) 'Marxism today and the unmaking of the British working class', *Public Policy Research*, 18(3): 151–57.

Kellner, D. (2003) *Media and the Triumph of the Spectacle.* London: Routledge.

Kidd, W. (2002) *Culture and Identity.* Basingstoke: Palgrave.

KILTR (2013) *KILTR, the cultural social platform.* Online. Available: <www.kiltr.com> (accessed 22 May 2013).

Klingmann A. (2007) *Brandscapes: architecture in the experience economy.* London: MIT Press.

Lanier, J. (2013) *Who Owns the Future?* New York: Penguin Group.

Lees, L. and Melhuish, C. (2013) *Arts-led regeneration in the UK: the rhetoric and the evidence on urban social inclusion.* European Urban and Regional Studies. DOI: 10.1177/0969776412467474

Mayer-Shonberger, V. and Cukier, K. (2013) *Big Data: a revolution that will transform how we live, work and think.* London: John Murray.

Massie, A. (2013) 'Independent Scotland: neoliberal nirvana or Scandinavian paradise?, *The Spectator.* Online. Available: <http://blogs.spectator.co.uk/alex-massie/2013/04/independent-scotland-neoliberal-nirvana-or-scandinavian-paradise/> (accessed 16 May 2013).

McQuivey, J. (2013) *Digital Disruption: unleashing the next wave of innovation.* Las Vegas: Amazon Publishing.

Pavoni, A. (2010, December) 'Erasing space from places. Brandscapes, art and the (de)valorisation of the Olympic space', *Explorations in Space and Society*, 18: 9–13.

Pine, B.J. and Gilmore, J.H. (1999) *The Experience Economy.* Boston: Harvard Business School Press.

Qualman, E. (2012). *Socialnomics: how social media transforms the way we live and do business.* Hoboken: John Wiley & Sons.

Raich, A. (2013) 'Pivotal role of culture in talking up independence', *The Herald.* Online. Available: <www.heraldscotland.com/comment/columnists/pivotal-role-of-culture-in-talking-up-independence.20270275> (accessed 15 May 2013).

Richards, G. (2013) 'Events and the means of attention', *Journal of Tourism, Research & Hospitality*, 2(2): 1–5.

Ritzer, G. (1993) *The McDonaldization of Society.* London: Sage.

Robertson, R. (1995) 'Glocalization: time-space and homogeneity-heterogeneity', in M. Featherstone, S. Lash and R. Robertson (eds.) *Global Modernities.* London: Sage, pp. 25–44.

Schmidt, E. and Cohen, J. (2013) *The New Digital Age: reshaping the future of people, nations and business.* New York: Alfred A. Knopf.

Solis, B. (2012) *The End of Business as Usual.* New Jersey: John Wiley and Sons.

Urry, J. (1990) *The Tourist Gaze.* London: Sage.

6 The future power of decision making in community festivals

Allan Stewart Jepson and Alan Clarke

Future points

- All festivals and events both now and in the future are connected by webs of power and decision making.
- Current research suggests that decision-making processes have demonstrated that the agenda of community festivals has been shaped by the powerful stakeholders rather than the powerless.
- Power has been revealed as set of forces that are both enabling and disenfranchising.
- Without analyses of the power relations we will only scratch the surface of those processes that shape the production and consumption of events and festivals.

Introduction

Researching cultural festivals reveals the existence of a multitude of stakeholder relationships, connected and enforced through different cultures. The one commonality is that they are all influenced by power, which in turn impacts on how festivals are constructed, delivered and consumed. The futures of community festivals and events will be determined by the decisions that are made, or not made, by the stakeholders in those communities, but alongside the factors identified in the other chapters in this collection, they will be shaped, manipulated, coerced and created by the power relations that come to define them. Power is necessary to underline and warrant the truth claims of the festival organizers and participants in ways that are not necessarily apparent until they are more closely scrutinized. This chapter will propose critical takes on the macrohistory of power generally used in festival, events, tourism, hospitality and leisure researchers, if indeed they recognize the significance of the concept and its applications.

As Inayatullah (1998: 381) argues,

> Futures studies, while strong at breaking humans out of the present, are often weak at contouring the parameters of the future possible. Macrohistory through its delineation of the structures of history – of the causes and

mechanisms of historical change; of inquiry into what changes and what stays stable; of an analysis of the units of history; and of a presentation of the stages of history – provides a structure from which to forecast and gain insight into the future.

Inayatullah also observes that futures studies are constructed within a particular frame, which is identified as that of the problem of modernity and postmodernity.

> In response to the needs of capitalism and the interstate system, futures studies have developed predictive models of economy and national security. At the same time, a counter hegemonic discourse has developed tied to deconstructing dominant forms of knowledge and creating dissenting futures. (Inayatullah 1998: 382)

Bergman and colleagues (2010: 858) recognize that there are difficulties: 'We do not give that term the pejorative connotation it has in post-modernistic and other radical relativistic theories. We do not, then, regard it as a sin to make truth claims.' The sin may be seen in the uncritical sense of acceptance of these claims. Systematic studies of how truth claims are formulated are thus an important part of our continued use of the typology and the mapping work that this entails.

Wendell Bell has this to say: 'the future is unknowable in the strict sense. Until it becomes the present, it is non-existent. There are no future facts'. Pentti Malaska is even more explicit:

> The presupposition that there exists a field of objects that belong to the senses, and can be observed and explained, is congenital to a scientific discipline. If it is possible to prove the existence of new empirical objects, it is possible to establish a new science or to create an enclave that is separate from the territory of prevailing sciences. The future field can do neither: its every essence is the lack of future objects to observe. (Presti 1996)

The implication behind this concept of the non-nature of future events is that futures studies are in some way at a disadvantage with respect to those sciences and disciplines that 'enjoy' more 'concretely demonstrable' objects, first and foremost, the historical and philological disciplines, with their immediate records, monuments and documents.

At the level of futures research, the *multiverse of realities* seems to translate the more genuine issues of a theory of complexity without eluding the mechanism of the empathic understanding of the observer. With his *multiverse of realities*, Mika Mannermaa (1988) emphasizes the function of the observer in the observer/actor system relationship. The theoretical basis behind scenario techniques conceptualizes the alternativity and conditionality of future prospects; the *multiverse of realities* redefines the present dimension of the observer in scenario seeking.

The simple may be complex even though it is not complicated. The present is conceptualized in terms of many contextual levels, which, in their diversity, can be placed in relation to the type of observer/actor. 'This means questioning the idea of one (and only one) universal reality and truth, which is thought to be discoverable by the means of scientific methods and thinking (Presti 1996: 898).

This chapter will explore power firstly as a result of the political nature of stakeholders often involved in the creation of local community festivals, and secondly it will examine how power or 'hegemony' can be exercised over minority ethnic groups or communities in society, thus restricting their desire to participate in community-based cultural events. The results of uneven power relationships have been widely documented particularly as they tend to create either mono-ethnic events or placeless festivals. The implication of this chapter for the future of events is that power is revealed as a pervasive and constructive set of forces that are both enabling and disenfranchising. Additionally it reveals that cultural diversity within local cultural festivals and events is only achieved through an integrated and inclusive event planning process. Finally, the chapter will seek to build on power discourses and look toward future decision-making processes employed within local community cultural festivals and events.

The approach to community festivals and events has been refined in the works of Clarke and Jepson (2009, 2010, 2011), Jepson, Clarke and Ragsdell (2012) and Clarke, Jepson and Wiltshier (2008). Their work has developed a focus on the way decisions are taken in and around community festivals and reviewed the definitions used in previous studies. None of the previous definitions referenced the conditions that create a community festival and therefore proposed a more critical and comprehensive definition that sees community festivals as a:

> Themed and inclusive community event or series of events which have been created as the result of an inclusive community planning process to celebrate the particular way of life of people and groups in the local community with emphasis on particular space and time. (Jepson and Clarke 2013: 7)

Researching cultural festivals reveals the existence of a multitude of stakeholder relationships, given meaning through different cultures. The factor that holds our analyses together is that the stakeholders are all influenced by power, which in turn impacts on how a festival is constructed, delivered and consumed. Church and Coles (2007) identify that power does not simply exist, but has to be created, and this is done through the relationships between the stakeholders. In the case of a community festival, this can be thought of as the 'social production of power', which also includes the spatial dimensions or 'sites of power' (Westwood 2002: 135).

Decision making has been influenced by power firstly as a result of the overtly political nature of some of the stakeholders involved in the creation of festivals, and secondly because the events themselves should be representations of local community cultures from various ethnically diverse groups. Research centred within community festivals is particularly interesting when one considers emergent power theories where equity can only be achieved through power sharing (Ryan 2002, cited in Coles and Church 2007), and the redistribution of power/power sharing in stakeholder coalitions is challenging (Thomas and Thomas 2005).

Stakeholder concepts

The term 'stakeholder' was invented by the Stanford Research Institute in 1963, where the notion was meant to refer to 'those groups without whose support the organization would cease to exist' (Freeman 1984: 31). Mitchell, Agle and Wood (1997) add a greater sophistication to this by suggesting that stakeholders may be identified by relational attributes of power, legitimacy and urgency. *Power* of a stakeholder can be identified in situations when the stakeholder can impose his or her own will on others through various means such as coercion, pressure, etc. '*Legitimacy* relates to the perceptions that the interests or claims of a stakeholder are appropriate or desirable, with these perceptions being based on socially constructed values and beliefs' (de Araujo and Bramwell 2000: 272). *Urgency* arises from 'the degree to which stakeholder claims call for immediate attention' (Mitchell, Agle and Wood 1997: 867).

Jamal and Getz (1995) do not propose to identify such a hierarchy of the various stakeholder groups, however; they refer to legitimate and relevant stakeholders, which suggests that there are key players that may not be legitimate. The decisive argument on the basis of when an actor is regarded as legitimate is the capacity to participate in collaborative tourism planning:

> a legitimate stakeholder is one who has the right and capacity to participate in the process; a stakeholder who is impacted by the actions of other stakeholders has the right to become involved in order to moderate those impacts, but must also have the resources and skills (capacity) in order to participate. (Gray 1985, cited in Jamal and Getz 1995: 194)

These arguments leave room for some questions about where claims to legitimacy can be grounded and justified, not to mention who has the power to enforce such definitions on the processes. Sheehan and Ritchie (2005: 733) conclude, 'Skill in stakeholder relationship building is increasingly important', which is worth exploring further in the context of community festivals.

The idea of stakeholders has become increasingly important in studies of tourism development, as well as in the larger field of management studies. It makes it possible to envisage a much wider range of actors and organizations being connected to the processes of development than was addressed in the traditional planning-dominated literature. The idea of stakeholders creates two critical changes within the analytical perspective. First, it opens out the range of actors and organizations that can be seen as having an interest in or being affected by tourism development. Secondly, it treats actors and organizations – stakeholders – as interests that also have agency, which means they are seen to have the capacity to shape tourism development in specific places. As Markwick (2000: 522) concluded:

> Exploration of the case of development conflict in Malta suggests that the complex intersections of stakeholders' interests require incisive yet flexible forms of conceptualization and analysis. Stakeholder mapping has been suggested here as one way in which academics might identify and analyse the interplay between stakeholders' differing interests and powers.

Macrohistories of power

Church and Coles (2007) also suggested that tourism has only had a selected involvement with the discourses of power, and that there was often no comment from tourism scholars on the epistemological, ontological or methodological implications of conceptualizations of power, and the comment could be easily applied to events research. In order to develop the agenda for future research the chapter will address these issues by returning to the macrohistory of some of the original theories of power. Analyses of the theories of Weber, Foucault and Gramsci for the discussion of power relations are included, with Clegg being included for his observations on power in practice in organizations.

It could be tempting to read power as the ability of one individual or small group, to get their own way, against the opposition of others. However, the study of power is by no means that simple, as Lukes (1974) observed in his classic study of the theories of power.

Lukes's seminal work reviewed the approaches to power, rejecting as simplistic both one-dimensional and two-dimensional views of power relations. In one-dimensional accounts, often associated with pluralist writings, one person or organization exercises power over another by making them do what they want. In two-dimensional readings power is not only about making someone do something, but it involves the act of suppressing other activities. The three-dimensional view of power that Lukes proposed is a critique of the behavioural focus of these two views. This theory incorporates the consideration of potential issues that are 'kept out of politics, whether through the operation of social forces and institutional practices or through individuals' decisions' (Lukes 1974: 24). Lukes argues that this can happen without observable conflict; therefore consideration must be given to latent conflict, which 'consists in a contradiction between the interests of those exercising power and the *real interests* of those they excluded' (1974: 25). He also claims that some forms of the power continuum like manipulation and authority do not necessarily involve actual conflict. Therefore what Lukes achieves is to move the focus from giving orders, taking orders and even controlling agendas to the coming together, or not, of communities in or around their festivals. Parsons (1957) also links power to authority but presumes that power is exercised only to achieve collective goals (which exist in consensus). Lukes also draws on Arendt's (1970) concept of power, which emphasizes the necessity of a group that can empower someone to act on behalf of the group. She argues that power is the property of a group, and power exists only as long as the group exists. Arendt is in favour of a concept of 'power to do something', i.e. power as a capacity, rather than 'power over somebody' (Lukes 1974). The demonstration of this comes, for example, in the accounts of the 'niceness' of the committee.

Weber: traditional, bureaucratic and charismatic

Weber's view on power presupposes that there is a defined group of people that will obey a kind of command (or all commands). In this sense, power is based on obedience (Erdélyi 1987). Furthermore, Weber places the exercise of power in the social context: 'Power (Macht) is the probability that one actor within a social relationship will be in a position to carry out his own will despite resistance, regardless of the basis on which the probability rests' (Eisenstadt 1968: 14). For community festivals, Weber poses a series of interesting challenges of the legitimacy of different kinds of authority. He argues that power is linked to authority, where the obedience towards the particular authority comes from two sources: a) any sort of motive to obey and b) belief in the legitimacy of the authority.

In the case of *traditional authority*, the person exercising the authority is appointed on the basis of the traditionally 'inherited' norms. It is inherent in the previous statement that obedience is owed to a person as opposed to an impersonal order. This person 'occupies the traditionally sanctioned authority and . . . is (within its sphere) bound by tradition' (Eisenstadt 1968: 46). The person elevated to authority is not a 'president' but an authority himself. The commands are legitimate because a) the content of the command is legitimate by tradition, and b) absolutism and despotism of the 'ruler' provides his legitimacy if the tradition allows for absolutism. Traditional authority is not underpinned by structured administration and skilled officials are also missing. In this form of authority staff are recruited on the basis of traditional relations, and tasks are 'allocated by discretion of master' (Hamilton 1993: 137). Laws are legitimated by tradition, and 'are considered to be part of previously existing norms' (Hamilton 1993: 137).

Weber also notes the existence of a bureaucratic hierarchy, where every person in authority has a 'superior' scrutinizing and controlling authority, and where the inferior bodies and persons also have the right to appeal and make official complaints. The procedures are regulated by technical rules and norms. However, the way to ensure that the implementation of these rules and norms are absolutely rational can be only through the work of skilled bureaucrats. Weber claims the purest form of power is the one that requires a bureaucratic management group. This group consists only of bureaucrats, who:

- are free in their person, and have only 'material' duties
- are placed in a fixed bureaucratic hierarchy
- have a fixed mandate
- are employed on a contractual basis
- are employed on the basis of their skills
- are paid in money
- have this post as their only or main job
- are under bureaucratic discipline and continuous control.

In the analysis of community festivals these ideas loom large when we consider the bureaucracies created to plan and implement events, which can be both internal to and external from those communities. The more externalized they are, the more rule bound they will appear.

The Weberian viewpoint of power stipulates that the power gained by 'winners' (i.e. those in charge or holding power) will be at the direct expense of 'losers'; all of these procedures are regulated by technical rules and norms. This is fine as long as it is not challenged within or around the festival. Indeed community festivals are generally seen as reinforcing the 'natural order' of the participating community. *Legal authority* presupposes that any arbitrary or need-based *rational* rules can become codified laws, which may claim to be respected by at least the members of the bureaucratic organization. This type of authority is characterized by continuous, rule-bound official – bureaucratic procedures. In the case of *traditional authority*, the person exercising the authority is appointed on the basis of the traditionally 'inherited' norms. The commands are legitimate because the content of the command is legitimate by tradition. The purest form of legal authority can be observed where the bureaucratic management group consists of appointed officials. As – at least in Weber's terms – bureaucracy means authority exercised on the basis of knowledge and skills, where no emotions and passions interfere with fulfilling the job, this is where its rationality is rooted.

Charismatic authority is based on the extraordinary abilities of a person. Originally, people with exemplary qualities (such as prophets, persons with the power to heal, etc.) were regarded as leaders. Obviously, charisma is only legitimate as long as it is 'proved', that is to say accepted by the followers. However, this acknowledgement of the charisma is not the base for the legitimacy; it is more seen as an obligation that comes from the enthusiasm or despararion of the followers (Erdélyi 1987). In this case, 'it is the charismatically qualified leader as such who is obeyed by virtue of personal trust in him and his revelation' (Eisenstadt 1968: 47).

It must be noted that authority never exists in the pure forms described above. The most typical form of everyday administration draws on traditional and legal and bureaucratic use of power: as it is 'tied to precedents transmitted from previous generations and [is] being bound by abstractly formulated universal principles' (Giddens 1972: 38).

Weberian futures

From the point of view of forecasting studies, it should be remembered that Weber adopts for the research a methodological underpinning that seems to suggest a way forward for historical investigation that could be referred to as a 'technique of ideal/type conditional frameworks'. Festivals and events will continue to draw on power claims within community festivals that are legitimized by Weberian guarantees. Bureaucratic organization will still be seen in the way festivals are structured within the communities.

The futures will also come to terms with the role of enthusiasms within community festivals. These enthusiastics come closer to Weber's notion of charismatic and will bring these characteristics to the fore in our understandings of the decision making and drivers of specific constructions of community festivals.

Clegg: frameworks of power

According to Clegg (1989: 189) 'power in organizations must concern the hierarchical structure of offices and their relation to each other, in the classical Weberian sense', and we see this in the organizations surrounding community festivals.

However, Clegg considers not only legitimate power but also the notion of illegitimate power, where the latter is understood as 'local struggles for autonomy and control', which do not threaten the formal, legitimated structure. Clegg argues for circuits of power rather than the static sources as Weber or Mann (1986) would suggest. However, Clegg is also determined to find the parallel in his circuits of the power sources identified by Mann. Mann's categories of 'ideological and the economic relationships' correspond with Clegg's 'circuits mobilizing relations of meaning and membership' (1989: 219), whereas the military and political relationships in Mann's terminology are equivalent to the 'techniques of production and discipline' identified by Clegg.

Discipline is found in the focus of modern power theories. Mintzberg (1983) emphasizes the importance of 'obedience' in the analysis of power in organizations. Obedience is closely linked to discipline or disciplinary practices. Several forms of these practices exist in everyday life: the various examples of surveillance include supervision, formalization, legislation, etc. These surveillance techniques all aim to 'effect increasing control of employees' behaviour, disposition and embodiment, precisely because they are organization members' (Clegg 1989: 191). In community festivals these employees are often doubly bound by being both local and volunteers.

Organizations have a 'real' structure; however, in practice authoritative structures rarely correspond to them, as things change over time in ways 'which are not captured by a static idealization; organizational membership changes and so particularly competent "power-players" may make more out of a position than a less competent predecessor, and so on' (Clegg 1989: 192).

Interest is regarded as a 'variable discursive formulation' (Clegg 1989: 195), and will be encountered in collective rather than individual terms. Clegg also suggests that in so far as interest representations characterize organizational life in terms of class and its social relations they will resemble the general conditions of economic domination and subordination in organization. However, 'general conditions of economic domination are also overlain in particular cases by forms of domination endured by specific groups of people' (Carchedi 1987, cited in Clegg 1989: 195). This domination may be experienced in terms of economic domination as well as other forms of general discrimination; nevertheless, it derives from a source outside the economy. There are future challenges here for how subcultures become centred in festivals, especially where host populations may not be overly sympathetic or tolerant of 'their' 'minorities'.

As Clegg (1989: 197) put it,

> Discretion may be thought of in terms of who may do what, how, where, when and in which ways to whatever objects and agencies. Customary and sometimes legally specific identities will be prescribed or proscribed for certain forms of practice. Embodied identities will be salient only in as much as they are socially recognized and organizationally consequent.

(Other forms of embodiment such as hair colour, size, etc. will become an issue only in special circumstances, for instance in organizations like the armed forces and the police.)

The organizations in and around community festivals are also the locus of decision and action. In general, 'organizations do things as a consequence of decisions to act in certain ways by certain other agents' (Clegg 1989: 197). Nevertheless, organizations also do things that are not a consequence of a decision so to act, if only because decisions are shaped by struggles around competing substantive objects. Organizational action is an indeterminate outcome of substantive struggles between different agencies: people who deploy different resources; people whose organizational identities will be shaped by the way in which disciplinary practices work through and on them, even in their use of such techniques; people who seek to control and decide the nature of organizational action and those many things to which they will routinely have recourse in their membership, work and struggles. Consequently, the interests of actors in organizations and the decisions that they make are necessarily contingent on various forms of organizational calculation. The complex and contingent conditions under which organizational action takes place must not be ignored.

According to Clegg (1989: 189), 'power in organizations must concern the hierarchical structure of offices and their relation to each other, in the classical Weberian sense'. Clegg considers not only legitimate power but also the illegitimate power, where the latter is understood as 'local struggles for autonomy and control', which do not threaten the formal, legitimated structure. Clegg argues for circuits of power rather than the static sources as Weber would suggest, with Clegg's 'circuits mobilizing relations of meaning and membership' (1989: 219).

Power can be seen as 'the rules of the game', which both enable and constrain action. Where rules are invoked, there must be discretion. The freedom of discretion requires disciplining if it is to be a reliable relay. Clegg (1989: 209) reinforces this when he observes:

> Rules will never be as static and idealized as in chess or some other game but will instead be far more fragile, ambiguous, unclear, dependent upon interpretation, and subject either to reproduction or transformation depending on the outcome of the struggles to keep them the same or to change them this way or that.

Clegg (1989: 200) suggests, 'Organizational locales will more likely be loci of multivalent powers than monadic sites of total control'.

Gramsci (1976) addressed the concept of 'hegemony', where power is seen to be exercised through consensus as well as through coercion. In effect the power relations are to be analyzed by what is thought 'proper' and what is excluded or denied in this definitional positioning. This has particularly serious repercussions for discussions of cultures, where the power to value and the power to deny can be very profound. Gramsci and Clegg both see the need for power to be analyzed in terms of networks, alliances, points of resistance and instability, which are also acknowledged by Foucault (1981). As Clegg continues (1989: 201), 'Power is implicated in authority and constituted by rules: the interpretation of rules must be disciplined, must be regulated, if new powers are not to be produced and existing powers transformed.' Nothing will ever be wholly stable; therefore resistance to discipline will not come from 'human nature' but 'because of the power/rule constitution as a nexus of meaning and interpretation which, because of indexicality, is always open to be re-fixed' (ibid).

Clegg's futures

Future authority in community festivals and events will make claims on the rules, even though the rules will have been amended and recontextualized. There is much work to be undertaken in untangling the circuits of power, and the communities will contribute great and even contradictory forces into the construction of the power relations in the events. These reconstructions will question the notions of power being defined as legitimate and with the involvement of distinct stakeholders from the community it will also be necessary to consider semi-legitimate and even illegitimate claims to power within the organizations. Such claims will have to be elaborated and unpacked in order for the future fields to be identified.

Foucault: discursive constructions

Any formulation of a macrohistory of modern power theories cannot be complete without the thoughts of Foucault. Cheong and Miller (2000) highlight how Foucault sees power as omnipresent, emphasising the construction of positions of power through discourse. They observe, 'Given the elusive character of power which is circulating and never localized here and there, never in anybody's hands, never appropriated as a commodity or a piece of wealth' a variety of people can possess and dispossess power in varying circumstances, and at different points in time and place (Cheong and Miller 2000: 376).

The genealogist therefore seeks to describe the economies of the said and the unsaid and provide insight into the power relations existing in the present. For Foucault, the existing power relations become most visible when the historian employs the strategy of 'shortening of vision', thereby bringing into focus the previously undisclosed. The notion of shortening of vision is in part constitutive of Foucault's notion of 'effective history': from the general notion, 'There is no "history" but a multiple overlapping and interactive series of legitimacy-v-excluded histories' (Wright 2002: 524). Foucault's conception of 'mixed genres' is understood as the inevitable byproduct of analyzing different types of data, which necessitates a reconciliation of empirical, interpretive, critical and the 'other-than-rational language' of myth and metaphor. Foucault 'alternates between detailed descriptions and reasoning, images and ideas' (ibid: 525).

According to one of the most quoted definitions that Foucault is credited with, 'power is actually the means whereby all things happen, the production of things, of knowledge and forms of discourse, and of pleasure' (Cassell 1993: 229). Foucault uses the negative definitions technique (Balázs 1998), whereby he makes assumptions rather than gives clear definitions. He argues that power cannot be identified with a belief system (as Weber suggests), and it is not a property that a person or a group could possess; rather, 'power is better conceived as a complex, shifting field of relations in which everyone is an element' (Fraser 1989: 29).

Foucault's main interest is the 'formation and functioning of incommensurable networks of social practices involving the mutual interrelationship of constraint and discourse' (Fraser 1989: 20). Modern power operates at all levels of society, in everyday social practices, and is not exercised by a central institution or person such as the state, the army or a king. It is not something 'given' that is exchangeable, it cannot be regained, but it is exercised, therefore it exists only in discourse (Balázs 1998). Foucault uses the term 'capillary' to capture the true characteristic of modern power, as he suggests that it is also continuous and productive. As Hollinshead (1999: 15) summarizes, 'since power circulates within the given body/collective/institution it may not be possessed and retained by particular individuals therein, but it may be accessed from innumerable points in the given circulatory regime-of-truth which many individuals participate in (Foucault 1984: 94)'. As power travels within and across an institution enwrapped with knowledge, it composes a 'gigantic moral imprisonment' of both the subjugated (i.e. those supposedly receiving the power in circulation) and the dominating (i.e. those supposedly wielding the power in circulation). The discourse and the praxis of both are controlled and mastered by this very power-knowledge dyad'. Foucault rules out the simple repressive hypothesis, which assumes that power operates essentially negatively, primarily through the means of censorship and denial. Foucault goes further and suggests that 'modern power is equally involved in *producing* all these things' (Fraser 1989: 27).

The dichotomy of the enabling and limiting or constraining nature of power is prevalent in every aspect of the Foucauldian power concept. On the one hand, he accuses the discursive regimes of using various forms of social restraints: 'the institutional licensing of some persons as authorized to offer authoritative knowledge claims and the concomitant exclusion of others' (Fraser 1989: 20). Foucault refers to the 'power to construct authoritative definitions of social situations and legitimate interpretations of social needs' as cultural hegemony (Fraser 1989: 107). On the other hand, he claims that power, besides limiting others' autonomy, also has an enabling character, which, therefore, widens people's freedom. As Hollinshead (1999: 13) summarized, '"power" is seen by Foucault to be the unspoken warfare which is waged silently and secretly through the language and the actions of that body's everyday routine and seemingly unspectacular enactments'.

Foucault says that power can be identified as a multiplicity of what he calls 'micropractices', the social practices that govern everyday life. These micropractices were developed in local disciplinary institutions, such as schools, prisons and hospitals, and were gradually integrated into 'macrostrategies' of domination. Therefore, he denies the claim that modern power regimes are imposed from the top down. Bramwell (2006: 961) observes,

Power is depicted as emerging through the interlocking of actors' projects . . . and this is influenced by the specific patterns of resource distribution and competition. It is argued that power is not simply possessed but rather is actively performed in social processes.

However, Foucault finds power techniques not only prevalent in all situations but also necessary. To believe that we are able to reach agreements and to continuously re-form traditions is only possible within the appropriate power constellation, with the necessary power techniques (Balázs 1998).

Bramwell (2006) utilizes the term 'discourse' in conjunction with a notion of 'knowledge frameworks' derived from Long's (2001) reading of Foucault (1972). A knowledge framework is a way of reading a relatively fixity and preconstructed way of interpreting actions and discourses. For Bramwell (2006: 961) they are 'the ways in which actors come to grips with the world in the context of the struggles, negotiations and accommodations between themselves and others.' As Fischer (2003) noted, it is important to recognize the context and the deliberative practices that underpin the operation of discursive politics. This is developed by Bramwell (ibid):

> there is often competition and conflict over resources, meaning and authority, with actors engaging in various struggles, such as the attribution of meaning in policy debates. In these relations individuals and groups may attempt to make space for themselves to pursue their own projects that run parallel to or challenge official government policies or the interests of other parties.

Long's arguments draw on Giddens's theory of structuration (1984) and echo Burns's proposal of the third way of tourism planning (2004). We are presented with the idea that

> Discourses are important within the larger knowledge frameworks. A discourse represents a set of meanings embodied in metaphors, representations, images, narratives and statements that advance a particular version of 'the truth' about objects, persons, events and the relations between them. (Long 2001: 51–52)

In policy debates, both knowledge frameworks and discourses influence what is included in the debates and also what is excluded, including the objects of concern, the preferred narratives for making sense of the issues, the actors that the policy makers consider and the agendas for action (Stenson and Watt 1999). Knowledge and discourses can delimit the 'possible', tending to steer thought and action in a particular direction (Bramwell 2006: 962).

It is also important to emphasize the dynamism of this view, as discursive practice can produce new constellations at any or all times and nothing should be seen to have any given permanence. Foucault's examples of what Hollinshead (1999: 16) termed the 'incommensurable systems of the way different institutions order or conceptualize things, not only distinct from other agencies or societies but differentially within the single agency or society over time' suggested that social constructions are 'precarious ensembles' (Merquior 1985: 77).

Foucault is undoubtedly complex but brings an interesting dimension to the study of community festivals. The implications of diffused power in everyday life and of the discourses deployed in the construction, maintenance and usages of power will need to be further examined in the future research. The discourses of power also allow a critical examination of some of the positions claimed by individuals and organizations in the tourism development processes, both to include and exclude players from the range of discourses that inform the processes.

It is important to recognize that these power relations are not necessarily about compliance but that community festivals could also create demonstrative resistance to those constructs of social control (Cohen 1982; Jackson 1988, 1992; Western 1992). Resistance can take many forms, but protests are usually the most likely form; however, voicing alternative cultures is another form of resistance and challenge if these positions can be constructed within the festivals themselves (Gramsci 1976).

Foucauldian festival futures

The most significant contribution that Foucault suggests for the multiversity of festivals and events is that of discursive analysis in understanding the construction and reconstruction of both the festivals themselves and the communities. The notion of empowerment has already played into the analyses of community festivals, but its logical corollary, disempowerment, has not been seen as often. The local communities will be bound within other discourses, which will seek to secure positions of power. Notably claims of professionalization, localness and authenticity will play through the development of the community festivals. Moreover there will be potential conflicts between the further professionalization of the community festival, its organization and its development, and the enthusiasm of local volunteers.

The future research agenda

Further research into the constructions of the agendas and contents of community festivals will be elaborated. Current research suggests that the decision-making processes have demonstrated that the agenda of community festivals has been shaped by the powerful stakeholders rather than the powerless. Hegemonic decisions have constrained the elements that have been showcased, marginalizing other minority cultures in the development of the festivals.

From the perspective of power future research concerning involvement and capacity development must approach these terms from a consideration that these processes are neutral. Considerations of power show that involvement is a focus of negotiation and even contestation over what and who can be involved in what roles and places. Similarly claims that festivals empower local communities require studies of the power relations in the creation, production and consumption of the festivals. The range of skills and competencies that the festivals can support are only realized if there is full involvement in the processes involved in the festivals. Cultural diversity within local cultural festivals and events is only achieved through an integrated and inclusive event-planning process.

Therefore studies of the power relations involved should also explore those situations where these communities may even feel marginalized and disenfranchised from these processes. This could be demonstrated in their lack of desire to participate in shaping the agenda of what could have become their own communities' festivals.

Further studies of power should illuminate the patterns of future decision-making processes employed within and around local community cultural festivals and events. This would explore the way in which festivals construct images of the communities and unpack how our societies have come to see so many mono-ethnic events and placeless festivals. Empowerment would help to ensure that festivals fully represent the multicultural nature of the communities and represent the full complex dimensions of the places that give support to those festivals. This would mean seeing the communities directly involved in funding decisions and event planning, not just performance.

Concluding remarks

The implications for the future of the event industry based upon the present and an understanding of the past are that organizers must become more aware of and sensitive to the wide range of stakeholders potentially involved in community festivals. They will have to look beyond the readily identifiable lists of the great and the good to uncover the dynamics within the communities themselves. Power has been revealed as a pervasive and constructive set of forces that are both enabling and disenfranchising.

Further analyses of power will be necessary to unpack the ways in which the events and festivals are put together, consumed and experienced in the changing moments of the future. This will involve exploring the ways in which the positions of power are constructed, challenged and reinforced. It becomes necessary to identify those who maintain and reinforce dominant positions within these processes and how they shape the involvement and exclusion of other stakeholders from the development of festivals.

Power must be seen as multifaceted and shifting. Stakeholders can build and contest positions based upon the construction and reconstruction of discursive practices. These arguments are pertinent in the evolution of community festivals, as the key players develop power from a number of different sources; the traditional bases of the established community may not equate to those in the local communities. The community values can suggest other ways of thinking and seeing the shape of the festivals in ways that recognize the meanings that are important within those communities.

Judd and Simpson (2003) identified 'independent centres of power' within which they observed that decision making often bypassed or limited democracy. This draws attention to the relationships between the public and private sectors involved in the development of festival projects. This further suggests that claims to democratic mandates or Weberian forms of absolutism have to be seriously scrutinized, especially where these claims are used to delimit opportunities. Swain (1995) draws attention to the patriarchal structures and male domination within planning processes that are evident in the processes of construction of festivals. Gender, sexuality and ethnicity discourses are vital to the construction of power locations. Within community festivals, it is possible to see terms used positively that have negative meanings in other contexts. The power of discrimination can be turned against traditionally dominant power bases where the strategy is not necessarily to empower the local communities.

Communities will benefit from involvement in festivals and events as they build skills and competencies in the context of the festival. This involves new discourses of power and recognizing new claims to legitimacy, and opening the organization to new stakeholders and their voices with possibilities of other ways of thinking about what is important in the festival. Analyses of the power relations between stakeholders will deepen the exploration of the ways in which a fuller range of voices come to be heard or not heard within the development processes.

Without analyses of the power relations supporting, challenging and driving the festivals, we will continue only to scratch the surface of those processes that shape the production and consumption of events and festivals. It should be noted that especially in community festivals this understanding is particularly important, as community values often challenge the dominant values expressed within the constructions of power in mainstream discourses. This project is essential to the understanding of the future development of festivals and events and underpins the research agenda.

References

Arendt, H. (1970) *On Violence*. London: The Penguin Press, Allen Lane.

Balázs, Z. (1998) *Modern Hatalomelméletek*. Budapest: Korona Kiadó.

Bell, W. (n.d.) 'An overview of futures studies' Available at: <http://master-foresight-innovation.fr/wp-content/uploads/2012/06/WBellOverviewofFS.pdf>

Bergman, A., Karlsson, J. C. and Axelsson, J. (2010) 'Truth claims and explanatory claims: an ontological typology of futures studies', *Futures*, 42: 857–65.

Bramwell, B. (2006) 'Actors, power and discourses of growth limits', *Annals of Tourism Research*, 33(4): 957–78.

Burns, P. (2004) 'Tourism planning: a third way', *Annals of Tourism Research*, 31(1): 24–48.

Cassell, P. (ed.) (1993) *The Giddens Reader*. Basingstoke: Macmillan.

Cheong, S. and Miller, M.L. (2000) 'Power and tourism: a Foucauldian observation', *Annals of Tourism Research*, 27(2): 371–90.

Church, A. and Coles, T. (eds.) (2007) *Tourism, Power and Space*. London: Routledge.

Clarke, A. and Jepson, A. (2009) 'Cultural festivals and cultures of communities', in C. Cooper (ed.) *Proceedings of the EUTO Conference 2008 'Attractions and Events as Catalysts for Regeneration and Social Change'*, Christel DeHaan Tourism and Travel Research Institute, University of Nottingham and The Centre for Tourism and Cultural Change, Leeds Metropolitan University, pp. 68–88.

Clarke, A. and Jepson, A. (2010) 'Power, hegemony and relationships within the festival planning and construction process', presented at *2010 Global Events Congress IV*, Leeds.

Clarke, A. and Jepson, A. (2011) 'Power and hegemony in a community festival', *International Journal of Events and Festival Management*, 2(1): 7–19.

Clarke, A., Jepson, A. and Wiltshier, P. (2008) 'Community festivals: involvement and inclusion', in *CHME 2008 Hospitality, Tourism and Leisure: Promoting excellence in research, teaching and learning*. Conference proceedings of the 17th Annual CHME Research Conference.

Clegg, S.R. (1989) *Frameworks of Power*. London: Sage.

Cohen, E. (1982) 'A polyethnic London carnival as a contested cultural performance', *Ethnic and Racial Studies*, 5: 23–41.

Coles, T. and Church, A. (2007) 'Tourism, politics and the forgotten entanglements of power', in A. Church and T. Coles (eds.) *Tourism, Power and Space*. London: Routledge, pp. 1–42.

de Araujo, L.M. and Bramwell, B. (2000) 'Stakeholder assessment and collaborative tourism planning: the case of Brazil's Costa Dourada Project', in B. Bramwell and B. Lane (eds.) *Tourism, Collaboration and Partnerships: politics, practice and sustainability*. Clevendon: Channel View Publications, pp. 272–94.

Eisenstadt, S.N. (ed.) (1968) *Max Weber: on charisma and institution building*. Chicago and London: The University of Chicago Press.

Erdélyi, A. (trans) (1987) *Gazdaság és Társadalom: Max Weber Közgazdasági és Jogi*. Budapest: Könyvkiadó.

Fischer, F. (2003) *Reframing Public Policy: discursive politics and deliberative practices*. Oxford: Oxford University Press.

Foucault, M. (1972) *Archaeology of Knowledge*. London: Tavistock.

Foucault, M. (1981) *The history of sexuality: volume I: an introduction*, trans. R Hurley. Harmondsworth: Penguin Books.

Fraser, N. (1989) *Unruly Practices: power, discourse and gender in contemporary social theory*. Cambridge: Polity Press.

Freeman, R.E. (1984) *Strategic Management: a stakeholder approach*. Boston: Pitman.

Giddens, A. (1972) *Capitalism and Modern Social Theory*. Cambridge: Cambridge University Press.

Giddens, A. (1984) *The Constitution of Society: an outline of the theory of structuration*. Cambridge: Polity Press.

Gramsci, A. (1976) *Selections from the Prison Notebooks*, ed. and trans. Q. Hoare and G. Nowell-Smith. London: Lawrence and Wishart.

Hamilton, P. (ed.) (1993) *Max Weber: critical assessments 1, volume III*. London and New York: Routledge.

Hollinshead, K. (1999) 'Surveillance of the worlds of tourism: Foucault and the eye-of-power', *Tourism Management*, 20: 7–23.

Inayatullah, S. (1998) 'Macrohistory and futures studies', *Futures*, 30: 381–94.

Jackson, P. (1988) 'Street life: the politics of carnival', *Environment and Planning D: Society and Space*, 6: 213–30.

Jackson, P. (1992) 'The politics of the streets: a geography of Caribana', *Political Geography*, 11: 130–51.

Jamal, T.B. and Getz, D. (1995) 'Collaboration theory and community tourism planning', *Annals of Tourism Research*, 22(1): 186–204.

Jepson, A.S. and Clarke, A. (2013) 'Community festivals and community development: inclusive or exclusive events', in R. Finkel *et al*. (eds.) *Research Themes in Events*. Wallingford: CABI, pp. 6–17.

Jepson, A.S., Clarke, A., and Ragsdell, G. (2012) 'Investigating the use of the Motivation-Opportunity-Ability (MOA) Model to reveal the factors which facilitate or inhibit inclusive engagement within local community festivals', *Global Events Congress: Conference Proceedings*, Stavanger, Norway, 13–15 June.

Judd, D. and Simpson, D. (2003) 'Reconstructing the local state: the role of external constituencies in building urban tourism', *American Behavioural Scientist*, 46(8): 1056–69.

Long, N. (2001) *Development Sociology: actor perspectives*. London, Routledge.

Lukes, S. (1974) *Power: a radical view*. Basingstoke: Macmillan.

Mann, M. (1986) *The Sources of Social Power, Vol. 1: a history of power from the beginning to A.D. 1769*. Cambridge: Cambridge University Press.

Mannermaa, M. (1988) 'Complexity and system thinking in futures research: from 'Neutral' scenarios to value considerations', *System Practice*, 1 (3): 279–95.

Markwick, M.C. (2000) 'Golf development, stakeholders, different discourses and alternative agendas: the case of Malta', *Tourism Management*, 21: 515–24.

Merquior, J.G. (1985) *Foucault*. London: Fontana.

Mintzberg, H. (1983) *Power in and Around Organizations*. Englewood Cliffs, NJ: Prentice Hall.

Mitchell, R., Agle, B. and Wood, D. (1997) 'Toward a theory of stakeholder identification and salience: defining the principle of who and what really counts', *Academy of Management Review*, 22(4): 853–86.

Parsons, T. (1957) 'The distribution of power in American society', *World Politics*, 10: 123–43.

Presti, A.L. (1996) 'Futures research and complexity: a critical analysis from the perspective of social science', *Futures*, 28: 891–902.

Sheehan, L.R. and Ritchie, J.R.B. (2005) 'Destination stakeholders exploring identity and salience', *Annals of Tourism Research*, 32(3): 711–34.

Stenson, K. and Watt, P. (1999) 'Governmentality and the 'Death of the Social'? a discourse analysis of local government texts in south-East England', *Urban Studies*, 36: 189–201.

Swain, M. B. (1995) 'Gender in tourism', *Annals of Tourism Research*, 22(2): 274 – 86.

Thomas, R. and Thomas, H. (2005) 'Understanding tourism policy-making in urban areas, with particular reference to small firms', *Tourism Geographies*, 7(2): 121–37.

Weber, M. (1948) 'The Religious rejections of the world and their directions', in *From Max Weber*, edited by H. H. Gerth, and C. Wright Mills. London: Routledge, pp. 323–24.

Western, J. (1992) *A Passage to England*. Minneapolis: University of Minnesota Press.

Westwood, S. (2002) *Power and the Social*. London: Routledge.

Wright, D.L. (2002) 'Applying Foucault to a future-oriented layered analysis in a post-bubble Japanese community', *Futures*, 34: 523–34.

7   Industry perceptions of events futures

Elisa Backer

Future points

- This chapter explores the perceptions of event managers of the future of events, and how the way they perceive future events may influence what future events will be.
- Events in the future are likely to witness increased professionalism, greater scrutiny, and increased difficulty obtaining sponsorships and volunteers, but be easier to access both through improved transport/transit routes and virtual experiences.
- Improved health and an ageing society are likely to result in events catering to a wider age bracket and have a wider age bracket of event staff.

Introduction

In 1939 Paul Valery said that 'the future, like everything else, is not quite what it used to be' (Doyle, Mieder and Shapiro 2012: 90). However, one thing that can be said with confidence is that 'the meetings and events industry will not be the same in ten years [sic] time' (Bergmann 2012). What that future will look like, and what industry thinks that future will look like, are relevant. After all, part of what the future of events will look like could be linked to the vision by industry. How event managers plan for the future, and change their events and their staffing to reach that perceived future, may indeed create a future.

This chapter discusses the perceptions amongst event managers concerning the future of tourism events and brings an important component to this book. Whilst the area of perceptions about events has received some research attention, perceptions by industry about the future of events remains a gap in the literature. This chapter outlines findings from empirical research to ascertain what event managers see in the future for events. The main visions for the future of events by event managers can be summarized as being:

- More use of social media
- Increased costs
- Increased demand for specific training/education courses

- Increased difficulty in obtaining sponsorships
- More occupational health and safety (OHS) and other legal/legislative safety requirements
- Saturated market
- Reduced travelling to events
- Greater professionalism

Background

Research into tourism events and festivals is not new. Interest from both an academic and practitioner perspective has grown dramatically over the past three decades. Despite this growth in research into events and festivals, the perceptions of industry, from a futures perspective, is absent from the literature. Further, often existing literature that purports to discuss the future of events ends up discussing the past. For example, Richards and de Brito (1996) provide a conclusion to an events book that is titled *The Future of Events as a Social Phenomenon* but is in fact a conclusion that collates the themes from the previous chapters. There is nothing about the future.

Thinking about the future is important, for both academics and practitioners. However, the role of event managers is necessarily tactical and focused on short-term goals; and therefore considering what their industry may look like in the future can be difficult. This chapter considers first the literature relating to perceptions of the events as well as relating to the industry of events from a professional perspective. As an empirically based chapter, it then outlines the method employed for the research, followed by discussing the results. The chapter concludes with a vision of the future of events informed by the results of the primary research.

Understanding events and festivals is important for researchers, educators, and industry. The volume of materials on events and festivals is now substantial, with large volumes of books, articles, and nonacademic reports. There is so much change through the 'industry' that the materials continue to be required to understand trends. This is why considering the future of events is so valuable, from both an academic perspective and an industry viewpoint.

Specific studies focused on festivals are growing. In 2010 a literature review identified 423 research articles focused on festival studies (Getz 2010). Whilst festivals are considered a subfield of events, specifically they can be considered to be an event in which 'visitors are likely to be seeking cultural enrichment, education, novelty, and socialization' (Crompton and McKay 1997: 429). Festivals (and events, more broadly) are important to destinations, as they 'create a demand for tourism services not only at a specific place but also at a specific time' (Andersson and Getz 2009: 848).

There has been an increase in the number of event tourism papers being included in academic journals, as well as an increase in academic journals dedicated to events (Getz 2008). There has also been growing interest in events from a tourism destination perspective, with communities increasingly allocating resources such as convention centres and events development officers, to pursue the events 'industry'.

Events are an important part of tourism, often forming part of the study of tourism in higher education. The growth of event management curricula at tertiary institutions has grown dramatically since the late 1990s (Dredge *et al.* 2012; Nelson and Silvers 2007; Thomas and Thomas 2013), fuelled by a realization of the economic benefits associated with holding events. As industry has realized the great benefits of holding events, this has led to a demand for events management professionals together with relevant professional qualifications (Dredge *et al.* 2012). Events have increasingly become part of the destination marketing strategies by Destination Marketing Organizations (DMOs). Yet, 'the majority of events have probably arisen for non-touristic reasons, such as religious holidays, competitions, community leisure, or cultural celebrations' (Getz 1989: 125).

There are many reasons why operators have become increasingly interested in events, and 'clearly there is a trend to exploit them for tourism and to create new events deliberately as tourist attractions' (Getz 1989: 125). Events are seen to provide considerable benefits to communities. Tourism events can increase visitation, length of stay, and expenditure, and can encourage repeat visitation, as well as reduce seasonality if events are strategically timed for off- or low-season periods. The development of tourism events can also provide the necessary stimulus to create additional infrastructure, and can also assist in building pride in a community by local residents.

However, events have also been the source of criticism. Sometimes an event that starts out to be a celebration of local culture in a community is destroyed through the pursuit of commercial interests. This debasement of local culture by commoditization has been recognized as one of the six negative social impacts of tourism (Leiper 2004). Also, despite widely popular statements from industry regarding the economic benefits relating to events, it is important to recognize the economic offsets from those benefits. Just as events can bring in visitors, they can also drive out residents and prevent potential visitors from coming to a region. Not everyone wants to be in a destination that is busy, and some people prefer to avoid the experience, and as such there can be an exodus and visitor detraction as a result. Events can also lead to diversion effects from business interruptions.

Perceptions about events

Whilst events can have both positive and negative benefits, they are an important component for communities. Perceptions about events have received a relatively small amount of research attention (Fredline and Faulker 2000; Ohmann, Jones and Wilkes 2006), but those studies conducted highlight the general support for events by residents. There have been a number of studies that have considered the perceptions of residents relating to a particular major event. Some of those studies have used secondary data, such as editorials/letters to the editor from local newspapers and records from the Courts (for example, Hall, Selwood and McKewon 1996; Hall and Selwood 1989). Other studies have undertaken primary research in order to directly gauge residents' perceptions.

Ohmann, Jones and Wilkes' (2006) study examined the perceptions of Munich residents relating to the 2006 Football World Cup. Findings from that study (n = 132) revealed that residents generally perceived the event positively, enjoying the atmosphere the event brought to the region, as well as urban regeneration and an increased sense of security (Ohmann, Jones and Wilkes 2006). Negative impacts were raised by a much smaller number of residents, who mentioned issues such as displacement of local residents, increased crime, and prostitution (Ohmann, Jones and Wilkes 2006).

Similarly, residents of the Gold Coast, Australia, were found to be generally supportive of the Indy car race (Fredline and Faulker 2000). Whilst residents acknowledged the negative impacts, they were highly supportive (88.5 percent) of its continuation (Fredline and Faulker 2000). In London, for the Olympic Games, residents were also found to be generally supportive of the event (Prayag *et al.* 2013; Ritchie, Shipway and Cleeve 2009), but did raise concerns such as anticipated traffic congestion, parking issues, and potential for the cost of living to increase (Ritchie, Shipway and Cleeve 2009).

More recently, a study in Macao revealed general support for major annual tourism events in the region (Chen 2011). The study considered a range of major events instead of taking a single-event approach, and revealed that 70 percent of residents felt that the events had a slightly more positive than negative impact on the region (Chen 2011).

Perceptions by event managers regarding risk management were considered in a recent study (Reid and Ritchie 2011) that focused on attitudes, beliefs, and perceived constraints of event managers in South-East Queensland (Australia). That study highlighted the great variation in perceptions by event managers. Events can be small and run entirely by volunteers; and they can be large and managed by professional organizations. These great variations can lead to enormously different perceptions as well as different levels of skills and resources. This was demonstrated by the differences in responses from respondents ranging from 'I have no idea [of what risk management means]' (Reid and Ritchie 2011: 335) up to articulating details of the strategies put into place.

Not only can perceptions of strategies vary amongst event managers, but also their perceptions regarding promotion and communication varies. Interestingly, although the perceptions of event managers and residents are important components when evaluating impacts of events and festivals, 'few studies focus on what managers think about the promotion and communication capacity of their festivals' (Karabag, Yavuz and Berggren 2011: 449). Whilst in general, festival managers tend to rate the impact of their festival on promotion and communication of the city as low (Karaba, Yavuz and Berggren 2011), local and international festivals have vastly different impacts on the promotion of cities, and 'not all festivals contribute to the promotion of cities in all market levels' (Karabag, Yavuz and Berggren 2011: 460).

Marketing and social media

A key part of promotion for many businesses is social media (Backer and Hay 2013). This has resulted in a massive shift in the way many organizations undertake promotions and the structure of their marketing budgets. Social media are particularly important platforms for tourism events because 'social media are now being used as a means of minimizing disappointment and to take the risk out of personal decisions' (Backer and Hay 2013: 1). Social media are an important form of word of mouth and one of the important aspects of it is its trustworthiness (Litvin, Goldsmith and Pan 2008). Its importance is then strengthened by the large base to draw upon (Backer and Hay 2013). However, social media also pose challenges to businesses, particularly with regards to reputation, which is something perceived very strongly by tourism managers (Ayen *et al.* 2012). Word of mouth, particularly via social media, can have major negative impacts on the success of tourism events and the perception of the local community in embracing this. Opponents to tourism events are particularly likely to be influenced by mass media (Weaver and Lawton 2013). As social media grows with new platforms and new audiences, the role that it has with impacting the perception of tourism events is likely to grow in the future, as long as social media are around.

Economic impacts

Economic benefits are an important component of events, and are a key factor that has led to the dramatic growth in events in the past two decades. There has been considerable research into the field of events, and 'to date, the majority of existing studies have focused upon the wider economic impacts' (Ohmann, Jones and Wilkes 2006: 2). Whilst the benefits are appreciated, it has been noted that research has tended to overstate the economic benefits associated with events and understate the social costs (Twynam and Johnston 2004). However, resident attitudes to regular events may become less negative after a period of time because the event organizers will become more experienced at reducing the disruptive impacts associated with the event and better at marketing the event to the local residents to engage with them (Fredline and Faulker 2000). It is also important to note that benefits from events, particularly when it comes to major events, can be quite broad and go beyond just economic benefits (Li and Jago 2012). Economic benefits are discussed in detail in the next chapter.

Social impacts

In addition to economic impacts, events hold social impacts, although the social dimensions of events have received far less research attention. Events can have social impacts such as community pride, changes in perceptions, altered understanding, social integration, and the development of social networks (Wilks 2006). Since events can be a celebration of interest and value, they are often seen more positively than tourism is. In fact 'much of the appeal of events is that they are never the same, and you have to "be there" to enjoy the unique experience fully; if you miss it, it's a lost opportunity' (Getz 2008: 404). It has been argued that 'the participants' experience is not exclusively individual, but rather rooted in a social and material interaction with other people and the environment' (Ryan and Wollan 2013: 110).

There are many different types of events. There are sporting events, private events such as weddings and milestone birthdays and anniversaries, business events such as meetings and trade shows, conferences, cultural events, political events, and entertainment events. The focus by most DMOs is on sporting and cultural events, which are seen as high yield and provide a strong focus on attracting visitors to the region. It has been recognized that major sport event management is 'too often associated with examples of mismanagement' (Emery 2010: 158). However, developing cultural pride and enabling celebrations of festivals that are meaningful to local residents is also cherished by many communities.

Some of those celebrations that have a strong cultural framework can cater more to residents than tourists, and this can have an impact on how the local community perceives the event. Events that cater strongly to the local community and are more of a community event than a tourism event may be rated higher by some residents than those events that have a stronger tourism focus. Also, the presence of tourists or second-homeowners, can have a direct impact on the timing of when some events occur (González-Reverté *et al.* 2012).

Tourism versus community events

Some local governments consider events in two categories – tourism events and community events – and may even have separate departments to focus on each 'type'. Tourism events are considered as events that will attract visitors to the region and accordingly are externally marketed. These are increasingly important to DMOs, as 'events attract tourists and motivate them to select a place where they can spend pleasant holidays or to revisit the place' (Holjevac 2010: 729). Community events are those that are seen to be primarily for the local community. However, whilst those events may not be marketed beyond the local community, if successful, they can still attract visitors, particularly daytrippers, and may also be successful in attracting people who are visiting friends and relatives (VFR travelers). The pivotal role that the local resident has with encouraging VFR travellers cannot be overstated (Backer 2008; Backer 2012). The importance of creating and growing events, regardless of their type, will no doubt continue into the future.

Volunteers

Whether events are classified as community or tourism events, the role of volunteers is very important. This can be particularly the case in regional areas, which are typically the most reliant on volunteers (White 2013). However, even when it comes to mega tourism events held in large cities, the role of volunteers is such that without them, many mega events could not take place (Kemp 2002). The numbers of volunteers involved in some recent mega events has been thought to be between 40,000 and 60,000 (Baum and Lockstone 2007). However, in regional areas that run smaller events that are less high profile, it can be difficult to attract volunteers, particularly educated volunteers (White 2013).

Given the trend in some communities towards increased difficulty obtaining and/ or retaining volunteers (White 2013), this may result in being a critical problem in the future, particularly for smaller tourism events in regional locations. One reason why it may be increasingly difficult to obtain/retain volunteers in the future could be in the way they are managed. Some managers do not understand the value of rewarding their volunteers (White 2013), and it is important that volunteers are not viewed simply as free labour (Gallarza, Franciso and Gil-Saura 2013). How well volunteers are managed, nurtured, and included in events, during and after, could be critical to retaining them. This could in turn have important impacts on the retention of those trained volunteers to ensure the success of tourism events in the future.

Sponsorship

One of the key ongoing issues for industry is that of revenue: something that will likely dominate into the future. The essential sources of revenue for events have been grants as well as sponsorship (Getz, Andersson and Carlsen. 2010). A high level of dependency on any one funding source can be highly risky and expose the event to potential failure (Getz 2003).

Whilst government grants may be a preferred option for event managers, they are not constant. A change of government, a change of economic conditions, a change of criterion: there can be many reasons why grants cannot be relied upon. As a result it:

> . . . makes government grants rather unpredictable, and reliance on grants equates to a dependency on the potential vagaries of government policy and fiscal capabilities. Accordingly, many festival managers seek corporate sponsorship even if they are philosophically inclined toward community service or the arts. (Andersson *et al.* 2013: 196)

One of the problems with the high need for sponsorships is the lack of information surrounding sponsorships. It is often difficult to know what is an appropriate fee to ask for, making it difficult for both potential sponsors and event manager to set reasonable levels (Andersson *et al.* 2013). Whilst sponsorship for some events is only a small proportion of their overall marketing budget, the growth rate of sponsorships is certainly 'outpacing advertising growth generally' (Andersson *et al.* 2013: 196).

Sponsorship is such an important part of running events. With such growth in events, with more events being developed and existing events growing, it would seem likely that event managers would find gaining sponsorships increasingly difficult. In order to find out what event managers thought about the future of events with regards to sponsorships, marketing, budgets, and other broad issues, an exploratory study was undertaken to support this chapter.

Method

The method employed for this research was qualitative, utilizing a structured survey instrument. As the research was exploratory, qualitative research was deemed most appropriate. The survey was developed as an online instrument, to allow busy event managers to answer the questions when they could best find available time. A structured questionnaire was developed that allowed open-ended responses, which allowed respondents to provide as must detail as they wanted to. The URL was sent to people who were involved in managing events, using industry networks within Australia. The URL was circulated through various industry groups, asking them to send it to appropriate contacts. A number of DMOs sent it to relevant members, and futures conference organizers also distributed it to select delegates who fitted the study purpose. Responses were analyzed using thematic analysis.

Results

This section discusses the key results from the primary research. There were 38 responses from the industry survey in total. To provide context, respondents were initially asked to state how long they had been involved working in events. The shortest time specified was 15 years, and the longest was 20 years.

Significant changes

Respondents were then asked, 'During your time working in events, what have been the most significant changes during the past five years in your opinion (consider the following in your response: competition – the number of events; the number of attendees, changes in demographics of attendees, changing costs – insurance etc)?'

A key theme that came through from the respondents was that events had become increasingly crowded spaces in which to compete. It was felt that events were a 'crowded market space' and that 'over the past five years with a larger number of other events it has made it far more difficult to attract participants' but that 'the demographic of our participants has not changed significantly'. The other theme that arose involved the rising regulations and requirements that made events more difficult for managing due to 'cost risk management regulations' and 'increasing OHS requirements – including increased associated costs for insurance etc'. It was felt that 'compliance is becoming a very large part of event organization, as is safety, working conditions, insurance and other non-core activities'. Further, it was identified that there was a 'greater legal responsibility for all aspects of events delivery' and that

> . . . running events have become extremely costly and with all the overhead costs increasing it makes it a lot harder to break even. With the economic climate as it is it is very hard to gain sponsorship and again break even.

It was also felt that people had 'higher expectations . . . for slick professional events', and that 'busy lives means people stay shorter times at events'.

Marketing budgets: past and future

The next question asked participants to indicate what proportion of their events marketing budget was dedicated to social media versus traditional marketing. The responses revealed that for many operators, social media were either only just starting to be used or had not been used at all yet. At the other end of the spectrum, some respondents showed that social media were already integrated into their traditional marketing stream.

The next question was 'In what way, if any, is your events marketing budget different to what it was five years ago?' Similar themes as arose from the previous question came through. The main theme was that budgets had either remained stable or had decreased. The manner in which marketing budgets were being directed had changed over the past five years according to all respondents. They had either had to make drastic changes due to significant budget cuts, or had reduced spending on print media to focus on social media even where their budgets had remained stable. No respondent stated that their budget had increased.

Respondents were then asked to consider how they thought their events marketing budget would change over the next ten years. This question was one that many respondents struggled with. The idea of looking forward ten years was considered difficult, as 'it is very difficult to forecast a ten year span'. However, a theme that did come through from respondents was that 'social media will most likely increase'. It was felt that 'social media will continue to rise and we will use more non-traditional media outlets. Our budget will be more contra based and our approach will shift from direct advertising to PR and partnerships'. Another respondent went as far as to say, 'I believe in ten years we won't advertise in publications or produce marketing collateral in the way of flyers etc. Everything these days is on social media and it is a much better cost effective marketing stream'.

Volunteers: past and future

Respondents were also asked to comment on what changes they had observed in the past five years in terms of recruiting volunteers and what changes they predicted in the next ten years with volunteers assisting on events. In terms of what changes had been observed in the past five years, the responses were mixed, with some respondents indicating that they 'have a strong volunteer base' and that 'volunteers are still easy to recruit if approached in the right way and rewarded for their efforts', whilst the majority found that volunteers are 'harder to secure' because 'fewer volunteers are available' and that there was a 'greater focus on gifts and benefits'. It was also highlighted that it was 'hard to get volunteers with the necessary credentials' and that 'no-one will volunteer their time or they commit and don't show'.

Responses were also mixed for predicting the next ten years. Again, similar to the previous question, many respondents could not predict that far in advance and simply said that the answer was 'unknown'. Others felt that 'greater demand for volunteers will make them harder to find and harder to retain', and there will be 'less and less use of volunteers as requirements make it more difficult to utilize them'. Consequently it was felt that 'we won't have any volunteers'. A small number of respondents stated they were 'hoping to increase our volunteer base over the next 10 years, and given social trend change I think this will be easy to do'. One respondent thought that there would be an 'increased payment of community groups to fill role as volunteers'.

Staffing: past and future

Respondents were then asked to comment on what changes they had observed in the past five years in terms of recruiting staff and what changes they predicted in the next ten years with recruiting staff. Once again, respondents struggled to consider what the next ten years may bring. Half the respondents said that the next ten years was 'unknown', whilst three respondents said there would be an 'increase in costs', and that 'professional staff will replace volunteers'. It was also felt that 'industry (is) becoming increasingly professionalized demanding specific training/education courses'. The issue of training and education also came through as a theme when respondents were reflecting on the past five years, stating that they had observed an 'improved skill level and knowledge base' and that 'staff are becoming more professional, better qualified and more impact full'. This was also noted as an area of difficulty though, as it was 'getting harder to find skilled event managers in regional areas, exacerbated by the increasing technical skills required by the industry'. Some respondents indicated that they 'do not employ staff', whilst contrary to that, others stated that there was 'more professional staff used to replace volunteers'.

Sponsorship: past and future

The next question involved asking about sponsorships, asking what changes had been observed over the past five years, and what changes were predicted to occur in the next ten years. All respondents except one highlighted the difficulty obtaining sponsorships, and that it was felt this situation would only get more difficult over time. It was felt that 'sponsorship requires a much more professional approach and you must provide valid reasons that the sponsor can put in to a business case. This will continue to be the case going forward'. It was also revealed that:

> ... sponsorship these days has to be organized a year in advance with budgets being locked in early. Companies don't have a lot of money to work with so it is very hard to get money though a lot are willing to come on board as in kind.

Whilst respondents acknowledged that obtaining sponsorship required a professional approach, successful sponsorship arrangements may be in part dependent on the event type (and the demographics that event attracts). Certainly in some sporting events, the proportion of spectators that were unaware of who the exclusive sponsor in the event was, has been revealed as high (Alexandris *et al.* 2008).

Clearly, 'if awareness is not achieved, sponsors cannot meet their subsequent objectives, such as image enhancement, positive behavioural intentions and increased sales' (Alexandris *et al.* 2008: 9).

Relationship between events and VFR

The next two questions involved asking respondents about the relationship between people visiting friends and relatives (VFRs) and events. Respondents were asked what proportion of people attending their event/s are linked to local residents (i.e. they are visiting friends and relatives). Responses varied widely. The lowest proportion mentioned was 17.5 percent, and the highest was 80 percent. Some respondents stated that it varied for their events and could be anywhere from '20% to as high as 80%'. When respondents were next asked if they have ever undertaken any marketing for their event/s to target people visiting friends and relatives in the local area, almost all respondents said that they had not. One respondent stated, 'yes – local print media advertising – signage – letterbox drop – newsletters', whilst another respondent stated, 'yes, we utilize the Geelong Tourism VFR campaign as part of our strategy and directly market "bring a mate" to our local audience'.

Significant negative influences: future

The next question asked respondents to indicate what issues they believed would hold the most significant negative influence on events in the next ten years. For some respondents this was 'unknown', but most respondents highlighted an increase in costs as being central. There were concerns about an 'increase in costs over regulation insurance focus' and 'increased costs, OHS and other legal/legislative safety requirements'. Also highlighted was that there was a 'saturated market of similar events' as well as 'reduced expendable income' and a 'reduction in travelling (to events)' mentioned.

Significant positive influences: future

The last question asked respondents to state what issues they believed would hold the most significant positive influence on events in the next ten years. Respondents seemed to find it more difficult to offer thoughts related to positive influences compared with negative influences, with most stating that this was 'unknown'. However, three respondents mentioned that 'social media represent[ed] a unique and cost effective niche marketing tool'. It was also felt that improved training was a positive aspect to create a 'more specialized and professional events industry'.

There was an opportunity for respondents to provide any other comments at the conclusion of the survey. Few respondents provided an additional comment. One stated that 'I believe that events, like anything in the tourism and hospitality industry, are subject to good management and good leadership. Badly led events will die, and well led events will thrive. Just as they always have'. Another interesting comment was that 'events are hard and expensive to deliver but can be very rewarding for regions that host them. If you have a good event, hang on to it. It is a lot harder to start one from scratch'.

Concluding remarks

The implications for the future of the event industry based upon the present are that tourism events will likely dominate the tourism agenda in future years. Whilst the field has already grown dramatically over recent years, and was seen by many event managers as being saturated, further growth was anticipated. However, that growth is likely to be dominated by events that are large and professional, with smaller community events becoming obsolete.

Those smaller events will likely be phased out as they increasingly struggle to meet rising costs associated with tough regulations, inability to recruit sufficient numbers of volunteers, and inability to obtain sponsorships. The difficulty in obtaining sponsorships was clearly identified by all but one respondent in this research. Given how important sponsorships are to events, this will need careful attention in the future by event managers.

Although event managers revealed how difficult it was to obtain sponsorships, and forecast this to continue and worsen in the future, it may only be partly linked to a growing events 'industry'. If event attendees are not paying attention to the promotion of event sponsors (perhaps because people increasingly tune out to 'static'), then it will require industry to rethink how they can provide benefits to sponsors in the future.

That also applies to volunteers. If event managers are finding it increasingly difficult to recruit and/or retain volunteers, they may need to develop new strategies in the future to make their volunteers feel valued. Volunteers, like sponsors, will need to feel that they are obtaining some benefit in order to stay involved.

Benefits should also be felt by the community because having residents' support for events is vital. People are increasingly conscious of negative impacts as lives get busier. Often both parents work, and people no longer 'switch off' because with today's technology, people are always 'on'. Technology in the future is likely to connect society more, and put increasing demands on employees to be responsive to emails, texts, and other future communication streams. It can trigger stresses because people don't have down time as they did in the past. Understanding these trends, event managers need to manage not only the economic constraints of the future, but the social constraints.

Those societal changes will likely result in expectations for events to be run more professionally, and as more training is created, the expectations will rise again. Legislation is likely to be tightened, and as such small community-based events could become a thing of the past, in the future. Just as society has seen with supermarkets (that a few large companies dominate and small corner stores become less common), events of the future may be run by a tighter number of professional 'expert' event companies.

Some other aspects may also be present in the future of events, which were not mentioned by the industry respondents. Some future events may be virtual, as already some organizations are seeing benefits from holding virtual events as a feasible way of promoting to people who may otherwise be unable to attend (Singh 2011). Globalization and the integration of cultures can bring about changes to the types of events staged (Bergmann 2012). There could also be a shift in the type of skills required by event managers, as technology potentially replaces some human resource components and creates new opportunities for highly skilled staff that can operate the technology. Continued improvements to health and an ageing population may also extend the age bracket of both event staff and event attendees.

Whilst many things are likely to change about events in the future, one thing is likely to remain constant, and that is the individualistic experience of being at an event. The event will always need to be lived to be appreciated and in order 'to experience such live events in our body, we have to travel to the sites where they occur, and then participate and play' (Ryan and Wollan 2013: 110). This is likely to be just as true in the future as it is today. Only the time it takes to travel there is likely to be shorter, as the future will almost certainly bring with it improved transit route connections.

References

Alexandris, K., Doukaa, S., Bakaloumia, S. and Tsasousia, E. (2008) 'The influence of spectators' attitudes on sponsorship awareness: a study in three different leisure events', *Managing Leisure*, 13(1): 1–12.

Andersson, T. and Getz, D. (2009) 'Tourism as a mixed industry: differences between private, public and not-for-profit festivals', *Tourism Management*, 30(6): 847–56.

Andersson, T., Getz, D., Mykletun, J., Jæeger, K. and Dolles, H. (2013) 'Factors influencing grant and sponsorship revenue for festivals', *Event Management*, 17: 195–212.

Ayen, J., Leung, D., Au, N. and Law, R. (2012) 'Perceptions and strategies of hospitality and tourism practitioners on social media: an exploratory study', in Fuchs, M., Ricci, F., and Cantoni, L. (eds.) *Information and Communication Technologies in Tourism 2012*, Proceedings of the International Conference. Helsingborg, Sweden, 25–27 January, pp. 1–12.

Backer, E. (2008) 'VFR travellers: visiting the destination or visiting the hosts?' *Asian Journal of Tourism and Hospitality Research*, 2(April): 60–70.

Backer, E. (2012) 'VFR Travel: it is underestimated', *Tourism Management*, 33(1): 74–9.

Backer, E. and Hay, B. (2013) 'Introduction: social media special issue', *Journal of Tourism, Culture & Communication*, 13: 1–4.

Baum, T. and Lockstone, L. (2007) 'Volunteers and mega sporting events: developing a research framework', *International Journal of Event Management Research*, 3(1): 29–41.

Bergmann, Y. (2012) *A Look into the Future: trends and developments of the meetings and events industry*. Online. Available <http://yashabergmann.com/2012/03/20/a-look-into-the-future-trends-and-developments-of-the-meetings-and-events-industry/> (accessed 7 January 2014).

Chen, S.C. (2011) 'Residents' perceptions of the impact of major annual tourism events in Macao: cluster analysis', *Journal of Convention & Event Tourism*, 12(2): 106–28.

Crompton, J.L. and McKay, S.L. (1997) 'Motives of visitors attending festival events', *Annals of Tourism Research*, 24(2): 425–39.

Doyle, C., Mieder, W. and Shapiro, F. (eds.) (2012) *The Dictionary of Modern Proverbs*, compiled. New Haven: Yale University Press.

Dredge, D., Benckendorff, P., Day, M., Gross, M.J., Walo, M., Weeks, P. and Whitelaw, P.A. (2012) *Influences on Australian Tourism, Hospitality and Events Undergraduate Education*, Issues Paper No.2. Sydney: Office for Learning & Teaching.

Emery, P. (2010) 'Past, present, future major sport event management practice: the practitioner perspective', *Sport Management Review*, 13(2): 158–70.

Fredline, E. and Faulker, B. (2000) 'Host community reactions: a cluster analysis', *Annals of Tourism Research*, 27(3): 763–84.

Gallarza, M., Franciso, A. and Gil-Saura, I. (2013) 'The value of volunteering in special events: a longitudinal study', *Annals of Tourism Research*, 40: 105–31.

Getz, D. (1989) 'Special events: defining the product', *Tourism Management*, 10(2): 125–37.

Getz, D. (2003) 'Why festivals fail', *Event Management*, 7(4): 209–19.

Getz, D. (2008) 'Event tourism: definition, evolution, and research', *Tourism Management*, 29(3): 403–28.

Getz, D. (2010) 'The nature and scope of festival studies', *International Journal of Event Management Research*, 5(1): 1–47.

Getz, D., Andersson, T. and Carlsen, J. (2010) 'Festival management studies: developing a framework and priorities for comparative and cross-cultural research', *International Journal of Event and Festival Management*, 1(1): 29–59.

González-Reverté, F., Gomis-López, J.M., Miralbell-Izard, O. and Viu-Roig, M. (2012) 'The role of identity in events scheduling', *Annals of Tourism Research*, 39(3): 1683–90.

Hall, C.M. and Selwood, H. (1989) '1989 America's Cup lost: paradise retained? The dynamics of a hallmark tourist event', In Syme, G.J., Shaw, B.J., Fenton, D.M. and Mueller, W.S. (eds.) *The Planning and Evaluation of Hallmark Events*. Aldershot: Avebury, pp. 103–18.

Hall, C.M., Selwood, J. and McKewon, E. (1996) 'Hedonists, ladies and larrikins: crime, prostitution and the 1987 America's Cup', *Visions in Leisure and Business*, 14(3): 28–51.

Holjevac, I. (2010) 'Business excellence and quality of tourism events', *Tourism and Hospitality Management*, May: 729–41.

Karabag, S.F., Yavuz, M.C. and Berggren, C. (2011) 'The impact of festivals on city promotion: a comparative study of Turkish and Swedish festivals', *Original Scientific Paper*, 59(4): 447–64.

Kemp, S. (2002) 'The hidden workforce: volunteers' learning in the Olympics', *Journal of European Industrial Training*, 26(2/3/4): 109–16.

Leiper, N. (2004) *Tourism Management*. 3rd ed. French's Forest: Pearson Education.

Li, S. and Jago, L. (2012) 'Evaluating economic impacts of major sports events: a meta analysis of the key trends', *Current Issues in Tourism*, June: 1–21.

Litvin, S., Goldsmith, R. and Pan, B. (2008) 'Electronic word-of-mouth in hospitality and tourism management', *Tourism Management*, 29: 458–68.

Nelson, K.B. and Silvers, J.R. (2007) 'Event management curriculum development and positioning: a path toward professionalization', *Journal of Hospitality & Tourism Education*, 21(2): 31–40.

Ohmann, S., Jones, I. and Wilkes, K. (2006) 'The perceived social impacts of the 2006 Football World Cup on Munich residents', *Journal of Sport & Tourism*, 11(2): 129–52.

Prayag, G., Hosany, S., Nunkoo, R. and Alders, T. (2013) 'London residents' support for the 2012 Olympic Games: the mediating effect of overall attitude', *Tourism Management*, 36: 629–40.

Reid, S. and Ritchie, B. (2011) 'Risk management: event managers' attitudes, beliefs, and perceived constraints', *Event Management*, 15(4): 329–41.

Richards, G. and de Brito, M. (1996) 'The future of events as a social phenomenon', in Richards, G., de Brito, M., and Wilks L. (eds.) *Exploring the Social Impacts of Events*. Hoboken: Taylor and Francis, pp. 219–35.

Ritchie, B.W., Shipway, R. and Cleeve, B. (2009) 'Resident perceptions of mega-sporting events: a non-host city perspective of the 2012 London Olympic Games', *Journal of Sport & Tourism*, 14(2–3): 143–67.

Ryan, A.W. and Wollan, G. (2013) 'Festivals, landscapes, and aesthetic engagement: a phenomenological approach to four Norwegian festivals', *Norwegian Journal of Geography*, 67(2): 99–112.

Singh, I. (2011) *Virtual Events and the Future of Tourism*. Online. Available <www.virtualeventshub.com/virtual-event-trends/virtual-events-and-the-future-of-tourism/> (accessed 9 January 2014).

Thomas, R. and Thomas, H. (2013) 'What are the prospects for professionalizing event management in the UK?' *Tourism Management Perspectives*, 6: 8–14.

Twynam, G.D. and Johnston, M. (2004) 'Changes in host community reactions to a special sporting event', *Current Issues in Tourism*, 7(3): 242–61.

Weaver, D. and Lawton, L. (2013) 'Resident perceptions of a contentious tourism event', *Tourism Management*, 37: 165–75.

White, D. (2013) *Regional Victorian Volunteer Managers and Their Opinions on Volunteer Retention*. Ballarat: Federation University Australia.

Wilks, L. (2006) 'Introduction', in Richards, G., de Brito, M. and Wilks L. (eds.) *Exploring the Social Impacts of Events*. Hoboken: Taylor and Francis, pp. 183–84.

8 Economic evaluation of special events
Challenges for the future

Larry Dwyer and Leo Jago

Future points

- This chapter demonstrates the importance of evaluating the contribution that special events make and that their economic contribution is but one dimension of this contribution.
- An overview of the techniques that have been used to assess the economic impact of special events is provided and the most credible approach recommended.
- 'Economic impact assessments' can give contradictory results to a cost-benefit analysis and techniques are needed to integrate the two methods to give more consistent outcomes.
- There is a need to broaden the base of special event evaluations so that the field is able to demonstrate its true potential and secure a more sustainable future.

Introduction

Special events are key drivers of tourism activity in many destinations around the world. As the staging of special events is often dependent on the financial or in-kind support of the public sector, it is critical for the long-term viability of special events that it is possible to demonstrate their contribution to the host community in credible ways. Although special events have broad-based impacts involving economic, social and environmental dimensions, there is still considerable focus on the economic contribution. Despite the fact that economic evaluation studies have been undertaken in numerous fields for many years, there is still considerable debate as to the approach that should be adopted for consistency and credibility. Failure to achieve this puts support for special events at risk and hence their viability in the future is also at risk.

This chapter seeks to:

- demonstrate the importance of evaluating the contribution that special events make and that their economic contribution is but one dimension of this contribution;

- identify and discuss the main policy reasons that destination managers may wish to achieve via their support of special events;
- overview the techniques that have been used to assess the economic impact of special events and recommend the most credible approach;
- highlight the fact that economic impact is not the same as economic benefit and that a cost-benefit analysis (CBA) is required to assess the economic benefit;
- present an overview of the key components of a CBA and how they should be assessed;
- show how 'economic impact assessments' can give contradictory results to a CBA and that techniques are needed to integrate the two methods to give more consistent outcomes; and
- highlight the need to broaden the base of special event evaluations so that the field is able to demonstrate its true potential and secure a more sustainable future.

Background

Special events provide important recreational opportunities for local residents and, in many destinations, they form a fundamental component of the destination's tourism development strategy. Special events increase the opportunities for new expenditures within a host region by attracting visitors to the region. They have the capacity to stimulate business activity, creating income and jobs in the short term and generating increased visitation and related investment in the longer term. They are valued by residents, directly and indirectly, and can enhance destination image. On the other hand, events are recognized to generate adverse environmental impacts such as various forms of pollution and adverse social impacts such as disruption to local business, congestion and crowding, and community backlash.

Given the diverse nature of event impacts, assessments of their contributions should be broad based to synthesize their economic, social and environmental impacts. The focus of this chapter is on economic evaluation where one might expect there to be some consensus on the method of evaluation. However, this has not been the case. Standard approaches to the economic evaluation of special events continue to be criticized for their use of inappropriate models and unrealistic assumptions, their narrow focus and their unsuitability to inform public policy and funding decisions (Dwyer, Forsyth and Spurr 2005, 2006; Jago and Dwyer 2006, 2013; Abelson 2011; Dwyer and Jago 2012). Given the range of activities that compete for government support, if these criticisms are not addressed to ensure that the credibility of economic evaluations of special events is enhanced, the public sector support for events will be at risk. Whilst the noneconomic impacts of special events are very important, the results of the economic evaluation of an event's contribution tends to be the key interest of the public sector, and this is likely to continue in the foreseeable future. It is critical for continuing support of special events by the public sector, therefore, that the consistent and widely accepted techniques be adopted for the economic evaluation of special events.

Governments are often asked to provide financial support for special events including the allocation of large expenditures to upgrade the required facilities for holding a special event. There are several possible policy objectives that destination managers may wish to meet by funding special events. The four main objectives are listed below (Abelson 2011):

1. To maximize gross domestic product (GDP) or gross state product (GSP).
2. To maximize the net income or consumption of existing households in the destination.
3. To maximize employment in the destination.
4. To maximize the net (welfare) benefits to residents of the destination.

The first three objectives require economic impact analysis to estimate the extent to which a special event fulfils funding goals. All governments have an interest in funding projects that promote economic development in a particular jurisdiction, defined by increases in GDP/GSP, household income and employment creation. For this purpose, economic impact analysis (EIA) can be used. Estimating the extent of achievement of the fourth objective, however, requires a different assessment technique – cost-benefit analysis (CBA).

It should be noted that in many destinations, government allocates a specific sum each year to the support of the attraction and sponsorship of events in that destination. Thus assessments of the economic impact of events are more relevant to the decision as to which events should be supported as opposed to whether or not events should be supported. That is, the performance of events is assessed in order to determine which ones should receive support and to what extent. Clearly, an exception to this approach applies to very large-scale events such as the Olympics, where government must decide whether to allocate additional funds to support the event and competition for these funds is from other sectors such as health and education.

As shall be argued below, it is researchers' failure to properly identify the objectives of event funding agencies that has been responsible for the use of economic assessment techniques that are inadequate to the task at hand. Compounding this problem is the propensity of consultants to deliver the biggest possible impact estimates for clients eager to develop events. To avoid the criticisms that continue to be levelled against the economic evaluation of special events, researchers need to explicitly identify these objectives and employ approaches that inform funding agencies about the extent to which these objectives are achieved by holding special events. This is the major challenge for the economic assessment of special events and an important direction in which the research agenda will develop in the future.

Economic impact analysis

To estimate the impact of a special event on each of the first three objectives listed in the previous section requires use of an economic model. The key input to economic impact analysis (EIA) is the amount of expenditure made by visitors, accompanying persons, organizers, delegates, sponsors, media and others. Only that expenditure representing an injection of 'new money' into an area is relevant to the estimation of the economic impacts on GSP/GDP, valued added, household income and employment (Dwyer and Forsyth 2005). 'New money' is defined as money that comes from outside the host region that would not have occurred had the event not been staged. The net injected expenditure that occurs as a result of an event is used as the input to an economic model, allocated to different industry sectors (accommodation, restaurants, tours, entertainments etc.) to determine the economic impacts on the destination. Since this injected expenditure will have secondary effects on the economy (indirect plus induced), multipliers may be used to determine an event's contribution to destination output, value added and employment. The type of model employed in economic impact analysis will determine the size of the multipliers and the estimates of changes in output, value added and employment resulting from holding the event.

As displayed in Figure 8.1, two main types of economic models can be used to estimate the economic impacts of an event, namely, input-output modelling and computable general equilibrium modelling.

The standard model used for economic impact estimation of special events has been the input-output (I-O) model (Crompton 2006, 2010). I-O tables show the various industries that make up the economy and indicate how these industries interlink through their purchase and sales relationships. In simple terms, they show for each industry the other industries from whom purchases are made and the other industries to which sales are made. In an I-O model, an exogenous injection of expenditure, such as an increase in visitor expenditure associated with the holding of a special event, brings about an increase in output in supplier industries. This requires in turn an increase in inputs supplied to those industries, which again requires an increase in outputs by industries supplying these inputs. An I-O model traces and estimates these input requirements among industries.

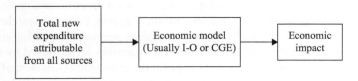

Figure 8.1 Economic impact of events

In recent years, a growing number of researchers have argued that, because of its simplistic assumptions, I-O modelling does not provide an accurate picture of the economic impacts of events, particularly large events. These researchers have argued that the EIA of special events should reflect contemporary developments in economic analysis, particularly regarding the use of Computable General Equilibrium (CGE) modelling. CGE models include more specifications of the behaviour of consumers, producers and investors, thus permitting specific models to be calibrated to actual conditions for a particular event in a particular economy. They are designed to capture the complex pattern of price changes, feedback effects and resource constraints, which exist in all economies following a demand side shock such as that occasioned by the holding of a special event (Blake 2005; Bohlmann 2006; Dwyer, Forsyth and Spurr 2005, 2006; Madden 2006; Victoria Auditor General 2007; Mabugu and Mohamed 2008). In contrast to I-O analysis, which always produces a positive gain to the economy, however disastrous the event, CGE modelling recognizes that price rises due to resource constraints may limit the increase in economic activity occasioned by a special event, and may even lead to contractions in economic activity in some sectors.

CGE simulations of the Formula One Grand Prix held in Melbourne in 2005 (VAG 2007) reveal that an increase in event-related expenditure of $58.4 million injected into the State of Victoria generated positive macroeconomic consequences, with real GSP up by $62.4 million, and 400 new jobs in the State (full-time equivalents). However, the grand prix crowds out activity in some industries both within the state and elsewhere in Australia. The modelling indicated that the event was associated with a substantial shift of resources and economic activity from the rest of Australia to Victoria, reducing GSP in other states by $60.5 million in total. Overall, the event generated a mere $1.9 million increase in GDP in Australia as a whole. According to VAG (2007), the 2005 grand prix delivered positive outcomes on the first three objectives as identified above.

The problem with EIA, which applies to both I-O and CGE modelling, is that it does not take full account of the opportunity costs of resources used to deliver an event and so does not provide 'the bottom line' for policy formulation. Thus, while EIA enables destination managers to estimate the extent to which a special event meets the first three policy objectives highlighted above, it fails to capture some significant welfare impacts. To estimate these welfare effects, and thus to address the fourth policy objective, cost-benefit analysis is required.

Cost-benefit analysis

The economic impacts of an event are not the same thing as its economic benefits. Economists know that prices do not always reflect full benefits from consumption or full costs of production. To enable the addition to GDP/GSP generated by a special event, inputs are needed – additional labour must be hired, additional capital must be made available, more land will be alienated and more natural resources will be used up, with attendant social and environmental effects.

The most comprehensive of the economic appraisal techniques is cost-benefit analysis (CBA). CBA is used to capture, measure, weigh and compare all expected present and future benefits of a policy, program or investment (such as a special event) with all its expected present and future costs. CBA is the preferred approach to event assessment, as it is holistic with (in principle) inclusion of all costs and benefits (welfare effects) associated with an event. In CBA, 'value' or 'benefit' is measured by willingness to pay – what people are willing to pay (or give up) to get what an event provides. In a CBA, welfare benefits are calculated by measuring the additional consumer surplus and producer surplus of a given option over the 'do nothing' or 'no event' case (Boardman *et al.* 2006). Economic costs are measured by 'opportunity cost' – what people or a society give up by investing capital and employing workers in event-related activities as opposed to the best alternative (Dwyer 2012). For a special event to be socially acceptable, the sum of the benefits to society (including private and social benefits) must exceed the sum of the costs to society (including private and social costs).

By quantifying the net benefits of projects, programs and policies in a standard manner, CBA improves the information base for public sector decision making, thereby assisting in the assessment of relative priorities. It is designed specifically to answer public policy questions. For special events, judgement can be made as to whether the economic benefits are greater than the costs, and to also judge whether the event would represent the best use of the funds, when funds are limited and alternative calls on funds exist. Economic impact analysis cannot do this.

Compared to EIA studies of special events, the literature on event assessment boasts relatively few CBA studies. Prominent studies include evaluation of the Eurovision Song Contest held in Israel (Fleischer and Felsenstein 2002) and the Vancouver Winter Olympics 2010 (Shaffer, Greer, and Mauboules 2003). The Victoria Auditor General commissioned a study of the 2005 Formula One Grand Prix. In contrast to the EIA, which estimated a $62.4 million increase in GSP for the State (see above), the CBA showed a net loss on the event (costs exceed benefits) of $6.7 million (VAG 2007: 81–126). A situation in which an EIA gives positive outcomes for a special event while a CBA indicates a net loss is not unusual (Shaffer, Greer and Mauboules 2003, Abelson 2011), and follows from the fact that the different methods have different objectives.

Some indicative types of costs and benefits of a special event are displayed in Table 8.1. These types of costs and benefits were identified in a CBA of the Formula One Grand Prix held in Melbourne, Victoria, from the perspective of the government of the state of Victoria (VAG 2007: 81–126).

Table 8.1 Indicative costs and benefits of a special event

COSTS

- Capital expenditures on event related infrastructure.
- Operating expenditures (for example, event management and staging, marketing/promotion and catering, administration).
- Other event-related costs incurred by government agencies such as road agencies, police and state emergency services.
- Social and environmental costs such as disruption to business and resident lifestyles, traffic congestion, road accidents, crime, litter, noise, crowding, property damage, environmental degradation, vandalism, congestion, air/water pollution, carbon footprint.

BENEFITS

- Payments to event organizers (ticket revenue, sponsorship and advertising revenue and media payments). The ticket sales and sponsor revenue received by the event organizer are a benefit to the taxpayer in that they offset the costs incurred in staging the event and reduce the size of the government subsidy to the event.
- Consumer surpluses of local households derived from attending the event. For many events, the price that patrons are willing to pay to attend the event exceeds what they are required to pay to attend and thus there is a net gain to the patrons from the event being available.
- Consumer surpluses of local households from attending associated offsite events/activities (satellite events, public screenings and off-site parties). Many events have such activities associated with them, which residents value as implied by their participation.
- Other benefits of local households from indirect enjoyment of the event. This refers to the pride and excitement that many residents derive, over and above any direct or indirect participatory benefits, simply because their destination plays host to the special event. Destination residents may be willing to pay something for such nonuse benefits rather than receive other social services. The source of such pride may be that the attention of the outside world is on them and their community, or it may be that their destination successfully managed a world-class event. Following earlier studies (Burns *et al.* 1986), this is sometimes referred to as 'psychic income'.
- Business (Producer) Surplus refers to the operating profits of local owners of visitor-related businesses (returns to locally owned capital) associated with the event. Producer surplus is the difference between the value of output and the cost of the factors of production (land, labour and capital), where their cost reflects their value in alternative uses.
- Labour Surplus refers to the net benefits to local labour (after compensation for working and tax) associated with the event. If an event results in the creation of additional employment in the destination, labour surpluses occur when labour is employed at a wage higher than what workers would be prepared to accept to enter into employment. When a worker would be otherwise unemployed or underemployed, the opportunity cost is the value of leisure foregone. The difference between the cost of labour, evaluated at the market wage rate, and evaluated at the shadow or reservation wage, is an additional benefit from the increased economic activity associated with an event.
- Follow-on benefits of future visitors to the tourism industry (brand benefit).
- Ongoing (legacy) benefits from construction of assets for the event.

Estimating costs of events

In general, the amount spent on producing an event is the cost of resources employed in terms of the value of other goods and services forgone. Major categories of organizer costs include: event management and staging, recurrent engineering, marketing/promotion, catering and administration. The cost of employing capital, land and labour for the event is the value of what those economic resources could have produced in their best alternative use.

Governments often allocate resources to support a special event. Event-related costs incurred by government agencies might include payments in respect of: roads and traffic authority, police, ambulance, fire brigade, emergency services and so on. Many relevant costs can be based on balance sheet figures of government departments and agencies. Any time devoted to event management issues by public servants has an opportunity cost, estimated with reference to some measure of average wages of public service employees.

Volunteers, who generally take leave from their employment to provide services at the event, would not be included as costs. While their time has an opportunity cost, there is no practical way of putting a value on it.

Estimating the social and environmental costs presents some difficulties. In each case, the valuation process requires two steps: estimating the amount of physical change (e.g. of recreation areas and amenity, traffic diversion and congestion, noise etc.), and estimating the value associated with that change. There are well-known methods for valuing temporary disruption to resident lifestyles through loss of land uses (VAG 2007), traffic congestion (Bureau of Transport and Regional Economics, 2007) and noise and air quality impacts on property values (Boardman *et al.*, 2006; Pearce, Atkinson and Mouranto 2006). Time lost due to congestion can be estimated and priced at average wage rates (Mackie, Jara-Díaz and Fowkes 2001). The increased incidence of crime associated with an event can be estimated from statistics for previous events, as can property damage, accidents and vandalism. Costs of removing litter and cleaning event sites can also be estimated. The standard economic method of valuing such benefits is willingness to pay or accept.

Similarly, the environmental impacts of events can be estimated. The generation of litter, noise, crowds, pollution and large carbon footprints are often associated with special events and need to be accounted for in an overall event assessment. Different events have different carbon footprints. Techniques for measuring the carbon footprint of an economic activity are available on the web.

A potential cost that is often emphasized by researchers is loss of local business trade and income due to event-created congestion and crowding out. However, in most cases, these switches are income distributional effects rather than efficiency effects, since consumers simply change the timing of their purchases or transfer their purchases to another location in the short run. This may create local winners and losers, but the net effect on businesses from switches in local purchases would generally be small (Abelson 2011).

Estimating benefits of events

Sales revenues

The estimated payments to event organizers are relatively straightforward. For most events, the largest benefit item is the payment to the event organizer through ticket sales.

Consumer surpluses

However, ticket prices may not reflect the maximum that many consumers may be willing to pay for a good or service. This willingness-to-pay amount represents the value of goods and services that consumers are willing to forgo to experience the event. Typically, the price that event attendees are willing to pay exceeds what they are required to pay, implying that they experience a net gain. This net gain, termed the consumer surplus, is the difference between the amount residents would be willing to pay for a ticket and what they actually pay. Thus, the monetary value of the benefits exceeds the revenues that the organizers are able to collect from the patrons, even with quite sophisticated pricing structures. The practice of ticket scalping is an indication that people are often willing to pay more than the official ticket price, and that consumer surplus exists. Free events can be valued entirely at Willingness to Pay (WTP) or Willingness to Accept (WTA).

Indirect participation at related (off-site) activities such as street parades, entertainments, etc. indicates that residents derive benefits from these activities. Since they would not exist if the event were not held, they must be counted as benefits to residents in addition to the consumer surpluses from event attendance itself.

Consumer surpluses from attending an event and other local household benefits from indirect participation may be estimated from event-specific surveys or information from other events (ACT Auditor-General 2002; VAG 2007).

A potential (nonuser) benefit would be civic pride or pleasure that residents experience in hosting a major event over and above participation benefits already valued. The contingent valuation method (CVM) is the most widely used method for estimating nonuse value. The method is called 'contingent' valuation because people are asked to state their willingness to pay (accept), contingent on a specific hypothetical scenario and description of the good or amenity. Through surveys or bidding games, CVM circumvents the absence of markets for certain goods by surveying consumers in hypothetical markets in which they have the opportunity to pay for the good in question. In contrast, the contingent choice method (CCM), a technique used to measure the value that respondents place on different attributes in a scenario, does not directly ask individuals to state their values. Instead, values are inferred from the hypothetical choices or trade-offs that people make between sets of attributes. By such means, resident values of events of different sizes and types could be estimated.

In the future, it is likely that both CCM and CVM will be increasingly employed to value the nonuser resident benefits associated with special events.

Producer surpluses

Business surpluses associated with a special event are the additions to operating profits (after tax) accruing to local owners of businesses. These gains are associated with additional expenditure by visitors less the cost of resources to service this expenditure.

VAG (2007: 115) provides an equation showing how business surpluses after tax (π) may be estimated:

$$\pi = [\Delta E \times (1 - IT)] \times (1 - CI) \times (1 - DT)$$

where

ΔE is the net injected expenditure generated by the event

IT is indirect taxes as a percentage of turnover

CI is the cost of inputs as a function of revenue less indirect tax

DT is direct company income tax rate.

Plausibly, if IT = 0.10, CI = 0.8, and DT = 0.3, the surplus after Commonwealth taxes would be 13 percent of the change in gross pretax injected expenditure. A figure of 13.5 percent was used in the CBA of the Formula One Grand Prix (VAG 2007).

Labour surplus

Additional employment can be an extra source of net benefit associated with a special event. A labour surplus occurs when jobs go to unemployed or underemployed resident workers to meet visitors' extra demand for goods and services, and these workers are employed at a wage higher than what they would be prepared to accept to enter into employment.

VAG (2007) offers the following formula to estimate labour surpluses:

$$LS = E \times A \times B \times C$$

where

LS = labour surpluses

E = net injected expenditure generated by the event

A = proportion of expenditure spent on labour (wages bill)

B = percentage of A that is done by extra local labour to meet the extra demand flowing from the event (that is not diverted from other employment in the destination)

C = percentage of wage that represents a surplus to the additional labour employed.

In VAG (2007), A × B × C equals 3 percent, i.e., 3 percent of new expenditure was denoted as labour surplus.

The ongoing legacy value (if any) of assets constructed for the event may also be estimated. This value is a function of the demand for additional event capacity less the costs of maintaining the assets. Consumer surveys can provide information on this.

Intangibles

Some outcomes of an event for a destination are not sufficiently well accepted or measurable to be included in a CBA. These are often referred to as 'intangible' outcomes. They include such items as increased business confidence, increased trade and business development, enhancement of business management skills, emergent values such as increased community interest in the issues relevant to the event 'theme', and enhanced destination image. Costs include the perception that events cause the destination to be crowded, with inflated prices, causing a loss of tourism and business to the host destination.

In respect of many such effects of events, it may be useful to study the perceptions that residents of the host community have of event-related phenomena such as traffic congestion, noise, pollution and parking availability as presented in Fredline, Jago and Deery (2003) and Fredline, Deery and Jago (2005). This recognizes that social costs may be as much psychological as physical. These authors also found that people's perceptions were a function of where they lived in relation to the event, and how they felt about the economic impacts of the event. Such information would be useful to destination managers, and social attitudes can be monitored using community tracking surveys to gauge the trend of support/ discontent for the event over time. More detailed study of the effect of resident perceptions on the measurement of event-related costs and benefits should be part of a future research agenda.

The so-called intangible costs and benefits, which are likely to vary from one event to another, depending upon size and type, are usually discussed as an addendum to a CBA (almost an afterthought). To date, research on the economic evaluation of special events has tended to neglect detailed research into these items or approaches to their measurement. Consequently, insufficient attention has been given to the role that CVM and CCM techniques may have in evaluating intangibles. There is an adage in the management literature: 'what is not measured is not managed'. Since informed policy making, however, requires that these intangibles be taken into account, incorporating these costs and benefits into CBA and EIA highlights an important research agenda for the future.

The literature on event assessment in recent years has begun to emphasize the need to adopt a triple bottom line or holistic approach whereby economic considerations are just one element among other criteria including social and environmental outcomes (Fredline *et al.* 2005). Many of the event-associated outcomes identified by these researchers would be labelled 'intangibles' in a CBA. The extent to which these approaches can inform, and in turn be informed by,

CBA represents another neglected area of study. More attention to the synergies of combining different approaches will help to progress the research agenda of special event evaluation.

An unresolved dilemma: integrating CBA and EIA

This chapter has argued that focus on EIA has led to a neglect of important items in event evaluation such as benefits of events to residents, businesses and workers. These effects are often ignored unless a particular effort is made to include them in a comprehensive event assessment. They represent, nonetheless, very real effects and must be recognized in an overall assessment of the costs and benefits of special events to the host destination. Events have important social and environmental effects on the quality of life of local residents. CBA comes closer to capturing quality of life effects than does a narrow EIA. The projected net benefits of a special event represent the 'bottom line' for determining the extent, if any, of support from public funds.

On the other hand, while conceding that the estimated economic impacts of a special event address narrower public policy objectives and provide an inadequate basis to decide on the level of public funding support (if any) that should be given, destination managers do regard economic impacts as key performance indicators of an event. So too do residents. As Fredline, Deery and Jago (2005) have argued, resident attitudes to events are a function of economic impacts, as surveys often show that economic impact is an important positive benefit in the minds of residents. Thus EIA and CBA are not independent even in the framework of a CBA.

CGE models were developed to estimate economic impacts such as the value of output produced (GSP) and employment. They also provide the government with estimates of the resulting net changes in taxation receipts associated with event funding (Madden 2006). These are important inputs to public policy decision making. The importance of EIA goes further than this, however. For large events in particular, CGE models can provide insights into how resources move between industries and the resulting changes in economic activity (Dwyer 2005, 2006), and provide useful inputs to a CBA. Recently, there have been calls to combine the advantages of using EIA (CGE models) to estimate the changes in economic activity associated with an event with the estimates of 'net benefits' offered by CBA to inform policy making.

There are two approaches that can be used, each of which represents an important area for future research.

The first approach to integration of EIA and CBA is to estimate producer and labour surpluses directly from the simulated outcomes of a CGE modelling of an event's economic impacts. In essence:

Impact of event on real GSP less costs of the factors of production (land, labour and capital)

= Business surplus

+ Labour surplus

= Net Economic Benefit of Event.

This complementarity perspective was recognized in Dwyer, Forsyth and Spurr (2006) and in the report by VAG (2007). More recently, Dwyer and Forsyth (2009) have argued that it is possible to use both assessment techniques in an 'integrated approach' to improve event evaluation.

The advantage of this approach is that the CGE modelling informs the destination manager about the direct and indirect economic impact effects of the event as well as inter-industry and taxation effects, while at the same time providing a basis for the estimation of the business and labour surpluses essential to a CBA. The approach requires the making of certain assumptions but is a way of integrating (to some extent) CGE and CBA. Of course, in any evaluation of an event, the effects on resident welfare should not be ignored, and the relevant consumer surpluses then need to be added for the cost-benefit calculation of net benefits. So too will any social and environmental costs and benefits need to be estimated.

A second approach involves the development of measures of economic welfare by adding additional assumptions to the standard CGE model. CGE models can include a welfare measure (Blake 2005). Some CGE models are explicitly designed to measure changes in welfare (Dixon 2009). In his study of the economic impacts of the London Olympics 2012, Blake (2005) includes a measure of resident welfare. Consistent with economic theory, Blake's model measures a change in welfare by Equivalent Variation (EV), which indicates how much the change in welfare is worth to the economy at the presimulation set of prices. Blake takes the Equivalent Variation (the nominal income the consumer needs at one set of prices in order to be as well off at an alternative set of prices) as a measure of economic welfare. He employs this as a monetary measure of the welfare effects of different policy scenarios. This measure takes the results from what may be quite complex effects of a simulation on a household and produces a single value to describe how much better (or worse) off the economy is as a result of such effects. It transforms the economic impacts into a measure of welfare based on various assumptions about labour supply and external inputs. This is an emerging area for CGE, and an emerging area of research interest for the evaluation of special events. However, it suffers from the same narrowness as the first approach. Comprehensive evaluation of an event requires that social and environmental effects be estimated so far as is possible. To date, the welfare measures used in CGE do not capture the full range of welfare effects associated with special events.

The 'net benefit' measures based on incorporating a welfare measure into CGE simulations or estimating business and labour surpluses from the model outcomes do not comprise the total net benefits; they form only part of a CBA since they do not meet the requirements of meeting the fourth public policy objective identified at the outset of this chapter. Benefits to consumers and benefits to residents, including effects on third parties, need to be added to the estimates of business and labour surpluses to provide a more comprehensive estimate of the net (overall) benefits of an event. It is also recognized that there are various other event-associated costs and benefits (social and environmental effects) that are not included in these measures. Notwithstanding the limitations of the combined or integrated approach to date, the use of CGE modelling incorporating welfare measures of household, business and labour surpluses that comprise important components of a CBA represents an important step in clarifying and reconciling the differences that often exist between EIA and CBA of a special event. It represents an important area for future research.

Concluding remarks

Employment of state-of-the-art economic evaluation techniques for special events will provide destinations with a competitive advantage over rivals in this growing tourism and recreation sector. The number of international tourist arrivals as a proportion of the world's population has increased from 6.2 percent in 1980 to 13.7 percent in 2008, a percentage that is expected to grow in the future (United Nations World Tourism Organization and European Travel Commission 2010). The presumed increase in the world's wealth over time will allow ever more people to engage in travel, both domestic and international. In the year 2000 there were 11.5 international tourist arrivals per 100 people. If this rate of travel were to remain stable, then population growth alone would see an increase in international travel of 20 percent to 2030. However, the UNWTO forecasts that the rate of international travel will increase to 20 trips per 100 people by 2020. Thus, the likely doubling of the rate of international travel, along with a 20 percent increase in population, suggests continued strong growth for international travel in the long-term future, with more people travelling more frequently (United Nations World Tourism Organization and European Travel Commission 2010). These same trends imply a healthy future for special events in meeting tourist needs given the importance being accorded to this sector in destinations globally. They also highlight the growing importance in an increasingly competitive global environment for evaluating the impacts of these events using appropriate assessment methods. In particular, these methods must recognize the importance of resident values. Destinations that neglect the importance of special events to their own residents cannot be expected to make informed decisions regarding either an appropriate 'events budget' or appropriate levels of funding for particular events that may be proposed.

In considering how to evaluate special events, it is important to be clear about objectives. This chapter has argued that this should be the welfare (or net social) benefits of the relevant community, not expected economic impacts such as generated GDP/GSP or household income. Economic impacts do not equate to net benefits. Moreover, in contrast to EIA, which ignores nonmarket consumption benefits and third-party effects, CBA measures the event-related changes in all sources of economic welfare, whether occurring in markets or as implicit values.

While economic impact assessments of events emphasize the injected expenditure associated with events as the basis for further analysis, a CBA recognizes that the consumer surpluses of residents may be important to event evaluation. In contrast to EIA, which treats resident expenditure on an event simply as 'transferred' expenditure, which is then ignored, CBA emphasizes that the residents of a destination may benefit from an event, alongside owners of capital and workers who might gain jobs. Therefore, it is insufficient just to focus on net injected expenditure and its economic impacts. In bringing residents' values back into the assessment, CBA thus improves the information base for public sector decision making, thereby assisting in the assessment of relative funding priorities. The challenges arising from the task of estimating the net benefits of special events should dominate the economic research agenda regarding special events in the future.

This chapter acknowledges that event assessment, which focuses only on economic impacts, is too narrow in scope to provide sufficient information to policy makers and government funding agencies. Where practical, a more comprehensive approach should be employed to embrace the importance of social and environmental impacts in addition to economic impacts. In particular, estimation tools required to measure welfare effects associated with special events need more detailed attention from researchers.

The standard approach to event evaluation has been for researchers and consultants to estimate the economic impacts of an event and then, alongside these, consider some of the possible wider effects of events that are not captured in the economic modelling, but that can be estimated using a formal CBA. This has resulted in a less than satisfactory approach to event evaluation since the EIA and the CBA can give conflicting results. An important topic for future research should be the issue of reconciling EIA and CBA. The recommended approaches bridge the gap between EIA and CBA in a way that has policy relevance for destination managers. Bridging this gap calls forth a host of challenges that must be met by researchers in the future.

References

Abelson, P. (2011) 'Evaluating major events and avoiding the mercantilist fallacy', *Economic Papers*, 30(1): March: 48–59.

ACT Auditor General (2002) *ACT Auditor General's Office Performance Audit Report V8 Car Races in Canberra: costs and benefits*, Canberra, ACT.

Blake, A. (2005) *The economic impact of the London 2012 Olympics*. Research report 2005/5, Christel DeHaan Tourism and Travel Research Institute, Nottingham University.

Boardman, A.E., Greenberg, D.H., Vining, A.R. and Weimer, D.L. (2006) *Cost-Benefit Analysis, Concepts and Practice*, 3rd ed. Prentice Hall: New York.

Bohlmann, H.R. (2006) *Predicting the economic impact of the 2010 FIFA World Cup on South Africa*, University of Pretoria, Department of Economics Working Paper Series: 2006–11.

Bureau of Transport and Regional Economics (2007) *Estimating Urban Traffic and Congestion Cost Trends for Australian Cities*, Working Paper 71, Department of Transport and Regional Services, Canberra.

Burns, J.P.A, Hatch, J.H. and Mules, T.J. (1986) *The Adelaide Grand Prix: the impact of a special event*, Adelaide: The Centre for South Australian Economic Studies.

Crompton, J.L. (2006) 'Economic impact studies: instruments for political shenanigans?' *Journal of Travel Research*, 45: 67–82.

Crompton, J.L. (2010) *Measuring the Economic Impact of Park and Recreation Services*. Ashburn, VA: National Recreation and Park Association, Research Series.

Dixon, P. (2009) 'Comments on the productivity commission's modelling of the economy: wide effects of future automotive assistance', *Economic Papers*, 28, 1 March: 11–18.

Dwyer, L. (2012) 'Cost benefit analysis', in L. Dwyer, A. Gill and N. Seetaram (eds.) *Research Methods in Tourism: quantitative and qualitative approaches.* Cheltenham: Edward Elgar, pp. 290–307.

Dwyer, L. and Forsyth, P. (2009) 'Public sector support for special events', *Eastern Economic Journal*, 35(4): 481–99.

Dwyer, L., Forsyth, P. and Spurr, R. (2005) 'Estimating the impacts of special events on the economy', *Journal of Travel Research*, 43(May): 351–59.

Dwyer, L., Forsyth, P. and Spurr, R. (2006) 'Assessing the economic impacts of events: a computable general equilibrium approach', *Journal of Travel Research*, 45: 59–66.

Dwyer, L. and Jago, L. (2012) 'Economic contribution of special events', in S. Page and J. Connell (eds.) *A Handbook of Events*, London: Routledge.

Fleischer, A. and Felsenstein, D. (2002) 'Cost-benefit analysis using economic surpluses: a case study of a televised event', *Journal of Cultural Economics*, 26(2): 139–56.

Fredline, L., Deery, M. and Jago, L. (2005) *Host Community Perceptions of the Impact of Events: A comparison of different event themes in urban and regional communities*, Gold Coast: CRC for Sustainable Tourism Pty Ltd.

Fredline, L., Jago, L. and Deery, M. (2003) 'The development of a generic scale to measure the social impacts of events', *Event Management: An International Journal*, 8(1): 23–37.

Fredline, E., Raybould, M., Jago, L. and Deery, M. (2005) 'Triple bottom line event evaluation: a proposed framework for holistic event evaluation', Paper presented at the Third International Event Conference, *The Impacts of Events: Triple Bottom Line Evaluation and Event Legacies*, UTS, Sydney.

Jago, L. and Dwyer, L. (2006) *Economic Evaluation of Special Events: a practitioner's guide*, Altona, Australia: Common Ground Publishing Pty. Ltd.

Jago, L. and Dwyer, L. (2013) 'Events as economic entities', in R. Finkel *et al.* (eds.) *Research Themes in Events*. Wallingford: CABI, pp. 68–77.

Mabugu, R. and Mohamed, A. (2008) 'The economic impacts of government financing of the 2010 FIFA World Cup', *Stellenbosch Economic Working Papers*: 08/08.

Madden, J. (2006) 'Economic and fiscal impacts of mega sporting events: a general equilibrium assessment', *Public Finance and Management*, 6(3): 346–94.

Mackie, P.J., Jara-Díaz, S. and Fowkes, A.S. (2001) 'The value of travel time savings in evaluation', *Transportation Research Part E: Logistics and Transportation Review*, 37(2/3): 91–106.

Pearce, D., Atkinson, G. and Mouranto, S. (2006) *Cost-Benefit Analysis and the Environment, Recent Developments*. Paris: Organization for Economic Co-operation and Development.

Shaffer M., Greer, A. and Mauboules, C. (2003) *Olympic Costs and Benefits*, Canadian Centre for Policy Alternatives Publication, February.

United Nations World Tourism Organization and European Travel Commission (2010) *Demographic Change and Tourism*, Madrid and Brussels: Author.

Victoria Auditor General (VAG) (2007, May) *State Investment in Major Events*. Victoria: Victorian Government Printer.

9 The greening of events

Exploring future trends and issues

Warwick Frost, Judith Mair and Jennifer Laing

Future points

- There is a growing trend towards green events, with a number leading the way in terms of adopting, promoting and encouraging sustainable practices.
- This chapter considers whether this trend will continue into the future, using a scenario planning approach focused on the year 2050.
- Three case studies of events that have won awards for their sustainable best practice are provided to illustrate the current situation.
- Four scenarios are developed, as potential futures, based on eight identified drivers.

Introduction

A growing number of events are incorporating *green* practices and objectives within their business planning (Laing and Frost 2010). This includes adopting environmentally sustainable practices and initiatives such as recycling, a small carbon footprint for venues and waste management. There is also a trend towards utilizing events to promote green and sustainable issues, directing persuasive messages towards attendees. Both of these types of developments are partly the result of pressure from sponsors, funding agencies and other key stakeholders or the need to comply with regulatory requirements. In other instances, they reflect the strongly held environmental values and ethos of organizers or managers. Some events have attracted plaudits and awards for their efforts in achieving sustainability.

At present, events are seen as being in the vanguard of sustainability and green issues. In this chapter, the term *green* is used as a synonym for sustainable, while *greening* refers to an 'investment in environmentally friendly facilities and practices' (Mair and Jago 2010: 78). There are many examples of events that promote good environmental practice and encourage participants to change their behavior and the world. However, this raises an important question of whether or not this trend will continue. If events are green at the moment, does that mean they also will be in the future?

Our aim in this chapter is to explore whether the phenomenon of greening associated with events is sustainable. To achieve this, our chapter is divided into three parts. The first details the current state of play, examining three contemporary events that have won awards for their sustainability. These are in the forefront of best practice and represent the direction that events are seemingly headed in at the moment.

The second and third parts of the chapter discuss the future for greening of events, using a scenario planning approach. Rather than speculating about one possible future, scenarios are a narrative or description of multiple futures (Yeoman, Galt and McMahon-Beattie 2005), based on various drivers, which are a mechanism to suggest how change might occur (Yeoman 2012). Accordingly, these provide future possibilities, rather than a set prediction. In the second part of the chapter, we present eight socio-political drivers of future change. Utilizing these drivers, in part three we suggest four possible scenarios to provoke and guide discussion of the future.

Using the example set by Yeoman (2012), the year chosen for our scenarios is 2050. This provides enough time (roughly two generations) for a more creative approach to scenario planning, where we indulge in open-minded, blue skies thinking about what possible futures might look like. It must be emphasized that these are not predictions but imaginings of what might happen based on the drivers. Following Bergman, Karlsson and Axelsson (2010), we have adopted *science fiction* as our 'paradigm of thought'. This refers to forecasts 'which make explanatory claims, but not truth claims' (Bergman, Karlsson and Axelsson 2010: 857). Our scenarios are meant to be imaginative, playful, and unconventional, as the aim is to challenge accepted modes of thought and lift readers out of their comfort zone.

The current situation

It is important to understand the current state of play in regards to events, as this provides a starting point and will allow comparison with the future scenarios. The successful management of events is increasingly distinguished by the ability to recognize and manage the *triple bottom line*, covering economic, social and environmental impacts (Hede 2007; Laing and Frost 2010), or even a quadruple bottom line, which also considers the impacts of corporate governance (Richards and Palmer 2010). However, it is clear that the economic impact of events has taken preference in research terms, and also in terms of the interests of event organizers and stakeholders (Laing and Frost 2010). While research has certainly examined both the impacts of events on local residents (Fredline, Jago and Deery 2003) and the impacts of events on the environment (for a full discussion, see Laing and Frost 2010), there remain significant gaps in our knowledge. For example, in terms of the environment, we are generally well aware of the practical steps that may be taken to improve the environmental performance of an event (see, for example, Jones 2012). However, we have relatively little knowledge of the impact that attending environmentally friendly events may have on attendees. Further, research on the impact of events on local residents has mainly focused on issues such as noise and overcrowding (Fredline, Jago and Deery 2003). We do not have the same level of understanding about the positive impacts of events in terms of social capital and social cohesion (exceptions include Arcodia and Whitford 2006 and Wilks 2011) or their effectiveness in promoting persuasive messages (Frost and Laing 2013).

Events are staged for numerous reasons, including celebrating special dates, or the passing of time; for social benefits; for entertainment and escapism; for religious reasons; celebrating or showcasing cultural traditions; acting as a focus for business; reflecting special interests; to encourage tourism; to raise money and awareness for charity and causes; and sometimes simply to make a profit (Frost and Laing 2011; Getz 2005). Therefore, raising environmental awareness and changing environmental behavior may not be key parts of the objectives of staging an event. However, as noted earlier, the opportunities offered by mass gatherings to target and reach large numbers of people at the same time mean that events can be viewed as potential learning spaces (Mair and Laing 2012; Frost and Laing 2013). It is proposed that there are three main elements of educational content at events – to raise awareness, to encourage behavior change as part of a larger campaign and to use the festival or event to play an advocacy role. Events are sometimes held as part of a larger social marketing campaign to underline a particular message that is aimed at behavior change (Andreasen 1994). This type of social marketing is more often seen in the health promotion area, where attendees are exposed to numerous behavior change messages – for example, the importance of healthy eating. Finally, and most relevant to this chapter, many event organizers feel very strongly that part of their role and responsibility in organizing an event is to emphasize issues that are personally important to them (Mair and Laing 2012).

To illustrate how contemporary events develop and utilize their green credentials, we consider three events that have won awards for sustainability. These are Bluesfest (Byron Bay, Australia), City of London Festival (UK) and the Manchester Festival (UK). Interviews were conducted with organizers or directors of each event. In all three case studies it is clear that the personal values and ethos of these individuals plays a significant role in driving the educational component of their events, leading to the events themselves becoming advocates for certain types of behavior change.

Festival vision

Bluesfest was one of the first music festivals in Australia to make greening an important part of the event, in the 1990s, at a time when green issues and recycling were not commonplace at mainstream events. The organizers feel very strongly that they have a responsibility to educate event patrons as 'we have a waste-wise message going out there . . . and you do see that the place is relatively neat and clean'. Sustainability does not stop at being green, but 'you've also got to talk about fair trade and you've also got to talk about social justice'. Bluesfest has also purpose-built their own venue site as a green community.

The City of London Festival takes a more holistic approach to greening, noting that 'sustainability is not just in terms of how we manage our events or run our office – you know, the practical levels – but also very strongly feeds into our artistic programming'. The desire to spread a message is also very visible here: 'We try to make attendees aware of what we are doing and why we are doing it'. This is tinged with an awareness of the scale of what they are trying to do: 'It's an ongoing process of trying to shift attitudes . . . hopefully as time goes by we could be chipping away at it a bit and be more successful'. The City of London festival runs in 62 venues and so attitudes towards greening vary between the venue managers. At times, the educational component of the City of London Festival is aimed as much at the venues and suppliers as at the attendees.

The prominence given to greening in their vision by the Manchester Festival shows how important sustainability is to them, including financial sustainability: 'We aim to be among the best international arts organizations in the world, and we aim to make the festival a sustainable event financially and sustainably [green]'. This prominence comes again (as is the case for Bluesfest) from the festival director: 'sustainability is championed by our director . . . we try to make sure it gets into the mindset of those who are working with us'. The Manchester Festival aims their education and advocacy at both the suppliers and the attendees:

> We try to advocate for sustainable event management amongst the sector in the city. We attach a series of guidelines to all of our suppliers which kind of says, here is what we mean by sustainable event management.

Social capital and social inclusion

For all three events, a social dimension is seen to be entwined with sustainability and environment goals. Festivals are often staged for broad social goals (Finkel 2010; Frost and Laing 2011; Wood 2005). It is believed that attendance at events can create social networks, which are helpful in the creation of social capital (Van Ingen and Van Eijck 2009). Arcodia and Whitford (2006) argue that festivals may facilitate the development of social capital in three main ways. They build community resources, encourage social cohesiveness and give people opportunities for public celebration. O'Sullivan and Jackson (2002) also suggest that leisure and events should be seen as a form of social integration, providing opportunities for social advantage and improving self-esteem. Social inclusion might be a potential outcome of a festival, in the sense of 'engaging sections of the community not commonly participating in community and political activities' (Johnson, Currie and Stanley 2011: 69), or breaking down barriers and building strong communities (Derrett 2003; Finkel 2010). A festival might also be an expression of acceptance of diversity or a focus for an otherwise marginalized group within a community (Gorman-Murray 2009). Finkel (2010: 277) observes that it is often these social inclusion goals or benefits 'that are a source of pride for organizers and a reason they decided to become involved in the festival in the first place'. Many local festivals are free or charge a nominal entry fee, giving greater access to lower socio-economic groups (Arcodia and Whitford 2006; Carlsen, Ali-Knight and Robertson 2007). Community involvement in volunteering, where people mix with others across a wide spectrum of backgrounds and interests, might also lead to greater social inclusion (Finkel 2010).

For Bluesfest, social justice is at the heart of the festival: 'We started by presenting blues music – that's the music of oppressed people! And we've extended what we do into having . . . indigenous Australia and Pacific Rim music'. As one interviewee said: 'How do we represent to people the different cultures that come from where we live? How in modern day Australia do we represent ourselves as being reflective of our community and our aspirations?' The issues of the local community are less obvious at the festival than the issues of fair trade and social justice.

The City of London Festival has an outreach program that targets the local community, particularly children, with the aim of upskilling people, and giving them opportunities to showcase their work. However, the organizers also feel that they play a wider role in encouraging people (locals as well as visitors) to use facilities within the City of London: 'It's about bringing people in, showing them the diversity, the history and the architecture as much as it is about the artistic works we put in the program'.

The Manchester Festival prides itself on the way it reaches out to the local community, making them a part of the celebration whether they physically attend the events or not:

> We run a community box office, with local cultural regeneration officers and some other partners, to offer tickets at a discounted rate across all of the festival shows to people who had some barrier to entry. We also deliberately made one third of the program free so that more people could attend elements of the festival. We also did a live relay of some of our events so that people who couldn't attend could still take part.

The festival also has a large volunteer program, involving around 330 volunteers who are part of the local community, and several of these volunteers have gone on to find full-time careers as a result of the opportunities that they had whilst volunteering.

Drivers

The events detailed above have developed in response to beliefs, issues and conditions at play in their current circumstances, which are – in essence – the drivers of what we have today. However, as we look towards 2050, these drivers may be modified and others may become more prominent, reshaping society. We propose a series of eight drivers that we believe may have a strong influence on the green events of the future. These drivers are based on extant literature (not confined to events), our current research on events, and accepted knowledge. They shape the scenarios depicted in the third part of the chapter.

1. Economic and demographic inequities

The rich countries get wealthier, the poorer countries get poorer. The division continues to get sharper (Sheehey 1996). Less developed countries are beset by overpopulation. Within them there is also a sharp divide between rich and poor, although a growing middle class is emerging in countries like India and China (Andrew and Yali 2012; World Economic Forum 2009), who are often Western educated and aspire for a better standard of living and access to consumer goods, particularly new technology. Environmental issues are arguably viewed as less important in the developing world. Consequently, the drivers and scenarios of green events considered here are very much placed in the context of the *developed* world.

2. Increasing urbanization

Almost 70 percent of the developed world now lives in urban settings (Yeoman 2012). This phenomenon is also seen in developing countries, notably many parts of Asia, where the growing middle class seek the employment benefits and breadth of amenities that a city provides. A move towards urbanization is likely to continue through to 2050, with the rise of China and India as world powers. Urbanization may result in an increasing desire and need to escape crowding and seek peace and quiet, underpinning interest in green spaces and a realization of its fragility and value to society. It may also fuel a growing environmental consciousness, referred to below, paradoxically as people become less connected to the natural world. City-based events might become more frequent, catering to the bulk of the population. Conversely, the lack of natural surrounds in everyday life might lead to an increasing interest in attending events held in rural or regional settings.

3. Existential authenticity

The quest for personal growth and fulfilment is often characterized as the desire to find one's authentic self, a concept labelled existential authenticity (Wang 1999, 2000). This occurs at a time when some are turning away from organized religion and seeking spiritual sustenance elsewhere. Self-help tomes have their own shelves in bookshops and regularly hit the bestseller list, catering to an audience desirous of finding themselves but also of being the 'best' version of themselves they can be. At an intrapersonal level, there are two aspects of this phenomenon: 'bodily sources of authentic self' and 'self-making' (Wang 2000: 67). Thus 'intense relaxation or recuperation, excitement, fun, and sensation seeking, can become the source of feeling authentic' (Voigt 2009: 81). Authenticity can also result from the achievement of self-awareness and identity construction (Laing, Voigt and Frost 2014). At an interpersonal level, existential authenticity exists where interaction with others engenders a sense of being one's true self. Social engagement fosters a sense of self-worth and self-esteem, associated with being valued by others.

4. Environmental consciousness

Rather than being constant, this ebbs and flows. Particular newsworthy incidents, such as chemical spills, nuclear accidents and extinctions, lead to heightened interest. At other times, economic and political issues may lead to a decline. At times there is a general scepticism, particularly when examples of *greenwashing* (false claims of ecological standards) gain publicity. While the concept of climate change has its detractors, there is mainstream acceptance amongst the scientific community and the general public that human intervention has had a deleterious effect on elements of climate leading to changes in temperature, rainfall, wind and the incidence and extent of severe storm activity resulting in natural disasters (Scott, Simpson and Sim 2012). Raising awareness of the effects of human behavior on the environment may be the aim of certain events, and this may be working to 'normalize' green behavior. Some events are held by local governments, primarily to raise awareness of certain issues, for example, climate change and the importance of pro-environmental (or green) behavior (Verplanken and Wood 2006). Other events are not themed around the environment but include some educational content on sustainability, often in the form of stalls providing information, or seminars and hands-on workshops (Laing and Frost 2010).

5. Regulatory paradigm

Public policy is driven by Neo-Classical economic thought. In particular, international and domestic schemes to address environmental issues follow the paradigm of changing behavior through financial penalties. Carbon trading, for example, taxes polluters and encourages countries and individual companies to take action to reduce their emissions. In turn, low polluters claim a credit, which they can sell. The prevalence of greenwashing amongst organizations has led to regulatory action in many countries to prevent claims that are difficult to verify or substantiate, exaggerations of the environmental benefit of products or services and the use of vague terms like 'eco-friendly' or 'earth-friendly' (Kewalramani and Sobelsohn 2012; Laing and Frost 2012; Mair and Laing 2012).

6. Green communities

Throughout Western countries, there is a trend towards small communities that identify themselves as green. They also identify themselves as creative, innovative and alternative (Florida 2005). Often named as *Villages*, they are clustered in two locations. The first is in inner-city neighbourhoods with nineteenth-century building stock. The second is in rural areas close to major cities, usually with natural amenities such as fertile soil, stable rainfall or attractive scenery. These communities are close knit and pride themselves on being tolerant, politically savvy and culturally sophisticated. They are home to many small businesses and syndicalist enterprises – typically cafes, food stores, bars, retail shops and artisans. Paradoxically, many of the inhabitants work in cities for governments or large corporations, and these communities provide the opportunity to live out an alternative identity. These communities are at the forefront of green thinking and innovation.

7. Growth in corporate social responsibility

Corporate social responsibility or CSR 'is a term increasingly employed to denote ethical behavior with respect to various shareholder, employee, consumer, supplier, and competitor stakeholder groups' (Dwyer and Sheldon 2007: 92). CSR often requires a balancing act, to address various needs and interests (Williams, Gill and Ponsford 2007). As an ethos, it underpins greater use of the triple bottom line approach by companies, where goals developed and outcomes sought are not merely in the financial realm, but also social and environmental. Organizations are increasingly anxious to be seen to be good corporate citizens (Williams, Gill and Ponsford 2007), not merely to meet the letter of the law. Those that adopt CSR policies may become 'employers of choice' (Deery, Jago and Stewart 2007). CSR arguably drives companies to want demonstrable, socially desirable results for their sponsorships, and some sponsors will only consider organizations or individuals that are a strong fit with their corporate values and ethical standards (Laing and Frost 2010).

8. Technological developments

The burgeoning of technology has seen a growth in connectedness through social media tools like Facebook and Twitter. Texting on mobile phones is part of the social fabric and the way many people arrange business transactions and appointments, as well as their social activities. There is more acceptance of the use of technology to receive as well as impart information and less reliance on human contact. Face-to-face meetings aren't as common in the business world as they once were, often replaced by teleconferences, video-conferences and platforms like Skype (Locke 2010; Weber and Ladkin 2004). Virtual conferences are also increasing in number. They leverage in some cases on technology creating a virtual world such as Second Life. This is seen as a way to address concerns about the environmental impacts of business events, but also accommodates a generation that is generally comfortable dealing online. Hybrid conferences provide the best of both worlds, combining a live segment for those attending in person, with an online component for a virtual audience (McLoughlin 2012).

Scenarios

Applying these drivers, we have imagined the following four scenarios for a future 2050. It is important to note that these are not predictions, but rather possible worlds designed to assist in planning processes.

In the *first scenario*, by 2050, mega events, particularly the Olympics and Soc-cer World Cup, find themselves receiving increasing criticism for tokenism and their failure to live up to claims of ecological responsibility. Corporate excessive-ness, breaches of human rights, pollution, waste and a poor record of achievement with respect to green issues, including the legacy left behind once the event is staged, are constantly discussed in the media. As a reaction to the inequities of host city selection, a coalition of perpetual bid losers has formed, utilizing their commitment to green issues and past successes in hosting green events as key planks in their platform. Labelled the Eco-Cities Alliance, they include Detroit, Istanbul, Chennai and Manchester. Arguing that they have *already* resolved their environmental problems, they claim it is their turn to share in the spoils of these mega events. Bidding for joint staging, they promise a new approach. Tellingly, they claim they will dramatically reduce the share of tickets going to sponsors and will focus instead on social inclusion. For the first time, tourism has been dropped as a means of attracting public funding, with the emphasis on providing for local people first. Technology is used to make more people feel connected to the event, and hybrid events are presented as a solution to the cost of staging mega events. Unsuccessful in their bid for the 2056 Olympics, they have promised to persevere.

The *second scenario* sees a role for events in addressing environmental con-cerns. After the Maldives finally disappear below the waves in 2046, as a result of rapidly increasing sea level rises, all doubts about the seriousness of climate change disappear. Mitigation of further greenhouse gas emissions becomes cru-cial, and novel ways to take action at an individual level become apparent. The device of selling tickets through a combination of money and individual carbon credits is pioneered by a number of popular music performers. This works effec-tively because potential fans are aware of and in tune with the environmental concerns of these stars, particularly through social media. The part payment through carbon credits demonstrates commitment, and the credits raised are uti-lized for projects in the developing world. Hybrid events are regularly staged, reducing carbon emissions. Events, like other businesses, are highly regulated in relation to their environmental footprint, and they must comply with a broad range of legislative requirements aimed at reducing and even eliminating their negative impacts on the environment. Most events exceed these requirements, conscious of their importance in minimizing future environmental damage.

The *third scenario* sees events as platforms of social change. Local festivals staged by green communities continue to be innovative, both in terms of technical and educational activities. By 2050, their focus has become much more outward looking. These green communities, such as those in Byron Bay, Manchester and parts of London have already reached high levels of environmental excellence. Their use of motorized transport is very low, and they have very high rates of recycling and the use of sustainable energy. Indeed, by this stage very little can be done to improve upon these. Accordingly, these communities have become more evangelical, utilizing partnerships and social media to spread environmental edu-cation. Their festivals are used as platforms for persuasive messages. They aim to advocate for social and environmental change at all opportunities.

Table 9.1 Linkages between scenarios and drivers

Scenario	Drivers
Multi-city bids for mega events.	1, 2, 4, 6, 7, 8
Events play an integral part in addressing and even helping to solve environmental concerns.	2, 3, 4, 5, 6, 7, 8
Events used as platforms for social change and learning spaces.	3, 4, 6, 7, 8
The demise of mega events and a consequential focus on smaller community events.	1, 2, 3, 6, 8

In the *fourth scenario*, mega events are not sustainable by 2050. Future economic collapse has precipitated the demise of large-scale mega and global events like the Olympics. Bankrupt economies can no longer afford them. Greece, whose modern economy was partly ruined by the Olympics, is an early example, but the problem spreads. As a reaction there is a shift to an increasing emphasis on smaller local events to fulfil the basic needs of entertainment, bringing people together and commemorating anniversaries, as well as making people feel more authentic, through discovering their roots and a sense of identity. Even then, many regional festivals (such as Bluesfest, London and Manchester) are put under pressure by declining sponsorship and government funding. This throws into question their ability to act as spaces for facilitating community and social cohesion. They must use technology such as social media more extensively and creatively, in order to create those feelings of connection and a sense of identity.

The following Table 9.1 summarizes the four scenarios above and links each of them to the drivers referred to in the previous section.

Concluding remarks

The implications of these scenarios for the future of the event industry based upon the present are four-fold.

Firstly, global economic forces may have the greatest impact on events, particularly mega events, which require massive amounts of underwriting by governments and are increasingly expensive to stage and attend. Individuals may not be able to afford the high entry prices, particularly when the online streaming is of such a high quality and provides the flexibility and convenience of watching the event when one chooses. The role of the big screen in the town square may become more important than attending the actual event. This may lead many mega events to turn away from a focus on the tourist dollar, towards providing social benefits and a green legacy for the local community. These drivers underpin scenarios one and four.

Secondly, the increasing visual evidence of climate change may act as a driver to encourage people to engage in sustainable behavior more generally and at events more specifically. Many of the arguments currently advanced for why people are loath to act to counter climate change revolve around the absence of visual cues and lack of a sense of being personally affected. There may also be issues of information overload. Events may help to cut through that and play their part as socially responsible entities, as well as acting as agents of social change. This is the backdrop to scenarios two and three.

Thirdly, there may be increased social capital among those living in places like green communities or villages, involving relatively closed social networks, juxtaposed with greater isolation and exclusion amongst those without access to these strong networks. This may make festivals even more important as spaces for bringing people together and forming the networks needed for healthy levels of social capital. These drivers can be seen at work in scenario 3, where the event becomes an advocate for environmental and social reforms, and in scenario 4, where mega events are increasingly replaced by smaller community events.

Fourthly, changes in technology may help in terms of the environment and limiting greenhouse gas emissions, and will facilitate online or virtual events, but this might come at the expense of the social aspects of attending events. To counter this, there may be a growing realization that face-to-face participation in events may offer greater opportunities for community bonding, and the excitement of taking part in a live experience provides a sense of authenticity that many seek in their leisure activities. All four scenarios developed in this chapter acknowledge both the potential and the threat of technology to social inclusion and the creation of community bonding.

References

Andreasen, A.R. (1994) 'Social marketing: its definition and domain', *Journal of Public Policy and Marketing*, 13(1): 108–14.

Andrew, M. and Yali, P. (2012) *The rise of the middle class in Asian emerging markets*, KPMG Report. Online. Available: <www.kpmg.com/cn/en/IssuesAndInsights/ArticlesPublications/Documents/Middle-Class-Asia-Emerging-Markets-201206-2.pdf> (accessed 4 January 2013).

Arcodia, C. and Whitford, M. (2006) 'Festival attendance and the development of social capital', *Journal of Convention and Event Tourism*, 8(2): 1–18.

Bergman, A., Karlsson, J. and Axelsson, J. (2010) 'Truth claims and explanatory claims: an ontological typology of futures studies', *Futures*, 42: 857–65.

Carlsen, J., Ali-Knight, J. and Robertson, M. (2007) 'Access: a research agenda for Edinburgh festivals', *Event Management*, 11: 3–11.

Deery, M., Jago, L. and Stewart, M. (2007) 'Corporate social responsibility within the hospitality industry', *Tourism Review International*, 11(2): 107–14.

Derrett, R. (2003) 'Making sense of how festivals demonstrate a community's sense of place', *Event Management*, 8: 49–58.

Dwyer, L. and Sheldon, P. (2007) 'Corporate social responsibility for sustainable tourism', *Tourism Review International*, 11(2): 91–5.

Finkel, R. (2010) '"Dancing around the ring of fire": social capital, tourism resistance and gender dichotomies at Up Helly AA in Lerwick, Shetland', *Event Management*, 14(4): 275–85.

Florida, R. (2005) *Cities and the Creative Classes*, London and New York: Routledge.

Fredline, L., Jago, L. and Deery, M. (2003) 'The development of a generic scale to measure the social impacts of events', *Event Management*, 8(1): 23–37.

Frost, W. and Laing, J. (2011) *Strategic Management of Festivals and Events*, Melbourne: Cengage.

Frost, W. and Laing, J. (2013) 'Communicating persuasive messages through slow food festivals', *Journal of Vacation Marketing*, 19(1): 67–74.

Getz, D. (2005) *Event Management and Event Tourism*, 2nd ed., New York: Cognizant.

Gorman-Murray, A. (2009) 'What's the meaning of Chillout? Rural/urban difference and the cultural significance of Australia's largest rural GLBTQ festival', *Rural Society*, 19(1): 71–86.

Hede, A.-M. (2007) 'Managing special events in the new era of the triple bottom line', *Event Management*, 11(1/2): 13–22.

Johnson, V., Currie, G. and Stanley, J. (2011) 'Exploring transport to arts and cultural activities as a facilitator of social inclusion', *Transport Policy*, 18: 68–75.

Jones, C. (2012) 'Events and festivals: fit for the future', *Event Management*, 16(2): 107–18.

Kewalramani, D. and Sobelsohn, R. J. (2012) 'The greenwashing domino effect', *Thompson Reuters News and Insight*, 2 March. Online. Available: <http://newsandinsight.thomsonreuters.com/Legal/Insight/2012/02_-_February/The_Greenwashing_domino_effect/> (accessed 30 January 2013).

Laing, J. and Frost, W. (2010) '"How green was my festival": exploring challenges and opportunities associated with staging green events', *International Journal of Hospitality Management*, 29(2): 261–67.

Laing, J., Voigt, C. and Frost, W. (2014) 'Fantasy, authenticity and the spa tourism experience', in C. Pforr and C. Voigt (eds.) *Wellness Tourism: A Destination Perspective*. London: Routledge, pp. 220–34.

Locke, M. (2010) 'A framework for conducting a situational analysis of the meetings, incentives, conventions and exhibitions sector', *Journal of Convention and Event Tourism*, 11(3): 209–33.

Mair, J. and Jago, L. (2010) 'The development of a conceptual model of greening in the business events tourism sector', *Journal of Sustainable Tourism*, 18(1): 77–94.

Mair, J. and Laing, J. (2012) 'The greening of music festivals: motivations, barriers and outcomes. Applying the Mair and Jago model', *Journal of Sustainable Tourism*, 20(5): 683–700.

McLoughlin, A. (2012) 'International events: attributes of a hybrid event – where physical meets virtual', In *Proceedings of the International Convention and Expo Summit*, 24–26 May, 2012. Hong Kong Polytechnic University, Hong Kong.

O'Sullivan, D. and Jackson, M. J. (2002) 'Festival tourism: a contributor to sustainable local economic development?', *Journal of Sustainable Tourism*, 10(4): 325–42.

Richards, G. and Palmer, R. (2010) *Eventful Cities*, Kidlington, UK; Burlington, US: Butterworth Heinemann.

Scott, D., Simpson, M.C. and Sim, R. (2012) 'The vulnerability of Caribbean coastal tourism to scenarios of climate change related sea level rise', *Journal of Sustainable Tourism*, 20(6): 883–98.

Sheehey, E.J. (1996) 'The growing gap between rich and poor countries: A proposed explanation', *World Development*, 24(8): 1379–384.

Van Ingen, E. and Van Eijck, K. (2009) 'Leisure and social capital: an analysis of types of company and activities', *Leisure Sciences*, 31(2): 192–206.

Verplanken, B. and Wood, W. (2006) 'Interventions to break and create consumer habits', *Journal of Public Policy and Marketing*, 25(1): 90–103.

Voigt, C. (2009) *Understanding Wellness Tourism: an analysis of benefits sought, health-promoting behaviours and positive psychological well-being.* Unpublished thesis, University of South Australia.

Wang, N. (1999) 'Rethinking authenticity in tourism experience', *Annals of Tourism Research*, 26: 349–70.

Wang, N. (2000) *Tourism and Modernity: a sociological approach*, Oxford: Pergamon.

Weber, K. and Ladkin, A. (2004) 'Trends affecting the convention industry in the 21st century', *Journal of Convention and Event Tourism*, 6(4): 47–63.

Williams, P., Gill, A. and Ponsford, I. (2007) 'Corporate social responsibility at tourism destinations: toward a social license to operate', *Tourism Review International*, 11(2): 133–44.

Wilks, L. (2011) 'Bridging and bonding at music festivals', *Journal of Policy Research in Tourism, Leisure and Events*, 3(3): 281–97.

Wood, E.H. (2005) 'Measuring the economic and social impacts of local authority events', *International Journal of Public Sector Management*, 18(1): 37–53.

World Economic Forum (2009) *Asian middle class to drive growth*, 18 June. Online. Available: <www.weforum.org/news/asian-middle-class-drive-growth> (accessed 4 January 2013).

Yeoman, I. (2012) *2050 – Tomorrow's Tourism*, Clevedon: Channel View.

Yeoman, I., Galt, M. and McMahon-Beattie, U. (2005) 'A case study of how VisitScotland prepared for war', *Journal of Travel Research*, 44: 6–20.

10 The future is green

A case study of Malmoe, Sweden

Hans Wessblad

Future points

- The chapter illustrates the greening of an event city: legitimate green or greenwashing.
- The process is in four movements: inspiration, actions, context, and institutionalization.
- The future event industry sustainability is based upon: personal enthusiasm, good attention, and evangelism.

Introduction

A week with me includes everything from unique artwork and exciting theater to concerts with both the greatest artists and the hottest newcomers. I have debates and conversations with famous guests, exciting competitions and shows. I have food from all over the world, cozy scenes and an extraordinarily festive mood! With 28 festivals behind me, I am the oldest festival in Sweden. With my 1.4 million visitors, I am also the largest in Scandinavia! (the Malmoe Festival, author's translation)

The personal, or rather personified, voice on the events website is an attempt to express the informal atmosphere significant for the Malmoe Festival. The approach in this chapter is to describe how an event destination makes the future greener. Making 'green' is used as a representation of sustainability ambitions in environmental and social, economic, cultural dimensions.

Malmoe has about 300,000 inhabitants, of which 30 percent are born in a foreign country. The history of Malmoe is the transition from a heavy industrial town up until the 1970s into something else; a rather new university college, an expanding service and knowledge industry, and a growing tourism business. Malmoe has an influential tourism organization, but not any distinct Destination Management Organization and thereby does not work with a defined event portfolio. The main event in the city is the Malmoe Festival – an event with a sustainability ambition. The social dimension was key from the start in 1985. From the beginning, the festival idea was once a year to lessen the segregation of Malmoe by welcoming everybody downtown. In recent years the festival has emphasized an environmentally friendly profile. The ambition today is to make the festival Scandinavia's largest event generating as little negative impact on the environment as possible. The social sustainability is still fundamental. The personified voice of the website quote above signifies the intended way to bring about change – a direct approach to everybody concerned.

The expressed objective of the project is to create green growth by greening the hospitality and events industries in Malmoe. The sustainability progress in Malmoe includes several projects, organized in single municipal efforts, in NGOs and in business endeavors as well as in different joint ventures, but without a strong unifying authority. Thereby the decision-making process is not related to a structure but rather to movements. The focus is on the event aspects of the municipality project, highlighting how the events industry needs to embrace the future given the scenario of scarcity of resources. To encourage change by setting a good example is also the strategy of the city.

Methodology

The material in this chapter stems from three sources: participation in the Malmoe sustainability movement (participating study: attending various meetings), interviews (major agents in the process), and secondary data (mainly websites). The study idea can be characterized as inductive in the sense of searching for the local rationality, and collecting individual perceptions of the phenomenon of Malmoe as a future sustainable hospitality and event destination (Silverman 1993).

The chapter, being a case study, is a broad picture and the author's story of a collage of voices, experiences, and texts. The induced categories are both field concepts and interpreted as theoretical concepts. The claims of the text are forecasting a probable future scenario. The strength in the prediction derives from both matters of fact happening in Malmoe (truth claims) and from aspects of interpretation (explanatory claims) (Bergman, Karlsson and Axelsson 2010).

Greening an event city

'Just so you know, Malmoe is Europe's new Green Room', declared the event sustainability officer from the municipal Environment Department, when explaining the city's sustainability ambition. Equally argued the events manager, when interviewed whether the European Song Contest in Malmoe could be a green event: 'Absolutely! Malmoe has the will, the ideas and the competence' (Malmoe News 2013). Being a city with an overall engagement in sustainability, Malmoe naturally needs a comparable approach in its tourism attraction system (Leiper 1990, 2008). The ambition is to become world leading in sustainable city development by the year 2025 (Malmoe 2025. The sustainable city).

Legitimate green

A sign of Malmoe's achievements is 'The Balancing Prize' in 2011, a Nordic Sustainability Award by the Ideas Bank Foundation, Oslo. The prize is given to Nordic municipalities or local communities that have excelled in creative contributions towards sustainable development. Malmoe has also received the UN prize 'Scroll of Honor 2009' as well as many other distinctions: number four of the world's green cities 2007 (Grist, Environmental Newsmill), one of thirteen cities listed in the Worldwatch Institute: 'State of the World 2007'; Malmoe 'Building a Green Future'; the Green Fleet Award: 'European Fleet of the year 2009'; and the EU Civitas Award: 'Best civitas city of the year 2006' (one city of three).

Green tourism, sometimes called eco-tourism, is not usually associated with urban tourism. But the municipal tourist organization continuously searches for sustainability tourist products (Weaver and Lawton 2007), locating sightseeing tours and mapping bicycle routes, and creating various guided tours exhibiting the sustainable Malmoe: climate smart tours. One way of enabling Malmoe to be accessible for green tourists is to be part of the global movement 'Green Map.' The Green Map allows online creation of locally generated maps of eco-adapted attractions and businesses. Another way of being a green tourism destination is to have eco-labeled hotels; Malmoe has 85 percent (in a comparable standard) – second best in Sweden.

In 2008 the Malmoe Festival received a diploma from the well-established Keep Sweden Tidy Foundation [Hall Sverige rent]. Applying for this diploma was more of a test of how well the event as such was developed in an environmentally friendly way. Getting the award involved tasks such as all personnel taking a course about the environment, using 100 percent renewable energy, and assigning all security personnel to use bicycles – all being examples of symbolic actions, part of a symbolic economy (Moller 2009). Later in 2012 Malmoe applied for 'A Greener Festival Award,' obtaining the second highest award: 'highly commended.' The not-for-profit award-giving company supports festivals in bettering their sustainability behavior, becoming more 'environmentally conscious' and 'adopting environmentally-efficient practices' (A Greener Festival). 'Yourope' is another event association of which Malmoe is a member. The two most relevant goals for the association are health and safety and environmental protection. In Malmoe this is pronounced as striving for safety and security.

Sustainability is a moving target. The principle behind the sustainability ambition is continuously to 'pick the easily reached fruits first; it creates a sensation of success and progress,' claims the event sustainability officer. Everybody engaged in the sustainability endeavor is to recognize his or her own progress. Then only when one's own progress becomes apparent, can one strive after more challenging tasks. This is the trick for making it possible for everybody to participate. Success with one challenge leads to encountering the next. Then the process is on, making the event and hospitality industries as sustainable as the rest of Malmoe is striving to be (Bell 2011; Mair and Jago 2010; Page and Thorn 2002).

Greenwashing

To some degree it is important to show the sustainability ambition before the full operation is established. Words and actions are not always synchronized. To make action happen, the green image has to be clear among all the different stakeholders related to the event and tourist destination. One perspective on the sustainability ambition is to view it as a 'sub-cultural attribute,' as the CEO of the city amusement park [Malmoe Folkets Park] expressed it. Sustainability is more important to some groups than to others. The city residents represent rather well-off groups among whom the sustainability issue is central. The principal role of the municipality is to create an image of the sustainability ambition, to show the good example, and thereby make the idea of sustainability become a general ambition in Malmoe. However, green words without green action is very close to greenwashing, namely, words claiming that the Malmoe destination is something that it is not yet (Pomering, Noble and Johnson 2011; Raska and Shaw 2012).

'I think greenwashing is good – if it is not the only thing you do' provokes the CEO of the City amusement park [Malmoe Folkets Park]. Quick fixes have to be combined with long-term investments – the pedagogical aspect is in the meantime very important. Due to the amount of people visiting and attending all the amusement sites and events of Malmoe, the symbolic, but sometimes substanceless, activities are important from an enlightening perspective. The CEO claims that any 'dirty laundry' cannot be hidden in the long run. Transparency in the sustainability ambition reveals areas where development is needed, agrees the tourism office CEO.

The tourism industries being related to mobility and irresponsible leisure behavior has a general obligation to become more sustainable. Malmoe has a sincere sustainability ambition, but not every stakeholder is fully green-dedicated yet. Malmoe is not 'bogus,' but not yet authentic (according to the Greenwashing index rating). If little progress occurs to make all relevant stakeholders take sustainability considerations into their business, then the Malmoe sustainability ambition starts to be suspect (Greenwashing index). Both the current Malmoe Festival project leader and the Environment Department officer perceive that they have set such high standards that not every participating business could comply. At the same time they are careful not to communicate success all the way. The ambition is 'to try and do the best we can' (CEO, the Malmoe Festival). There is some criticism about what is not done. What the Malmoe Festival achieves today is the best that can be done at the time. Being convinced with this approach makes all the nonfulfilled actions just something left to deal with as soon as possible. In Malmoe, sustainability is a moving target where individual conviction interacts with an institutionalization of major stakeholders, step by step, becoming greener (Harris and Crane 2002). Both the greening process so far and the aspects of greenwashing are matters of facts and predict somewhat a future state in the city.

The process in four movements

From the goal of sustainability for the major event in Malmoe to being developed in other events in the city; there is a progression through four different movements (identified by the author): inspiration, actions, context, and institutionalization. The greening project aims to involve most major event and tourism operations in the city of Malmoe. 'All events in Malmoe should affect everyone – in all respects,' as a consultant declares. In the following the four different movements are interpretations of aspects that will explain why Malmoe most probably will end up in a greener state over an amount of years.

The inspiring example

The centerpiece of the sustainable tourism ambition in the city is the Malmoe Festival. The event is very well established in the city's different communities. The event is small enough to be run by a slim management, small enough for individual commitment to make a difference. In spite of this it is expressed to be the largest event in Sweden.

The first movement involves the successful management of the Malmoe Festival. The event is chosen as the basis for reflecting over sustainable hospitality and events on a city scale. The Malmoe Festival, being the largest and oldest event in the city, becomes a point of reference when the greening of the overall event city started to be evident in 2009: '. . . if we can run this festival sustainably, we could do a lot,' claimed the event sustainability officer. As in most changing processes, it often boils down to individual commitment – the driving force in the beginning is foremost personal.

In 2009 a new manager started at the Malmoe Festival. Her title as the festival manager was (in direct translation from Swedish) 'project leader.' There is definitely a distinction from being a project manager. The difference in short is to *lead* a group of people by aligning them around a shared, inspired vision, versus to *manage* a group of people completing the tasks assigned to them (Bennis 1989; McLean and Weitzel 1991; Covey 1991). The event manager, was definitely more 'project leader' than 'project manager' in the sustainability work. The good cooperation with the Environment Department was productive and driven by a vision. With the accomplishment of the festival, the idea emerged of modeling the rest of the events in Malmoe accordingly. However, such an idea demanded an overall approach.

Without a distinct event portfolio ambition in Malmoe, the sustainability model did not influence other events in the city (Ziakas and Costa 2011a, 2011b). One reason lies in the split event organization in the municipality. The outdoor events, such as the Malmoe Festival, are administered by the 'Public Streets and Parks' [Gatukontoret]. The indoor events are governed by the 'Recreation Department' [Fritidsfoervaltningen]. This is a significant divide. As in most cities, the municipal management of the different administrations often acts as if separated in watertight compartments.

However, some changes go straight through. Such a thing as only serving ecological and fair-trade coffee and tea is now taken for granted. Equally successful is the overall heightened waste management amongst everything from individual food stalls to music performances, claims the new (2013) festival project leader.[1] Her ambition is that wherever sustainability could be developed, at least an attempt is made and that often leads to a change in operation.

Because of thorough communication, which the festival organizers are proud of, everyone drinks tap water. It is called 'bring your own bottle.' Water taps are spread all over the event. The same idea was introduced at the Eurovision Song Contest 2013 (arranged in Malmoe). Empty bottles are to be found all over, even in lounges and back stage. Drinking tap water could be seen as something insignificant. Nevertheless, it is a symbolic action; everybody from attendee to artist performs some kind of sustainability. It is not just the organizations that have to adapt. Everybody is participating.

Actions that drive development

The second movement is when the event project leader and her colleague at the Environment Department created a strict agenda over the sustainability aspects to be taken into consideration at the Malmoe Festival (Choi and Sirakaya 2006). A city festival is perhaps more than any event a conglomerate of different players. Some are direct stakeholders; others represent indirect stakeholder interests (Bell and Morse 2004). The direct stakeholders represent the municipal organizations (everything from the police force and the fire department to the street cleaning and water/electricity distribution) and private organizations (everything from major artists to food stall keepers). Then all the residents in and out of the city need to be mentioned – being all the attendees. However, behind all these, there is the whole city representing the indirect stakeholders of the festival. All are supposed to be influenced by the sustainability agenda (Quinn 2006).

Communicating with all the stakeholders becomes as essential as doing thorough documentation of the work: communication is done before and documentation after. The challenge is to communicate with the large unorganized groups of stakeholders. All the attendees as well as the plentitude of different vendors have to understand the message of the sustainability agenda (Chávez-Cortéz and Alcántara Maya 2010). One example is the internal waste management system at the Malmoe Festival introduced by the previous food and beverage manager before she became CEO of the festival; the garbage separation is done by the different food stalls and other attractions, and thereafter the festival picks up the waste directly at the place. The gain is two-fold: the food stall or attraction has an easy way to get rid of the waste, if they separate thoroughly, and the event can secure good garbage separation.

A trickier issue is changing the attendee's behavior. At the Malmoe Festival the individual has to walk some hundred meters to the nearest waste separation station. The stations are spread out all over downtown during the festival. The attendees have to be convinced of a win for themselves in throwing away the litter at the waste station. The attendee has to be confident about his/her own sustainability actions. The dual attendee issue of the festival is to change the behavior and to inspire further green considerations at the same time. A third aspect is that some sustainability is imperative. One example is that only fair-trade and ecologically grown coffee is available. Another example is the 2012 increase of all participating fees with two hundred Swedish crones (approx. 25 €) (naturally surcharged the attendees). The funds are used to buy carbon offsetting.

To work with festival sustainability is mostly a matter of documentation. But the development is due to figuring out ways to progress and give advice accordingly. The different participating organizations – both on the procurer and the delivery side – were largely positive to the various directives. 'They seem to understand how we reason,' claims the event sustainability officer. Issues of avoiding bottled water and favoring locally produced goods were unproblematic. To a great extent, change is a matter of knowledge and competence, thus, whether the participating organizations have the capacity to prepare their personnel or not.

When the stakeholders in the city first heard the sustainability messages, the words were taken as standard environmental concern comments; one listens to the message, but with little impact. However, changes were to come. The stakeholders realized that the sustainability messages influenced their commercial prosperity. Sustainability starts to be seen as good business (Fraj, Martinez and Matute 2011). Attention to the Environment Department's missives and presentations slowly grows by the day. The perceived trend among most stakeholders in the event business in Malmoe is pro-sustainability.

The sustainability context

The third movement in Malmoe is making sustainability understood as is only possible with good safety and security. Safety and security are related to sustainability. It is claimed by several informants that Malmoe should to be chosen as an event site due to sustainability in addition to a sense of safety and actual security, and thereby the city can live up to all three aspects. The sustainability ambition becomes less of labeling the city and more of continuously strengthening safety and security in the city, easing the social unrest concurrently with bettering the sustainability matters (Quinn 2006).

Becoming a sustainable hospitality and event city is a continuous process. Documentation is central in all quality enhancements, as is evaluation of the progress. Since environmental work does not always show obvious progress, there is a vital need for objective reference points. An example is the weight of garbage. If the garbage is not decreasing but even increasing, then one should start to ask questions. Documenting opens up a problematizing process as well as making people and organizations responsible. Even if the development shows little progress, the documentation enables possibilities for change, by facilitating analysis and evaluation.

The 2011 decision to expand the sustainability ambition further than the singular Malmoe Festival becomes a matter of both the venues and the event organizers. Some of the event organizers and other direct stakeholders joined to form a core group of people who were to meet regularly, operating jointly as a test-bed for new ideas. The other matter of venues called for an inventory: which are used, which are adaptable to sustainability, and to what extent could the others be upgraded?

Several new venues have been built recently. Most of these are constructed through sustainability considerations.

The Eurovision Song Contest 2013 is a one-time special event. Sometimes implementing sustainability gets all the attention and the symbolic actions become forgotten. The ambition in Malmoe is to highlight sustainability so that it becomes a common concern. When hosting the Eurovision Song Contest, Malmoe wanted to make a lasting impression on the attendees, on the artists, on all the different actors. The organizers' idea is that a sustainability relay will start in Malmoe and will create continued development at coming Eurovision Song Contest cities. Malmoe hopes that its environmental commitment will be inspiring to the coming Eurovision Song Contests. Both the Eurovision Song Contest 2013 and the Women's Forum 2014 (in Malmoe) are sustainable-certified events. These two events work as the good examples of managing future events in Malmoe. The idea for the future is to make Malmoe attract larger events that request a distinct sustainability profile.

Institutionalization by certification and funding

The event sustainability officer divides the sustainability efforts into 'hygiene factors' and 'motivators' (probably referring to Herzberg). The prioritized goal is to create an overall sensation of safety and actual security in the city; this is fundamental and is seen as a hygiene factor. Safety and security are defined by criteria that have to be reached. Thereafter the sustainability work could be arranged into motivating steps for creating an increasing attraction for Malmoe. The progress toward greater sustainability may be seen as moving further up the steps (see previous section on 'Legitimate green').

The top level is the ISO-certification of the city according to ISO 20121. The interpretation of the process is an institutionalization of an approach towards the social, ecological, economical (and cultural) environment (Wright 1998). The economical dimension has not always been emphasized. There was an opinion that the municipality was poor in understanding the business setting. A consultant claimed that economic sustainability is when good ideas survive due to thriving businesses. One aspect of this is social entrepreneurship, and it creates opportunities. Any development starts and ends only with what is available; there are not resources enough to create new contents in a future hospitality and events Malmoe, the consultant argued (Tassiopoulos and Johnson 2009).

Sustainability is to be implemented and knowledge spread in related organizations so they will be self-propelled, thereby those personnel engaged in sustainability efforts could move their positions further. This is what has happened. The Malmoe Festival project leader and the sustainability officer who both previously worked with the Malmoe Festival moved on to manage the Eurovision Song Contest.

Getting started making an event sustainable meant getting funding. After an application to Sweden's Innovation Agency, VINNOVA (Swedish Governmental

Agency for Innovation Systems) for seed money for further larger applications, the seed money was used to investigated the state of event sustainability in Malmoe. The initial question was which businesses to include and which not to include in the sustainability venture. Not even the hotel and restaurant businesses were evident. The core group of organizations was to be more tightly related to events. Some central municipal organizations and other principal businesses showed little interest. Taking in the sustainability concept starts with realizing that there is an external demand.

However, at this stage there is no special municipal funding for the whole sustainable event project in Malmoe. The project is supposed to be funded externally. The first national application (VINNOVA) ended up with seed money for developing a full application; however, Malmoe's application was not chosen in 2012. A similar application was placed with the EU Programme LIFE+ and granted for 2013.

Malmoe may be large enough to focus on the substantial EU funding instead of the lesser national grants. Depending on the type of project, the EU funding is more accurate. The LIFE+ programme seemed suitable to the city-scale sustainability project. Malmoe has experience from previous EU LIFE-projects, mainly in the local investment programs and climate investment programs (e.g. green tools for urban climate adaption, climate friendly healthcare, Climate Living in Cities Concept). The main funding of the larger projects, especially on climate issues, comes from EU. Nonetheless the direction is set. The vision was to become a sustainable event city. However, without the EU funding and other external funding the progress would be narrower and slower. But it was claimed that it is just one way to go, towards sustainability. The sustainability progress is becoming an institutionalized part of Malmoe (Kronsell 1997). There is an ecology in both the city's environment and among the city's organizations (Singh, Tucker and Meinhard 1991).

Concluding remarks

The implications for the future of the event industry based upon the present are matters of fact, such as personal enthusiasm, good attention, and instilling the belief inside the municipality.

In Malmoe the progress towards sustainability includes several projects, organized in single municipal efforts, in NGOs and in business endeavors as well as in different joint ventures. To understand how the progress occurs without there being a strong unifying authority, one can break down the process into essential pieces. The ambition to become a city of sustainable events 'is like a puzzle'; numerous bits and pieces have to find their places (Our Malmoe, January 2013).

The first type of puzzle piece to the future is to understand individual commitment. The personal antecedents differ in e.g. values, lifestyle, motives, education, and experience. The case of Malmoe shows that an idea, in this case *sustainability*, is carried by persons. The endless striving for an enduring society rests on a personal stand on sustainability. Before an individual takes a stand, no sincere sustainability can be developed. However, removing barriers and reducing constraints are required, plus the decision to make this happen (Getz 2012). Apart from everything, a real commitment is crucial. In Swedish there is a saying of these enthusiasts being 'fiery souls' [eldsjaelar]. These real enthusiasts need both supporting organizations and a multitude of opportunities to voice their ideas (Wessblad 2010). The Malmoe case shows that the sustainability ambition would have been much less without these, often female, fiery souls.

A second type of puzzle piece for sustainable progress is to realize that the topic has to be voiced in contexts where it is understood. Both the internal and the external contexts of the municipality must have a maturity; the sustainability principle has to be institutionalized in the organizations. The good attention Malmoe has achieved for sustainability is due to identifying grounds where the topic is hot. When the sustainability ambition starts to be incorporated in everyday operation, it drives the organizations involved. Getting good attention, through good publicity, works as a catalyst in reducing (the author's interpretation) the barriers to progress. Thereby actors, other than the sustainability movers, communicate the progress; these external voices are better heard internally than the insider declarations. Each step results in a more sustainable event destination (Mair and Jago 2010).

A third type of piece is to promote sustainability 'evangelism' inside the municipality. Sustainability is a question of belief. Belief creates engagement and thereby progress. The religious aspect is not emphasized even though there is such a dimension (Harper 2011). Giving reasons for sustainability and spreading these innovative ideas among the different stakeholders seems to be fundamental to progress (Djupe and Gwiasda 2010).

The lesson learned from Malmoe is that progress towards sustainability takes time. On the other hand, it is the only road to take. To enforce a sustainability policy on a municipality just creates what can be expected, a creation of only the policy followers and little progress actually achieved (Andersson, Shivarajan and Blau 2005). Having patience and being persistent in changing people's minds will help Malmoe become the sustainable hospitality and event city it is reaching to be.

So all in all, the development of a sustainable event and hospitality destination of Malmoe is not a planned process. It is both an institutionalized and cultural phenomenon – some tipping points tilt in favor of the sustainability idea and some against (Bell 2011). It is a movement with a distinct global connection and with a locally clear intention.

Note

1. CEO and Project Leader of the Malmoe Festival 2013 and onward.

References

A Greener Festival Award (2012), Available at: <www.agreenerfestival.com/2012/11/final-greener-festival-awards-2012-announced/>, accessed 2013 January 2.

Andersson, L., Shivarajan, S. and Blau, G. (2005) 'Enacting ecological sustainability in the MNC: a test of an Adapted Value-Belief-Norm Framework', *Journal of Business Ethics*, 59(3): 295–305.

Bell, S. (2011) 'From sustainable community to big society: 10 years of learning with the imagine approach', *International Research in Geographical and Environmental Education,* 20(3): 247–67.

Bell, S. and Morse, S. (2004) 'Experience with sustainability indicators and stakeholder participation: a case study relating to a "blue plan" project in Malta', *Sustainable Development,* 12: 1–14.

Bennis, W. (1989) *On Becoming a Leader,* New York: Addison Wesley.

Bergman, A., Karlsson, J. and Axelsson, J. (2010) 'Claims of truth and explanatory claims: an ontological typology of future studies', *Futures,* 42(8): 857–65.

Chavez-Cortés, M. and Alcántara Maya, J.A. (2010) 'Identifying and structuring values to guide the choice of sustainability indicators for tourism development', *Sustainability,* 2: 3074–099.

Choi, H.C.C. and Sirakaya, E. (2006) 'Sustainability indicators for managing community tourism', *Tourism Management,* 27: 1274–289.

Covey, S.R. (1991) *Principle-Centered Leadership,* New York: Summit Books.

Djupe, P.A. and Gwiasda, G.W. (2010) 'Evangelizing the environment: decision process effects in political persuasion', *Journal for the Scientific Study of Religion,* 49(1): 73–86.

Fraj, E., Martinez, E. and Matute, J. (2011) 'Green marketing strategy and the firm's performance: the moderating role of environmental culture', *Journal of Strategic Marketing,* 19(4): 339–55.

Getz, D. (2012) *Event Studies: theory, research and policy for planned events,* Oxon: Routledge.

Greenwashing Index, Available at: <www.greenwashingindex.com/green-britain>, accessed 2 January 2013.

Harper, F. (2011) 'The energy transition: religious and cultural perspectives', *Zygon,* 46(4): 957–71.

Harris, L.C. and Crane, A. (2002) 'The greening of organizational culture: management views on the depth, degree, and diffusion of change', *Journal of Organizational Change Management,* 15(3): 214–34.

Kronsell, A. (1997) *Greening the EU: power practices, resistances and agenda setting,* Lund: Lund University Press.

Leiper, N. (1990) 'Tourism attraction systems', *Annals of Tourism Research,* 17: 367–84.

Leiper, N. (2008) 'Why "the tourism industry" is misleading as a generic expression: the case for the plural variation, tourism industries"', *Tourism Management,* 29: 237–51.

Mair, J. and Jago, L. (2010) 'The development of a conceptual model of greening in the business event tourism sector', *Journal of Sustainable Tourism,* 18(1): 77–94.

Malmoe News (2013) ESC – A green European event [ESC - Ett grönt, europeiskt arrangemang], Available at: <http://www.malmo.se/Nyheter/Forvaltning/1-28-2013-ESC-Ett-gront-europeiskt-arrangemang.html> , accessed 30 January 2013.

McLean, J.W. and Weitzel, W. (1991) *Leadership: Magic, Myth or Method?* New York: AMACOM.

Moller, P. (2009) 'The influence and flow of culture: aspect politics in the city [Kulturens inflytande och utflytande: Aspektpolitik i staden], conference paper at *Natuce – Culture: Conference for cultural studies in Sweden* [Natur –kultur: Konferens foer kulturstudier i Sverige] 15–17 June 2009: Advanced Cultural Studies Institute of Sweden.

Our Malmoe (2013) Available at: <www.malmo.se/Kommun--politik/Vart-Malmo/Vart-Malmo-artiklar/1-24-2013-Gront-pussel-for-hallbara-fester.html>, accessed 10 February 2013.

Page, S.J. and Thorn, K. (2002) 'Towards sustainable tourism development and planning in New Zealand: the public sector response revisited', *Journal of Sustainable Tourism,* 10(3): 222–38.

Pomering, A., Noble, G. and Johnson, L.W. (2011) 'Conceptualising a contemporary marketing mix for sustainable tourism', *Journal of Sustainable Tourism*, 19(8): 953–69.

Quinn, B. (2006) 'Problematising "Festival Tourism": arts festival and sustainable development in Ireland', *Journal of Sustainable Tourism*, 14(3): 288–306.

Raska, D. and Shaw, D. (2012) 'When is going green good for company image?', *Management Research Review*, 35(3): 326–47.

Silverman, D. (1993) *Interpreting Qualitative Data: methods for analyzing talk, text and interaction*, London: SAGE Publications.

Singh, J.V., Tucker, D.J. and Meinhard, A.G. (1991) 'Institutional change and ecological dynamics' in W.W. Powell and P.J. DiMaggio (eds.) *The New Institutionalism in Organizational Analysis*, Chicago: The University of Chicago Press, pp. 361–422.

Tassiopoulos, D. and Johnson, D. (2009) 'Social impact of events' in R. Raj and J. Musgrave (eds.) *Event Management and Sustainability*. Wallingford: CAB International, pp. 76–89.

Weaver, D.B. & Lawton, L.J. (2007) 'Twenty years on: the state of contemporary ecotourism research', *Tourism Management*, 28(5): 1168–79.

Wessblad, H. (2010) *Effective Events Are Sustainable Experiences: performance and communication, from vision to vitality*, Kalmar: Tourism Research Unit, Linnaeus University.

Wright, P. (1998) 'Tools for sustainability analysis in planning and managing tourism and recreation in the destination', in C.M. Hall and A.A. Lew (eds.) *Sustainable Tourism*, Harlow, Essex: Addison Wesley Longman Ltd., pp. 75–91.

Ziakas, V. and Costa, C.A. (2011a) 'The use of an event portfolio in regional community and tourism development: creating synergy between sport and cultural events', *Journal of Sport & Tourism*, 16(2): 149–75.

Ziakas, V. and Costa C.A. (2011b) 'Event portfolio and multi-purpose development: establishing the conceptual grounds', *Sport Management Review*, 14: 409–423.

11 The future of local community festivals and meanings of place in an increasingly mobile world

Kelley A. McClinchey and Barbara A. Carmichael

Future points

- Postmodern urban spaces will become increasingly diverse premised on the consumption of varied forms of culture, arts and entertainment.
- Increasing cultural mobilities, uneven power struggles and lack of connection with place will have implications for the future of festivals.
- The future of community multi-ethnic festivals is dependent on locals' conceptualizations of urban space, place and identity.
- As identities become fluid and lives more mobile, there is a desire for simplicity, a search for authenticity and engagement with local culture that will impact local festival experiences.

Introduction

Postmodern urban spaces include multiple forms of cultural representation, as arts/culture/entertainment have become key markers of the postmodern city (Bramham and Wagg 2010). The growing number of festivals and events may seem like any other component of a postmodern urban leisure landscape, yet little attention has been paid to the true meaning of festivals and the impact globalization has on festivals now and in the future. There is a concern that the effects of increased cultural mobilities will lead to homogenous undifferentiated places and weakening ties between culture and place (Rankin 2003). Furthermore, an increase in festival production and commoditization of culture may produce generic placeless festivals (McLeod 2006).

Growing attention needs to be directed at festivals in the future, as postmodern urban spaces are wrought with complexity and change. Increasing cultural mobilities, uneven power struggles and lack of connection with place have implications for the future of festivals. The future of festivals may require rethinking them as spaces premised on movement and interaction. Through an empirical analysis of a multicultural festival in a multi-ethnic urban space, this chapter presents a conceptual model of an urban festival as a cultural space of flows. It is suggested that the future of urban festivals lies in their ability to conceptualize space differently and ground place and its meaning through locals' cultural flows. The aim of this chapter is to discuss how postmodern urban space and increased cultural mobilities will impact local cultural festivals in the future. The discussion forecasts explanatory claims (Bergman, Karlsson and Axelson 2010) based in multiple truths and realities, thus it critically envisages multiple futures and determines the ways in which our actions and the actions of others contribute (Patomaki 2006).

The Multicultural Festival in Kitchener-Waterloo, Canada, provided the context for examining festival and sense of place perceptions, and mobility behaviours of ethno-cultural group leaders (festival participants). Findings revealed valuable themes that were subsequently used to apply a model of a cultural space of flows. This model demonstrated how the future of community cultural festivals depends on the grounding of place in urban space through local cultural flows from festival exhibitors at the festival, to the urban community and beyond to the global space (countries of origin).

Postmodern urban leisure space

Icons of the postmodern city include postmodern architecture; heritage conservation; mass transit systems and cultural investments in cinema, art galleries and festivals/events (Soja 1989, Dear 2000, Bramham and Wagg 2010). Harvey (1989) identified key elements of a global postmodern city such as the precinct, plaza or mall, gateways and landmarks, waterfronts and business, retail and science parks. At first believed to exist only in major urban centres these markers of postmodern urban space are being developed in small to mid-sized urban areas as well. Postmodern urban spaces are becoming both cosmopolitan and ethnic spaces. Postmodern spaces break down the boundaries between class, race, gender and ethnicity. They favour public, open and welcome spaces with varying styles of architecture, arts and culture and entertainment forms. There is less of a dichotomy between high and low forms of culture and more emphasis on diversification and variety (Bramham and Wagg 2010).

Specifically, 'Ethnoscapes' are ethnic residential neighbourhoods and/or retail spaces including ethnic grocers, cafes, restaurants and retail shops, with an increasing number of special events and festivals promoted for a diversified urban population (Appadurai 1996). However, this form of city boosterism of relocation and restructuring around the postmodern, argued by Harvey (1989), acts like a 'carnival mask' to conceal deep rooted class divisions with ensuing privatization of social, cultural and political forms and spaces. Similarly, commercialized forms of ethnic culture are sometimes presented in 'anesthetized' or 'sanitized' form for the purposes of entertainment and enjoyment, what Hage (2000) referred to as cosmomulticulturalism. Likewise, commoditization of culture and increasing numbers of festivals may cause festivalization where festivals lose distinctiveness and authenticity (Getz 2007). Ethno-cultural events and festivals, a component of the postmodern urban space, can serve as a stimulus and justification for local development, urban regeneration and place marketing (Andranovich, Burbank and Heying 2001). They can be used as a social strategy to combat feelings of insecurity, senselessness and placelessness often felt in public spaces (Andranovich, Burbank and Heying 2001; Hughes

1999). Yet, festivals and events can also have marked social consequences like promoting a tourist gaze consisting of a 'sanitized' city and 'purified' festival landscape (Atkinson and Laurier 1998). Waitt (2008) discussed these geographies of hype qualified through 'geographies of helplessness' and 'geographies of hope'. Geographies of helplessness conceptualize festivals as an oppressive social force excluding and including certain people from 'public spaces' (Harvey 1989; Waitt 2008). Geographies of hope temporarily suspend social relations allowing for sites of negotiation and hope. Positive and negative impacts of festivals will exist in the future, as class, race and ethnic power relations will still exist and as they may get increasingly masked by the postmodern urban landscape.

Other predictions for the future of festivals in postmodern urban space link to Libeskind (2012) who described what urban space will look like in the next 25 years; mass production is out and customization will be attainable for all. This customization will be important for the vast number of urban cultural festivals that continue to be developed now and in the future. However, urban leisure space is changing so rapidly that customization may seem redundant as everyone demands the same level and variety of consumption, constantly and continuously at a faster pace than ever before (see Yeoman *et al.* 2012).

Postmodern urban landscapes have become the backdrop for an increasing number of festivals planned in the urban space. If this unleashed trend continues, it could have both positive but also negative implications for the future of local cultural festivals. According to Patmore (1983), the greatest changes to impact the future of urban leisure have taken place in two opposing directions. Firstly, the growing scale and direction of mobility in personal leisure means that people are able and willing to travel greater distances for leisure opportunities. This may negatively impact local festivals as residents travel more frequently outside of their own community. In contrast, it may benefit community festivals as nonresidents are motivated to travel farther to attend smaller-scale festivals. Secondly, postmodern leisure space has changed from collective space to more individualized space (Bramham and Wagg 2010). This may negatively impact festivals as individuals no longer see value in spending quality leisure time socializing at events in public spaces, much like activities in piazza and plaza culture including the Italian Passeggiata (e.g. Chessell 2002). Thirdly, a future trend in postmodern urban leisure space is about being out in a cosmopolitan setting and living the consumer life to the full, participating in metropolitan cafe society in a city that never sleeps (Bramham and Spink 2010). Subsequently, there is a shift occurring in the revitalization of downtowns in the emergence of the 'compact city' to resist urban sprawl, improve public transit, and develop brown field sites (Bramhan and Spink 2010). There is also a shift in planning for creative cities based on authenticity and 'thick' community involvement (Duxbury 2004). However, a reduction in state-regulated development and increases in neo-liberalism are capitalizing on the very aspects of the creative economy meant to be diversified and authentic. Moreover, globalization, a condition of postmodernity, is also affecting the future of urban and festival spaces.

Cultural globalization

Globalization may be the concept, *the* key idea by which we understand the transition of human society into the third millennium (Dyck and Kearns 2006). Cultural globalization can be defined as the intensification of worldwide social relations, which link distant localities in such a way that local happenings are shaped by events occurring many miles away (Giddens 1990). Globalization is obliterating difference and the world is being reorganized into a global economic system with media and culture firmly implicated in the exploitation and inequality wrought by capitalism (Harvey 1989; Sklair 1991). Two main components in the discourse of cultural globalization that have impacts for urban space in general and in relation to festivals and the future are increased physical, cultural and social mobility to far-reaching spaces of the world and the impact of global processes on local place.

Increases in mobility

Due to globalization, it is argued that current migration flows are taking place on a larger scale and in a shorter time than in previous periods (Mitchell 1997). Migration patterns across the globe are expected to be more diverse, and the number of migrants is expected to increase (Somerville 2009; Statistics Canada 2011). In 2011, Canada had a foreign-born population that represented 20.6 percent of the total population, the highest proportion among the G8 countries (Statistics Canada 2011). Asia, including the Middle East, was Canada's largest source of migrants during the past five years. More specifically, Canada is experiencing an influx of migrants from the Philippines, China, India, Pakistan, Iran, Colombia and Mexico (Statistics Canada 2011). These mobility flows are expected to increase in the future due in part to the dichotomy between rich and poor nations, regional political instability, famine/drought and civil strife. Migrants tend to be attracted to Canada because of its multiculturalism policy, which grants immigration status based on a points system. It also has a strict set of guidelines for ways in which private businesses and public services can incorporate policies based on equity and inclusion. The 2009 objectives for the multiculturalism program focused on building an integrated, socially cohesive society and making institutions more responsive to the needs of Canada's diverse population (Citizenship and Immigration 2012). Despite this, the multiculturalism policy has received criticism for its oversimplification of the issues experienced by migrants (Li 2005; Goodhart 2008; Kymlicka 2010) even though there is strong evidence that it has played a positive role in the successful integration of ethnic minorities (Kymlicka 2010; Bloemraad 2006).

However, present and future conditions of physical mobility create change in terms of cultural mobility as well. These increased cultural flows mean that settlement areas are becoming more ethnically diverse, thus requiring adjustments to current urban development policies such as multicultural planning and increases in social services such as settlement liaisons, language interpreters, multicultural education initiatives and employment training. Even though Canada has many of these planning initiatives in place, more attention will need to be paid to these positions as mobility flows increase in the future. This is especially true for the needs relating to community festivals, leisure organizations and ways to encourage sense of belonging and community for new migrants in urban areas. Ninety-two percent of Canada's new migrants live in one of Canada's 33 census metropolitan areas (CMAs) (Statistics Canada 2011). Research has yet to acknowledge the impact of multiculturalism policies on ethnic-specific and nonethnic specific leisure pursuits (Karlis and Karadakis 2005).

Libeskind (2012: 40), who designed the Royal Ontario Museum in Toronto, Canada, explained how urban space has changed: 'cities reinvented themselves as the world became more pluralistic – places are competing for recognition within the old national border'. Increased mobility of people, products and communication through globalization has resulted in a concept that steps beyond the traditional binary perspective of migration. The idea of a circuit is used to emphasize how migration may not just be a set of movements to and from distant places and perhaps across national borders, but a continuous circulation of people, money, goods and information through which various settlements have become so closely woven together that, in an important sense, they have come to constitute a single community across a variety of sites (Rouse 1991). Thus, globalization provides the context, possibility and motivation for transnational practices (Zhou and Tseng 2001). Transnational flows and increases in physical and cultural mobility impact migrants' sense of place and identity (Louie 2000). In the future, these transnational practices are expected to continue and expand especially because of a unquantifiable economic downturn. These unfavourable economic conditions have caused unsettling and uneven global migration patterns, not to mention challenges in trying to meet the needs of a decreased yet specific job market. For instance, increased migration in challenging economic times may result in skill shortages: the need to still meet both low and high end positions as well as the pressure to fulfil positions left by an aging demographic (Somerville 2009). Furthermore, as immigration networks expand they beget further immigration creating denser ethnic networks.

Presently in Canada specifically, ethnic organizations and urban development projects have responded to current migration settlement patterns by increasing the number of community events and leisure festivals to help contribute to senses of belonging and community.

Some research has explored festivals, ethnicity and mobility in urban space (Shukla 1997; Chessell 2002). Jeong and Santos's (2004) study discussed the conflicts that exist among globalization, tradition and place identity with regard to the Kangnung Dano festival in Korea. The festival acted as a political instrument reconstructing regional identities due to contested meanings of place (Jeong and Santos 2004). In another case, Chacko (2009) compared and contrasted the politics of identity related to festivals such as Chinese New Year and the Ethiopian New Year (Inqutatash) celebrated in Washington, DC. Migrants fashioned hybrid identities of both ethnic and American culture (Chacko 2009). Hannerz (1992: 218) suggested that, 'it must now be more difficult than ever, or at least more unreasonable, to see the world . . . [as] separate pieces with hard, well-defined edges. Cultural interconnections increasingly reach across the world' and thus impact our sense of place.

Sense of place and placelessness

People attach meanings to place; they feel a sense of belonging to place, and place plays an important role in the formation of our identities (Holloway and Hubbard 2001). Relph (1976) and Tuan (1980) have referred to this humanistic approach to place meaning as having a *sense of place*. Relph's (1976) thesis involved a conceptual framework for how economic and cultural globalization and large-scale mobility transforms the relationship between people and place, and how place and place making should be theorized. He discussed experiences of 'outsiderness' and 'insiderness'. Relph used these concepts to examine the notion of 'authentic' place making and 'inauthentic' place making (placelessness). Relph (1976: 90) defined placelessness as 'weakening of the identity of places to the point where they not only look alike, but feel alike and offer the same bland possibilities for experience'. Similarly, Ritzer (1993) suggested that particular distinctive places disappear only to be replaced by universal homogenous 'non places'. In the context of global mobility flows, Massey (1991) suggested that we embrace change and global cultural mobilities rather than perceive places as becoming placeless due to cultural globalization. Massey (1991) viewed places as the complex intersections and outcomes of power geometries that operate across many spatial scales. Places and the social relations within and between them, then, are the result of particular arrangements of power, whether it is individual and institutional or imaginative and material. Massey's progressive concept of place recognized the open and porous boundaries of place as well as the myriad linkages and interdependencies among places. Massey suggested embracing this progressive sense of place and being aware of how cultural mobilities impact local place rather than become reactionary. However, global mobility processes are occurring at rates faster than ever predicted; thus it is no wonder that individuals and specific ethnic groups become reactive when their place identity is conflicted or challenged. This is especially true for new migrants who have left a country of origin where religious, racial or ethnic identity was repressed. In the new settlement area, they may feel the need to grasp at local place identity and need to display their ethnic difference in order to regain a sense of belonging and self-identity. This is where the need to showcase and share cultural traditions through ethnic festivals and events becomes increasingly important presently and in the future.

Previous academic work on festivals has shown that they can contribute to sense of place, belonging, identity and community, although more understanding is needed on the impacts of globalization on the future of festival and event places (Getz 2007; Derrett 2003; De Bres and Davis 2001; Quinn 2003). In the context of the festival, MacLeod (2006) discussed the complex processes relating to the concepts of place and community in an era of postmodernism. MacLeod suggested that festival promotions lead to commoditized and socially meaningless cultural performances, further contributing to feelings of placelessness and placeless festivals. Research on cultural festivals and meanings of place warrants further attention by researchers, especially considering that factors such as globalization, increases in migration and dramatic political and social changes greatly influence one's understandings of place (MacLeod 2006). In particular, shared identity and sense of belonging are considered important indicators of the effectiveness of multiculturalism policy in Canada (Bush 2008), but this has yet to be examined empirically.

The multicultural festival, Kitchener, Canada

Kitchener Census Metropolitan Area (CMA) is located in Southwestern Ontario, approximately 100 kilometres from Toronto, Ontario, and 200–300 kilometres from the US border. Toronto has traditionally been one of the 'global gateways' for immigrants to Canada (Li 2006). Toronto's immigrant statistics depict a highly diverse city with approximately half of its total population (46 percent) being non-Canadian born (Statistics Canada 2006). While the number of migrants per total population in Toronto is substantial, neighbouring urban centres are also experiencing an influx in new migrants and this includes the Kitchener CMA. This is because new migrants, traditionally settling in Toronto, often migrate from the GTA to take advantage of affordable housing, safe neighbourhoods, opportunities for employment and education, and availability of services (Chui, Tran and Maheux 2007). Furthermore, the federal government encourages recent migrants to settle outside of large metropolitan areas (Citizenship and Immigration Canada 2012).

Kitchener-Waterloo CMA has grown noticeably in the past decade both in terms of number of people and diversity of population. The Kitchener CMA has the fifth highest proportion of foreign-born population in Canada, behind Toronto, Vancouver, Hamilton and Windsor (Statistics Canada 2006). Ethnic backgrounds of migrants to Kitchener CMA have also changed. The majority of these migrants arrived before 1996 from the following countries of origin: Yugoslavia, Romania, India, Poland and El Salvador. However, new migrants are arriving from several different regions around the world, namely South and Southeast Asia and Latin America (Central and South America) (Statistics Canada 2006). Future trends in migration in Kitchener-Waterloo mirror that of the rest of Canada.

The Multicultural Festival in Kitchener is one of many festivals and special events established in cities across Canada in 1967 to mark and celebrate Canada's Centennial. The Multicultural Festival began as a result of members of the Kitchener-Waterloo Multicultural Centre, located in downtown Kitchener, wanting to create something special to help celebrate Canada's 100th birthday (www. kwmc.on.ca). As stated on the Multicultural Centre website, there are four components to the festival: international cuisine, traditional folksong and dance, artefacts for sale from around the globe in an international marketplace and community participation. The festival 'brings together several ethno-cultural groups and community organizations in an effort to build a more comprehensive working model of the area's cultural mosaic' (www.kwmc.on.ca). It enables these groups to raise funds for their individual organizations, while other initiatives have raised money for causes such as the Walkerton Relief Fund, the Heart and Stroke Foundation, Rotary Club of Canada and many others. While the Multicultural Centre hosts the festival, its success is the result of countless hours of preparation from each of the festival's participants. As the Multicultural Centre website states, 'it is a community event in the true sense of the word.'

The Multicultural Festival takes place in Victoria Park, downtown Kitchener. It is an urban public park operated by the City of Kitchener. At one end of the festival grounds is the stage surrounded by the food tents showcasing ethnic foods from ethno-cultural groups in the region, and on the pathway closest to Victoria Pond is the international marketplace, which offers artefacts and crafts for sale. It is a large urban green space surrounded on three sides by single-dwelling heritage neighbourhoods and on the other it is adjacent to the downtown commercial district.

In the past 10 years, postmodern urban development in downtown Kitchener has occurred at an alarming rate, consisting of professional postgraduate training schools, technology companies, revitalization of factories into loft apartments, brown-field site redevelopment, beautification of King St, ethnic restaurants, cafes and bars and new public spaces (see Harvey 1989; Dear and Flusty 1998). Future trends in the postmodern urban landscape continue toward maintaining and increasing residential loft development in the downtown core – commercial development pertaining to arts/entertainment, specifically special events. Data from personal interviews with key informants, not-for-profit ethno-cultural/community group leaders (festival exhibitors), provided the context for the study. Respondents were asked questions pertaining to the festival in general, their sense of place perceptions, and their mobility behaviours (communication and travel to their country of origin). Wording of questions was obtained through a review of the literature as well as a pilot study of the questions (e.g. Quinn 2003; Manzo 2005; Shamai and Ilatov 2005; Jorgenson and Stedman 2005). Results were analyzed using NVIVO 8 software. Data were systematically coded to allow themes to emerge (Charmaz 2009; Glaser and Strauss 1967), and names of key informants have been changed to protect anonymity. Themes are discussed in relation to their connection to global processes such as mobility flows and place meanings and in the creation of the cultural space of flows model. Words in italics are the actual words/themes raised by respondents themselves.

Connecting local and global mobilities – maintaining a sense of place identity

Ethnic group leaders had important sense of place perceptions that were influenced by their everyday experiences and mobility behaviours. Several of the respondents perceived that a sense of place meant a sense of belonging, a *place to belong* or where *you feel you belong*. Alani described it as 'a sense of belonging with an individual group with the same language in your own community'. But this sense of belonging was difficult to articulate due to deep feelings and emotions often related to their identity. The theme of identity was conceptualized as identifying with one's roots or origins or being 'back home'. They simply said 'it is part of who I am' or 'it is who I am'. Sandra mentioned her attachment to the west and could describe some aspects of why she found it meaningful more so than for her home in Waterloo. Respondents, in some instances, did not know why they have these feelings of attachment. Sense of place was also conceptualized as having a dual identity or being attached to two places. Samuel, from Bulgaria described this as:

> When you are happy where you are it's mostly home but then when you become disappointed it is like you are in limbo. We have dual citizenship. I've been here almost 20 years so I feel we've built a home here but when you are in one place or the other you miss them both.

All multi-ethnic urban areas of the new millennium, not just global cities, are home to various migrant groups who fashion hybrid social/cultural identities as they settle into their adopted environments (see Chang 2005). Festival spaces allow ethnic groups to modify traditional modes of cultural production to inscribe new meaning and cultural identity on the urban fabric (Chacko 2009). The breaking down of social and cultural boundaries creates conflict over place identity. In this Multicultural Festival space place identity is less about hybridity and more about dualism. Sense of place is contested and conflicted at times due to the attachment and identity with two places. Massey (1991) discussed the complexities associated with a sense of place especially in an age wrought with power geometries and inequalities associated with time-space compression. This has led to reactionary measures to senses of place identity (Massey 1991). Festivals can offset feelings of placelessness by giving ethnic migrants a reason to maintain cultural traditions, attend ethnic group events and connect with other community members. Cultural festivals can also help contribute to geographies of hope by giving marginalized ethnic groups justification for maintaining ethnic traditions, a purpose for practicing cultural activities and a motivation for staying involved with their ethno-cultural groups (Waitt 2008). This in turn provides a sense of belonging in the community and increases their contact with relatives in their country of origin. Massey argued that there is a lot more shaping our 'sense of place' than the bounded experiences contained in place, and it is a relative and relational concept, open to movement and flow. Such ideas begin to theorize place as 'articulated moments' in globalized networks, places as nodes caught up in a global 'space of flows' (Castells 1996).

Festivals are shown to contribute to sense of place, community and identity (De Bres and Davis 2001; Quinn 2003), and it was a factor for ethnic group leaders in this study, to a degree. But more accurately, the festival enabled respondents to connect with their place identity on a fluid level (i.e. whether it was for the city, their country of origin or some other meaningful place). It allowed ethnic migrants to connect with other ethnic group members and festival visitors, thus contributing to their sense of community and belonging. The festival also gives them a concrete purpose in being able to practice (all year long) and perform their ethnic traditions for others in the community. The Multicultural Festival connects the movement and flow of ethnic culture within the urban space (local place) to ethnic spaces throughout the globe.

Multicultural festival as a cultural space of flows

Globalization and its predecessor postmodernity have diminished boundaries, allowing the increase of physical, cultural and social mobility. But we need place and cultural boundaries as a form of identity making. This model shows how these flows can be grounded to ensure senses of place are maintained and the meaning sustained and not forgotten. Festivals in urban public spaces provide this grounding yet allow culture to flow by maintaining cultural ties through ethnic group organizations, performances, practices, music and costumes and by encouraging travel to their country of origin. A conceptual model shows how festivals can combat feelings of placelessness despite globalization processes. A space of flows, once seen as placeless, needs to be reconceptualized in terms of increasing mobility processes and connectivity among places and larger global flows (Castells 1996).

Flow 1: Ethnic groups – festival visitors

The Multicultural Festival plays an important role in allowing for *communication*, *education* and *cultural exchange*, and in enabling groups to *pass on culture*. It is *informative* and *increases our awareness*. The festival provides an opportunity for *showcasing*, *representing*, *seeing* or *observing* other cultures. Krystina, a first-generation Croatian Canadian, explained that 'it exposes people to different cultures . . . the festival allows us to demonstrate that we are an active community and active members of the community'. Thomas, from Serbia, explained that the festival lets 'other people know about us and to appreciate us, our awareness is not that high so to show that we are present in Canada'. Marvan, leader of a Sri Lankan group, explained that 'the Multicultural Festival's purpose is to bring all diversity, all groups under one umbrella, to showcase the talents, culture and food'. Chacko (2009) suggested that festivals can be bridging events that underscore home and host cultures and identities. The Multicultural Festival allows cultural group leaders to communicate, educate, exchange, display and showcase ethnic cultural information to festival visitors. There is a flow of information from ethnic groups to other ethnic groups and to visitors.

Flow 2: Festival visitors – urban space – family/friends – ethnic entrepreneurs – travel

Ethnic culture is showcased, displayed and exchanged at the festival in terms of the wide variety of ethnic foods, music, dancing and crafts available at the festival. 'Yes, I believe it opens doors for diversity and allows you to pass on culture to the world, people come and buy food and they really enjoy it' (Sonia from Jamaica).

The cultural festival experience, including the arts performances, ethnic products and food, is communicated to the visitor, and he or she leaves, perhaps with a desire to continue the flow. This may consist of festival visitors sharing some new knowledge with family/friends in the urban space. It may translate through cooking a new recipe or searching up information on the Internet. This cultural flow may translate into a network such as purchasing ethnic food products from ethnic entrepreneurs or going to an ethnic restaurant. It could also translate into a network where visitors actually travel to one of the countries and learn even more about the culture, bringing back products or new knowledge. Krystina commented that after visiting the exhibitor booths at the festival, she researches these countries in more detail, deciding where she would like to travel next.

Flow 3: Ethnic group leaders – next generation/youth – future mobility

The festival connects ethno-cultural group members with the next generation. Many respondents' role as cultural group leaders is to teach the younger generation ethnic traditions such as playing instruments, singing, learning dances, craft making or cooking that they then perform or exhibit at the festival. Lou, a Chinese Canadian stated that 'it is the personal experience where people step into cultures, especially for children, they could possibly change their perceptions. It could facilitate the future of their lives'.

In this study, ethnic migrants communicate with family and friends in their country of origin, travel back as often as they can and bring back food products, clothing and handicrafts for use during the festival and in their everyday experiences. Several group leaders stated that if they did not return to their country of origin due to financial or time constraints, they would send their children instead. This is a continuation of the cultural flow and network. Marvin further described how important it is to instil a sense of place for the next generation because they are really living in two different worlds:

> You see, a sense of place for us is two different worlds – we need to be in touch with two different worlds but for kids sense of place is here. We need to introduce the sense of place for the other place. There is always a possibility things will erode but it depends on the people who participate in our culture/arts.

The festival gives migrants the opportunity to teach the next generation about ethnic culture by giving them a reason for learning cultural traditions and performing these traditions for the Multicultural Festival and for other cultural events in the urban space.

Flow 4: Local–global connections

The products ethnic group leaders bring back from their trips to their country of origin were food products like spices, chocolate or sweets, clothing, fabrics or music specifically for their artistic performances and handmade crafts presented at the festival. Samuel, from Bulgaria, described their experiences:

> We travel back as much as we can but it is not easy. Last year I went back but not my wife and son. We have family and relatives there and we email and phone regularly. We used to bring back products from Canada and they were so excited to bring stuff but now they can get it cheaper there. We do bring back spices and all the customs [we are used to].

While ethnic group leaders send emails regularly and sometimes make phone calls to friends and family in their country of origin, all respondents stated that the items they used in the festival came directly from their country of origin. Sonia from Jamaica describes their recipes for jerk and curry chicken: 'none of the other islands have jerk chicken, they may have adopted the recipe themselves but it is from Jamaica'.

There was a connection between the cultures (or even foods/songs/dances) of the world all coming together in one location, here at the festival. Albert shared eloquently the festival as communicating an understanding of global places in a local space. He talks about our world being 'small': 'you get to understand the whole world in a small area and you mix and mingle with the Chinese people, for example, and you get to understand their world and that it is a rather small world – that there is diversity in the city'.

An ethnic or multi-ethnic festival as a space of cultural flows contradicts the idea that increases in mobilities and flows weaken ties between culture and place. In this instance, flows and mobility behaviours strengthen ties among culture, place of origin, the new urban space and the next generation. But it is not without collective and personal conflict. Waters (2001) stressed that there is not one single global culture – nor hermetically sealed local ones – but that everywhere there is a complex interaction of local and global. These interactions are grounded locally in festival spaces and, by being cognizant of their potential role in contributing to sense of place, may be how they survive global processes in the future.

Concluding remarks

The implications for the future of the event industry based upon the present are that local cultural festivals need to be modeled as a cultural space of flows grounding local place in a future of increased global mobility.

As a result, strategic community planning should mirror a fluid, rather than static, response to the development and management of multi-ethnic events supporting funding, authentic content and locally driven promotion. 'Sense of place'–based planning initiatives in relation to leisure/arts/entertainment should take precedence over media-driven mass-produced product promotion for cultural tourism (Thorne 2012). The postmodern *may* celebrate difference, but its contours are projected onto existing unequal power relations of race and ethnicity (Bramham and Wagg 2010).

Urban spaces, including festival spaces, are still sites of constant negotiation and renegotiation. If based as strategic sites, festivals enable ethnic migrants to feel grounded in place while feeling connected to culture through mobilities and flows. This space of cultural flows model demonstrates how cultural festivals contradict the discourse of globalization that renders spaces placeless. Instead, a cultural space of flows encourages the movement of culture and the maintenance of tradition, thus contributing to senses of place and belonging for the urban space and beyond. The Multicultural Festival as a space of cultural flows allows ethnically diverse participants and visitors to showcase and share cultural traditions, thereby connecting identity with place and with their sense of place in Kitchener and somewhere else far away (e.g. their country of origin).

Festival and urban space needs to be viewed differently, especially as consumption patterns change due to postmodernity and globalization increasing mobility even faster than ever before. Rather than focus on capital gain through economic flows in financial capital-driven space, a focus needs to be instead on cultural/social capital in cultural spaces that are fluid. For example, the urban space of a public park during the Multicultural Festival is temporarily transformed into an ethnic leisure space, an educational space, and a fluid space (for mobilities and flows). It also becomes a place that affords great meaning for individuals and groups. More specifically, this notion of fluid cultural space should be explored further as a way to diversify cultural capital in urban space. Conceptualizations of space must change as senses of place become increasingly more important in a future based on mobility and flows. For example, the Royal Ontario Museum in Toronto, Canada, is no longer just an educative cultural space during day hours for school groups, tourists and family leisure travel; it is also an entertainment/social space in the evenings for 20- to 30-somethings as they mingle, socialize, have cocktails and wander through the exhibits.

As migration flows increase both in numbers and diversity, new migrants will need special events and leisure festivals that best fit their cultural needs. In many instances, ethnic groups have initiated their own special events as part of grassroots innovative movements at a very local level (e.g. neighbourhoods). This may in fact be a future trend for community festival development. The future of multiethnic festivals will be to articulate meanings of hope, pride and celebration yet allow on a deeper level local ethnic organizations the ability and fortitude to practice, perform and organize cultural traditions authentically. This could give them a sense of self-governance and belonging, justifying their right to sustain ethnic culture and performance in postmodern urban space in the same regard as high culture.

Ethnic group leaders in this particular study overwhelmingly referred to the constraints of finding funding for their ethno-cultural groups to pay for rental space for meetings, dance practices, costumes and food products:

> Funding is a major issue. Well there are big corporate sponsors but for small diverse groups a challenge is money. This is especially true when the economy goes bad then there is even less money and the commercial sponsors don't look at you because they feel you don't contribute much because we are a small group. Really it's a matter of survival. (Marvin)

Despite being an open and welcome Multicultural Festival, power relations do exist for small ethnic groups who are constrained. Moreover, multiculturalism policy in Canada may garner rights for equality and diversity, but marginalizations still exist for migrants in terms of labour relations and employment training, affordable housing and social services including ethnic leisure and recreation. These challenges are expected to exist in the future, as critics of multiculturalism in Canada and across the globe question its success.

The postmodern is intent on breaking boundaries between high/low cultures, but where does ethnic culture fit in the arts/entertainment mix of the postmodern urban leisure space, authentically? As postmodernity brings about pluralism fewer seem interested in specific forms of high culture, and it seems futile to continue justifying their continual exorbitant funding models by state organizations. For example, the Waterloo Clay and Glass Museum has been saved from bankruptcy twice in 2010, with the city giving it over $150,000 (Canadian dollars) in funding. It also has a 50-year rent-free lease on its city property and building (Outhit 2010), whereas ethno-cultural organizations must pay high rental fees to rent space in city-operated facilities to hold meetings and host festivals and events. Similarly, the KW Symphony has had to be saved from bankruptcy a number of times in the past five years.

Postmodernism may thus continue to perpetuate a mobile way of life that facilitates capital and labour flows and also erodes a sense of history, a sense of community and a sense of place (Hay 1998). Amin and Thrift (2002) pointed out that, while official attempts to differentiate places are problematic (e.g. through place promotion), the success of localities in a global economy will depend upon their ability to embrace the global.

Due to increases in mobility processes occurring from the local to the global, and vice versa, one may question the importance of being rooted in place. But Yeoman (2010) stated that in the future, as identities become fluid and lives more mobile, there is a desire for simplicity, a search for authenticity and engagement with local culture. The questions of 'where we are' and 'who we are' will become increasingly more important and more difficult to answer. But it is these roots, these connections to culture and place, that form our identity. This is especially important for migrants fashioning dual place identities. We are most passionate about those aspects of ourselves (and others) that connect us with our self and place identity. It is these reasons why local, real, distinct cultural festival experiences are vital for the future of festivals in urban space. The festival provides a space for connecting visitors and participants with a small glimpse of the places that our fellow community members find meaningful and that in turn create a more meaningful urban space. Thus, the future of local community festivals depends on their ability to grasp cultural flows enabling urban space to be fluid yet grounded in locals' conceptualizations of place.

References

Amin, A. and Thrift, N. (2002) 'Cities and ethnicities', *Ethnicities*, 2(3): 291–300.
Andranovich, G., Burbank, M.J. and Heying, C.H. (2001) 'Olympic cities: lessons learned from mega-event politics', *Journal of Urban Affairs*, 23(2): 113–31.

Appadurai, A. (1996) *Modernity at Large: Cultural dimensions in globalization.* Minneapolis: University of Minnesota Press.

Atkinson, D. and Laurier, E. (1998) 'A sanitised city? Social exclusion at Bristol's 1996 International Festival of the Sea', *Geoforum*, 29(2): 199–206.

Bergman, A., Karlsson, J. and Axelson, J. (2010) 'Truth claims and explanatory claims', *Futures*, 42(8): 857–65.

Bloemraad, I. (2006) *Becoming a Citizen: incorporating immigrants and refugees in the United States and Canada.* Berkeley: University of California Press.

Bramham, P. and Spink, J. (2010) 'Leeds: becoming the Postmodern City' in P. Bramham and S. Wagg (eds.) *Sport, Leisure and Culture in the Postmodern City.* Surrey, England: Ashgate, pp. 9–32.

Bramham, P. and Wagg, S. (eds.) (2010) *Sport, Leisure and Culture in the Postmodern City.* Surrey, England: Ashgate.

Bush, N. (2008) *Multicultural Nations: issues of race and national identity in Britain and Canada.* Unpublished MA Thesis. Toronto: Ryerson University.

Castells, M. (1996) *The Rise of the Network Society: the information age: economy, society and culture.* Volume I. Oxford: Blackwell.

Chacko, E. (2009) *Spaces of Celebration and Identity: ethnic festivals in the public spaces of Washington, DC.* Washington, DC: American Association of Geographers Annual General Meeting.

Chang, T.C. (2005) 'Place, memory and identity: Imagining "New Asia"', *Asia Pacific Viewpoint*, 46(3): 247–53.

Charmaz, K. (2009) *Constructing Grounded Theory: a practical guide through qualitative analysis.* London: Sage Publications.

Chessell, D. (2002) 'Italian festivals in Australia's Little Italy's: the use of public spaces in Italian-Australian commercial precincts to create a cosmopolitan "sense of place"' *Events and Place Making: Proceedings of International Event Research Conference*, Sydney.

Chui, T., Tran, K. & Maheux, H. (2007) *Immigration in Canada: a portrait of the foreign-born population, 2006 Census.* Catalogue no. 97–557. Ottawa: Statistics Canada.

Citizenship and Immigration (2012) *Facts and figures 2012: immigration overview: permanent and temporary residents.* Online. Available <www.cic.gc.ca/english/resources/statistics/facts2012/index.asp> (accessed 12 March 2013).

De Bres, K., and Davis, J. (2001) 'Celebrating group and place identity: a case study of a new regional festival', *Tourism Geographies*, 3(3): 326–37.

Dear, M. (2000) *The Postmodern Urban Condition.* Oxford: Blackwell.

Dear, M.J. and Flusty, S. (eds.) (1998) *The Spaces of Postmodernity: readings in human geography.* Oxford: Blackwell.

Derrett, R. (2003) 'Making sense of how festivals demonstrate a community's sense of place', *Event Management*, 8: 49–58.

Duxbury, N. (2004) *Creative Cities: principles and practices.* Ottawa: Canadian Policy Research Networks, Inc.

Dyck, I. and Kearns, R.A. (2006). 'Structuration theory: agency, structure and everyday life', in S. Aitkin and G. Valentine (eds.) *Approaches to Human Geography.* London: England: Sage, pp. 86–97.

Getz, D. (2007) *Event Studies: theory, research and policy for planned events.* Oxford: Butterworth-Heinemann.

Giddens, A. (1990) *The Consequences of Modernity.* Cambridge: Polity.

Glaser, B.G. and Strauss, A.L. (1967) *The Discovery of Grounded Theory: strategies for qualitative research.* New Brunswick: Aldine Transaction.

Goodhart, D. (2008). 'Has multiculturalism had its day?' *Literary Review of Canada*, 16(3): 3–4.

Hage, G. (2000) *Against Paranoid Nationalism: searching for hope in assimilating society.* Annandale: Pluto Press.

Hannerz, U. (1992) 'The global ecumene as a network of networks', in A. Kuper (ed.) *Conceptualizing Society.* London: Routledge, pp. 140–60.

Harvey, D. (1989) *The Condition of Postmodernity.* Oxford: Blackwell.

Hay, R. (1998) 'A rooted sense of place in cross-cultural perspective', *Canadian Geographer*, 42(3): 245–66.

Holloway, L. and Hubbard, P. (2001) *People and Place: the extraordinary geographies of everyday life.* Harlow, England: Pearson Education Ltd.

Hughes, G. (1999) 'Urban revitalization: the use of festival time strategies', *Leisure Studies*, 18: 119–35.

Jeong, S. and Santos, C. (2004) 'Cultural politics and contested place identity', *Annals of Tourism Research*, 31(3): 640–56.

Jorgensen, B.S. and Stedman, R.C. (2006) 'A comparative analysis of predictors of sense of place dimensions: attachment to, dependence on, and identification with lakeshore properties', *Journal of Environmental Management*, 79: 316–27.

Karlis, G. and Karadakis, K. (2005). *Canadian-Based Research on Leisure and Ethnicity: current state of condition.* Canadian Association of Leisure Studies. Eleventh Canadian Congress on Leisure Research. Nanaimo, British Columbia.

Kymlicka, W. (2010) *The Current State of Multiculturalism in Canada and Research Themes on Canadian Multiculturalism 2008–2010.* Ottawa: Department of Citizenship and Immigration Canada.

Li, W. (2005) 'Beyond Chinatown, beyond enclave: reconceptualizing contemporary Chinese settlements in the United States', *Geojournal*, 64(1): 31–40.

Libeskind, D. (2012, December) 'Historic cities will get modern', *Conde Nast Traveller*, 40.

Louie, A. (2000) 'Re-territorializing transnationalism: Chinese Americans and the Chinese motherland', *American Ethnologist*, 27(3): 645–69.

MacLeod, N.E. (2006) 'The placeless festival: identity and place in the post-modern festival', in D. Picard and M. Robinson (eds.) *Festivals, Tourism and Social Change.* Clevedon, England: Channel View Publications, pp. 222–37.

Manzo, L.C. (2005) 'For better or worse: exploring multiple dimensions of place meaning', *Journal of Environmental Psychology*, 25: 67–86.

Massey, D. (1991) 'A global sense of place', *Marxism Today*, 38: 24–29.

Mitchell, K. (1997) 'Transnational discourse: bringing geography back in', *Antipode*, 29(2):101–14.

Outhit, J. (2010) 'Waterloo gives struggling Clay and Glass $51K Boost', *K–W Record*, 23 August. Online. Available <www.therecord.com/news/article/291882–waterloo-gives-struggling-clay-and-glass-gallery-51k-boost> (accessed 5 January 2013).

Patmore, J.A. (1983) *Recreation and Resources: leisure patterns and leisure places.* Oxford: Blackwell.

Patomaki, H. (2006) 'Realist ontologies for futures studies', *Journal of Critical Realism*, 5(1): 1–31.

Quinn, B. (2003) 'Symbols, practices and myth-making: cultural perspectives on the Wexford Festival Opera', *Tourism Geographies*, 5(3): 329–49.

Rankin, K.N. (2003) 'Anthropologies and geographies of globalization,' *Progress in Human Geography*, 27(6): 708–34.

Relph, E. (1976) *Place and Placelessness*. London: Pion.

Ritzer, G. (1993) *The McDonaldization of Society: an investigation into the changing character of contemporary social life*. Thousand Oaks: Pine Forge Press.

Rouse, R. (1991) 'Mexican migration and the social space of postmodern', *Diaspora*, 1: 8–23.

Shamai, S., and Ilatov, Z. (2005) 'Measuring sense of place: methodological aspects', *Tijdschrift Voor Economische En Sociale Geografie*, 96(5): 467–76.

Shukla, S. (1997) 'Building diaspora and nation: The 1991 cultural festival of India', *Cultural Studies*, 11(2): 296–315.

Sklair, L. (1991) *Sociology of the Global System: social change in global perspective*. London: Harvestor Wheatsheaf.

Soja, E. (1989) *Postmodern Geographies: the reassertion of space in critical theory*. London: Verso.

Somerville, W. (2009) *Future Immigration Patterns and Policies in the United Kingdom*. Washington, DC: Migration Policy Institute.

Statistics Canada (2006) *Census Data*. Online. Available <www.statcan.gc.ca> (accessed 13 April 2010).

Statistics Canada (2011). *Census Data*. Online. Available <www.statcan.gc.ca> (accessed 27 July 2013).

Thorne, S. (2012) 'Place-based cultural tourism: a new planning paradigm', *Economic Development.org*. Online. Available <http://economicdevelopment.org/2012/10/place-based-cultural-tourism-a-new-planning-paradigm/> (accessed 29 December 2013).

Tuan, Y. (1980) 'Rootedness verses sense of place', *Landscape*, 24: 3–8.

Waitt, G. (2008) 'Urban festivals: geographies of hype, helplessness and hope', *Geography Compass*, 2(2): 513–37.

Waters, M. (2001) *Globalization*. 2nd ed. London: Routledge.

Yeoman, I. (2010) 'Tomorrow's tourists: fluid or simple identities?' *Tourism Insights*. Online. Available <www.insights.org.uk/articleitem.aspx?title=Tomorrow%E2%80%99s+Tourists%3A+Fluid+or+Simple+Identities%3F> (accessed 1 June 2013).

Yeoman, I., with Tan, R., Mars, M. and Wouters, M. (2012) *2050: Tomorrow's Tourism*. Bristol, United Kingdom: Channel View Publications.

Zhou, Y. and Tseng, Y. (2001) 'Re-grounding the "Ungrounded Empires": localization as the geographical catalyst for transnationalism', *Global Networks*, 1(2): 131–53.

12 Developing brand relationship theory for festivals

A study of the Edinburgh Festival Fringe

Louise Todd

Future points

- This chapter illustrates the relevance of the brand relationship paradigm to future festivals through the present setting of the Edinburgh Festival Fringe.
- A typology of Fringe-consumer brand relationships is presented.
- The chapter provides a predictive forecast of a future festivalscape scenario, iterates the significance of festival-consumer brand relationships to this future and highlights consumers' symbolic engagement with festival brands.

Introduction

Relationship principles prevail in consumer marketing practice where brands are imbued with human traits to strengthen their consumer appeal. The brand-as-a-person metaphor has gained momentum in consumer research (Aaker, J. 1997; Aaker, J., Benet-Martinez and Garolera 2001; Aaker, J., Fournier and Brasel 2004; Azoulay and Kapferer 2003; Patterson 1999). Consequently, the related concept of consumer–brand relationships has attracted interest (Aggarwal 2004; Fournier 1998, 2009; Hess and Story 2005; MacInnis, Park and Priester 2009). Tourism research has applied brand personality constructs to destination branding and image (e.g. Ekinci and Hosany 2006; Hosany, Ekinci and Uysal 2006; Murphy, Moscardo and Benckendorff 2007). Nevertheless, brand relationship theory remains unused in developing equitable and differentiated festival brands contributing to future survival and success (Aaker, D. 1991).

This chapter proposes the significance of brand relationship theory to future festivals. With forecasted shifts in festival marketing, production and consumption (Ringland 2006; Schultz 2006) it is essential for festivals to foster strong, competitive and resonant future brands. These can competitively differentiate festivals and build valuable equity with consumers (Aaker, D. 1991). Further, positive, sustainable, stable and interactive festival–consumer brand relationships can successfully engage consumers (Fournier 1998).

A study of the Edinburgh Festival Fringe (The Fringe) is presented to illustrate the potential value of the festival–consumer brand relationship paradigm. Fournier's (1998) consumer–brand relationship research is applied to the setting of the Fringe and its consumers where phenomenological interviews reveal a typology of festival consumer–brand relationship forms. Although specific to the Fringe setting, this application of brand relationship theory provides a revealing account of consumers' engagement with festival brands. This is relevant and applicable to future festivals in contributing to theory and brand management practice.

In considering the significance of contemporary Fringe consumer–brand relationships to future festivals, this chapter applies marketing scenario planning principles (Pattinson and Sood 2010; Ringland 2006). It also draws upon Bergman, Karlsson, and Axelsson's (2010) ontological typology of future forecasts. The application of these to statements on the future assists in understanding the future of festivals, as this may be. The present study thus presents a prediction forecast of a future festivals scenario. Its drivers are based upon a potential scenario exploring the future (Ringland 2006) while founded on today's standard world (Khan and Wiener 1967). This chapter therefore presents a future view where the festival brand relationship paradigm will be a useful and rewarding strategic marketing approach to engage consumers.

The future festivalscape

Porter (1998: 234) emphasizes the importance of strategic planning in an uncertain future. While forecasting is complex and contingent on unknown variables, 'scenarios' provide 'discrete, internally consistent views of how the world will look in the future'. Scenario planning anticipates real life and is a useful in expressing tacit and explicit future visions of a particular phenomenon (Ringland 2006). It involves pushing 'thinking to a place (or space) . . . to start to explain possible future developments' (Pattinson and Sood 2010: 418).

Festivalscapes are where festival benefits are produced and consumed. They involve cues that are intrinsic, such as the physical environment; and extrinsic, including brand perceptions (Bitner 1992; Lee *et al.* 2008). This chapter forecasts a future festivalscape scenario based on truth and explanatory claims and applies scenario planning principles to develop a predictive forecast described in terms of external driving forces (Bergman, Karlsson, and Axelsson 2010; Pattinson and Sood 2010). It continues by illustrating the significance of the present Fringe-consumer brand relationship typology to the future in relation to this envisioned festivalscape.

Drivers of future change

In marketing and branding practice increased consumer empowerment is facilitating a power shift away from brand owners (Yeoman and McMahon-Beattie 2011; Ind 2003). Indeed, as consumers are progressively individualized (Yeoman, Greenwood and McMahon-Beattie 2009), festival brands are correspondingly co-created amongst consumers and stakeholders rather than managed by their owners (Ind and Todd 2011). This is influenced by greater consumer choice, accessibility (Yeoman *et al.* 2009), growing ease of digital communications and social networking, as society becomes increasingly interconnected (Ind 2003; Schultz 2006).

In a 'standard world context', entrenched by 'salient features of the real world' (Khan and Wiener 1967: 8) the expected primary generators of future change in marketing and branding will be: technological advancements, challenges of channel fragmentation and the growing shift of power from brand owners to consumers (Schultz 2006). The particular key drivers shaping the future of festival brands will therefore be: provision and consumption modes, the future festival consumer and increased substitutability fuelled by digital connectivity. This forecast is framed by competitive forces of: future festival provision and consumption, the power and nature of consumers, competitive rivalry and threats to the future festivalscape from emerging entrants and substitute experiences (Porter 1998).

The future festivals scenario

Future festival consumers will face greater choice than they presently do, being 'increasingly exposed to and influenced by events' of all forms (Yeoman *et al.* 2009: 388). Accordingly, managers must not be complacent in marketing accessible and engaging experiences (Fyall 2011). The polarization of global-local-ization (Yeoman *et al.* 2009) suggests that festivals and events will witness paradigmatic shifts in their tangible provision and consumption. Consequently, festival managers must be responsive and equipped to build brands (Fyall 2011) demonstrating consumer-facing values that are 'trustworthy, ethical and sustainable' (Yeoman *et al.* 2009: 389).

Underpinning festival provision is postindustrial society's prevailing leisure and service orientations (Bergman, Karlsson, and Axelsson 2010; Khan and Wiener 1967). In this context future festival consumers will have excess time to experience festivals and events. Nevertheless, sustainability will remain a concern (Yeoman *et al.* 2009) with consolidation and collaboration as future drivers across the festival industry. Similarly, alienation, crises, fear of natural disasters and terrorism – tempered by prolonged global economic concerns, rising fuel costs and taxes – will feature in an uncertain global future (Fyall 2011). Conflicts between consumer conscience and desire to travel may impact on global festival tourism (Getz 2012). The ability to provide physical and virtual festival experiences will therefore be essential to future survival. Maintaining differentiated brands with trustworthy and sustainable values (Yeoman *et al.* 2009) will assist in building positive equity with consumers (Aaker, D. 1991).

Being societally and individually significant (Getz 2012), festivals address intrinsic consumption motivations and consumers' social and experiential needs (Crompton and MacKay 1997; Gelder and Robinson 2009). As today's festival consumer has unique motivations, those of the future will also be highly individual with bespoke preferences, expectations and behaviours (Yeoman *et al.* 2009), and this will impact on industry trends and practices. In predicting future festival consumers' traits it is useful to consider today's emerging Generation Y cohort, born between 1979 and 1994 and sharing life and time characteristics

(Kupperschmidt 2000). Research reveals distinct character traits and expectations influenced by rapidly emerging technological servicescapes of the late twentieth and early twenty-first centuries (Neuborne and Kerwin 1999). For example, 'Gen Y' consumers are highly brand aware but lack brand loyalty (Bakewell and Mitchell 2003). Further, expectations of heterogeneity in service provision leads Gen Y to seek co-created personalized experiences that resonate with their own identities (Beckendorff and Moscardo 2010). In engaging this cohort recent efforts include branded 'Lates' events where attractions have created special Gen Y–focused events (Leask and Barron 2012). In the future festivals must be able to adapt to new consumers' traits and expectations, e.g., increased customization and co-creation (Fyall 2011). Such features will be most evident in brands that resonate personally with a range of consumers (Aaker, D. 1991; Fournier 1998).

Consumption modes and distribution channels will be altered and fragmented within the future festivalscape (Fyall 2011). The continued importance of the experience economy (Pine and Gilmore 1998) will increase desire for authenticity (Yeoman *et al.* 2009). Today's wifi, 3G and 4G technologies allow 'virtual' experiences to be 'authenticated' though live streaming and social media. The recent (re)emergence of 3D (as well as 4D and 5D), augmented reality, podcasting and similar technologies have formalized a perceptible shift in how events are encountered. Now consumers can experience the reality of arts and cultural exhibitions, the *Bolshoi Ballet*, and *National Theatre Live* productions at their local cinema. Indeed, entertainment, arts and events are already being distributed simultaneously 'live' via cinema, mobile platforms, television, DVD and the Internet (Picturehouse Entertainment 2013). Consumers' desire for authenticity and co-created experiences, countered by time, mobility and sustainability (Yeoman *et al.* 2009) means that future festivals will be conceptualized, produced and consumed in these ways. Rapidly evolving technologies will facilitate a vividly competitive environment amongst existing industry players and an unprecedented provision of substitute and virtually authentic arts and entertainment experiences. Festival brands must strive hard to differentiate themselves in this congested marketplace (Fyall 2011).

This is a briefly envisioned future festivalscape scenario, as precise future variables are not yet known. Nevertheless, this chapter argues that in successfully engaging future consumers, festivals must recognize the importance of building and maintaining trustworthy and sustainable brands (Yeoman *et al.* 2009). Such brands must resonate across functional, symbolic and experiential domains, addressing consumers' identity needs, while being purposive and dynamic relationship partners (Fournier 2009).

The brand concept

Brands communicate and differentiate products while enhancing equity and image. Their specific personality characteristics can facilitate formation of consumer relationships (Richards and Palmer 2010). Despite being owned by organizations, brands 'only properly exist in the minds of consumers and represent the totality of experience' (Ind 2007: 79). On these bases it is vital for festivals to manage their brands effectively to engender positive consumer perceptions, focus upon strategic approaches and build upon competitive advantage (Aaker, D. 1991).

Brands are ambiguous concepts (Haigh 2006), being collections of tangible, intangible and often experiential attributes correlating with consumers' needs (Park, Jaworski and MacInnis 1986; Rosenbaum-Elliot, Percy and Pervan 2011). Functional elements include names and logos, and symbolic elements are loyalty, equity, image and personality. Positive brand equity is desirable in building consumer loyalty, dependent on the particular assets and liabilities that consumers link to functional brand names or logos (Aaker, D. 1991). It is defined as 'the differential effect of brand knowledge on consumer response to the marketing of the brand' (Keller 1993: 2). Brand knowledge is composed from consumers' brand awareness, and brand image and is 'conceptualized according to the characteristics and relationships of brand associations' (Ibid: 8).

Consumers' awareness and perceived image of brands are central to forming relationships (Fournier 1998). Both involve memory, as brand awareness relates to consumers' recall and recognition, while brand image is 'a set of associations usually organized in some meaningful way' (Aaker, D. 1991: 109). Strong, favourable and unique associations (Keller 1993) result in the formation of 'pictures which are wholly resident in the consumer's mind' (Patterson 1999: 412) and a positive brand image.

Brand image is supported by two constructs. Firstly, brand personality is an emotional aspect, where consumers' personification of particular brands generates emotions with personal meanings (Aaker, J. 1997; Ekinci and Hosany 2006; Keller 1993; Patterson 1999). The second construct, consumer image or 'self-concept' (Burns 1979: 2), is underpinned by principles of interpersonal attraction, meaning consumers favour others they perceive as being congruent to themselves (Backman, Secord and Peirce 1963; Burns 1979). There is theoretical justification to suggest consumers also prefer brands they perceive as similar to themselves. This is termed 'self-image congruency' and in such situations consumers' brand preferences can expedite the attachment of personal meanings to the corresponding products, services and experiences (Belk 1988; Chon 1992; Ross 1971; Sirgy 1982; Solomon 1983).

Self-concept and self-image congruency are aligned with experiential brand elements, adhering to consumer 'desires that provide sensory pleasure, variety, and/or cognitive stimulation' (Park, Jaworski and MacInnis 1986: 136). On this foundation consumers' brand choice involves communicating and reinforcing their social identities (Aron, Paris and Aron 1995; Hirschman 1992; Richins 1994; Rosenbaum-Elliot, Percy and Pervan 2011), contributing to 'symbolic self-completion' (Schouten 1991: 412).

Festival brands are particularly complex, being symbolic of their host destinations, and of significance throughout lived experience, social worlds and subcultures (Getz 2012). They are high in experiential elements, encompassing consumers' perceptions of a festival and what it promises (Bowdin *et al.* 2011). Engagement with festival brands therefore addresses consumers' tangible,

symbolic and experiential needs, serving as expressions of self-concept in situations of festival brand-self-image congruency (Belk 1988; Belk, Wallendorf and
Sherry 1989; O'Cass and Frost 2002; Solomon 1983; Xue 2008). Accordingly,
effective management of festival brands is fundamental to positioning strategies
(Park, Jaworski and MacInnis 1986). As such, festival managers must develop
and nurture strong, equitable brands that resonate with consumers on a personally
meaningful level. The brand relationship paradigm is a useful means of achieving this.

Brand relationships

To compete and survive in the future festivalscape scenario, festivals must
develop positive, reciprocal and enduring brand relationships with their consumers. Fournier (1996) pertinently describes the role of brand relationships as
'soothing the "empty selves" left behind by society's abandonment of tradition
and community and (providing) stable anchors in an otherwise changing world'
(Fournier 1996, cited in Keller 2008: 8). Future festival brands must strive therefore to provide continuity and self-image congruency with consumers to ensure
engagement and loyalty.

Brand relationships are complex and purposeful constructs, existing between
consumers and brands. They have numerous characteristics, meanings and related
motives (MacInnis, Park and Priester 2009). The theory is grounded in 'consumers as active meaning makers' (Fournier 2009: 5), reframing the brand personality
construct (Keller 2008) and expressed in the context of the brand-as-a-person
(Rosenbaum-Elliot, Percy and Pervan 2011). The underpinning proposition is
consumers and brands have similar connections and characteristics to interpersonal relationships such as relatives, friends, partners and enemies (Fournier
1998, 2009). Such relationships evolve over time and are not mutually exclusive. They are influenced by lived experiences and identities and characterized
by measures of interdependence, temporality and perceived commitment (Hinde
1979). The interpersonal relationship norms of interactivity, continuity and mutuality are applicable to consumer-brand relationships (Aggarwal 2004; Hess and
Story 2005). Brands are thus viable partners, contributing to purposive, multiplex
and dynamic relationships with features characterized by loyalty and trustworthiness (Fournier 1998, 2009) and imbued with personal meanings based on
equity, interaction, affinity and stability levels (Aaker, J., Fournier and Brasel
2004). Consumers have portfolios of brands with which they have relationships.
These are influenced by life-worlds and identities, linked to self-concept and act
as meaning-based communication systems (Fournier 1998).

Brand relationship theory has gained interest in its proposition (Bengtsson 2003;
Breivik and Thorbjørnsen 2008; Jevons, Gabbott and de Chernatony 2005; Smit,
Bronner and Tolboom 2007), in consumer and in psychology contexts (Aggarwal
2004; Esch *et al.* 2006; Heath, Brandt and Nairn 2006; Ji 2002; Kates 2000; Morgan-
Thomas and Veloutsou 2011). In *The Handbook of Brand Relationships*, MacInnis,
Park and Priester (2009) present selected research in this area. Despite this interest

there has been little consideration of brand relationships between festivals and consumers. Nevertheless, it is suggested that brands with unique and exciting personalities have the potential to be strong relationship partners (Smit, Bronner and Tolboom 2007). This feature is seen in festivals' embodiment of experiential brand elements. Brand relationship theory is therefore a significant conceptual framework for future festivals to apply to the festival-consumer domain.

In presenting the significance of brand relationships to the success of future festival brands, Fournier's (1998) pioneering interpersonal brand relationship paradigm (MacInnis, Park and Priester 2009) is applied to the setting of the Fringe and its consumers. This research involved phenomenological interview case studies of three women and the brands they use to develop relational phenomena in the consumer products domain. A typology of distinct and meaningful forms of consumer-brand relationships was developed by studying the women's in-depth brand relationship accounts.

Consumer–brand relationship forms

Fournier (1998) identified the fundamental continua of relationship elements as: voluntary–imposed; positive–negative; intense–superficial; enduring–short-term; public–private; formal–informal; and symmetric–asymmetric. These opposing elements were applied to the development of 15 meaningful relationship types, based upon theoretical interpersonal relationship forms. These are characterized in dimensions of 'friendships', 'kinships', 'affect-based' relationships, 'interim' relationships and a series of 'dark-side' relationships.

In Fournier's (1998) typology of relationship forms, the first series identified are friendships, classified as 'best friendships', 'casual friendships', 'childhood friendships' and 'compartmentalized friendships'. 'Kinships' are defined as family-based relationships. Affect-based relationships range from 'committed partnerships', to 'arranged marriages', 'marriages of convenience' and 'secret affairs'. 'Interim relationships' are characterized as 'flings' or 'courtships' and a final range of 'dark-side' relationships, are 'dependencies', 'enmities', 'enslavements' and 'rebounds'.

These consumer-brand relationship forms may be applicable to one individual across different brands or to one brand across individual cases. Each form is characterized by particular dimensions and further defined by a multifaceted Brand Relationship Quality (BRQ) construct, indicating relationship strength and depth (Fournier 1998; Keller 2008; Smit, Bronner and Tolboom 2007). These are: love and passion; self-concept connection; interdependence; commitment; intimacy; and partner quality (Fournier 1998).

Research setting and approach

The Fringe and its consumers

The Fringe first occurred in 1947 when eight theatre groups, not invited to Edinburgh's new postwar International Festival, decided to perform independently

(Moffat 1978). As an open-access, nonprogrammed arts festival, many features of the Fringe have since developed organically (Ind and Todd 2011), with even its brand name not a strategic decision, but designated by playwright Robert Kemp, writing in 1948 of the activities: 'round the fringe of the official Festival drama' (Moffat 1978: 17).

The contemporary Fringe brand demonstrably contributes to Edinburgh's experience economy and festival city reputation (Pine and Gilmore 1999; Richards and Palmer 2010). The 2013 Fringe featured 45,464 performances of 2,871 shows in 273 venues, with an estimated 1,943,493 tickets issued (Edinburgh Festival Fringe 2013). As one of 12 citywide festivals it accounts for half of Edinburgh's four million annual festival attendances (Festivals Edinburgh and BOP Consulting 2011). The Fringe provides a rich example of a festival with longevity and a mature and recognized brand.

Those stakeholders most engaged in consuming the Fringe were relevant to this study and were accordingly differentiated as primary or secondary (Clarkson 1995; Reid and Arcodia 2002). The 21 consumers interviewed were members of at least one of five primary groups (Table 12.1), based on their self-perceived primary role, although there was considerable overlap amongst groups (Todd 2010, 2011).

Fringe brand relationship interviews

In applying Fournier's (1998) existing consumer brand relationship forms to the 21 Fringe consumers, the original theoretical underpinning and methodological approach was adapted to the present setting. The interview process was based on Fournier's (1998) approach, sharing the concern of entering informants' worlds without preconceptions and focussing on lived experience from a first-person perspective (Fournier 1998; Kvale and Brinkmann 2009). This phenomenological

Table 12.1 Fringe consumer categories and informants

Fringe consumer group	Examples of roles within group	Number of informants (assigned pseudonyms)
Organizing consumers	Fringe Society staff, volunteers, board members	Three (Susan, Margaret and Mark)
Participating consumers	Performers, venue workers, managers, programmers	Seven (Emma, Jenna, Alison, Lydia, Gordon, Alistair and John)
Attending consumers	Audience, ticket-buying public, attendees	Four (Robert, Sophie, Kate and Neil)
Supporting consumers	Government/civic organizations, grant funders, independent sponsors	Five (Clare, Daniel, Catherine, Moira and Robin)
Supplying consumers	Ticketing/design agency	Two (Tom and Andrew)

method was applied to understanding consumers' lived experiences of the Fringe brand (Thompson, Locander and Pollio 1989).

The sampling technique was 'snowballing', where initial informants recommended others of theoretical relevance (Goodman 1961). Loosely themed questions were developed in a semi-structured format and interviews were audiorecorded with consent. During the interviews, complimentary information was sought in the Fringe brand context, i.e., 'a first person description of the informant's brand usage history and . . . contextual details concerning the informant's life world' (Fournier 1998: 357).

Analysis involved verbatim transcription and assignation of pseudonyms to informants. The transcripts became the basis of a hermeneutical circle 'part-to-whole mode' of interpretation (Thompson, Locander and Pollio 1989: 141). A cross-case analysis identified themes that were compared with the dimensions and qualities of Fournier's (1998) specific brand relationship forms. Emerging brand relationship themes varied, but commonly encountered were Fringe brand loyalty, image/personality, and Fringe-self-image congruence.

A typology of Fringe–consumer brand relationships

The typology of Fringe–consumer brand relationship forms is based on the interview findings. The revealed Fringe-consumer brand relationships forms align with Fournier's (1998) dimensions and BRQ measures. The 21 informants' Fringe-consumer brand relationships correspond to 11 of Fournier's (1998) 15 existing consumer-brand relationship forms. These are categorized in terms of brand relationship form dimensions.

Best friendship: Susan

'Best friendships' are voluntary and based on reciprocity, with high self-image congruency and endurance ensured through positive rewards. There was one example of a Fringe-consumer 'best friendship' and this involved Susan (organizing consumer). Susan has a close and positive relationship with the Fringe. A former reviewer, performer and venue manager, she has been involved for 18 years. Susan is highly enthusiastic about the Fringe and the personal opportunities it has brought. She believes the Fringe reflects her own personality and has high affect for it, saying, 'I feel very involved. I feel this is just not a job here. I feel very affectionate towards it and also quite protective of it'.

Casual friendship: Emma

'Casual friendships' are characterized by infrequent engagement with low intimacy and few expectations for reciprocity. There was one case of a Fringe-consumer 'casual friendship' with Emma (participating consumer), a performer of more than 20 years. In the past she had 'superb fun' in amateur productions. She characterizes her emotional connection with performing as stronger than her commitment to the Fringe: 'I'm not very loyal at all!'

Childhood friendships: Clare, Robert and Sophie

While 'childhood friendships' are high in affect, they involve infrequent engagement, which would have been regular previously. Being reminiscent of earlier times, they yield comfort and security of past selves. Three instances were evident. The first was with Clare (supporting consumer) whose Fringe 'childhood friendship' was previously based on 'common associations' through sponsorship. Once close, this relationship has grown distant, which she attributes to a change in organizational direction: '(The Fringe) was like a good friend. It was reliable . . . you could talk . . . there was communication. But I don't think that that's there anymore, we're quite remote now!'

Robert (attending consumer) has 15 years' history with the Fringe as an audience member and previously worked with the Fringe. He describes himself as 'an audience member now, but one who is definitely interested in the success of the Fringe'. Robert has fond Fringe memories and attributes his experiences to contributing to his development and career. Robert is 'sadly, less involved now', but acknowledges since growing older he has had to move on: 'I don't think I'll ever see 40 shows in a festival again!' He describes his relationship as 'a close friend who you trust and can rely on, but don't have to be in contact with all the time!'

Sophie (attending consumer) considers herself as an audience member, although plans to become a performer. She also has eight years' history working with festival organizations. Sophie describes her relationship with the Fringe as 'buddies . . . we'd catch up when we're in town . . . I think it would be long term, but it wouldn't be weekly. It'd probably be seasonally'.

Compartmentalized friendships: Tom and Jenna

'Compartmentalized friendships' are highly specialized and situationally confined. Endurance is due to interdependence through contractual obligations. There are socio-emotional rewards associated with these relationships, but having lower intimacy than other friendships, they are easily accessed and exited.

There were two 'compartmentalized friendships'. The first was Tom's (supplying consumer). Tom's organization has supplied the Fringe for three years, contracted in a specialized role. He describes a strong attachment with rewarding opportunities to work creatively, saying: 'Financially we couldn't just work for the arts. The Fringe is unique, and it's such a high profile thing, it's something we're very keen to be involved in'. Jenna (participating consumer) manages independent venues leased to production companies during the Fringe. These otherwise operate differently. She depends on having a 'trusting and open relationship' with the Fringe, saying that 'it does bring a lot into the organization'.

Kinships: Mark, Daniel, Catherine, Moira and Robin

'Kinships' are nonvoluntary unions with lineage ties, and such family-based relationship forms were seen across five cases. The first was seen between Mark, a venue manager (organizing consumer), and the Fringe. Mark described a 'close-knit family . . . we're all part of a big dysfunctional family and people support each other'.

Four 'kinships' were seen between the Fringe and supporting consumers. Daniel's organization supports Edinburgh's festivals. He describes the relationship as 'nurturing but challenging', a kinship because of mutual necessity, explaining: 'you're not just choosing to be together, you have to be together'. Catherine's organization supports the Fringe. She describes their relationship as siblings: 'I'm not saying we're the bigger brother, but maybe the older brother'. Similarly, another supporting consumer, Moira, describes her brand relationship with the Fringe as being 'a close partnership' and 'trusted'. Her role involves working with related organizations. Finally, Robin also represents a supporting organization and describes a family network: 'we're part of a big family, cousins rather than brothers and sisters'.

Committed partnerships: Andrew, Alison and Lydia

'Committed partnerships' were seen in four cases. These are long-term, exclusive and voluntary in character with high commitment levels, so are true partnerships being socially supported with high affect, intimacy and trust. The first was Andrew's (supplying consumer). His organization has exclusively supplied the Fringe for 17 years. He works closely with it on a trusting and bespoke basis: 'we wrote our systems specifically for the Fringe'.

Alison (participating consumer) is an independent venue producer of more than 20 years and works exclusively with the Fringe: '(it) gives you that opportunity to create your own professional history through determination'. As another participating consumer, Lydia is a Fringe venue producer. Involved from childhood, she first performed in the 1970s and has been an artistic programmer for more than 20 years. She describes herself as 'sensationalist' about the Fringe, seeing it as 'a phenomenon'.

Arranged marriages: Margaret

'Arranged marriages' are nonvoluntary and generally third-party imposed. These are long-term, exclusive and tend to be relatively low in affect. Margaret (organizing consumer) is in an 'arranged marriage' with the Fringe. She was elected to her post with the Fringe Society more than ten years ago. Margaret has an exclusive relationship with the Fringe. Admitting a low previous emotional connection, she is now, however, 'hugely proud of it'.

Marriages of convenience: Gordon and Alistair

These relationships are long term and committed in nature but influenced by environmental forces. There were two 'marriages of convenience', both between participating consumers and the Fringe. Gordon, a former actor and current producer, has attended the Fringe since its beginning. Involved in amateur dramatics for 40 years, Gordon was previously a keen audience member, saying: 'personally it was the highlight of the year.' Now the survival of his theatre company depends on the Fringe: 'today it's purely commercial'. Alistair programmes an independent arts venue. He sees opportunities to produce new creative work specifically for the Fringe, saying: 'it's completely different to what we do normally'.

Dependencies: Kate

These 'dark-side' relationships are defined as obsessive and emotional. They evoke feelings of irreplaceability and separation anxiety, described as selfish attractions with high tolerance of transgressions. There was one 'dependency' Fringe-consumer brand relationship, seen in Kate (attending consumer). An audience member, Kate is a lifelong theatre goer. Seeing the Fringe as an intensive opportunity to attend productions by local amateur dramatic companies, Kate is emotional about the Fringe, saying: 'it's very important to me. If it wasn't there I would absolutely hate it . . . If it wasn't there, it would be awful. What would I do with myself in August?' Kate prefers to attend performances alone: 'I am selfish! I go to shows myself, because then I don't have to worry about anybody else enjoying it!' While Kate believes the Fringe has become 'over-commercial and over-priced' in recent years, this does not deter her.

Flings: Neil

As interim relationship forms, 'flings' are characterized as short term or time bounded. While emotional reward is associated with flings, they lack commitment and reciprocity. Neil (attending consumer) is in a 'fling' with the Fringe. An audience member, Neil is 'not loyal'. Rather, he enjoys the Fringe atmosphere, saying: 'I see that huge kind of buzz and vibrancy and lots of activity as being good thing. I wouldn't want it all year round, but . . . that to me signifies the festival is here!'

Courtships: John

'Courtships' are also interim relationships; however, these will develop into future committed partnerships. John (participating consumer) is a founding member of a young theatre company that has performed at the Fringe for the past three years. John's 'courtship' brand relationship with the Fringe is based upon opportunities counterbalanced with financial and personal risk. As John's company becomes established, this relationship is likely to develop into a partnership. Presently he sees the Fringe as 'very welcoming but very demanding . . . it has all the honey you can have, but it's also got all the bees that can sting you!'

Discussion

Fringe–consumer brand relationship forms are varied with the majority defined in dimensions of friendship, kinship and marriage. There was evidence of three distinct organizing consumer–brand relationships an: 'arranged marriage', 'kinship' and 'best friendship', all sharing elements of longevity and characterized by exclusivity and intensity. Susan's voluntarily formed, intense and enduring 'best friendship' was the strongest relationship with high affect and reciprocity levels. Susan viewed her own interests and background as being highly congruent to the Fringe and her brand relationship was perhaps the most positive of all 21.

Of the seven participating consumers, there were five brand relationship forms identified across this broadly characterized group: a 'courtship'; 'casual friendship'; 'compartmentalized friendship'; two 'committed partnerships'; and two 'marriages of convenience'. All were positive in their dimensions. Both supplying consumers had enduring Fringe-consumer brand relationships. Andrew's 'committed partnership' had developed throughout the years and was characterized by high levels of reciprocal and exclusive support, commitment and trust. A well-established relationship, this would endure adversity because of its inherent intimacy. Tom's supplier brand relationship was a 'compartmentalized friendship', although it had potential to become more established. Within the attending consumers group there were three forms of Fringe-consumer brand relationships: two 'childhood friendships', a 'fling' and a 'dependency'. A homogenous series of brand relationships was seen in the five supporting stakeholders interviewed with four demonstrating 'kinships' of 'non-voluntary unions with lineage ties' (Fournier 1998: 362). This similarity was unsurprising, as these organizations work in a network.

The future significance of these festival consumer-brand relationship forms deserves further investigation as brand relationship quality and strength alters over time in line with personal perceptions, experiences and external forces (Fournier 1998). It may be possible to identify particular factors contributing to festival-consumers' 'courtships' evolving into longer-term brand relationships; or to determine why close, frequently engaged brand relationships can become 'childhood friendships'. Examination of the festival–consumer brand relationship setting is required to establish any incidences of Fournier's (1998) 'dark' brand relationships, those secretly held, or based upon dimensions of addiction, pain and compulsion. One 'dependency' Fringe-consumer relationship form was identified, although without the associated negative dimensions. It may be that such relationships do not have a natural fit with festival consumers who are engaged in brand relationships on voluntary and public bases. This is a worthy question for future festivals, meriting further investigation in festival–consumer brand contexts, where consumers have intrinsic motivations to attend.

Being a contemporary investigation in the Fringe setting, this study would benefit from longitudinal consideration of consumers' changing roles and the consequent impacts upon brand relationships. As this chapter aims to present the relevance of brand relationship theory to future festivals, it should be highlighted the findings presented here summarize existing Fringe–consumer brand relationship forms. These may provide an initial grounding for future festivals research in this area.

Conclusions

The implications for the future of the event industry based upon the present are manifold. Brands are 'no longer made by organizations. Rather they are constructed in a space in which organizations are influencers and listeners' (Ind and Todd 2011: 47). Based on the standard world context, the forecast future festivalscape scenario envisioned in this chapter predicts an increasingly fragmented festivals market. Communications will be led by new technological abilities and numerous substitute experiential offers available by various means. The future festivalscape will therefore be highly competitive and consumer led. As this future evolves, the successful engagement of consumers with festival brands, as equitable and viable relationship partners, is essential to the survival of festivals.

Actively assuming a brand relationship perspective rather than a traditional marketing approach allows enhanced understanding of the role of brands in consumers' lives (Breivik and Thorbjørnsen 2008) with advantages of: 'reduced marketing costs, ease of access, acquiring new customers, customer retention, brand equity and more profit' (Smit, Bronner and Tolboom 2007: 627). In developing future festival brand concepts managers must build profitable, mutually beneficial and reciprocal relationships with consumers through effectively leveraging functional, symbolic and experiential conceptual brand dimensions. The present Fringe-consumer brand relationship typology provides evidence of such brand relationships within the setting of a festival-consumer setting and this is relevant to successful future festival brand managers.

Being an exploratory study of festival–consumer brand relationship, this chapter provides evidence of Fringe–consumer brand relationships across various roles and stages. The resulting Fringe–consumer brand relationship typology contributes to future knowledge by presenting this conceptual framework. Although an initial study and specific to the empirical Fringe setting, it is applicable to future festivals in its methodological approach and findings. There is strong evidence of a series of positive Fringe–consumer brand relationship forms across the sample that are rewarding and reciprocal, rather than negative. These share core dimensions of Fournier's (1998) consumer brand relationships. There may be much to learn from these and further questions to ask in terms of application to future management practice.

Returning to Fournier's (1998) BRQ measures of: love and passion; self-concept connection; interdependence; commitment; intimacy; and partner quality, there are potential benefits to considering this matrix as an alternative to consumer brand loyalty levels. Furthermore brand personality theory may be useful in shaping future marketing decisions. Despite receiving little attention in festival settings to date, future consideration of these constructs is recommended. As noted, there is evidence of these in the present Fringe-consumer brand relationships, based upon friendship, marriage and kinship forms. It is timely to question the most effective means of applying these concepts to the future marketing of festivals.

This chapter closes by emphasizing the relevance of the interpersonal relationship paradigm to future festivals. This is particularly in terms of its potential deep resonance with consumers who are seeking highly personalized, self-image-congruent, attached and intrinsic experiences with festival brands (Park *et al.* 2009). While there is much to be discovered about this important construct, managers of festivals should act now to harness this approach and develop their own brands as future-proof festival–consumer brand relationship partners, contributing to purposive, multiplex and dynamic relationships with consumers.

References

Aaker, D. (1991) *Managing Brand Equity: capitalizing on the value of a brand name.* New York, London: The Free Press, Maxwell Macmillan.

Aaker, J. (1997) 'Dimensions of brand personality', *Journal of Marketing Research*, 34(3): 347–56.

Aaker, J., Benet-Martinez, V. and Garolera, J. (2001) 'Consumption symbols as carriers of culture: a study of Japanese and Spanish brand personality constructs', *Journal of Personality and Social Psychology*, 81(3): 492–508.

Aaker, J., Fournier, S. and Brasel, A. (2004) 'When good brands do bad', *Journal of Consumer Research*, 31(1): 1–16.

Aggarwal, P. (2004) 'The effects of brand relationship norms on consumer attitudes and behaviour', *Journal of Consumer Research*, 31(1): 87–101.

Aron, A., Paris, M. and Aron, E. (1995) 'Falling in love: prospective studies of self-concept change', *Journal of Personality and Social Psychology*, 69(6): 1102–112.

Azoulay, A. and Kapferer, J. (2003) 'Do brand personality scales really measure brand personality?', *The Journal of Brand Management*, 11(2): 143–55.

Backman, C., Secord, P. and Peirce, J. (1963) 'Resistance to change in the self-concept as a function of consensus among significant others', *Sociometry*, 31(2): 102–11.

Bakewell, C. and Mitchell, V. (2003) 'Generation Y female consumer decision-making styles', *International Journal of Retail and Distribution Management*, 31(2): 95–106.

Belk, R. (1988) 'Possessions and the extended self', *The Journal of Consumer Research*, 15(2): 139–68.

Belk, R., Wallendorf, M. and Sherry, J. (1989) 'The sacred and the profane in consumer behavior: theodicy on the Odyssey', *The Journal of Consumer Research*, 16(1): 1–38.

Benckendorff, P. and Moscardo, G. (2010) 'Understanding Generation-Y tourists: managing the risk and change associated with a new emerging market', in P. Benckendorff, G. Moscardo and D. Pendergast (eds.) *Tourism and Generation Y.* Cambridge, MA: CAB International. pp. 38–45.

Bengtsson, A. (2003) 'Towards a critique of brand relationships', *Advances in Consumer Research*, 30: 154–58.

Bergman, A., Karlsson, J. and Axelsson, J. (2010) 'Truth claims and explanatory claims: an ontological typology of futures studies', *Futures*, 42(8): 857–65.

Bitner, M. (1992) 'Servicescapes: the impact of physical surroundings on customers and employees', *The Journal of Marketing*, 56: 57–71.

Bowdin, G., Allen, J., O'Toole, W., Harris, R. and McDonnell, I. (2011) *Events Management.* 3rd ed. Oxford: Elsevier Butterworth-Heinemann.

Breivik, E. and Thorbjørnsen, H. (2008) 'Consumer brand relationships: an investigation of two alternative models', *Journal of the Academy of Marketing Science*, 36: 443–72.

Burns, R. (1979) *The Self-Concept: theory, measurement, development and behaviour.* London: Longman Group Limited.

Chon, K. (1992) 'The role of destination image in tourism: an extension', *Tourism Review*, 47(1): 2–8.

Clarkson, M. (1995) 'A stakeholder framework for analyzing and evaluating corporate social performance', *Academy of Management Review*, 20(1): 92–117.

Crompton, J. and MacKay, S. (1997) 'Motives of visitors attending festival events', *Annals of Tourism Research*, 24(2): 425–439.

Ekinci, Y. and Hosany, S. (2006) 'Destination personality: an application of brand personality to tourism destinations', *Journal of Travel Research*, 45(2): 127–39.

Edinburgh Festival Fringe (2013) *World's Largest Arts Festival Draws to a Close for Another Year*. Online. Available <https://www.edfringe.com/news/world-s-largest-arts-festival-draws-to-a-close-for-another-year> (accessed 27 August 2013).

Esch, F., Langner, T., Schmitt, B. and Geus, P. (2006) 'Are brands forever? How brand knowledge and relationships affect current and future purchases', *Journal of Product and Brand Management*, 15(2): 98–105.

Festivals Edinburgh and BOP Consulting (2011) *Edinburgh Festivals Impact Study*. Online. Available <http://www.festivalsedinburgh.com/sites/default/files/Edinburgh%20festivals%202010%20Impact%20Study%20Report.pdf> (accessed 30 July 2013).

Fournier, S. (1998) 'Consumers and their brands: developing relationship theory in consumer research', *Journal of Consumer Research*, 24(4): 343–53.

Fournier, S. (2009) 'Lessons learned about consumers' relationships with their brands', in D. MacInnis, C. Park and J. Priester (eds.) *Handbook of Brand Relationships*. New York: ME Sharpe Incorporated, pp. 5–23.

Fyall, A. (2011) 'Destination management: challenges and opportunities', in Y. Wang and A. Pizam (eds.) *Destination Marketing and Management: theories and applications*. Wallingford: CABI International, pp. 340–57.

Gelder, G. and Robinson, P. (2009) 'A critical comparative study of visitor motivations for attending music festivals: a case study of Glastonbury and V Festival', *Event Management*, 13(3): 181–96.

Getz, D. (2012) *Event Studies: theory, research and policy for planned events*. 2nd ed. Oxford: Elsevier Butterworth-Heinemann.

Goodman, L. (1961) 'Snowball sampling', *The Annals of Mathematical Statistics*, 32(1): 148–70.

Haigh, D. (2006) 'Scenarios in brand valuation and brand portfolio strategy' in G. Ringland and L. Young (eds.) *Scenarios in Marketing: from vision to decision*, Chichester: John Wiley & Sons, pp. 101–18.

Hess, J. and Story, J. (2005) 'Trust-based commitment: multidimensional consumer-brand relationships', *Journal of Consumer Marketing*, 22(6): 313–22.

Heath, R., Brandt, D. and Nairn, A. (2006) 'Brand relationships: strengthened by emotion, weakened by attention', *Journal of Advertising Research*, 46(4): 410–19.

Hinde, R. (1979) *Towards Understanding Relationships*. London: European Association of Experimental Social Psychology, Academic Inc.

Hirschman, E. (1992) 'The consciousness of addiction: toward a general theory of compulsive consumption', *The Journal of Consumer Research*, 19(2): 155–79.

Hosany, S., Ekinci, Y. and Uysal, M. (2006) 'Destination image and destination personality: An application of branding theories to tourism places', *Journal of Business Research*, 59 (5): 638–42.

Ind, N. (2003) *Beyond Branding*. London: Kogan Page.

Ind, N. (2007) *Living the Brand: how to transform every member of your organization into a brand champion*. London: Kogan Page.

Ind, N. and Todd, L. (2011) 'Beyond the Fringe: creativity and the city' in F. Go and R. Govers (eds.) *International Place Branding Yearbook 2011: reputation under pressure*. Chippenham: Palgrave Macmillan, pp. 47–59.

Jevons, C., Gabbott, M. and de Chernatony, L. (2005) 'Customer and brand manager perspectives on brand relationships: a conceptual framework', *Journal of Product and Brand Management*, 14(5): 300–09.

Ji, M. (2002) 'Children's relationships with brands: "True love" or "One-night" stand?', *Psychology and Marketing*, 19(4): 369–87.

Khan, H. and Wiener, A. (1967) *The year 2000: a framework for speculation on the next thirty-three years*. New York: Macmillan.

Kates, S. (2000) 'Out of the closet and out on the street! Gay men and their brand relationships', *Psychology and Marketing*, 17(6): 493–513.

Keller, K. (1993) 'Conceptualizing, measuring, and managing customer-based brand equity', *Journal of Marketing*, 57: 1–22.

Keller, K. (2008) *Strategic Brand Management: building, measuring and managing brand equity*. 3rd ed. Upper Saddle River, NJ: Pearson Prentice Hall.

Kupperschmidt, B. (2000) 'Multigeneration employees: strategies for effective management', *The Health Care Manager*, 19: 65–76.

Kvale, S. and Brinkmann, S. (2009) *Interviews: Learning the Craft of Qualitative Research Interviewing*. Los Angeles, London, New Delhi, Singapore: Sage Publications.

Leask, A. and Barron, P. (2012) 'Engaging with Gen Y at museums', in M. Smith and G. Richards (eds.) *Handbook of Cultural Tourism*. London: Routledge, pp. 396–403.

Lee, Y. K., Lee, C. K., Lee, S. K. and Babin, B. (2008) 'Festivalscapes and patrons' emotions, satisfaction, and loyalty', *Journal of Business Research*, 61(1): 56–64.

MacInnis, D., Park, C. and Priester, J. (2009) 'Introduction: what brand relationships?', in D. MacInnis, C. Park and J. Priester (eds.) *Handbook of Brand Relationships*. New York: ME Sharpe Incorporated, pp. ix–xxi.

Moffat, A. (1978) *The Edinburgh Fringe*. New York: Johnston and Bacon.

Morgan-Thomas, A. and Veloutsou, C. (2011) 'Beyond technology acceptance: brand relationships and online brand experience', *Journal of Business Research*, 66(1): 21–7.

Murphy, L., Moscardo, G. and Benckendorff, P. (2007) 'Using brand personality to differentiate regional tourism destinations', *Journal of Travel Research*, 46(1): 5–14.

Neuborne, E. and Kerwin, K. (1999) '*Generation Y: Today's teens – the biggest bulge since the boomers – may force marketers to toss their old tricks*. Online. Available <www.businessweek.com/stories/1999-02-14/generation-y > (accessed 20 January 2012).

Park, C., Jaworski, B. and MacInnis, D. (1986) 'Strategic brand concept-image management', *The Journal of Marketing*, 50: 135–45.

Park, C., Priester, J., MacInnis, D. and Wan, Z. (2009) 'The connection-prominence attachment model (CPAM): a conceptual and methodical examination of brand attachment' in D. MacInnis, C. Park, J. and J. Priester (eds.) *Handbook of Brand Relationships*. New York: ME Sharpe Incorporated, pp. 306–27.

Patterson, M. (1999) 'Re-appraising the concept of brand image', *Journal of Brand Management*, 6(6): 409–36.

Pattinson, H. and Sood, S. (2010) 'Marketers expressing the future: scenario planning for marketing action', *Futures*, 42(4): 417–26.

Picturehouse Entertainment (2013) *Available Now*. Online. Available <www.picturehouse entertainment.co.uk/available-now/alternative-content.html> (accessed 31 July 2013).

Pine, J. and Gilmore, J. (1998) 'Welcome to the experience economy', *Harvard Business Review*, 76: 97–105.

Porter, M. (1998) *Competitive Strategy: techniques for analysing industries and competitors*. New York: The Free Press

O'Cass, A. and Frost, H. (2002) 'Status brands: examining the effects of non-product-related brand associations on status and conspicuous consumption', *Journal of Product and Brand Management*, 11(2): 67–88.

Reid, S. and Arcodia, C. (2002) 'Understanding the role of the stakeholder in event management', in *Proceedings of: Events and place making. UTS Business: Event Research Conference, UTS Australian Centre for Event Management*. University of Technology, Sydney, Australia in Association with CRC in Sustainable Tourism. Sydney. 15–16 July, pp. 479–515.

Richards, G. and Palmer, R. (2010) *Eventful Cities: cultural management and urban revitalisation*. Oxford: Elsevier Butterworth-Heinemann.

Richins, M. (1994) 'Special possessions and the expression of material values', *The Journal of Consumer Research*, 21(3): 522–33.

Ringland, G. (2006) 'Introduction to scenario planning' in G. Ringland and L. Young (eds.) *Scenarios in Marketing: from vision to decision*. Chichester: John Wiley & Sons, pp. 1–18.

Rosenbaum-Elliott, R., Percy, L. and Pervan, S. (2011) *Strategic Brand Management*. 2nd ed. Oxford: Oxford University Press.

Ross, I. (1971) 'Self-concept and brand preference', *The Journal of Business*, 44(1): 38–50.

Schouten, J. (1991) 'Selves in transition: Symbolic consumption in personal rites of passage and identity reconstruction', *The Journal of Consumer Research*, 17(4): 412–25.

Schultz, D. (2006) 'Marketing communication: Radical or rational change?' in G. Ringland and L. Young (eds.) *Scenarios in Marketing: from vision to decision*. Chichester: John Wiley & Sons, pp. 119–39.

Sirgy, M. (1982) 'Self-concept in consumer behavior: a critical review', *Journal of Consumer Research*, 9: 287–300.

Smit, E., Bronner, F. and Tolboom, M. (2007) 'Brand relationship quality and its value for personal contact', *Journal of Business Research*, 60(6): 627–33.

Solomon, M. (1983) 'The role of products as social stimuli: a symbolic interactionism perspective', *Journal of Consumer Research*, 10(3): 3–19.

Thompson, C., Locander, W. and Pollio, H. (1989) 'Putting consumer experience back into consumer research: the philosophy and method of existential-phenomenology', *The Journal of Consumer Research*, 16(2): 133–46.

Todd, L. (2010) 'A stakeholder model of the Edinburgh Festival Fringe' in *Proceedings of: UK Centre for Events Management, Global Events Congress IV: Festivals and Events Research: State of the Art*. UK Centre for Events Management, Leeds Metropolitan University, Leeds. 14–16 July.

Todd, L. (2011) *Festival Images: brand image and stakeholders' brand relationship types at the Edinburgh Festival Fringe*. School of Marketing, Tourism & Languages, Edinburgh Napier University, Business School (Unpublished PhD Thesis).

Xue, F. (2008) 'The moderating effects of product involvement on situational brand choice', *Journal of Consumer Marketing*, 23(2): 85–94.

Yeoman, I., Greenwood, C. and McMahon-Beattie, U. (2009) 'The future of Scotland's international tourism markets', *Futures*, 41(6): 387–395.

Yeoman, I. and McMahon-Beattie, U. (2011) 'The future challenge' in N. Morgan, A Pritchard and R. Pride (eds.) *Destination Brands*. 3rd ed. Oxford: Butterworth-Heinemann, pp. 169–182.

13 Exploring future forms of event volunteering

Leonie Lockstone-Binney, Tom Baum, Karen A. Smith and Kirsten Holmes

Future points

- This chapter uses a literature review to identify key trends and challenges for event volunteering.
- Key trends affecting the future of event volunteering include demographic change, increased time pressures, corporate volunteering, pressure to increase diversity and advances in information and communications technology.
- These trends suggest that the future event volunteer market will be more segmented and differentiated, and event volunteering will take more diverse forms.
- The chapter proposes new forms of event volunteering that may emerge in the future including event volunteer junkies, virtual event volunteers and corporate event volunteers.

Event volunteering: current understandings

Event volunteering has grown in popularity as an area of research interest in recent years. Sporting and mega events, in particular, have been afforded significant attention as the backdrop to event volunteering studies. Common topics of interest across the field include a focus on examining event volunteer profiles, motivations and expectations (Farrell, Johnston and Twynam 1998; Strigas and Jackson 2003; Twynam, Farrell and Johnston 2002/03); experiences and satisfaction (Farrell *et al.* 1998); aspects of commitment (Cuskelly *et al.* 2004; Elstad 2003; Green and Chalip 2004) and trends and management issues (Coyne and Coyne 2001; Smith and Lockstone 2009). There is, however, a dearth of studies examining dominant and alternative models of event volunteering.

As the setting for hosting event volunteers, event organizations are different from more traditional organizations, as they require a large workforce for a short period of time. There is a period of rapid hiring before the event, a labor-intensive workload during the event, and dismissal after the event (Yufang 2005). For a one-off event, such as many mega events are, the organization is time limited and the workforce, including volunteers, is employed only once (although there may be a central governing body that oversees the operation of an event that moves between locations). For periodic events that recur on a regular basis, these organizations can be described as 'pulsating' (Hanlon and Jago 2004), as they hugely expand their structure and personnel numbers for the event before quickly contracting back to their original size. In many cases, it is volunteers who provide much of the increase in staff during the event. Volunteers might be involved just once, or may return to volunteer at the event each time it is held.

The size of the event influences how volunteers are involved and managed. Broadly speaking, mega and major events have complex organizational structures and a formalized and structured approach to volunteer management, which reflects the dominant event volunteer management approach, the program management model. According to this model, volunteers are recruited and assigned to roles, which meet the needs of the program, rather than attempting to meet the needs of the volunteers (Meijs and Hoogstad 2001). This model seeks to replicate the Human Resource Management practices used for paid staff with a volunteer workforce. Unlike their smaller counterparts, mega event volunteer programs are typically massively oversubscribed (Baum and Lockstone 2007); for example, the 2012 London Olympics received over 240,000 applications for 70,000 volunteer places. In smaller-scale event organizations, volunteer management is usually informal, ad hoc and often insufficiently resourced. The type of event organization is also important. Not-for-profit organizations commonly run many smaller-scale events and are also involved in larger-scale events, especially in the cultural sector. They will involve volunteers in governance roles as a board of trustees (Saleh and Wood 1998) and may be completely volunteer based with no paid staff. Volunteers are also involved with commercial events that are run on a profit-making basis and although this can cause tensions and raise ethical considerations, these issues are rarely discussed (Ferdinand 2008; Nogawa 2004).

Smith and Lockstone (2009) discussed different models of volunteer recruitment at cultural festivals. They identified two main sources of new volunteers: individuals and groups, with individuals recruited through word-of-mouth and special interest groups. They also noted that some events commission third parties such as volunteer centers or bureaux to recruit individual volunteers on their behalf. When recruiting groups of volunteers, event managers can work with established groups within their communities, such as community organizations, education institutions and businesses (including employer-supported volunteering programs). These groups provide volunteers for a particular role – for example, taking responsibility for a functional area such as stewarding or ticket sales.

Method

Having laid the groundwork for the reader's understanding of event volunteering and its management, this paper adopts an exploratory approach to envisage the forms that event volunteering may take in the years leading up to 2025.

The study is underpinned by a comprehensive literature review. The qualitative method that has been deployed is used widely in conducting foresight studies (Popper 2008) and has been supplemented where possible with relevant quantitative data (Karlsen and Karlsen 2013). The researchers reviewed the relevant academic and industry literatures on event volunteering and its parent field of volunteering, using search terms such as 'future', 'trends' and 'patterns'. The results were used to determine the key drivers affecting event volunteering and volunteering in general, with a view to assessing their ongoing impact.

The researchers propose a series of prospective future forms of event volunteering on the basis of these inputs and four key assumptions. These are:

1. There will be still be events and they will essentially mirror the current form and content of established event types despite some incremental development. A thorough discussion of the drivers affecting future events is beyond the scope of this chapter and is covered elsewhere in this edited collection.
2. Volunteering will remain an important and universally recognized cornerstone of civil societies (United Nations Volunteers 2011).
3. There will still be a need for, daresay a dependence on, volunteers for the success and survival of all types of events.
4. Mega and major events will continue to rely on the program management model with some incremental development to recruit, train, deploy and reward the tens of thousand of volunteers involved in these events. Given the established dominance of this model, it is not separately discussed as a future form of event volunteering, although it is acknowledged that for mega events in particular, with the increasingly long lead times from bidding to host city announcement and actual hosting of the event (often a cycle in excess of 10 years), organizers will have to factor in a decade or more of social, economic and political change that might affect the future efficacy of this currently accepted model.

Seven future forms of event volunteer result, and are labelled event volunteer junkies, outsourced, corporate, virtual, invisible, offset and bring your own (BYO) event volunteers. The authors do not emphasize the prevalence of any one future form relative to another. In practice, different configurations of the forms may eventuate (and even others that are not considered here). Though the forms provide alternative pictures and narratives for the years leading to 2025, the researchers do not propose precise timeframes. In particular the authors accept Yeoman's position (2012) that the future becomes increasingly unclear when imagined over an extended timeframe, with scenarios for the distant future akin to Bergman, Karlsson and Axelson's (2010) science fiction paradigm.

The authors acknowledge the limitations of this exploratory method. As a means of providing foresight a literature review is frequently used to accompany other techniques. This is commonly the case at the preliminary stage as an input into later stages of the foresight process, with more complex foresight methods involving the collection of primary data. Popper (2008: 68), for example, proposed an alignment of the literature review with the first stage of the foresight generation process, namely 'exploration', which is used to 'identify and understand important issues, trends and drivers'. The proceeding stages of 'analysis' and 'anticipation' establish the links between drivers and map out future scenarios using techniques such as expert panels, extrapolation, modelling and scenarios. Noting this caveat, the exploration detailed in this chapter provides grounding for researchers who wish to proceed to the subsequent stages of analysis and anticipation and to develop scenarios in the true sense of the futures/foresights literature. Having laid the groundwork for the future forms to be presented, the chapter now turns to discussion of the key trends influencing volunteering and event volunteering in particular, as identified in the literature review.

Trends affecting volunteering

Recognition is growing within academic and policy circles of the central importance of volunteering as a contributor to resilient, civil societies. The United Nations' *State of the World's Volunteerism Report* (United Nations Volunteers 2011: 2) highlights the universal nature of volunteerism in that 'it is an integral part of every society'. Given its centrality, various researchers have examined the major trends affecting volunteering so as to ensure its sustainable future (Evans and Saxton 2005; Finlay and Murray 2005; Merrill 2006). The key themes that emerge across these studies include demographic change, increased choice and time pressures, advances in information and communications technology (ICT), new forms of volunteering and increased diversity. Each trend will be briefly reviewed before its impact on future forms of event volunteering is considered.

Demographic change

Demographic change offers both possibilities and limitations for event volunteerism. The large pool of baby boomers (those born between 1946 and 1961/1962) has been highlighted as a plentiful source of volunteers (Rochester, Ellis Paine and Howlett 2009). In Australia, for example, approximately one-quarter of the population is predicted to be over 65 years of age by 2050, up from 13.5 percent in 2012 (Australian Government 2012). The most educated, affluent and discerning generation to retire, they are likely to expect more from their retirement activities than previous generations. Nevertheless, declining pensions, increased retirement ages and labor shortages in some sectors mean that volunteer organizations will need to compete with each other, continued paid work, other leisure options and family commitments for volunteers' time (Finlay and Murray 2005). There is recognition of the need to engage this cohort as they set their retirement priorities (Volunteering Australia 2007). These individuals have high expectations that will need to be understood and met. Short-term roles such as event volunteering are more likely to appeal to them than ongoing, regular volunteering.

Demographic change will also mean that many developed countries have fewer young people as a proportion of their population. Young people may view volunteering instrumentally, as a means of gaining skills or work experience, particularly as educational institutions increasingly move to embed student volunteering placements as a form of service learning in degree programs (Haski-Leventhal, Meijs and Hustinx 2009). Event organizers are well placed to take advantage of this trend including working with students on the increasing number of event management degree programs in the United Kingdom, Australia and the United States (Barron and Leask 2012), many of which include compulsory or optional work placement programs.

Increased choice and time pressures

Increased choice among the various free-time options available to people today and in the future means that volunteering is in competition with a multitude of other activities. This has been exacerbated by a reduction in many governments' services and an increased reliance on volunteering (United Nations Volunteers 2011), which leads to increased competition among organizations for the pool of willing volunteers. Volunteers are likely to seek more flexible roles and commitments (Lockstone, Smith and Baum 2010; Evans and Saxton 2005) and also desire more enriching volunteer experiences (Finlay and Murray 2005). In order to achieve this, volunteering needs to improve its image (Rochester *et al.* 2009), as research shows that the word most strongly associated with volunteering is 'commitment', and tomorrow's volunteers are likely to be cause driven rather than time driven (Evans and Saxton 2005). Event volunteering, which is associated with novel, chance of lifetime experiences (Farrell *et al.* 1998), is likely to offer a more attractive image of volunteering than other forms.

Event volunteering can benefit from the emergent trend of episodic volunteering (Macduff 1991, 2005), driven by changing leisure and work patterns, demographic trends and perceived time pressures (Merrill 2006). Holmes and Smith (2009: 40) define episodic volunteers as 'those with flexible volunteering patterns who volunteer with an organization on an infrequent, occasional, or short-term basis'. This temporally bound commitment distinguishes episodic volunteers from their volunteer counterparts undertaking more traditional regular and ongoing commitments. The episodic nature of event volunteering may see volunteers of all ages engage as a one-off activity or return to an event organization in a series of episodic reengagements (e.g., volunteering once a year at an annual event), a pattern called 'bounce-back' by Bryen and Madden (2006).

Advances in information and communications technology

ICT offers opportunities for virtual volunteering and for individuals to assist an organization remotely, but ICT also has implications for the management of volunteer programs – for example, volunteer recruitment via matching websites. ICT tools such the Internet and mobile communication technologies offer a means to engage new volunteer markets, for example, by using social networking sites to reach young people (Commission on the Future of Volunteering 2008). ICT can enable people with disabilities or mobility constraints to get or stay involved in a volunteer program (Rochester *et al.* 2009), which is important in light of the documented link between personal well-being and volunteering (Mellor *et al.* 2008). ICT eliminates the need for face-to-face contact, providing greater flexibility for volunteers to engage wherever and whenever they want (United Nations Volunteers 2011). Online volunteers typically engage in tasks such as fundraising, website development and maintenance and research (Rochester *et al.* 2009; United Nations Volunteers 2011), all of which are essential to event organizations.

Corporate or employee volunteering

Employee volunteering or corporate volunteering as also been cited as both a trend and an opportunity, which has hitherto been underexploited (Commission on the Future of Volunteering 2008). Encouraging employees to commit their time and expertise to volunteer activities undertaken during or outside of working hours, to date large commercial companies and public sector agencies have taken most advantage of these programs as an expression of their commitment to corporate social responsibility (CSR) (Haski-Leventhal *et al.* 2009; United Nations Volunteers 2011). There is the potential, however, for volunteer organizations to devise programs that both appeal to, and are flexible for individuals and groups of employees who seek to fit their volunteering within or around their working day. This form of volunteering, as with student volunteering mentioned earlier, has been challenged in terms of its 'voluntary' nature. Rochester *et al.* (2009) highlight that employees may feel compelled to participate and that nonparticipation may be viewed as negatively affecting future performance appraisals. They go on to suggest that employees ultimately may be undertaking projects of their employers' choosing, thereby obviating any personal choice they would have had as to where they 'volunteer' their time.

Corporate volunteering programs can provide large numbers of employees as volunteers, but they often want a distinct project that can be completed in a short period of time. Event organizations offering flexible and episodic opportunities could thus benefit from employee volunteering.

Increased diversity

It has been argued that volunteering should and will become more diverse (Commission on the Future of Volunteering 2008; Finlay and Murray 2005). This does not just mean more diverse in terms of the individuals who volunteer but also in the ways in which they become involved with an organization, evident from the trends discussed in this chapter. As such, volunteering and volunteer management will become more complex and demanding, will require resources and interventions but can bring rewards to the volunteer and organization, as well as have positive impacts for communities and society more generally.

Combined, these trends point to an increasing and continued market for event volunteering opportunities in the future. This chapter will now explore the potential diverse forms of event volunteering.

Future forms of event volunteering

Based on the literature review findings, the ensuing discussion highlights a number of future forms event volunteering might take in the years leading up to 2025.

Event volunteer junkies

This future form focuses event volunteer junkies as serial event volunteers that in most cases are less committed to a specific event type but are 'addicts' of the generic event volunteering experience. This high level of multiple reengagements may be viewed as an extreme form of Bryen and Madden's (2006) 'bounce-back' concept or as akin to Handy, Brodeur and Cnaan's (2006) categorization of 'Habitual Episodic Volunteers'. A management model for harnessing the interest of event junkies is highlighted in Nichols and Ralston's (2012: 173) case study of the organization Manchester Event Volunteers (MEV). Established in the wake of the 2002 Commonwealth Games, this legacy initiative operated by Manchester City Council 'acts as a broker between volunteers and event organizers by maintaining a database of 1500 volunteers, advertising events to them and, once they have expressed interest, passing their contact details on to the event organizers'. Nichols and Ralston (2012) go on to note that the initiative annually supports approximately 150 events. In further findings, they suggest that MEV's role suits the episodic desires of serial volunteers to reengage when they want and that on the other side of the coin, event organizers value the event-specific experience and training of MEV recruited volunteers.

Whilst the MEV model can usefully serve event junkies who volunteer with events in their local community, there will be a smaller cohort of extreme event junkies that travel the world following the path of globally roaming mega events. Research already attests to their existence (Fairley, Kellett and Green 2007; Lockstone and Baum 2009); however, key challenges affecting air travel more generally, including climate change and rising oil prices, might curb this form of extreme event volunteering into the future.

Outsourced event volunteers

Identified by Smith and Lockstone (2009), this future form of event volunteering is predicted to grow in importance to the mutual benefit of all parties involved. For the event organizer, increasing time pressures will lead them to seek recruiting shortcuts to established cohorts of potential volunteers, dealing only with key gate-keepers to each group (not individual volunteers) in the process. In outsourcing functional roles or areas to community organizations and educational institutions, event organizers can incidentally increase civic engagement in their events. For the community groups (e.g., Rotary, Lions) that are allowing access to their members, the event organizer typically rewards this support with a financial contribution towards group projects or causes. As Smith and Lockstone (2009: 161) note, 'in this model, individuals may feel more commitment towards their club or group rather than the event, and while this is not necessarily a problem, it is an area that warrants further investigation'. Similar concerns regarding commitment may be raised by the increasing prospect of student volunteers recruited by way of the growing number of event management (and related) education programs to undertake work placements at events. However, the highly temporal nature of events, combined with student's desires to 'taste' a range of event experiences, may lessen the importance of their commitment needing to be directed to a specific event. This is particularly the case if the student (in gaining skills and experience), the education institution (in ensuring their students gain work experience as part of a formal qualification) and the event organizer (in getting the contribution of students' time) each get want they want out of the limited engagement. In terms of a broader commitment to volunteering, however, it has been argued that service learning opportunities 'have better long-term impact if they are optional rather than compulsory' (Haski-Leventhal *et al.* 2009: 151).

Corporate event volunteers

There is definite scope for events to target corporate volunteering programs given that event volunteering can offer distinct, one-off and flexible experiences and that the pressure on companies to act as good corporate citizens is unlikely to diminish. In the context of major events, corporate volunteering programs may increasingly align to corporate sponsorship of events, so that organizations give both cash and in-kind (staff) support to certain headline events. This trend could evolve into cash for contribution schemes where companies match their sponsorship dollars to the hours of volunteering committed. For small and medium-sized enterprises that have been slower to engage with employer-supported volunteering schemes (United Nations Volunteers 2011), similar value may lie in partnering with community events, whereby employees feel their volunteering is directly benefiting the local community, whilst the company benefits from the visibility afforded from being one of a smaller number of event sponsors (say, compared to major events).

It must be acknowledged that the majority of corporate event volunteering will likely take place outside of normal business hours, as the events space exists beyond Monday–Friday, 9am–5pm. Rochester *et al.* (2009: 109), in reference to Tschirhart's (2005) work, highlights that 'to what extent the activity [corporate volunteering] takes place in work time; it can be seen as more or less "voluntary"'. This timing issue can be easily compensated for in terms of recognized HR practices (e.g., offering days off in lieu for time volunteered on weekends), thereby ensuring that corporate event volunteering is truly an informed personal choice on the part of the employee. Coming from the corporate world with specialist financial, marketing and planning expertise, this volunteer cohort can support events separately or in addition to the operational level by way of specific management projects or short-term contributions to board subcommittees.

Virtual event volunteers

Virtual event volunteers, like their corporate counterparts, will also likely engage with events beyond immediate event operations. Their virtual, distant presence in the context of 'real' events allows these volunteers to engage in tasks such as fundraising, website management and research for event organizations at a time and place of their choosing. Increasingly, event organizers may use virtual event volunteers to engage on their behalf with social networking sites such as Twitter and Facebook to generate online word-of-mouth.

Virtual event volunteers may be a misnomer in the context of Bergman, Karlsson and Axelson's (2010) science fiction paradigm of future studies. It is not suggested that there will be 'virtual volunteers' working at 'virtual events' in the foreseeable future. Whilst the use of haptic technologies (Yeoman 2012) might make this a possibility by enabling through touch and feel the sensation of volunteering at virtual events all from the comfort of one's home, it seems for the most part an exercise in futility. Events operating in a 'virtual environment' have no concrete need or dependence on volunteers for their livelihoods.

Invisible event volunteers

Event organizers driven by cost pressures may increasingly involve event audiences in the co-production (Bitner *et al.* 1997) of event experiences, shifting tasks done traditionally by paid staff or specifically recruited event volunteers onto the audience with or without their tacit knowledge. This blurring of service boundaries could see attendees become 'invisible volunteers' through their engagement with events. For example, festival goers could be involved in providing backstage support to the artists such as transport or refreshments. This could be sold to audiences as an opportunity to get close to the performers and see behind the scenes at the event. Innovative event organizers will be best placed to take advantage of this future form by holistically (front- and backstage) evaluating engagement opportunities at the service interface between events and their audiences.

Offset event volunteering

Increasing recognition of the environmental impacts of events may see 'offset event volunteering' arise as a viable and accepted future form. Research highlights that much of the environmental impact of event attendees is generated by travel to and from events (Collins, Jones and Munday 2009; Collins, Munday and Roberts 2012). Event organizers can promote 'offset event volunteering' as a donation of volunteer time by audiences to compensate for travel-related and on-site environmental impacts. This donation would most logically go towards cleanup efforts at the site to return it to its pre-event state.

Bring your own (BYO) event volunteering

Grassroots sporting organizations, in particular, will increasingly rely on the BYO model to recruit volunteers. Increased competition for a shrinking pool of 'time poor' volunteers, in particular people in the 35–44 years age group who sports organizations heavily rely upon (Australian Bureau of Statistics 2011) to support their events, will lead to athletes/competitors having to supply a volunteer (mostly likely a friend or family member) as a prerequisite to event participation. The BYO volunteer model is already in place at some sporting events but offers opportunities for any event or festival that is participant, rather than spectator, driven.

Implications and conclusion

The analysis of current trends and forecasting of certain future forms of event volunteering offers significant implications for the event industry. These will be dependent on the size, scale and frequency of the event; the event's profile and the resources both available to the event and needed for its success. For example, high-profile and well-resourced events are better placed to market themselves to corporate volunteering programs. Regular events can develop good, ongoing relationships with community organizations and local companies to recruit 'bounce-back' and outsourced volunteers. Events with strong levels of participant commitment will be able to make the most use of BYO volunteering.

The trends suggest that the future event volunteer market will be considerably more differentiated and segmented than it is at present. Future event volunteers will be able to engage in events in many different ways, via one or more of the forms discussed here. This means that volunteer management could become more complex and most efficiently achieved by recruiting different segments of volunteers to take on specific tasks. A festival manager could recruit virtual event volunteers to assist with the pre-event marketing; a corporate team to help set up the festival site; a group of invisible event volunteers to assist on the day in shepherding the artists and have the site cleaned and bumped out by a team of offset event volunteers (under supervision). In contrast, a local sports event may recruit event volunteer junkies from a government-run broker service to steward the event; outsource running of the car parking to a local community organization and mandate that participants supply their own volunteer to help pack up the site afterwards.

Many of the future forms will challenge the traditional definition of volunteering as increasing levels of obligation pervade these forms and the ensuing commitment of volunteers. The questions that will need to be asked in the future replicate many that are already being examined, such as will the volunteer be committed to the event or their club (in the case of the outsourced model), or their family member competing (in the case of the BYO model) or their company (in the case of corporate volunteering)? Will corporate or outsourced groups be best managed by one of their own? How can BYO volunteers receive the necessary training, and how will this affect the tasks that can be assigned to them? What rewards will be needed for volunteers who are participating as part of a group or out of obligation (e.g., BYO volunteers)? Volunteer managers will need to rethink both the management and the rewards offered to volunteers. Event volunteering, regardless of form, will persist to 2025 while needing to meet the challenges described in this chapter and ones yet to be envisioned.

References

Australian Bureau of Statistics (2011) *Voluntary Work, Australia 2010. Cat No. 4441.0 2010.* Canberra: ABS.

Australian Government (2012) *Australia in the Asian Century.* Canberra: Commonwealth of Australia.

Barron, P. and Leask, A. (2012) 'Events management education', in S.J. Page and J. Connell (eds) *The Routledge Handbook of Events.* Abingdon: Routledge, pp. 473–88.

Baum, T. and Lockstone, L. (2007) 'Volunteers and mega sporting events: Developing a research framework', *International Journal of Event Management Research*, 3(1): 29–41.

Bergman A., Karlsson, J. and Axelson, J. (2010) 'Truth claims and explanatory claims: An ontological typology of future studies', *Futures*, 42: 857–65.

Bitner, M.J., Faranda, W.T., Hubbert, A.R. and Zeithaml, V.A. (1997) 'Customer contributions and roles in service delivery', *International Journal of Service Industry Management*, 8(3): 193–205.

Bryen, L. and Madden, K. (2006) *Bounce-back of Episodic Volunteers: what makes episodic volunteers return?* Unpublished manuscript, Brisbane.

Collins, A., Jones, C. and Munday, M. (2009) 'Assessing the environmental impacts of mega sporting events: Two options?', *Tourism Management*, 30: 828–37.

Collins, A., Munday, M. and Roberts, A. (2012) 'Environmental consequences of tourism consumption at major events: an analysis of the UK stages of the 2007 Tour de France', *Journal of Travel Research*, 51(5): 577–90.

Commission on the Future of Volunteering. (2008) *Report of the Commission on the Future of Volunteering: manifesto for change*. London: Volunteering England.

Coyne, B.S. and Coyne, E.J. (2001) 'Getting, keeping and caring for unpaid volunteers for professional golf tournament events', *Human Resource Development International*, 4(2): 199–214.

Cuskelly, G., Auld, C., Harrington, M. and Coleman, D. (2004) 'Predicting the behavioural dependability of sport event volunteers', *Event Management*, 9: 73–89.

Elstad, B. (2003) 'Continuance commitment and reasons to quit: a study of volunteers at a jazz festival', *Event Management*, 8: 99–108.

Evans, E. and Saxton, J. (2005) *The 21st Century Volunteer*. London: nfpSynergy.

Fairley, S., Kellett, P. and Green, B.C. (2007) 'Volunteering abroad: Motives for travel to volunteer at the Athens Olympic Games', *Journal of Sport Management*, 21(1): 41–57.

Farrell, J., Johnston, M. and Twynam, D. (1998) 'Volunteer motivation, satisfaction and management and an elite sporting competition', *Journal of Sport Management*, 12: 288–300.

Ferdinand, N. (2008) 'The benefits of using student volunteers for small businesses in the event industry: the use of student volunteers at Concert Live', *Journal of Tourism, Sport and Creative Industries*, 1: 39–53.

Finlay, J. and Murray, M. (2005) *Possible Futures: changes, volunteering and the not-for-profit sector*. Sydney: The Smith Family.

Green, B.C. and Chalip, L. (2004). 'Paths to volunteer commitment: Lessons from the Sydney Olympic Games', in R. Stebbins and M. Graham (eds) *Volunteering as Leisure/Leisure as Volunteering: an international assessment*. Oxfordshire: CABI Publishing, pp. 49–67.

Handy, F., Brodeur, N. and Cnann, R.A. (2006) 'Summer on the Island: episodic volunteering', *Voluntary Action*, 7(3): 31–46.

Hanlon, C.M. and Jago, L.K. (2004) 'The challenge of retaining personnel in major sports events organizations', *Event Management*, 9: 39–49.

Haski-Leventhal, D., Meijs, L.C.P.M. and Hustinx, L. (2009) 'The third-party model: enhancing volunteering through governments, corporations and educational institutes', *Journal of Social Policy*, 39(1): 139–58.

Holmes, K. and Smith, K.A. (2009) *Managing Volunteers in Tourism: attractions, destinations and events*. Oxford: Elsevier.

Karlsen, J.E. and Karlsen, H. (2013) 'Classification of tools and approaches applicable in foresight studies', in M. Giaoutzi and B. Sapio (eds) *Recent Developments in Foresight Methodologies*. New York: Springer, pp. 27–52.

Lockstone, L. and Baum, T. (2009) 'The public face of event volunteering at the 2006 Commonwealth Games: The media perspective', *Managing Leisure*, 14(1): 38–56.

Lockstone, L., Smith, K. and Baum, T. (2010) 'Volunteering flexibility across the tourism sector', *Managing Leisure*, 15(1): 111–27.

Macduff, N. (1991) *Episodic Volunteering: building the short-term volunteer program*. Walla Walla, Washington: MBA Publishing.

Macduff, N. (2005) 'Societal changes and the rise of the episodic volunteer', in J. L. Brudney (ed) *Emerging Areas of Volunteering: ARNOVA Occasional Paper Series*. Indianapolis: ARNOVA, pp. 49–61.

Meijs, L. and Hoogstad, E. (2001) 'New ways of managing volunteers: Combining membership management and programme management', *Voluntary Action*, 3(3): 41–61.

Mellor, D., Hayashi, Y., Stokes, M., Firth, L., Lake, L., Staples, M., Chambers, S. and Cummins, R. (2008) 'Volunteering and its relationship with personal and neighbourhood well-being', *Nonprofit and Voluntary Sector Quarterly*, May: 1–16.

Merrill, M. V. (2006) 'Global trends and the challenges for volunteering', *The International Journal of Volunteer Administration*, XXIV(1): 9–14.

Nichols, G. and Ralston, R. (2012) 'Lessons from the volunteering legacy of the 2002 Commonwealth Games', *Urban Studies*, 49(1): 169–84.

Nogawa, H. (2004) 'An international comparison of the motivations and experiences of volunteers at the 2002 World Cup', in W. Manzenreiter and J. Horne (eds) *Football Goes East: business, culture and the People's Game in China, Japan and South Korea*. Abingdon: Routledge, pp. 222–42.

Popper, R. (2008) 'How are foresight methods selected?', *Foresight*, 10(6): 62–89.

Rochester, C., Ellis Paine, A. and Howlett, S. (2009) *Volunteering and Society in the 21st Century*. Basingstoke: Palgrave Macmillan.

Saleh, F. and Wood, C. (1998) 'Motives of volunteers in multicultural festivals: The case of Saskatoon Folkfest', *Festival Management and Event Tourism*, 5(1/2): 59–70.

Smith, K.A. and Lockstone, L. (2009) 'Involving and keeping event volunteers: Management insights from cultural festivals', in T. Baum, M. Deery, C. Hanlon, L. Lockstone and K. Smith (eds) *People and Work in Events and Conventions: a research perspective*. Wallingford, UK: CABI International, pp. 154–67.

Strigas, A. and Jackson, N. (2003) 'Motivating volunteers to serve and succeed: design and results of a pilot study that explores demographics and motivational factors in sport volunteerism', *International Sports Journal*, 7(1): 111–21.

Tschirhart, M. (2005) 'Employee volunteer programs', in J. L. Brudney (ed) *Emerging Areas of Volunteering: ARNOVA Occasional Paper Series*. Indianapolis: ARNOVA, pp. 13–29.

Twynam, D., Farrell, J. and Johnston, M. (2002/03) 'Leisure and volunteer motivation at a special sporting event', *Leisure/Loisir*, 27(3/4): 363–77.

United Nations Volunteers (2011) *State of the World's Volunteerism Report*. Germany: United Nations Volunteers.

Volunteering Australia. (2007) *Involving Baby Boomers as Volunteers: take a closer look*. Melbourne: Volunteering Australia.

Yeoman, I. (2012) *2050 – Tomorrow's Tourism*. Clevedon: Channel View Publications.

Yufang, S. (2005) 'An analysis of the characteristics and management of Olympic volunteers', *China Volunteer Service Journal, Special English Edition*: 40–49.

14 The future of surveillance and security in global events

Vida Bajc

Future points

- Security and surveillance have taken center stage in global events as a synergetic strategy to minimize uncertainty through control of collective behavior.
- This synergy subjects every aspect of global events to the specifications of the surveillance and security apparatus.
- The apparatus imposes its own vision of secure social order on global events through the process called *security meta-ritual*, a transformation of social and physical spaces into a sterile zone of safety within which every person's movement and communication are monitored and managed.
- *Security meta-ritual* will likely shape the future of global events and their aftermath by fostering legitimacy in the apparatus and encouraging sacrifice of democratic principles in exchange of security.

Introduction

Surveillance and security in global events comprise a synergetic strategy for imposing a vision of secure social order on collective public activity. In this strategy, surveillance is the means through which the vision of order is imposed, while security provides this ambition with a sense of urgency. The surveillance and security apparatus imagines the order it imposes through obtaining information about past human behaviour using data-mining techniques and then processing this information using computer modelling, statistical analysis, and computational mathematics. The goal is to minimize uncertainty by controlling social behavior that is yet to transpire. In this process, security becomes the dominant ordering principle, a *meta-frame* according to which every aspect of the event is planned and performed. *Security meta-framing* is applied to a wide variety of social situations. In the context of global events, the design and the performance of secure order have a specific form called *security meta-ritual*. The *security meta-ritual* will likely shape the future of global events through the following factors: the dynamics through which security comes to be elevated to the top of collective priorities in anticipation of the event; the role of the media in this process; the reference to collective and institutional memory; the urge to mobilize all possible resources;

the expectation that all event participants must cooperate; the creation of a sterile zone of safety; and the socialization into this vision of secure social order. Resistance and public protests are likely to be the single most important factors in countering the effects of *security meta-ritual*.

Surveillance, security, and global events: a conceptual clarification

The increasing association of security and surveillance with global events has come to be known as 'major event security.' While popularized in the mass media and the professional jargon of many practitioners and more often than not also uncritically adopted by scholars, the expression obscures more than it reveals. To think about how metal detectors, personnel in uniforms featuring the sign 'Security', surveillance cameras, unmanned aerial vehicles equipped with high-resolution cameras, special forces, undercover agents, background checks, identity cards, surveillance data bases, anti-aircraft missiles on residential rooftops, hidden sharpshooters, a chain of fences, and metal barriers may shape the future of global events, it is necessary to first disentangle three closely related but distinct phenomena: global events, surveillance, and security.

Global events as capacity to perform a planned collective activity under controlled conditions on a global scale

Global events can be thought of as large-scale, mass-mediated collective happenings with limited duration and potentially significant transformative capacities that reach well beyond their physical location (see Bajc 2012). Such events may be planned or unexpected. Planned global events are spectacular demonstrations of the power to meticulously design and then perform in a controlled way the planned order of a collective human activity on a huge scale during a specified period of time in a designated place. In contrast, unexpected events tend to have a shocking effect by exposing vulnerability and unpredictability and making us aware of the limits of human capacity to control social life. The security imperative and technologies and practices of surveillance have become an intimate part of both types of global events. In this chapter, the focus is on planned global events.

In anthropological terms, planned events of this kind are rituals, versions of which are found in all cultures and historical periods. For scholars of ritual, such collective happenings are central for understanding of collective social life, particularly how group members relate to each other and to members of other groups. This is so for a number of reasons (see Handelman 1990), two of which are particularly relevant for the study of surveillance and security. Rituals foster group sentiments and in this way separate those who belong to the group from all others. This sense of belonging on the part of ritual participants is shared through meanings and communicated through symbols and shared experiences. Rituals also facilitate social change and transformation and communicate ideas about social order and rules of social behavior. In this way, rituals are important means through which members of a group are socialized into a particular socio-cultural order.

Given the importance of rituals for collective social life, it is not surprising that in late-nineteenth-century Europe there were attempts to simply invent rituals that would have the capacity to unite large populations (Hobsbawm and Ranger 1983). Sports competitions, festivals, parades, expositions, and other such highly visible public rituals contributed to the articulation of the process of national identity formation and recognition by other emerging nation-states. Following Maurice Roche (2000), then as today, such events are used as opportunities to articulate ideologies and models of governance. Neo-liberal economic ideas are particularly salient, as cities and their state governments seek to capture the world's attention in a highly competitive global market for consumer attention, political power, and corporate investment. So, too are models of global order, as local power elites project and promote their status in the global network of governing power structures by demonstrating the ability to produce a highly controlled event of enormous complexity. With the emphasis on control, global events have become exemplifications of a vision of secure social order, confidence in the ability to design such social order, and the power to control its process at such a massive scale (Bajc 2012).

Surveillance as bureaucratic means of imposing secure order on a complex collective public activity

In most basic terms, surveillance is a bureaucratic means of population planning and control on a massive scale by using information collected about human behavior in the past to project, anticipate, and preempt human activity in the future (see Bajc 2007a, 2010). In the context of global events, surveillance is the ability of credentialed professionals to identify and classify individuals and groups for the purposes of monitoring, tracking, blocking, and otherwise controlling their movement into, out of, and within a designated geographical area for the duration of the event (Bajc 2007b, 2011b, 2014). This ability to control by planning, anticipating, projecting, and preempting depends on systematic and ongoing accumulation of information about individual and group behavior and then processing this information using computer modeling, computational mathematics, and statistical analysis. The goal is to develop technologies and devise procedures, policies, and rules that help reinforce the planned order of the event and preempt human activity that does not correspond to these plans.

The historical roots of surveillance are in the development of the modern state, particularly its exclusive claims to a territory with clearly delineated boundaries and sovereign authority to govern the population on that territory. This required a capacity to manage the population by separating people who belonged to the state from others through a passport regime (Torpey 2000) and subjecting aspects of lives of individuals within the territory to state regulation (Foucault 2008). For these purposes there developed ways of methodical and systematic accumulation of information about each person and modes of statistical analysis to process this information (Desrosières 1998). Through this way of governing developed the modern bureaucracy, a cadre of professionals the work of which depends on the mastery of gathering and processing of information. Surveillance as a means of controlling participation at global events is an extension of these processes of population management. As Gilles Deleuze (1992) pointed out, it is also a manifestation of the shift toward control on a global scale for political and economic purposes.

Central to the ability to collect and process information were two developments: *individuation* of each person as identifiably unique and *exclusionary classification* to sort out the information collected (see Bajc 2007a; 2010). *Individuation* refers to assigning to each person a unique set of identifiers, which make it possible to differentiate between individuals. Early on it was family and given name, date and place of birth, and some kind of a number. Technological and scientific innovations yield ever more perfected identification signs from mug shots to fingerprinting, retina scan, and, most recently, a DNA sequence. Only after a person has been so identified does it become possible for information about this individual to be systematically collected, mobility monitored in space and through time, and access denied.

Exclusionary classification is the sorting of this information into clear-cut, exclusive categories. This process works in two directions: from individual behavior to a category and from a category to an individual behavior. Every time a person scans her identification card, swipes her credit card, completes a business transaction, dials a number on her cell phone, sends an e-mail from her own account, accesses an Internet website from her own computer, or sends or receives a Tweet through her own account, that information is fed into centralized databases where it can be accessed on demand. So-called data analysts can classify this information about past behavior into various categories such as safe, dangerous, public protester, terrorist, or hooligan on the basis of which a given individual can be denied access to a global event at some future date. This is how individuals find themselves on a no-fly list, particular soccer fans are barred from attending a game, protesters against G8 meetings are denied entry into the country where the meeting is held. *Exclusionary classification* also allows the operatives to profile, which means to invent categories based on imaginary characteristics of a social group – for example mob, hooligan, or terrorist. Behavior of individuals in sports stadia or on streets and plazas surrounding the event, which resembles imagined characteristics of that category, is flagged out and individuals so identified removed from this space.

With technological developments in data storage capabilities, access to databases of various communications service providers, and sharing of data between surveillance and security apparatuses worldwide, as well as advancements in computational and complex systems analysis, data analysts are able to mine various centralized databases in search for patterns that are used to reconstruct the past and project into the future. Retrospectively, patterns of behavior of a particular individual or social group are reconstructed after the fact. Prospectively, future human behavior is envisioned by thinking out acts of human beings before the fact. Such computer programs help simulate every conceivable scenario, design drills and exercises of disruption management and preemption, and calculate potential risks (Amoore 2011). The goal of these calculated imaginaries is to mitigate or preempt envisioned human activity that was not planned by the event organizers.

Security as the meta-frame

This ambition to control through the means of surveillance is given a sense of urgency thorough the notion of 'security'. Security is a socio-cultural construct that has the capacity to become the dominant ordering principle of social organization in such a way that it is able to push in the direction of collective understanding that all means necessary should be employed to ensure that global event will take place as planned and with no unintended disruption. In this process, security battles against other values associated with global events such as equal access, open participation, festivity, spontaneity, interpersonal bonding with other participants, the right to protest, or privacy. The author calls this struggle for security to dominate the organization of social life *security meta-framing* (Bajc 2011a). In a meta-framing dynamic, the prefix 'meta' signifies that there is a necessary hierarchy. In this hierarchy, security dominates as a logic to reduce social complexity in order to minimize uncertainty. This logic is based on *exclusionary classification* and exclusionary thinking in that it generates categories of human activity that are either acceptable or not acceptable. Through *security meta-framing*, the public is presented with mutually exclusive options of either security or danger, where security is interpreted as an obvious choice. But what is 'security'?

While surveillance can be articulated as technologically and expertly informed bureaucratic practice of ordering and controlling present and future social life, security has no such tangible manifestation. This is so because security is a perception of reality that is internalized as an emotion or a worldview and politically articulated as an ideology or an agenda (Bajc 2013). Security is a domain of experience in which there are embedded specific cultural assumptions about safety and danger and cultural sentiments about what is and is not orderly. As a meta-framing process, security becomes a logic according to which *exclusionary classifications*, such as hooligan, terrorist, alien, state enemy, or VIP, are invented as means to reduce social complexity in order to minimize uncertainty. In this way, whether internalized and politically articulated by individuals or institutions, lay people or national security advisers, security is a cultural construct that profoundly shapes the way people live their everyday lives (Bajc and de Lint 2011).

This capacity of security to become a meta-frame is related to a number of developments. On the part of the public there is a general expectation that something must be done to tame uncertainty and to ensure safety in participation at global events. This public sentiment about uncertainty, characteristic perhaps of late modernity (see Beck 1992), is merging with other historical shifts. On the part of the state, institutions responsible for matters of state sovereignty, such as the military and intelligence services, work under the assumption that threats to security of the state are existential and therefore require the use of all possible means to preempt such threats from materializing (Buzan, Waever and de Wilde 1998). Internally, a different set of state institutions was put in place, such as the police, which was to be primarily concerned with involvement with local communities to ensure safety and retrospectively respond when the law is not followed (see Zedner 2009). Today there is a tendency to treat all sorts of social situations, including global events, as security problems rather than issues of safety and legality (Waever 1995). As well, there is a push to integrate institutions previously ascribed to different spheres of responsibility into one network of security authorities and experts (Bigo 2012). In this process of articulation of what is and is not a matter of security, economic interests also tend to play a prominent role (Neocleous 2006).

Crucial for the study of *security meta-framing* is an understanding of its capacity to dominate collective life in a huge variety of social settings, from military occupation, colonial ambitions, ethnic conflict, class disparities, or racial tension, to global events (see Bajc 2013). The challenge in the study of *security meta-framing* is to understand the dynamics of how security comes to dominate as a particular kind of logic to minimize uncertainty by controlling human behavior through surveillance, what kind of social order this generates in particular social settings, and what the consequences of this social order may be for the life of communities and individuals. In the case of global events, *security meta-framing* enables a specific kind of transformation that has a ritual form. This form is called *security meta-ritual* (Bajc 2007b, 2011b).

Security meta-ritual and the future of global events

Security meta-ritual is a process in which the surveillance and security apparatus performs its vision of secure social order in the context of global events. This is a process of change from routine everyday life, which the apparatus deems dangerous, into a different kind of social order, which the apparatus envisions as secure. This transformation involves changes of physical as well as social spaces. As others have observed, this change can be intensely visual to the point of resembling a spectacle (Boyle and Haggerty 2009). Looking at the nature of this transformation more closely, however, it becomes evident that these dynamics themselves have a ritual form. Approaching these dynamics from the standpoint of ritual theory has important empirical and theoretical implications for understanding the past, the present, and the future of surveillance and security in global events. What follows is an outline of the *security meta-ritual* model derived from empirical and theoretical research on global events so far (Bajc 2007b, 2011b, 2012b, 2014, forthcoming). *Security meta-ritual* is likely to shape the future of global events particularly in terms of changing the aesthetics of our living environment, the notions of privacy of event participants, the ways in which people relate to each other in public spaces, and not the least, the very nature of global events.

Shift of attention

When the public is made aware that preparations are underway to organize a global event in a given metropolitan area, there is a shift of attention from routine daily life toward the event. With this cognitive shift there emerges a dynamic of *security meta-ritual* as an attempt to set the parameters and the conditions for the organization and performance of the event. For institutions, this is a shift from routine responsibility toward how human and other resources are to be diverted toward preparations for the event. In some cases, particularly when the event is noncyclical, the period of time between the breaking of the news that an event is forthcoming and the dates of its actual performance can be extremely short. Such a shock notice leaves the public with limited means to question the imperative of security and its exclusionary logic. It may also shorten internal debates within various security-related agencies and institutions of political leadership. Cyclical events, in contrast, particularly those of huge complexity, tend to be scheduled years in advance, opening a prolonged international and local spotlight on the organizing elites and the host country through investigative journalism and public scrutiny (Bajc forthcoming). Given the symbolic power of events, this shift of attention will continue to bring to the fore struggles over issues related to marginality and disadvantage that would otherwise remain in the background and to create spaces for social protests against the organizing elites. These dynamics will vary according to different political, social, and cultural circumstances of the location of the event.

The role of the media

In this process, the media play a crucial role. Investigative reporting draws attention to public protests, grievances by minority groups, treatment of the poor and the homeless, and various forms of corruption. Closer to the time of the event, mass media become the means through which the apparatus communicates to the public the parameters of how the new social order will be implemented, including what is permitted and what is not allowed, changes in road traffic patterns, restrictions of airspace, information about operatives and agencies involved in pursuit of the planned order, and other detailed instructions and descriptions of the workings of the apparatus. Journalists also pay close attention to how the surveillance and security apparatus is implementing its vision of secure social order for the event by scrutinizing its failures and uncovering corruption. For those who will take part in the event via live broadcasts into their homes, sports bars, clubs, or individual mobile devices, these reports may be the only awareness of the workings of the *security meta-ritual*, while others attending in situ or living near the event's physical location are likely to have a very different experience of this process. Which details are conveyed through these broadcasts varies widely around the world (Moragas, Larson and Rivenburgh 1995), and viewings are often organized as occasions of their own (Dayan and Katz 1992). In addition to investigative reporting of failure of the apparatus, social media will continue to offer new possibilities for transmission of images, texts, and other expressions of the experience of *security meta-ritual* to the publics worldwide. This is so despite the fact that social media are often prohibited inside the sterile zone of safety.

Collective and institutional memory

Security meta-ritual draws on collective and institutional memories related to failures of the apparatus to preempt a disruption. Collective memory here refers to a mode of experience through which people are able to share memories of events past by creating awareness in each person that there are others who identify themselves in relation to particular narratives about past events (see Bajc 2006). Referring to such collective memories has the goal of reassuring the workings of the apparatus and to strengthen the validity of *security meta-ritual*. Institutional memory refers to what has come to be called 'best practices' and 'lessons learned', the tendency on the part of the apparatus to accumulate knowledge about how its vision of secure social order was planned and carried out in the past and passing that knowledge to others. Disruption to the performance of the 1972 Munich Olympics is often said to have created a historical shift in *security meta-framing* of global events and seems to be one of the catalysts for the emergence of *security meta-ritual*. There are wide variations in what is remembered and by whom about specificities of interruptions of particular global events. The huge casualties that resulted from the apparatus attempting to crush student demonstrations in Mexico City days before the 1968 Olympics and the bomb that exploded during the Atlanta 1996 Games, with incomparably fewer casualties, are two examples of such differences in remembering.

Mobilization of all resources

Disruption to the planned event is considered a failure of the performance of the apparatus in that it undermines its claims to the ability to control the future. In the marketplace of security enterprise, such failure can also have real financial consequence. Thus there is a push for constant vigilance in identifying and envisioning threats to security, the urge that all preventive measures necessary must be taken to preempt such scenarios, the pressure that no resources be spared to this end, and the tendency to entrust these matters to private enterprise. To this end, there will continue to be a pressure to perfect surveillance techniques, implement the latest technologies available on the market, and mobilize all institutions. In some states, this process has been legally sanctioned through classifications such as 'national special security event', which help to streamline allocation of resources. Such classifications also create a legal space for anti-democratic legislation that is aimed at restricting or prohibiting unplanned collective public expressions. The host country itself can be put under pressure by global institutions, raising important questions about how host states maintain their sovereignty in the face of such global power. These dynamics will be playing out differently in different states and host cities, as they will experience financial crises, their institutions forced to deal with budget cuts, and the population expected to cover the losses.

Cooperation of all involved

A smooth and efficient performance of the planned order on the part of the apparatus depends on the willingness of all involved to cooperate toward the common goal. On the part of the public, this means getting people to agree to adjust their behavior in accordance with the parameters of the *security meta-ritual*. Similarly, various institutions are made to work together, including the military, the police, undercover agents, special forces and national intelligence agencies from multiple states, and various security services corporations and enterprise. This subordination of public behavior as well as the workings of a wide variety of institutions toward the common goal is a multilayered process that varies widely depending on the host city and state as well as the type and the complexity of the planned event. Those who are able to obtain permission to attend any part of the event must comply with the specifications of the apparatus or else risk being excluded. Others who live in the area where the event is taking place may find these specifications disruptive to their daily routine life, prompting a variety of public responses. Institutions, in turn, each have their own organizational culture so that to be able to work together effectively there needs to develop some form of a shared way of doing things. There are wide variations in terms of which among these organizational cultures comes to dominate for the duration of the project, how others are made to adjust, and what kind of consequences there may be for dissent. In all of this, host countries will continue to aspire to prove themselves capable of such organizational cooperation at this scale in the eyes of the global elites. In this push for cooperation at the global scale another phenomenon is emerging that will likely continue to expand, namely, a set of global 'security experts'. These are surveillance and security operatives with access to information, policy makers, and political elites, which enable them to compile institutional memories to be able to emerge as a 'go to' service in the organization of the next event (see Richards, Fussey and Silke 2011).

Purification of participants and physical and social spaces

The purification process involves physical and social spaces as well as individuals and objects. This process has different stages. In a designated urban area, a physical space is carved out from the routine life and sectioned off for the process of transformation in preparation for the event. In this space, existing architecture and landscape are altered through construction of event infrastructure, aestheticization of residential and commercial neighborhoods, removal of structures that are at odds with the envisioned order, and implementation of surveillance-friendly public spaces and landscaping. Purification of physical space is accompanied by purification of social life. This is a process of removal of disadvantaged individuals and dislocation of entire social groups, the activities of which do not conform to the order as envisioned by the apparatus. As the time of the event nears, this space is sectioned off by an impermeable boundary and within this enclosure no stone remains unturned to ensure a purified, sterile zone of safety. This enclosure has specifically designated entrances through which the chosen participants are made to enter and be positioned in a particular location to which they are assigned. To enter, each preselected individual undergoes a process of purification by being subjected to varying degrees of identity checks, metal detectors, body searches, inspection of personal belongings, and surveillance cameras. The zone is itself divided into a hierarchy of subspaces, each with its own designated entrance through which only those may pass to whom this subzone has been assigned. In this way, within this sterile zone of safety, participants are ordered hierarchically in terms of privilege of access. Ways in which participants and institutions will resist this purification will vary, as will their results and consequences.

Socialization effects

Consequences of the *security meta-ritual* vary according to the scope and complexity of the event. A number of trends can be observed (see also Barnard-Wills, Moore and McKim 2012). Surveillance-friendly architectural and landscape design and fortified infrastructure reflect a particular security aesthetics, which will continue to shape the way people inhabit urban environments. Intervention into the community life of populations deemed dangerous or otherwise not fitting the vision of security-sanctioned social order will continue to create new forms of social exclusion and redefine the way people relate to each other in public spaces. The surveillance systems and policing strategies left in place after the event will continue to shape people's conceptions of privacy and their notions of the self. *Security meta-ritual* promotes a vision of secure social order in which every individual is controlled in space and through time where spontaneity is discouraged and unstructured festiveness deemed dangerous. This order fosters legitimacy and trust in the surveillance and security apparatus, nurtures fear of strangers and open public spaces, and discourages cosmopolitanism.

Concluding remarks

Today, planned global events have become above all spectacular demonstrations of the capacity to meticulously design and then perform under highly controlled conditions the planned order of a collective public activity at a global scale (Bajc 2012). This chapter advanced the following argument: given that uncertainty is seen by the organizers as a threat to such staging of global events, security and surveillance have taken center stage as a synergetic strategy to control collective behavior to be able to minimize uncertainty. In controlling social behavior, the surveillance and security apparatus imposes its own vision of social order using security as the sentiment that has the effect of creating a sense of urgency and surveillance as the means through which security is to be achieved. The process through which the apparatus imposes this order on a global event is referred to as *security meta-ritual*. This is a process of transformation of social and physical spaces into a sterile zone of safety within which every aspect of a global event is subjected to the specifications of the surveillance and security apparatus.

This security-sanctioned order in planned global events observed to date suggests a particular future trajectory: People will likely continue to be divided into insiders and outsiders, those who will be allowed to participate at the event and all others who will be barred from attending. Inside the sterile zone of safety and around its perimeter, every person's movement and communication will continue to be managed and controlled with the hopes to be able to prevent unplanned activity from happening. Breaches of this social order tend to lead to policy recommendations that more should have been done to prevent such disruptions from occurring. Such policies support the urge to mobilize all conceivable resources to enforce this vision of secure social order and are likely continue to encourage allocation of ever larger amounts of public resources and collective good to implement ever more perfected surveillance technologies and techniques for controlling human behavior in public events. So, too, locally specific as well as globally initiated forms of resistance and protest against these practices will likely continue.

Given its ritual nature, the *security meta-ritual* will likely shape social life in at least two ways: first, by fostering legitimacy in the ways of the surveillance and security apparatus; and second, by socializing participants and observers alike not only in what it takes to have safety but also that democratic decision making, freedom of movement and assembly, and the right to privacy should be worth sacrificing in exchange for a secure social order. Despite the tendency to shroud surveillance procedures and security considerations into secrecy, resistance and public protest will likely be the single most important factors in countering the effects of *security meta-ritual*. In light of all this, event practitioners, scholars, participants, and observers alike will be faced with important ethical concerns about their own role in the implementation of this vision of secure social order.

References

Amoore, L. (2011) 'Data derivatives: on the emergence of a security risk calculus for our times', *Theory Culture and Society*, 28(6): 24–43.

Bajc, V. (ed.) (forthcoming) *Surveilling and Securing the Olympics: from Tokyo 1964 to London 2012 and beyond.* New York: Palgrave Macmillan.

Bajc, V. (2013) 'Sociological reflections on security through surveillance', *Sociological Forum*, 28(3): 615–23.

Bajc, V. (2012) 'Events, global', in M. Juergensmeyer and H. Anheier (eds.) *Encyclopaedia of Global Studies*. London: Sage.

Bajc, V. (2011a) 'Introduction: security meta-framing: a cultural logic of an ordering practice', in V. Bajc and W. de Lint (eds.) *Security and Everyday Life*. New York: Routledge, pp. 1–30.

Bajc, V. (2011b) 'Collective activity in public spaces: the Pope John Paul II in the Holy City', in V. Bajc and W. de Lindt (eds.) *Security and Everyday Life*. New York: Routledge, pp. 49–76.

Bajc, V. (2010) 'On surveillance as solution to security issues', in G. Cassano and R. Dello Buono (eds.) *Crisis, Politics, and Critical Sociology: essays on resistance and social practices*. Leiden and Boston: Brill, pp. 183–96.

Bajc, V. (2007a) 'Introduction: debating surveillance in the age of security', Special issue Watching Out: Surveillance, Mobility, and Security. *American Behavioral Scientist*, 50(12): 1567–91.

Bajc, V. (2007b) 'Surveillance in public rituals: security meta-ritual and the 2005 U.S. Presidential Inauguration', Special issue Watching Out: Surveillance, Mobility, and Security. *American Behavioral Scientist*, 50(12): 1648–73.

Bajc, V. (2006) 'Collective memory and tourism: globalizing transmission through localized experience', Special issue Collective Memory and Tourism. *Journeys: The International Journal of Travel and Travel Writing*, 7(1): 1–14.

Bajc, V. and de Lint, W. (eds.) (2011) *Security and Everyday Life*. New York: Routledge.

Barnard-Wills, D., Moore, C. and McKim, J. (eds.) (2012) 'Introduction: spaces of terror and risk', Special issue. *Space and Culture*, 15(2): 92–7.

Beck, U. (1992) *Risk Society: towards a new modernity*. London: Sage.

Bigo, D. (2012) 'International political sociology', in P.D. Williams (ed.) *Security Studies: an introduction*. 2nd ed. London: Routledge.

Boyle, P. and Haggerty, K. (2009) 'Spectacular security: mega-events and the security complex', *International Political Sociology*, 3: 257–74.

Buzan, B., Waever, O, and de Wilde, J. (eds.) (1998) *Security: a new framework for analysis*. Boulder, CO: Lynne Rienner.

Dayan, D. and Katz, E. (1992) *Media Events: the live broadcasting of history*. Cambridge, MA: Harvard University Press.

Deleuze, G. (1992, Winter) 'Postscript on the societies of control', *October*, 59: 3–7.

Desrosières, A. (1998) *The Politics of Large Numbers: a history of statistical reasoning*. Cambridge: Harvard University Press.

Foucault, M. (2008[2004]) *The Birth of Biopolitics: lectures at the Collège de France, 1978–1979*. G. Burchell (trans.). New York: Palgrave Macmillan.

Handelman, D. (1990) *Models and Mirrors: towards and anthropology of public events*. 2nd ed. New York: Berghahn Books.

Hobsbawm, E. and Ranger, T. (eds.) (1983) *The Invention of Tradition*. Cambridge: Cambridge University Press.

Moragas, M., Larson, J. and Rivenburgh, N. (1995) *Television and the Olympics*. London: John Libbey.

Neocleous, M. (2006) 'From social to national security; on the fabrication of economic order', *Security Dialog*, 37(3): 363–84.

Richards, A., Fussey, P., and Silke, A. (2011) *Terrorism and the Olympics: major event security and lessons for the future*. London: Routledge.

Roche, M. (2000) *Mega-events and Modernity: Olympics and expos in the growth of global culture.* London: Routledge.

Torpey, J. (2000) *The Invention of the Passport: surveillance, citizenship and the state.* Cambridge: Cambridge University Press.

Waever, O. (1995) 'Securitization and desecuritization', in R.D. Lipschutz (ed.) *On Security.* New York: Columbia University Press, pp. 46–86.

Zedner, L. (2009) *Security.* New York: Routledge.

15 A perspective on the near future

Mobilizing events and social media

Peter Bolan

Future points

- This chapter identifies the importance of social media and mobile apps to events, including developing and harnessing aspects such as QR code technology, augmented reality, gamification and Wi-Fi connectivity.
- How such digital media applications can be used to market and promote events is analyzed.
- The chapter illustrates how these digital media applications can provide an alternative to attending the event.

Introduction

Questions such as 'what will happen?', 'what can happen?' and consequently 'how will changes affect society and industry?' are central to futures studies and research (Bergman, Karlsson and Axelsson 2010). New media technology, essentially referred to under the umbrella of digital media, is changing the face of not only how we market and promote events but also the very nature of events themselves. According to authors such as Richards and Palmer (2010), such new forms of digital media are beginning to have a substantial impact on the way in which events are produced, consumed and distributed. Organizations are continually under pressure to get themselves on social media platforms and to consider whether or not they should delve into the world of mobile apps to cater to the ever-growing appetites of those who increasingly use their smartphones to stay connected. Kietzmann *et al.* (2011: 241) states, 'Given the tremendous exposure of social media in the popular press today, it would seem that we are in the midst of an altogether new communication landscape'.

According to Weber (2009: 3), 'Learning to market to the social web requires a new way to communicate with an audience in a digital environment'. Whilst this presents challenges to those in the events sector, it also provides enormous opportunities. Event planners and organizers must engage with the popular forms of social media if they are to ensure success in today's competitive marketplace. Furthermore, they must consider how best to do this through the mobile device (smartphones and tablet computers such as the iPad) and to what extent specially designed apps may boost their audience, enhance event experience and develop their business success. What has also become referred to as eWOM (electronic word of mouth) by authors such as Zhang, Jansen and Chowdhury (2011) can have huge influences on business success, and managers must ensure their organizations engage in the eWOM process as both initiators and active participants. The next section discusses the key forms of digital media technology that those involved in the future of event management must be engaging with.

Digital media technology

One of the real game-changers in terms of new technology adoption in recent years has been the advent of social media. Social media is '. . . a type of media dispersed through online social interactions and takes a variety of forms including social networking sites, blogs, wikis, podcasts, photo and video sharing, social bookmarking and virtual environments' (Fletcher and Lee 2012: 505). In terms of social media popularity and usage it is dominated by what have become known as the big '5', namely: Facebook, Twitter, LinkedIn, blogging and YouTube. Whilst others are now gaining ground (such as Google+, Pinterest and Instagram), it has been Facebook in particular that has led the way so far. According to Nair (2011: 46), 'It took 38 years for the radio to attract 50 million listeners, and 13 years for television to gain the attention of 50 million viewers. The Internet took only 4 years to attract 50 million participants, and Facebook reached 50 million participants in only one-and-a-half years'.

Mobile applications or 'apps' are '. . . increasingly being used on smartphones or other devices (such as tablets) to access news, games, entertainment, weather and other information' (Brown 2012: 231). As early as 2007 it was becoming apparent to researchers such as Lascia (2007) that the world was becoming a truly mobile information society and that new mobile-enabled capabilities were changing people's behaviour and starting to shape cultural values and norms within daily life. This has very much continued and grown, and mobile apps have now captured the public imagination. Uptake and desire for them has been phenomenal, with Apple announcing in January 2010 that 3 billion apps had been downloaded in just 18 months following the launch of the App Store (Chaffey and Ellis-Chadwick 2012). The festival and event sector cannot afford to ignore such a fact, especially when so much of what they do lends itself to these applications.

QR codes or 'Quick Response' codes are two-dimensional barcodes that can be scanned by smartphone cameras and are used to provide fast and efficient access most commonly to URLs. They were originally created as far back as 1994 by the Japanese corporation Denso Wave but have only begun to gain more widespread use in recent years. According to Hoy (2011: 296), QR codes have several distinct advantages over traditional barcodes, namely that 'they can store far more information, they can be scanned at high speeds in any direction and orientation, and they have built-in error correction features that allow them to be read even when partially obscured'. Such a system for smartphone usage has been gathering pace in terms of usage, particularly so in Europe. European usage of QR codes by smartphone users has doubled in just 12 months (Smart Insights: Sept 2012). Such codes allow tagging of items or places in the physical world with additional data/information or links to online material though connecting to relevant URLs, etc. In essence they provide a fast and efficient link from the physical world to the electronic through smartphone technology (Hoy 2011).

Augmented reality is another form of digital media technology that has developed in line with smartphone capabilities. Augmented reality (AR) 'blends real-world digital data capture typically with a digital camera in a smartphone to create a browser-based digital representation or experience mimicking that of the real world' (Chaffey 2011: 706). Such technology is now being utilized in areas such as heritage-based visitor attractions where ruined buildings can be viewed through the mobile phone camera and overlaid with what the original structure would have looked like centuries before. In this way such aspects can be 'brought to life' and provide a more immersive experience for the visitor. There are a number of ways this technology can also be used in the field of events, which is explored in the following sections of the chapter, but authors such as Hyun, Lee and Hu (2009) state that animated-based mobile applications have the highest interactivity and vividness and therefore the greatest appeal to users.

Gamification is now proven to be a useful technique in marketing, especially mobile marketing. This emerging concept known as gamification '. . . involves applying game-based thinking to a brand, business or organization to engage and develop loyalty' (Chaffey and Ellis-Chadwick 2012: 321). Essentially this technique is about developing and providing interactive games and quizzes (increasingly through mobile technology), which can serve to help market and promote a business, its products/services or indeed an event. A recent example of this was developed for the Irish Open Golf Championship at Royal Portrush (Northern Ireland) where an interactive Irish Open 2012 Quiz was available on mobile platforms that visitors to the event could play to test their knowledge about golf and the event and to learn more about what was happening across the three days of the tournament.

Wi-Fi (wireless fidelity) and advances in this area is also of high significance for the world of events and festivals. Wi-Fi is the shorthand used to describe a high-speed wireless local area network (Chaffey 2011). Businesses and organizations from airports to coffee shops to hotels now offer Wi-Fi 'hotspots', which allow people Internet access through their laptops, tablets and smartphones. People are increasingly expecting and demanding such access at either low cost or indeed for free, especially if they are a customer spending money in other ways. Event venues also need to be offering such a service these days, particularly if they are to maximize use of social media and other apps through smartphones amongst event goers whilst attending the events.

Marketing and promoting the event

Social media provides huge opportunities to those involved in the marketing and promotion of events and festivals. The ability to harness user-generated content and directed activity will and can have huge implications for events, but to assess the impact Web 2.0-derived user platforms can have, a closer understanding of the social media landscape is necessary. Social media in business can bring dangers for those who do not properly understand how to use it effectively. It '. . . converts consumers into marketers and advertisers, and consumers can create positive or negative pressure for the company, its products, and its services' (Akar and Topcu 2011: 36). As long as businesses are cognizant of the possible dangers of using social media (i.e. the power it provides the consumer) and realize that it is about a two-way conversation and regular engagement rather than a marketing channel to talk at the customer, then there are immense opportunities than can be realized.

In relation to this field, core ways to promote an event utilizing social media (Web 2.0 and related applications) include a number of key applications. These include blogging about the event (before, during and afterwards); putting the event on Facebook; tweeting the event and creating a group page on LinkedIn. Furthermore, creation of an online event based game/quiz (gamification), as well posting photos on Flickr, Pinterest or Twitpic, can bring very beneficial impacts. Uploading a short video to YouTube; live streaming the event online and placing QR codes in magazines, posters and around the event venue itself will further develop and enhance potential. It is also the combination of these different social media rather than just using one or two in isolation that can truly lead to maximizing success and harnessing the Web 2.0 landscape for event success.

Santomier (2008) discusses how new media and technology have provided avenues to assist sport businesses in adding value and competitive advantage to sport sponsorship. This is further supported by the work of Dees (2011: 275) who states, 'Fans do not want to sit passively and read or listen to advertisements, but rather interrelate with teams, sponsors and brands'. This interactivity that social media, and especially social media through mobile devices, provides is crucial for event planners and organizers to harness, not only prior to an event, but during and afterwards as well. The marketing of the event, especially in this digital age, doesn't end when the event starts but continues much longer.

Enhancing the event experience

The power of digital media to enhance the event experience itself for those attending is growing at a phenomenal rate. Dees (2011) discusses how fans and event goers now use in-venue devices (usually their own smartphones) to access sport content while they are attending the event itself and that various forms of digital media content provide these fans with constant access to information, stories, statistics and video clips all in the palm of their hands. Such use of technology in this way enhances and provides a more immersive experience for the event goer. An example already in use in terms of sporting events is 'FanVision', which displays audio and video content, instant replays, team and match statistics and other related content. The system, however, uses it own specially developed handheld device, which fans can either rent at the event itself or buy for future use (FanVision 2013). The digital media device is already used relatively widely in the United States, particularly in the sports of American football and NASCAR.

It has also recently become available for use with Formula 1 motor-racing events and includes features such as access to on-board cameras and real-time telemetry.

With regard to such use of digital media whilst in attendance at events, another form that has been developed in the field of sports events is 'Yinzcam', which, according to authors such as Dees (2011: 279), is '. . . a mobile video application that allows fans in all parts of the stadium regardless of their viewpoint to enjoy every facet of the live sports experience'. A key difference with this system is that it is free to users and works on their smartphones or tablets through a Wi-Fi network in the event arena, enabling them to easily view live video, action replays, alternative camera angles, etc., on their own mobile device. Again this application is in widespread use in North America, particularly in American football's NFL and also basketball's NBA.

Combining specially designed applications like these with other social media–based apps and features such as GPS location-based services opens up yet further scope and potential for the event goer such as finding your way to your seats, finding your friends at the event and sharing comments and opinions of the event, as well as the possibility for the event organizers to tie in with various concessions, merchandising and sponsorship. Gamification (such as the example previously quoted for the Irish Open Golf 2012) can add to this further still by providing a fun interactive element (in the form of games, puzzles and quizzes) to proceedings that can boost interest and enjoyment of the event. In short, what used to be simply a case of 'being there' and soaking up the atmosphere of such events can now be greatly enhanced and the experience made more interactive, enjoyable and immersive through mobile digital technology.

Augmented reality (AR) can also come into play here. Imagine waiting for a music event to start and viewing the empty stage through your smartphone or tablet and having the stage come to life using AR to place previous singers and bands on the stage performing excerpts from their well known hits. Imagine visiting your favourite football stadium even when it is empty and being able to view the pitch through your mobile device and have AR superimpose images of your favourite players and excerpts from important matches with footage of goals scored, etc. All of this is now possible, and the signs are that the market for it is out there with the necessary mobile devices. It simply requires the willingness, innovation and creativity to have it developed in the right way to meet the needs of the events industry.

To ensure maximum uptake amongst event audiences and by extent maximum enjoyment of the enhanced event experience, there needs to be good Wi-Fi connectivity in the event venue. It is absolutely vital that event venues offer free Wi-Fi and that it is of a sufficient strength and capacity that event goers can use smartphones or tablets to their hearts' content. Many event venues have not yet made this a priority and yet in light of what has been discussed here in the chapter so far it seems rather remiss if they do engage in some of the strategies outlined but then fail at this final hurdle to provide the technological architecture and infrastructure to support such ventures.

Providing an alternative to attending the event

Another side to what such digital media can do is to provide a worthwhile experience of the event without actually being there. Whilst some might see this as competition in relation to ticket sales and attendance at the actual event itself, it can be seen as way to greatly expand the audience for the event and to gain more coverage and exposure. Richards and Palmer (2010), in their work on eventful cities, make note of a BBC music event that was tied strongly to the notion of online or virtual music festivals and was hosted through the online game 'Second Life'. As the event featured real music artists and ran in parallel with a real music festival – BBC Radio 1's One Big Weekend event – comparisons can be drawn. Some 30,000 people attended the real 'live' event, with some 400 attending the cyberspace version. Such an example serves to prove that the balance of interest still lies very much with the desire for the real actual experience. However, as digital media and the plethora of Web 2.0 tools become more widespread and accepted, such a balance will inevitably shift, though most will likely always favour the 'real' experience if possible.

For those who cannot attend the event, however, they may still gain some of the event experience if it is live streamed online (during the event) or if highlights are available afterwards through the organization's own website, social media pages or through general video platforms such as YouTube. This can be further enhanced through blogs and photo-sharing sites such as Flickr and Pinterest. Whether this is free or users are required to pay a fee for certain aspects will be up to event organizers. For example, it may prove a useful additional revenue stream if users are charged to watch the event if it is broadcast live online. This would also help offset any threat to actual ticket sales for the event itself, i.e., those who can't attend can still see it live but not for free. Providing video clips or highlights post-event and other aspects such as photo sharing should not incur a charge, though, as consumers would expect an element of this for free these days.

Through such mechanisms event organizers can expand their audience, get key brand imagery and messages across to consumers (including those from sponsors), capitalize on merchandising opportunities and through social media in particular get a real 'buzz' going about the event or festival, which can encourage those not attending 'this time' to attend actual events in future. Development of an event app for use through smartphones and tablets could tie a number of these aspects together and provide a further 'talking point' and indeed potential revenue stream.

A source of market research and a tool for eCRM

The event planner and organizer who embraces and utilizes digital technology in these ways will also have a readily available source of market research at his or her fingertips and the means to develop and establish a strong element of eCRM (electronic customer relationship management). Regular engagement with event goers through social media will provide an excellent source of feedback on events in terms of what people enjoyed, the experience they had and any negative aspects or areas for improvement. Event goers will inevitably comment through such media anyway, but it is much better for the business to get involved. As many social media marketing experts such as Weber (2009) say, the conversation about your business is happening online anyway; the business's challenge is to join in that conversation and when it does it needs to add value and say something meaningful.

Using other techniques such as web analytics, those in the event management business can harness all the readily available online data that sits 'behind the scenes' of their website, their social media pages and their photo image platforms. Web analytics can be defined as the measurement, collection, analysis and reporting of Internet data for purposes of understanding and optimizing web usage (Chaffey 2011). It is not just a tool for measuring web traffic but can also be used for business and market research, and to assess and improve the effectiveness of an organization's web presence across multiple digital channels.

In such ways event planners can stay connected to what their audience thinks, foster and develop meaningful eCRM and use such collected and analyzed data to inform changes to future events and how they are marketed and indeed experienced by the event goer. It's all about harnessing digital media through social platforms to be better informed and maintain better relationships rather than simply be at the mercy of what the organization's event goers say online without any involvement or engagement from the business.

Concluding remarks

The implications for the future of the event industry based upon the present are inextricably tied in to recent and emerging advances in digital and mobile technology. What can be termed the social media landscape is fraught with dangers and pitfalls, especially for unsuspecting organizations and businesses who do not fully understand it and how to harness its business potential (Weber 2009; Chan and Guillet 2011; Constantinides and Fountain 2008). The world of mobile apps is also still a very new and misunderstood one to many in the business world. Lack of knowledge or fear of the dangers must not hold back those involved in event and festival planning, organization and management, however. The benefits that can be gained are immense, and we are entering a period where the consumer will begin to expect and demand this.

Harnessing and using this technology is already changing the face of events and the experience for the event goer and it is only getting started. New technologies are constantly emerging, most recently Google glasses, for example. In a sense these provide a wearable computer with an optical head-mounted display that displays information in a hands-free smartphone style format directly on the glass itself. Applications for this in the events field are potentially huge and could take areas discussed in this chapter such as augmented reality and gamification to another level yet again. We are indeed moving into an incredibly exciting and dynamic time for the future of events and festivals, which will be shaped and developed by technological advances and the resultant consumer thirst for how such technology is used and applied.

This chapter has examined the diverse ways in which mobile technology and social media can and should be used in the field of events. There is a lack of research on such usage and on its impact in business generally but particularly so in the area of mobile apps and especially so with regard to events and event management. The author hopes that what has been presented here clarifies both existing possibilities and future potential for those involved in aspects of event management from both a practitioner and academic research viewpoint. There is a great need for more research to be conducted into these fundamentally important areas.

With regard to how this could evolve further, virtual events (those taking place in cyberspace) are already beginning to happen and could be the next big game-changer, building on what has been discussed here, yet further still.

References

Akar, E. and Topcu, B. (2011) 'An examination of the factors influencing consumers' attitudes toward social media marketing', *Journal of Internet Commerce*, 10(1): 35–67.

Bergman, A., Karlsson, J.C. and Axelsson, J. (2010) 'Truth claims and explanatory claims: an ontological typology of futures studies', *Futures*, (42): 857–65.

Brown, S. (2012) 'Mobile apps: which ones really matter to the information professional?' *Business Information Review*, 29(4): 231–37.

Chaffey, D. (2011) *E-Business and E-Commerce Management: strategy, implementation and practice*, 5th ed., Harlow: Pearson.

Chaffey, D. and Ellis-Chadwick, F. (2012) *Digital Marketing*, 5th ed., Harlow: Prentice Hall.

Chan, N.L. and Guillet, B.D. (2011) 'Investigation of social media marketing: how does the hotel industry in Hong Kong Perform in marketing on social media websites?' *Journal of Travel & Tourism Marketing*, 28(4): 345–68.

Constantinides, E. and Fountain, S.J. (2008) 'Web 2.0: conceptual foundations and marketing issues', *Journal of Direct, Data & Digital Marketing Practice*, 9(3): 231–44.

Dees, W. (2011) 'New media and technology use in corporate sport sponsorship: performing activational leverage from an exchange perspective', *International Journal of Sport Management and Marketing*, 10(2/4): 272–85.

FanVision (2013) *About*. Online Available <http://www.fanvision.com/about.html> (accessed 4 February, 2013).

Fletcher, A. and Lee, M.J. (2012) 'Digital heritage: current social media uses and evaluations in American museums', *Museum Management and Curatorship*, 27(5): 505–21.

Hoy, M.B. (2011) 'An introduction to QR codes: linking libraries and mobile patrons', *Medical Reference Services Quarterly*, 30(3): 295–300.

Hyun, M.Y., Lee, S. and Hu, C. (2009) 'Mobile-mediated virtual experience in tourism: concept, typology and applications', *Journal of Vacation Marketing*, 15(2): 149–64.

Kietzmann, J.H., Hermkens, K., McCarthy, I.P. and Silvestre, B.S. (2011) 'Social media? Get serious! Understanding the functional building blocks of social media', *Business Horizons*, 54(3): 241–51.

Lascia, J.D. (2007) *The Mobile Generation: global transformations at the cellular level*, Report of the Fifteenth Annual Aspen Institute Roundtable on Information Technology, Washington DC: Aspen Institute.

Nair, M. (2011) 'Understanding and measuring the value of social media', *The Journal of Corporate Accounting & Finance*, March/April: 45–51.

Richards, G. and Palmer, R. (2010) *Eventful Cities: cultural management and urban revitalisation*, Oxford: Butterworth-Heinemann.

Santomier, J. (2008) 'New media, branding, and global sports sponsorship', *International Journal of Sports Marketing and Sponsorship*, 10(1): 15–28.

Smart Insights (2012) *The Who, Why and Where of Using QR or Action Codes for Marketing*. Online. Available <http://www.smartinsights.com> (accessed 4 February 2013).

Weber, L. (2009) *Marketing to the Social Web: how digital customer communities build your business*, 2nd ed., London: Wiley.

Zhang, M., Jansen, B.J. and Chowdhury, A. (2011) 'Business engagement on Twitter: a path analysis', *Electronic Markets – International Journal of Electronic Commerce Business Media*, 21(3): 161–75.

16 The future is virtual

Debbie Sadd

Future points

- The transformational power of technology will impact the design of events.
- Events as gatherings will still need interaction for co-creation.
- The fusion of virtual and real, with blended technology, will be the way forward.
- Technology usage will enable competitive position within the events industry and will assist sustainable development.

Introduction

Over the past ten years, the speed at which events have seen graphics and entertainment formats develop has continued at a fast rate. Professor Steve Feiner is quoted in an article (2011) as saying that he believed augmented reality still had some way to go and stated,

> I honestly believe that at some point in the future we're going to have AR eyewear that's sufficiently light weight, comfortable, visually appealing, high quality enough and at the right price that people will want to wear while walking around. It has to be socially acceptable and desirable.

It is interesting to see that only two years later, in 2014, the Google glasses technology will be available (having been put back from 2013) but with an initial price tag of around $1,000. Maybe not a commercially viable price, yet the product is still predicted to be extremely popular and demonstrates how quickly advances in technology are being made.

Haptic technology is advancing the experience through touch (without the need for verbal communication) and is highly developed in gaming technologies such as Xbox, Xbox One, PS3, PS4 Wii (Robles-De-La-Tour 2009). Recently academics are proposing that technology-based events (techno-events) have the power to move beyond physical laws, space, time and memory (Frew and McGillivray in press). Therefore, they blur the distinctions between reality and fantasy, which can lead to resistance from some sections of society as a destabilizing force. It is no longer 'science fiction' (ibid), but more parallel worlds of sensory digital avatars and second life immersion. However, from where does the belonging and togetherness often seen as a driver for attending events arise in this scenario?

Development of virtual technologies

Historically, much of the 'virtual' technological developments have proceeded with support from military organizations, (e.g. the STRICOM programme, in the United States), with battlefield technology requirements. Barrilleaux (1999) described, more than a decade ago, how augmented reality allowed vehicle crews to see virtual vehicles and weapon effects and was a crucial component of the two-way simulation, which therefore allowed live and virtual vehicles to interact in real time on the same battlefield. Considering this type of technology was available in 1999 for the military, it has taken a relatively long time to transfer into the commercial entertainment world. An example of how this has been developed into events applications is the CroMAR project (mobile augmented reality for supporting reflection on crowd management) described by Mora, Boron and Diviniti (2012). Mobile augmented reality is used to support crowd management initiatives by using it to layer information about the event itself onto a simulated platform at the same physical location. This is, however, problematic, as Brown *et al.* (2004) argue that the full power of mobile augmented and virtual reality systems is realized only when these systems are connected to one another. Therefore these connections need wireless networks and so the effect is only as good as the technology providing the access.

Frew and McGillivray (2008) proposed that events in general continue to be in awe of what they referred to as 'the transformational power of technology' in allowing escapism and fantasy in event design. Considering these observations were made six years ago, this applies more than ever today, with further developments seen in technology on a daily basis of which augmented reality is at the leading edge.

Augmented reality

Augmented reality (AR) by definition is the concept whereby the view of reality is modified in some way by computer-generated sensory input such as sound, video and graphics in live real-world environments and searches for new ways to interact between physical and virtual worlds (Arthur 2010). Therefore, the technology enhances the perception of reality for the recipient of the augmentation and builds upon developments in the virtual world. Whereas previously it was developed for military and medical uses, now it is seen in many applications from gaming to sports, travel, education, construction, industrial design architecture and archaeology. Whilst it has many applications in the entertainment field, it is relatively new to the meetings and business conference market where it allows for interaction and communication with customers and clients through understanding their behaviour and preferences.

It is the augmentation of the reality that distinguishes it from virtual reality, whereby the technology replaces the real world. In addition, augmented reality allows the environment to be interactive and digitally manipulated, with artificial information being overlaid onto the real world. Such popular examples include sponsor advertising available only to TV audiences seen directly in the field of play at rugby and cricket matches. Furthermore, it can be a combination of both real and virtual adding the original image with layers of digital information. This can be seen during competitive swimming, whereby the TV viewers see the position of the swimmers in relation to world records appearing ahead of the competitors as they swim along.

The history of augmented reality has developed out of mobile technologies and desktop technologies to now being a crucial component of live event experiences, whereby it is not an addition but a fundamental part of the experience. Azuma (1997) describes it more as a seamless integration of virtual and real, calling it mixed reality. Ever more discerning audiences are requesting more emotive experiences from events to enhance the consumer experience but also for the organizer to gain competitive advantage over rivals with groundbreaking technology. However, the concepts of augmented and virtual reality have been seen in movies as far back as *Total Recall* and even the 'Star Wars' movie franchise in the 1980s. Duran Duran's December 2000 'Pop Trash' live concert tour used a variety of real-time visual effects developed specifically for the band to demonstrate prototypes of new developing AR technologies (Pair *et al.* 2002).

Whilst there have been many advances in the new types of technology, with most developments being ways of using technology to complement other means of communication, there are few developments commercially available that allow for total connectivity in the virtual world. There are silent discos and headsets, but these only allow one-way interaction where the experience is unique to each user as he or she chooses the music he or she wishes to have relayed through his or her individual headsets. The overall effect is quite amusing seeing a room of people all dancing to different music! Even holograms and augmented reality do not allow two-way interactions. Furthermore, returning to the movie *Total Recall*, Sharon Stone took tips from her virtual coach, but she wasn't given feedback. In the intervening years technology is still being developed to allow this two-way interaction, as seen with the testing of Google glasses, yet augmented reality is still only one way and not interactive. Recent demonstrations of how far the technology has developed include the recent CONFEX exhibition in London, where a hologram of the American singer and music producer, Will-i-am, was shown at the finals of the Eventice (student job hunt) competition. Whilst the imagery was outstanding, he could only move sideways on the stage and not forwards and backwards. His reaction with the audience is nonexistent and his engagement with his audience one way. However, these developments are progressing on a daily basis, and when we get used to one form of augmented reality we then start to search for ever more exciting developments and seeing new things.

The live streaming of events is growing so fast it is now becoming a commonplace development, especially in sport. The additional creation of live sites to facilitate the experience has expanded the ways in which people can engage in events. Live streaming even allows for the event to be accessed from home, but again the enjoyment and experience is not the same as being at the actual event for a variety of sensory touch points (Arthur 2010). Allowing attendance at 'sold out' events in this way allows for marketing and brand extension beyond those attending but without the true interconnectivity and co-creation.

Technology incorporated into the events experience will allow for competitive advantage, as espoused by Porter (1982). Innovation and the concern for 'newness' is prevalent within the events market especially in highly competitive and economically stretched markets. In strategy studies, Porter states that continuous innovation is needed to maintain competitive advantage, yet festivals and events need to differentiate their product by the level of service they offer and the level of innovation they can afford. There appears, according to Quinn (2013), a dichotomy here, as traditional festivals tended to relate to celebrating the 'old' yet increasingly need innovation, which is all about the new. With anthropological studies showing how events are about celebration and rituals, acknowledging the need to follow rites and rituals thus perhaps conflicts with the need to innovate and try new things (Getz 2007).

Justifications for the inclusion of augmented reality

Within the study of events, and the planning of events, much has been written within consumer behaviour and marketing about the anticipation and the journey involved in waiting for events (Schmitt, 1999). Similarly, much has been written about the shared experience of the event itself, whether festivals, product launches, conferences or shows because in both the journey and in the event experience itself, human interaction is central for the co-creation (Rihova *et al.* 2013). However, will virtual events and augmented reality substitute for this co-creation, allowing each individual to interpret their experiences differently?

Hall (2013), in discussing the views of Ben Nasher, a computer expert, proposes that the use of AR (in his example the use of iPad-like devices mounted on Segway bikes allows for virtual tours around venues) allows people to avoid having to travel to events, thus satisfying sustainability advocates. However, will this 'remote' access allow for networking and some of the interconnectability required to actually do business? In contrast, Bulearca and Tamarjan (2010) suggest that is in the use of AR in experiential marketing events that makes them memorable and thus useful within Client Relationship Marketing to gain customer loyalty, rather than perhaps as innovative developments. This polar argument needs to be viewed in the context of the typology of events under discussion. For instance, corporate events and business conferences are both places that need physical contact, as sometimes the best deals consist of a handshake agreement, whereas in economically stringent times there is a need for long-distance engagement in events due to restrictions in travel budgets. On the other hand, festivals will always be gatherings of people, yet these people are continually seeking ever more stimulating experiences, and so technology is being used more and more to provide this. The social reality within events is not objective, 'but highly subjective and shaped by our perceptions', according to Bulearca and Tamarjan (2010: 237); thus often AR is used within events to raise the level of experience for the attendee in order to engender some customer benefits/loyalty within marketing terms. Therefore, the AR is part of a promotional tool kit offering perceived added value to the customer/attendees through developments in near field communication with trade shows and fairs using AR through mobile platforms such as smartphones and tablets (Greenwald 2012) and now retailers such as Macy's are incorporating AR into sales experiences (Bizwire 2011).

As was already mentioned, the development of Google glasses, with their technological innovations, is causing a stir, but the high base price makes it the type of technology that will not initially gain widespread adoption. Headphones for silent discos are more affordable compared to these glasses at present, but with future developments the price may become more affordable, yet it will be crucial as to how they enhance the event experience. The argument will be that as technology develops, so will consumer expectations. What is considered a 'wow' factor in 2013 will become mainstream very quickly – see Feiner's 2011 predications about optical technology. It will be interesting to see where the value will be added, as social media now allows digital footprints to be part and parcel of the event experience. The need for a 'live' event setting could be more important than ever in an increasingly digitalized world. Perhaps with generation 'C' (connected, communicating, content-centric, computerized, community-oriented, always clicking; Booz & Co, 2010) and their technological engagement and dependency, the face-to-face enjoyment and experience through live events will be the trend for the future. This drives the industry to think of ever more ways to foster interconnectivity. According to Getz (2007) and Goldblatt (2002) and their definitions of events, with virtual augmentation and people's lives being more connected than ever on a daily basis with technology, perhaps only events will allow for the 'real' and the necessary opportunities for social interaction. However, for Pine and Gilmore (1999), with their 'experience economy' notions and then the further development of the arguments into transformational economies, the transformation comes from the personal interaction rather than with technology. There will still be a space and a need for more virtual participation in some aspects of events through online engagement, due perhaps to constraints preventing the attendees from being there in person (hence leaving a zero footprint at the physical site of the event). However, can the 'live' performance create the same engagement and interaction using digital technologies? In marketing and sponsorship terms, smart tools are constantly being integrated into campaigns, as they add value and therefore are often an important part of these events' design. As previously mentioned, the specific use of this technology in conferences is growing, as it has allowed through technology the opportunity for delegates to spend more time in building relationships with people but still perhaps requiring physical attendance (Ibrahim, 2011).

Sustainability concerns

Whether technology could ever totally replace the 'gathering' of people is perhaps too far in the future to propose, especially with 2013 being the 'Year of the Gathering' (a year-long celebration of everything Irish (www.thegatheringireland.com). Elements of the event industry will be constantly reviewed in light of environmental and sustainability issues. Legislation will constantly need to be reviewed to ensure up-to-date standards are maintained within the industry and society as a whole. Indeed BS8901, the original UK industry standard, has as a result of the London 2012 Games morphed into ISO 20121 Sustainable Event Management policy (BSI, 2012) based on the groundbreaking environmental developments seen in the planning of and the running of the 2012 Olympics (Bioregional Development Group, 2012). The independent Commission for a Sustainable London 2012 believes that London has been the greenest Olympics ever, especially through its recycling and regeneration. However, it further added that much more could be done to minimize the impact on people and the planet of future Olympics.

All events now are encouraged to be organized in a sustainable manner and the Rio Declaration (1992) states it is about minimizing the negative impacts and accentuating the positive. However, this is not just environmental, as economic and social impacts too need to be considered in the triple bottom line evaluation. Events on the whole have been late to adopt the sustainability agenda, yet now there is more impetus with the adoption of ISO 20121 with the controlled use of resources and consideration given around levels of waste and efficient management of waste systems. The radical argument would be that all virtual exposure to events would minimize these waste systems, yet the very nature of the virtual and augmented technology requires energy to run them, which in itself has a carbon footprint. Therefore there is a weak argument to be made for total substitution.

Getz, Andersson and Larson (2007) suggest that in twenty-first-century life, the very socio-cultural, economic and political fabric of society rests on events being a core component of cultural consumption and a vital part of everyday life. This is even more important when reviewing the growth in large-scale events. These cannot always be attended by everyone, and so technology whether actual, virtual or augmented engagement can be a powerful way of bringing these events to bigger audiences.

What does the future hold?

'Events technology consultant Adi Ben-Nesher has discussed the "mind blowing" ways that augmented reality can be used at events' is the headline from 5th February 2013 in *CIT Magazine* (Hall, 2013), one of the United Kingdom's leading trade publication, thus illustrating an example of how it has become a key supporting tool within event design.

For the meetings and conventions market virtual product displays are increasing with exhibitors visualizing physical products in on-stand environments. As already mentioned near field technology is allowing the incorporation of recognition systems to acquire reference representation of the real world. When trying to sell destinations, venues or hotels, immersive technology is transporting the 'guest' into 360-degree representations and thereby allowing experiences to be gained whilst at a show or convention (EIBTM, 2013).

In an article called 'Five Predictions: What's Next in Event Management Technology and What It Means', Doug Matthews, known as 'The Special Event Guru' in the United States (an industry spokesperson), predicted in November 2012 that the big five developments for event management would include the use of apps to provide in-app advertising related to the event in question, with special reference to augmented reality in mobile applications in handheld displays. In addition multiplatform integration of technology, through projectors allowing multiple viewing angles, will be part of the daily enhancement of experiences whether through business applications or personal enjoyment. Finally he supports the social media usage within mobile apps as a crucial continuing development area in event management. Tangible user interfaces will augment the physical world experience – supporting the argument for blended technology. Interestingly in his predictions, the events all still have physical attendees with no virtual substitutions. In addition, the future predictions from top technology experts include technology as an enabler, cloud technology and tablets as the platform to connect. Goudreau (2013) reports that the CEO of IBM, Ginni Rometty, believes that the big technological developments will be data analytics revolutionizing decision making; social networks will drive value and customer segmentation will revert to individual segmentation. The implications here for the events business are how personal each event attendee will then customize their experience to be, and perhaps this is where the advances in technology will allow this. However, Robinson, Wade and Dickson (2010) have predicted in relation to the events industry that twenty-first-century events will be dominated by three distinct genres of events: local, carbon neutral sustainable events; global mega events and the development of virtual events using new and emerging technologies that would not only satisfy the media dependencies of generation 'C' (create, connect, consume, communicate and contribute), but also those who would like the traditional event personal interface.

Frew and McGilivray (In Press), in contrast, believe that future technological developments could be incorporated into event designs through realms of fantasy and therefore may lead to a future when the 'end user'/event attendee never needs to physically attend the event to experience the event. The co-creation and co-production is through the technology. Future opportunities to engage in events through virtual walkways where attendance is not possible will allow virtual attendees to immerse themselves to gain an experience of sorts, yet how will this experience ever be a true substitute for the real thing? It could still be argued that the experience of attending an event is more than just the physical being there through the co-creation (Rihova *et al.* 2013). Perhaps experiencing virtual Glastonbury in a pod somewhere else will not afford the same experience of traveling to the event; the anticipation leading up to the acts appearing; the mud, wet and rain or the interaction with fellow attendees. This can already been seen, as it is possible to enter a world of computer games in 3D, and through unique headsets a virtual world of entertainment where total immersion is part of the experience. Human experiences have traditionally been expressed through words and pictures, and now advances in technology allow for this data capturing to be presented in the form of AR through emotional interfaces.

Conclusion

Whilst the environmental lobbyists have seen major changes within the sustainability agenda with the staging of the London 2012 Olympics, the connectivity and interaction seen at events will never force them off the agenda totally, as humans still need to meet and interact. This interaction will remain a crucial component of the events industry, as festivals and celebration dating back thousands of years have always involved humans, sometimes traveling over great distances, to interact culturally, historically and religiously or on a business interface, and this will continue to do so, incorporating technological advances, the rationale being that technology cannot yet allow for total connectivity and immersion and that integral face-to-face human reaction, co-creation and co-production are crucial elements of the event experience. Technology is being developed yet arguments abound as to whether these innovations will ever be totally immersive. Technology will continue to enhance enjoyment in society, through an innate desire to experience ever more cutting edge developments and furthermore younger generations thrive on connectivity with technology. Haptics, nonverbal communication involving touch, virtual and augmented reality are all evolving within events, yet the cost of being at the cutting edge does preclude many people and the investments required for the events industry to make these developments part and parcel of everyday event experiences; that is still some way in the future. As the cost of these developments become more affordable, more and more events will be a fusion of the real with the virtual as a norm. The future points more to a blending of live setting, virtual/augmented technology and online engagement.

Significance of this chapter's contribution to the future of events

Technology is now transforming every aspect of our lives, and in particular generation 'C' (Solis 2012) thrives on its evolution. As our lives are becoming more dependent upon advances in technology, what will events of the future be able to offer in relation to experiences and transformation? Whilst ever more remarkable technological developments are being delivered on a daily basis, the design of event experiences will need to fit into this highly evolving environment. Commercial applications of augmented and virtual reality have been seen within military training, sports coverage and marketing promotions; it is only certain event concepts that support those developments at present, but the market is changing.

The future of events in relation to this technology could go down the route of total immersion, with haptic technology being developed even further to embrace all five senses. Alternatively, events could be the one opportunity for real inter-action and experience on a face-to-face level in worlds where otherwise we will become insular. The co-creation and co-production needed to experience events will only be possible with real time – real-life integration of which technology, whether augmented, virtual or both, will be a part of the experience – but not the whole experience.

References

Arthur, C. (2010) Augmented reality – it is like real life but better. *The Guardian*, 10 September. Online. Available <www.guardian.co.uk/technology/2010/mar/21/augmented-reality-iphone-advertising> (accessed 28 November 2013).

Azuma, R.T. (1997) 'A survey of augmented reality', *Presence: Teleoperators and Virtual Environments*, 6(4): 355–85.

Barrilleaux, J. (1999) *Experiences and Observations in Applying Augmented Reality to Live Training*. Online. Available <www.jmbaai.com/vwsim99/vwsim99.html> (accessed 28 November 2013).

Bioregional Development Group (2012) *The Towards a One Planet Olympics Initiative Revisited*. Online. Available <www.bioregional.com/files/publications/towards-a-one-planet-olympics-revisited.pdf> (accessed 27 August 2013).

Bizwire (2011) 'Macy's introduces augmented reality experiences in stores across country as part of its 2011 "Believe" campaign', *Business Wire*. Online. Available <www.businesswire.com/news/home/20111102006759/en/Macy%E2%80%99s-Introduces-Augmented-Reality-Experience-Stores-Country> (accessed 28 November 2013).

Booz & Co (2010) *The Rise of Generation C Implications for the World of 2020*. Online. Available <www.booz.com/media/file/Rise_Of_Generation_C.pdf> (accessed 24 August 2013).

British Standards Institution (BSI) (2012) *ISO 20121 Sustainable Event Management*. Online. Available <www.bsigroup.co.uk/en-GB/iso-20121-sustainable-events-management> (accessed 27 August 2013).

Brown, D.G., Julier, S.J., Baillot, Y., Livingstone, M.A. and Rosenblum, L.J. (2004) 'Event-based data distribution for mobile augmented reality and virtual environments,' *Presence: Teleoperators and Virtual Environments*, 13(2): 211–21.

Bulearca, M., Tamarjan, D. (2010) 'Augmented reality: a sustainable marketing tool?', *Global Business and Management Research: An International Journal*, 2(2/3): 237–52.

EIBTM (2013) *Augmented Reality Is Coming to an Event Near You*. Online. Available <www.eibtm.com/en/News-and-Media/Blog/Augmented-Reality-is-coming-to-an-event-near-you/> (accessed 24 August 2013).

Feiner, S. (2011) 'Augmented reality: a long way off?', *AR Week. Pocket-lint*. 3 March.

Frew, M. and McGillivray, D. (2008) 'Exploring hyper-experiences: performing the fan at Germany 2006', *Journal of Sport & Tourism*, 13(3): 181–18.

Frew, M. and McGillivray, D. (In press) 'From fan parks to live sites: mega events and the territorialisation of urban spaces', *Urban Studies*.

Getz, D. (2007) *Event Studies*. Oxon, UK: Routledge.

Getz, D., Andersson, T. and Larson, M. (2007) 'Managing festival stakeholders: Concepts and case studies', *Event Management*, 10: 103–22.

Goldblatt, J. (2002) *Special Events: global event management in the 21st century*, 3rd ed., New York: John Wiley & Sons.

Goudreau, J. (2013) IBM CEO Predicts Three Ways Technology Will Transform The Future Of Business, *Forbes.com.* Online. Available <www.forbes.com/sites/jennagoudreau/2013/03/08/ibm-ceo-predicts-three-ways-technology-will-transform-the-future-of-business/> (accessed 28 November 2013).

Greenwald, W. (2012, February) 'Augmented reality takes centre stage at Toy Fair 2012', *PC Magazine,* London UK.

Hall, T. (2013, 5 February) 'Augmented reality has a "mind blowing" future for events, says technology expert', *CIT Magazine,* London, UK.

Ibrahim, M. (2011, June) 'Smart tools that add value', *Technology*: 20–21.

Matthews. D. (2012) *Five Predictions: what's next in event management technology and what it means.* Online. Available < http://specialeventguru.blogspot.co.uk/2012/11/five-predictions-whats-next-in-event.html> (accessed 28 November 2013).

Mora, S., Boron, A. and Diviniti, M. (2012) 'CroMAR: Mobile augmented reality for supporting reflection on crowd management', *International Journal of Mobile Human Computer Animation,* 4(2): 88–101.

Pair, J., Wilson, J., Chastine, J. and Gandy, M. (2002) 'The Duran Duran Project: the augmented reality toolkit in live performance'. *The First IEEE International Augmented Reality Toolkit Workshop.*

Pine, J. and Gilmore, J. (1999) *The Experience Economy.* Boston: Harvard Business School Press.

Porter, M. E. (1982) *Cases in Competitive Strategy.* New York: Free Press.

Quinn, B. (2013) *Key Concepts in Event Management.* London: Sage.

Rihova, I., Buhalis, D., Moital, M. and Gouthro, M.-B. (2013) 'Social layers of customer-to-customer value co-creation', *Journal of Service Management,* 24(5): 553–66.

Robinson, P., Wale, D. and Dickson, G. (2010) *Events Management.* Oxford: CABI.

Robles-De-La-Torre G. (2009) 'Virtual reality: touch/haptics', in B. Goldstein (ed.) *Sage Encyclopaedia of Perception.* Thousand Oaks CA: Sage Publications.

Schmitt, B. (1999) 'Experiential marketing', *Journal of Marketing Management,* 15(1–3): 53–67.

Solis, B. (2012) *Meet Generation C: the connected customer.* Online. Available <www.briansolis.com/2012/04/meet-generation-c-the-connected-customer/> (accessed 24 August 2013).

U.N.D.E.S.A. (1992) *Rio Declaration on Environment and Development.* United Nations Conference on Environment and Development. Rio de Janeiro, 3–14 June 1992. Online. Available <http://www.un.org/documents/ga/conf151/aconf15126-1annex1.htm>, accessed 12 June 2013.

17 Leadership and visionary futures

Future proofing festivals

Martin Robertson and Steve Brown

Future points

- An understanding of the event's audience is the primary factor in the success of the event, now and in the future.
- Aided by a visionary future, new levels of directorial leadership will emerge.
- The rise of the practitioner academic will have significant implications for the direction of future event research.
- Co-creativity and the demand for bespoke experiences will increase, while the impact of new technologies will decrease.

Introduction

David Bowie's 1974 album *Diamond Dogs* offered a dystopian vision of the world in which '. . . fleas the size of rats sucked on rats the size of cats and ten thousand peoploids split into small tribes coveting the highest of the sterile skyscrapers . . . ' (Bowie 1974).

Thankfully, neither this predictive vision nor the one encapsulated in George Orwell's novel *1984* (published in 1949 and on which Bowie based his album) came to pass. The danger of any attempt to predict the future is that the only real way to know what will happen is to be there to experience it – and to bring tomorrow back to today. The rest is, for most people, educated guesswork, guesstimation.

However, we should not condemn eminent futurists as offering only apocalyptic farewells, such as the pronouncement, 'I'll be back!' by the T-800 Model 101 cyborg assassin, played so successfully by Arnold Schwarzenegger in the film *The Terminator*. We should feel comfortable, rather, that whatever surprises the future might bring, designing an event based on an understanding of the event's audience will still ensure that the event practitioner will have the optimal chance of delivering a successful and sustainable event that meets or exceeds it stated aims and outcomes (Brown 2010).

The authors contend that analysis of the future is not only exceptionally valuable as part of contingency planning and strategic foresight for the management of festival and events – and thus avoiding failure (Getz 2002) – generally, it is also vital for the sustainability of this social form, a form which holds increasing power in the societies of 2020, 2030 and 2040.

Conceptual base and methodological position

Further, the authors propose that visionary futures are vital in a rapidly changing world in which co-creativity and a myriad of technological infusions will change the way people live and contribute to new economic models, new working relationships and new social regulation processes (Robertson and Yeoman 2014). We contend that when considering the future of festivals, a prediction of what will happen in the future is likely to fail (Bauer 2013). Instead, a *vision* is required to forecast a future to work towards.

There are seven vision types, each with different purpose and characteristic (van der Helm 2009). These are humanistic, religious, political, business/organizational, community, policy and personal. The researchers have undertaken one that takes on the characteristics of the business/organization, and thus involves leadership and is convergent in nature.

Vision formation is more successful when it supports a cause rather than a specific goal (Byrne and Shipman 2010). To legitimize a vision it is important that it is able to motivate and bring support, that the vision is shared and that it expresses higher-order aspirations (Bezold *et al.* 2009) (rather than attempt to predetermine exact outcomes). The vision forwarded here has been extrapolated from formal surveys and from discussion with event leaders (festival directors, event designers, artistic directors, creative producers and event managers) from organized events in Australia, China, New Zealand, Sweden, the United Arab Emirates, the United Kingdom and the United States of America. For a festival, one likely cause is assuring the most enlightened and sustainable event design possible. This requires leadership that is vision orientated and adaptable to changes as they occur.

While certainly a broadly behaviourist analysis, this work is both scoping and normative in nature. It looks at past and present applications of design – in areas both directly and indirectly relating to festivals. The researchers then identify current and potential trends and determine the relationship of these with the design of festivals. These are reviewed in respect of identified drivers and trends. Together they form a normative commentary on the future design of festivals and event.

Directorial leadership of the event

While innumerable elements of society and the event industry are certain to change – a decade's hence, even a year's hence – and there will be numerous surprises for even the most prescient of futurists, one factor will be a constant: the creation and staging of event experiences will necessitate an audience. A deep understanding of the audience is, therefore, a critical factor in being able to respond to, and proactively design for, the change that will occur. Event Design is the practice that embodies, embraces and engages with that deep understanding – it is 'audience-centric' by definition – and the future event practitioner will therefore need to be an event designer first before any other aspect of his or her professional practice.

For festivals the role of the director (whom we can also refer to as leader or leaders) is immensely important (Ensor, Robertson, and Ali-Knight 2007, 2011; Robertson 2012a). In the contemporary event industry 'leader' can mean event designer, artistic director, creative producer or even event manager, but directorial (leader) vision is always crucial. The work here, then, takes a normative position as a way in which festival leaders may choose to affect a visionary future rather than a predictive one.

In an early personal investigation by one of the authors' it was found that early adoption of this leadership role (and adoption of the idea of event design itself) came from those event industry practitioners who had already held a leadership role as a director or producer in either theatre (where the majority had prior experience), television or film, i.e. three industries where an understanding of the audience is primary and where directorial vision *is* the role.

These directorial leaders will be multi-practitioners working between filtering trends and facilitating trends. They will need the skillset to enable them to design for the live and design for the virtual – part marketer, part audience behaviourist, always an event designer. They will be working in an environment where the sustainable consumption of events is the norm and sustainable event practice is so deeply embedded in professional practice it is no longer thought of as needing a green tick as a badge of compliance or honour.

A vast array of event design software and hardware will be available to leaders. Accordingly, as with existing lighting design software, the leaders will apply their vision and generate a 3D digital model of the venue and place design elements on screen. They will see how the event works before creating the plans and program to implement the design. Ultimately, as exists for lighting, the program can also run the event. Expanding that capability in the future, not only lighting, but every element of the design can be designed (and run) virtually. For audiences unable to attend live they can simply download the virtual event or experience it online.

Live and online audiences will be connected via a variety of sensors evaluating both physiological and psychological arousal and response rates. Receiving such immediate and iterative feedback from the audience, the event designer (or the automated software program) modifies the event's program in real time to change the shape, structure and program of the event to ensure that arousal levels are maintained and an optimal experience is achieved for each and every member of the audience.

On a quiet day, tired after an evening of managing and designing multiple events on multiple live and virtual stages, the event designer looks to the software to provide ideas and inspiration for a new event that is being developed. After the designer enters the initial parameters of the event, most importantly the demographic and psychographic profile of the audience, the software generates a long list of event ideas; event names and the basic event marketing, management and safety plans. Narrowing down to two or three options, the event designer tweaks the parameters until three separate events exist digitally, choosing one for the event being developed and uploading the other two for immediate virtual consumption.

The experiential and liminal nature of events: future vision

There is a large body of knowledge relating to the experience economy, both as it influences the individual and its relation to the wider business and management environment (Pine and Gilmore 1998, 2011). Tarssanen and Kylänen (2009) proposed an Experience Pyramid Model for the tourism, cultural and entertainment industries (Figure 17.1), which is included here to animate understanding of the product experience. While the vertical axis indicates the core levels of experience, and is important, for concision key reference is made to the horizontal axis: individuality, authenticity, story, multisensory perception, contrast and interaction. They are looked at as they relate to the principles of designing an event (Brown and James 2004) and as they determine the vision.

Planned events (festivals and artistic performance events) offer a transmission of experience unlike any other products (Getz 1997; Hall 1992; Ryan 2012). They are immensely popular because of their capacity to offer the audience member an experience, one that is 'betwixt and between' ordinary experiences (Turner 1977). They offer liminal capacity (Turner 1977), a sense of otherness. Further, this sense of otherness may prevail in a great number of event types – ranging from dramatic art performance to sport competition to business conference or training (Ryan 2012).

As these organized events are recognized for their liminal capacity, many stakeholders support them in anticipation of their offering this quality while also serving their own purposes – political and economic, short term and long term (Ryan 2012;

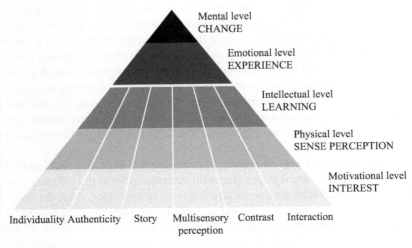

Figure 17.1 Experience pyramid

Yeoman, Robertson, and Smith 2012). This is particularly true for major public events, hallmark events or mega events. The danger is that the outcome (political or as part of business communication strategy) may take precedence over the core strength of the event itself, its uniqueness and authenticity (Crespi-Vallbona and Richards 2007; Richards 2007).

It is difficult to immerse an event in a range of external functions and required outcomes without expecting the experience to be affected. And so it is that many events and festivals (particularly music festivals) have failed because the experience offered is a replica of many others (that are generic) in a market that looks now to be oversupplied, as a variety of stakeholders and/or entrepreneurs attempt to gain advantage. This is of particular significance for music festivals at which liminal qualities are seen as particularly important (Hawkins and Ryan 2013; Packer and Ballantyne 2011).

The state of liminal experience is not best suited to constraint. Brown and James (2004) warn of the dangers of failing to understand experience, and designing events with stakeholders in mind rather than the community or attendee group it should nurture and respond to. As Brown and Hutton (2013: 43) state, the 'creation and staging of the event experience – the realm of event design – is predicated on an understanding of the psychosocial domain of the audience'. Necessarily, however, organized events have, as stated, become bound to their required outcomes. Further, given that change normally comes with additional cost, it has also meant that new events require more stakeholders and strategic alliances able to fund these necessary changes (Robertson and Wardrop 2012). This, unfortunately, adds more strain when attempting to design in a way that captures uniqueness, authenticity and the experiential needs of the event participants. This is likely to remain the case for the near to mid-term future.

So, experience management for organized events will become as much about creative management (as an exacting and responsive process) as it is an act of being creative. Accordingly, designing an event experience will become more multifarious – and more demanding – than ever before. Looking into the future as we do in this work, it is important to understand that these changes will occur with new pressures. These are discussed further.

Co-creativity and the bespoke event

To add to this future view, the authors propose that these demands will work in conjunction with an increased level of participation by audiences. While responses to the experience economy have become more common in academic literature, its inclusion by practitioner academics in the field of event management is more recent and opens 'a rich new field' of exploration (Brown and Hutton 2013: 44).

Further, co-creation (creative collaboration) and the need for interaction of the audience member with the performance is very important but has received limited acknowledgment in regard to the way that it can be applied to the festival/live event environment. It is evident, however, that for a festival to gain a longer-term identification – with high levels of meaning and sustained interest (Ryan 2102) – festival and event goers and other stakeholders will only commit themselves to co-creative activity where each has a part in generating value (Ramaswamy and Gouillart 2010). Moreover, the co-creative environment is a competitive one, one in which arts and festivals may be stratified not only because of perceived limitations of collaborative contribution but also if there is a failure to recognize the difference in levels of collaborative capacity (Walmsley 2013). There is far more segmentation and value adding for festival attendees to be made from understanding the multiple forms of co-creative opportunity that can be facilitated – and the risks (and negatives) that can arise from audience-led creativity.

The notion of co-creativity has emerged from stage production. So as active involvement of the audience in theatre can bring forward a better performance (Ryan 2012), so too the active involvement of the attendee is vital for the degree to which the festival is memorable. In theatre stage production this has resonated around the actor's 'sixth sense', the subliminal awareness of the audience (Hagen 1991; Jean 2006). In the same way it is observed that scenario planning, as one form of normative futures research, offers an organization insight and preparedness for its future that is like the actor's sixth sense (van der Heijden 2002).

Audiences already have the opportunity to co-create in real time both live and virtually. A marked characteristic of contemporary audiences (certainly those considered Generation X and later) is their ability and preference to multitask (in terms of attentional focus) at events. Audiences at the national touring music festival, Big Day Out (like many similar events) continually posted messages via social media throughout the live performance. Television audiences use social media to chat while watching their favourite 'soap'. Live theatre uses voting devices so that the audience can determine exactly what happens next (Brown and Hutton 2013: 52). Co-creation is at a very low level certainly, but as new technologies develop and the level of personal data available about an individual audience member increases, event designers are able to respond immediately (with or without the knowledge of the individual) and modify the experience for them – and maybe just for them alone. Audiences already: are tracked via GPS embedded in their tickets (MySki-Star 2012); have their experiences and feelings (and behaviour) recorded and evaluated for a time and space at the event (Pettersson and Getz 2009; Pettersson and Zillinger 2011) and have their physiological and psychological response to the multiple stimuli of an event environment evaluated (Brown and Hutton 2013). There will be an unprecedented opportunity for event designers to design events for an individual and for that individual to make changes and influence that design (co-creation) resulting in an event that is theirs and theirs alone (the bespoke event).

The impact of existing and likely new and emerging technologies, together with increasing globalization of culture will, however, mean that the number of possible experiences available to any individual (whether live or virtual) is also likely to increase exponentially. On the one hand this matches a trend identified where there is likely to be an increase in 'the number of occasions human beings choose to celebrate' (Yeoman 2013: 250), but as the number of these possible experiences increases, audiences will not only begin to drown in choice but those choices will also become increasingly generic and limited.

As has already occurred in the music industry, individuality is often suppressed in favour of similarity. Like 'festivalisation' (Benneworth and Dauncey 2010;

Steinbrink, Haferburg and Ley 2011; Robertson 2012b), music producers watch the charts and mimic production styles based on those records that are seen to be succeeding commercially. In the late 1990s, popular artist Cher had a world-wide hit with 'Believe' (Cher 1998), which used a new recording effect based on deliberately alternating the vocal tone with auto-tuning software. Cher's use was original but the effect can now be found on hundreds of female (and male) vocal recordings. Once any new event design is in the global marketplace, the success-ful, original idea will be observed via social media postings and or web-wide media (e.g. YouTube) and used repeatedly by others.

The worldwide franchise of the television reality show *Big Brother* has run as a virtual event successfully since 1999. Apart from the language it is broadcast in, audiences share the same experience and can influence the outcome by voting people out of the *Big Brother* house. Producers can evaluate the telephone polling to make determinations about which cast members should remain in the house and their decision can be informed by evaluating the social media that is generated by viewers. This occurs for a myriad of other shows (e.g. any show where the viewer votes) and each will have attendant social media including live chat rooms and even purpose-built software (e.g. FANGO; http://au.fango.yahoo.com/) for viewers' interaction. It would be a reckless producer, indeed, who ignored the wishes/views/postings of his or her viewer(s). Journalists who are now intercon-nected with a global audience via Facebook and Twitter accounts are rated by their employers depending on the amount of 'traffic' that they generate. 'Top' stories are those that generate the most 'hits' and the news is consequently popularity driven as are many of the cultural and social aspects of our society. Popularity, however, does not necessarily determine whether something (in our case an event) is good or bad, just that it has reached a numerical target.

Knowing that an event design will be successful because the target audience is designing it for themselves may well be one way of ensuring economic sus-tainability, but for the individual everything becomes artificial and so the rise of authenticity as a key event design principle can be predicted to occur. As face-to-face, social interaction diminishes with an increase in virtual events, audiences will seek to connect with real people. A virtual mosh pit maybe safer than a real mosh pit, but the risky behaviour that is part of the makeup of the male adolescent will be a negative frustration leading to possibly higher levels of risky behaviour rather than a positive health and safety outcome.

Faced with seemingly limitless 'choice' of a 'wide range of the same', audi-ences can respond in one of three ways:

- Do nothing (i.e. not make a choice) and not engage with any (planned event) experience;
- Want to be told what to do and 'choose' *that* experience; or
- Prefer authentic experiences that are 'bespoke' (and that may only be avail-able to a narrow cohort of friends and family).

Many events will claim to be authentic, to capture the sense of 'magic nostalgia' and to provide opportunities for an audience member to show the world their 'exceptional choices' (Yeoman 2013: 251–253). It is likely, however, that the majority will remain within the generic range simply because of the economic imperative.

There may be an initial shift to (virtual) bespoke experiences where the audience member dials up or keys in the parameters of the event design. But we argue that this will be followed by bounce back to real experiences (experienced live and in location) with other audience members. Whether virtual or 'real', many bespoke events will be relatively easy to achieve, at least to a certain level.

So, the event may be generic but can also be modified by the individual audience member (you) who determines the music, the performers, the setting, the timing, the duration, even the climate in which it takes place.

Sitting in the centre of a 360-degree, floor-to-ceiling screen with a 250-speaker sound system and with each surface able to make minute changes in terms of texture, vibration, temperature and tilt angle, you can design every parameter of the event. The future air conditioning system adjusts the temperature according to the vision requested, and subtle scents are introduced to match the narrative of the experience. Given advance notice, AmazonFutureFood.com can deliver the same banquet that all the other guests are tasting – unless they like anchovies, and you don't. You have decided upon the 2050 equivalent of Brad Pitt to be the drinks waiter and, like the holodeck on the Starship Enterprise, there he is in all his holographic glory, ready to serve. If you think the event design is a little ordinary, then pay the premium (unless you are already a member of the Event Gold Class) and you can have your dreams caught and translated to the experience (Stokes 2014).

Should all this decision making be too much for you, let the software do it for you. 'They' already have all they need to know about you on the database based on everything you have posted or purchased or chatted about or selected during your entire lifetime. Web bots crawl the virtual event industry for just the right event for you and set up the parameters. A 3D printer prints out any props required and you can tweak the program a little just to feel as if you are in control of your experience. As the event unfolds, you respond to the little personal messages ('Eat Food Item #23 now!') and if you need a comfort break, just press hold.

Alternatively, the performance of Peter Brook's 'The Mahabharata', staged in an open air quarry for the 1988 Adelaide Festival, began in the early evening and ran uninterrupted until dawn the next day (and this author didn't notice the time and didn't need a comfort break).

A successful event designer will be that (brave) person who observes the trends but ignores those in favour of providing almost the opposite – unique, authentic experiences, that are bespoke and personalized. These will become the high end of events, the most expensive and the most sought after, as they are rich experiences using all five senses in real time.

The future audience

Van Boven and Gilovich's investigation into well-being found that 'spending money on experiences may lead to greater well-being than the purchase of material possessions' (2003: 1194). Although Howell and Hill's investigation into what makes people happy after their basic needs are met discovered that while it was not material things *per se* that satisfied us, if money was spent on experiences, then happiness might be argued to follow (Howell and Hill 2009: 521). If the experience can satisfy, then understanding how to capture and engage the audience with a positive and meaningful experience (Brown 2012) is the goal.

The degree of involvement in the festival or event varies greatly, dependent on a number of audience profile issues (both demographic and lifestyle related). In each, the metaphor of the fourth wall can be used to understand the relation between the audience and the performer/performance, i.e., the relation between the fictional context and the real context. This is to say that fiction and reality are often merged through a shared narrative (e.g. current question/answer period, voting on possible theatrical outcomes by the audience and opportunity for improvisation by actors in response to this) to ensure positive engagement (Jean 2006). It is a postmodern manifestation (Alraek and Baerheim 2005) and has been understood and used in both theatre and education (Jean 2006) and applied to museum design (Brown and Hutton 2013).

The reference to theatre, in particular, throughout this work is significant. A theatre, like a festival, is both a business and a purveyor of experience. Similarly, they rely upon and are measured by performance; they offer a range of experience components, layers of service and are often site specific. The application of the dramaturgical (Goffman, 1959), i.e., an understanding of the interaction with the total performance environment is central.

Extending Goffman's (1959) dramaturgical perspective, and applying both Kotler's (1973) *Atmospherics* and Bitner's (1986) Servicescapes concepts, Nelson (2009) offers a valuable base for understanding and prospectively enhancing the experience of business event attendees. Further, Brown and Hutton (2013) offer a guiding summary of the body of knowledge for (and theoretical constructs that form) the methodologies that may be used for investigating 'audience behaviour'.

The democratization of the festival experience

While one outcome of the aforementioned desire for co-creative value is that the increasing cost of new festivals may be reduced with the involvement of a greater number of the community (either through a communal acceptance of less elaborate and costly activity, or through a greater spread of cost bearing), it is not the case that the application to design of the event the will be any less important – far from it. The capacity to compare and accumulate experience, and to measure those experiences as part of personal cultural capital, becomes ever more important (Yeoman 2013; Yeoman, Robertson and Smith 2012). The use of technology to this end is very important. Indeed technology will have impact that few of us can imagine. But to suppose that it is both cultural leveller and a force to democratize the whole world is too simplistic.

While it is true that there will be greater access to arts and festival experience as a result of technology (Yeoman 2013), this does not mean that there will be one level of performance or one level of audience enjoyment. Yeoman (2013) reflects that there will be a 'no brow' culture, indicating that there will be an equalization of arts consumption. Evidencing the proliferation of co-creation and multicultural consumption does support this. However, other indications are that (art) festival consumption has a variety of co-creative dimensions, responding to different personal as well as group or community needs. As with all leisure experience, forms and the depth of participation will still be determined by personal perceptions, by the social and circumstantial position of a festival goer and the real or perceived opportunity cost of the event and related activity (Robertson 2004; Torkildsen 2002) and by the levels of knowledge they have and the sense of risk they perceive (Cheron and Ritchie 1982; Hay 2013; Robertson 2004; Slovic 2013). We argue, thus, that technology and new design will facilitate greater capacity for personalized, peer reviewed, individual, community, group specific, amateur, professional, co-creative, serviced, rewarding, differentiating, therapeutic, traditional, modern and cosmic experience than ever before, i.e., the future of festival and art performance design and its near seamless interrelation with technology will offer an infinite number of opportunities to aid the *future vision*.

The important notion that events are examples of bounded liminality (Ryan 2012), in which the experience has defined space, time and composition, is very important. The raucous and carnivalesque nature of events can be provided within the context of experience needs and audience type and preference. A good starting point to understand this is Ryan's (2012: 257) *matrix of event meaning duration of interest* (see Figure 17.2). For Ryan (2012) the venue is the nexus. This may also be true in the virtual and hybrid environment, although it does need adaptation to make this more understandable.

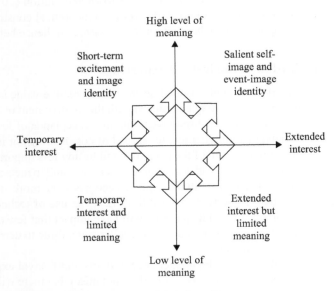

Figure 17.2 Matrix of event meaning and duration of interest

The impact of new technologies

It is rare that all the senses are managed as part of a large outdoor event per-formance. But so it was in the 2014 New Year celebrations for London that multisensory elements were added to the event. Tastes and smells of fruit were added to the display and, in a sense, wrapped 'guests in a cocoon of experience as color, fragrances and sound weave tighter to create the atmospheres clients seek' (Hancock as cited in Nelson 2009: 127).

Providing stimulation to the five senses is, of course, a primary function of the event designer, and there are multiple examples of this being executed effectively at both indoor and outdoor events now. Tomorrow, holograms, fog screens, water screens, data goggles, 3D contact lenses and more will also enhance the visual experience by providing data, images, alerts, explanations, subliminal messages and signals to motivate action and modify your behaviour.

Face recognition software identifies you on arrival at the event and your favou-rite music starts to play in your embedded, under-skin speakers (head phones, literally) that provide sound into the ear passages and vibrations and reverb to provide bass definition and sense of place, position and movement – even if you are stationary. Instantaneous translation arrives via the same speakers, creating the real-world equivalent to the *Babel Fish* (Adams 1979) and first introduced in a more rudimentary way by the American army as a way to negotiate more suc-cessfully in global operations.

Synthetic odours and scents arrive through site-wide diffusers or inserted nasal capsules that are synced via GPS and the event's time code to release synthetic scent molecules of exactly the right type at exactly the right time.

Your nano-skin suit modifies your body temperature and applies pressure to match a light breeze off the Alps or a stinging sand storm off the desert. The tightness in your chest in the scary part of the adventure may not be your own physiological response to the situation.

To accentuate the bass response and feel of the event soundscape, subtle vibra-tions travel through the soles of your feet via your slip-on event shoes. Your feet feel cold and wet when you walk through the virtual puddle. You feel (and hear) the crunch of the gravel that you can see, and you can even taste the dust that rises as you walk – all in the comfort of your carpeted lounge (event) room.

Once the dusty taste has gone, you can taste and feel the bubbles of the Bollinger Champagne you are not drinking. Infinitesimally small electrical impulses stimu-late the five tastes and general mouth feel of anything you are meant to be eating or drinking via a minute cap appended to a single tooth. You have gourmet tastes and a giant appetite but you emerge from the experience calorie free.

Event design practitioners of the future will need to be keen observers of their audience and trends in a wide range of fields (e.g. technological, political, social, cultural, economic, etc.) as if undertaking an ongoing and extensive situational anal-ysis. The successful event design practitioner will be the one who also looks closely at the other side of the coin. Accordingly, if mass, globalized events delivered via digital media are the trend, then investigate personalized, face-to-face events. If the majority of events incorporate groundbreaking technology including writing with a Thought Pen (where just thinking about the word puts it onto a screen), then investigate how your audience can touch, hold and use a pencil and paper.

Long before you decide on an event to attend, you will have generated an enormous amount of data about yourself. You will have access to much of this and much will be knowingly generated with your permission, of course. However increasing amounts of data (so called 'big data') will be hidden from you and used by event designers to design just for you. You will have extraordinary access to choices from the range offered to you (which is already based on your choices and preferences). If you depart from that range, then that, too, will be flagged, noted and acted upon. It will be an ongoing and ever-present iterative data collection process of monumental proportions that captures your likes and dislikes, your networks (both social and business), your tastes and preferences, your recent and past behaviours and anything and everything you have ever consumed (in whatever form that consumption takes). Events will be marketed to you at home, at work, at play, while your sleep, on your wrist, behind your eyes via retinal imaging, subcutaneously and sensationally in every possible way. It will be impossible to ignore.

The rise of the practitioner academic and the implications for future research

Like many of the professional degrees and courses being offered at universities, event design and management courses actively seek the engagement and involvement of professional practitioners to provide insights into the contemporary best industry practice and to inform (if not undertake) the teaching in those programs. Early models of this engagement saw event industry practitioners engaged with curriculum advisory committees, guest lecturing and even the establishment of full courses. The practitioner, however, remained 'from industry' and the engagement was often transitory. Over time, as more and more (event) industry practitioners became more deeply engaged with the academy, there was an expectation (from the academy) that practitioners would gradually increase their involvement with the university while decreasing their role in industry (Brown 2014). More recently there has been the rise of the *practitioner academic* (Simendinger *et al.* 2000), where both roles – industry practitioner and academic – are embraced by the academy and equal weight is given to time spent in both fields.

The rise of the practitioner academic within universities also provides opportunities for current academics to engage with the event industry and the event industry professional to engage with the academy (as has occurred with both authors). This is vital at a time when event studies has reached an impasse (Baum, Lockstone-Binney and Robertson 2013) and related research may be in a transitionary phase, as important new dimensions and academic disciplines are likely to become aligned to the event management foundations (Getz 2012).

From the research perspective, practice-led research and research-led practice (Smith and Dean 2009) each inform the other, leading to an iterative development of research that is based on contemporary best practice, that is in itself informed by rigorous academic research that is also based on contemporary best practice.

The nature of future research is, therefore, likely to be undertaken by practitioner academics with the results of that research applied and immediately implemented. If data storage capacity, rapid information retrieval systems and complex evaluation software continue to develop at current rates, massive amounts of data will be collected in real time and will be exhaustively comprehensive. Evaluation will be continuous, i.e. every minute of every hour of every day of every year of every event and of every audience member. We will know minute details about our audiences and our events. There will be immediate evaluation and continual response to the data coming in and continual modification of event designs to improve levels of satisfaction, safety and operational effectiveness. There will be more research data and analysis available than any individual event designer can deal with.

The implications for future research are that event designers may push back against the data overload and prefer to operate on 'gut instinct', their own personal experience and by trial and error. New, sophisticated software systems and processes will enable event designers to filter information effectively to automatically evaluate the data, as no individual or research team can individually manage the volume of data coming in. Very specific issues pertinent to a single event designer can thus be identified and explored. Conversely, very broad trends can also easily be identified, as the population for the data collection will be global – the research population will, after all, be the entire world.

Limitations of the future vision

This investigation is part of a larger study in which the practitioner academic is seen as having a more vital role and that looks well beyond 2030, so the results from this study are limited by: the relatively short visionary period (looking only to 2030); the duration in which the data has been collected (over a four-year period) and by the fact that the data collection was exploratory rather than exhaustive. A strength of this approach, however, is that the visions have been extrapolated from small groups or survey responses from individuals and consequently there have been few factors to stifle imagination or to precipitate one-sided 'groupthink' (Stevenson 2006).

Nonetheless, while the Vision does draw both on utopian visions (elicited from leaders, current research and news, technological development, science and science fiction), it has not been held in a way as to collectively stretch ideas far beyond current realities, nor has it determined a specific time frame. Given that this investigation is exploratory with a relatively short visionary period (looking to 2030), determining a specific time frame and stretching ideas beyond current realties will strengthen and make the vision more forceful (Bezold 2009).

Concluding remarks

The implications for the future of the event industry are that the design of events does have a clear relation to the y-axis of the Experience Pyramid (Tarssanen and Kylänen 2009; Figure 17.1). Understanding the audience is imperative, and certainly requires a response to and facilitation of people's need for individuality (and sense of uniqueness) when experiencing an event. The event designer must continue to offer experiences which are credible, i.e. authentic. Indeed, we suggest that increased interaction with the experience and increased opportunity for event or festival visitors to either create their own cocktail of experience or choose to pass greater responsibility to the event design professional, will ensure a greater propensity for authentic experiences in the future.

While alternative hybrid and virtual event experience will grow, the desire to connect with others will not dissapear. States of liminality will be found both with and without physical, face-to-face activity. Most people will join events to be with other people. This is necessarily central in the formation of futures vision for an event or festival – as social mechanisms (valves) their continuity is vital.

As technological change continues with an accellerating pace into the future, so too technological advancement is normalized. Its impact on the activities of the day will be asynchronous rather than revolutionary. So, also, event experiences will have at their core the same needs and desires. They will not change quickly. Accordingly, even when considering that the perfomer of 2030 may be a cyborg, or that technology allows the audience member to communicate his/her preferences to a digital storyboard filter for inclusion in a drama being performed right in front of him/her (in reality or virtually), the desired effect of an event (whether a festival, sport events, training event, etc.) is still determined by the audience member.

Increasingly accessible, more people will be able to be involved in organized events (whether they be music festivals, football, peformance arts or a celebrity cooking class) at the level they wish, more of the time. With less inhibitions, event visitors are not likely to be segmented by demographic or lifestyle factors. There will be a democratization of many events and event activities, which will see an evolution of audience profiles completely different from those seen today.

New levels of directorial leadership for events will emerge to meet the new expectations of the audience. As has always been the case, this will require understanding of new specialisms and new levels of professionalism in each area to ensure optimal event design. These may or may not include collaborative involvement with audiences. As Ryan's (2012) model (Figure 17.2) illustrates, event goers are motivated in different ways and so event designers will need to understand and address these motivations. The 'experientialist practioner', therefore, will emerge as a core professional (perhaps formally trained in specialist theatre business colleges). The experential and liminal needs of an event require similar skills to those of a good storyteller, and the physical and/or cerebal involvment of the audience member with the event will still need to be stimulated in 2020 and 2030, just as it occurs now.

The rise of the practical academic and the emergence of new professions and skills to expedite a dynamic festival and events future is clear, but the form and function of these have yet to be developed.

References

Adams, D. (1979) *The Hitchhiker's Guide to the Galaxy*. New York: Harmony Books.

Alraek, T.J. and Baerheim, A. (2005) 'Elements from theatre art as learning tools in medical education', *Research in Drama Education*, 10(1): 5–14.

Bauer, J.C. (2013) *Upgrading Leadership's Crystal Ball: five reasons why forecasting must replace predicting and how to make the strategic change in business and public policy*. Hoboken: Taylor and Francis.

Baum, T. Lockstone-Binney, L. and Robertson, M. (2013) 'Event studies: finding fool's gold at the rainbow's end?', *International Journal of Festival and Event Management*, 4(3): 179–85.

Benneworth, P. and Dauncey, H. (2010) 'International urban festivals as a catalyst for governance capacity building', *Environment and Planning C: Government and Policy*, 28(6): 1083–100.

Bezold, C. (2009) 'Aspirational futures', *Journal of Futures Studies*, 13(4): 81–90.

Bezold, C., Peck, J., Bettles, C. and Olson, B. (2009) 'Using vision in futures planning', in J.C. Glenn and T.J. Gordon (eds.) *Futures Research Methodology V.3.0* (Vol. 3) Washington: The Millenium Project.

Bitner, M.O. (1986) 'Consumer responses to the physical environment in service settings', in M. Venkatesan, D.M. Schmalenseem and C. Marshall (eds.) *Creativity in Services Marketing*. Chicago: American Marketing Association, pp. 89–93.

Bowie, D (1974) 'Future legends', on *Diamond Dogs* (CD), EMI Records Limited.

Brown, S. (2010) *Event Design: creating and staging the event experience* (Vol. 1). Adelaide: Visible Management Pty Ltd.

Brown, S. (2012) 'Expert opinion', in D. Getz (ed.) *Event Studies: theory, research and policy for planned events* (2nd ed.) Oxford, UK: Routledge, pp. 222–23.

Brown, S. (2014) 'Emerging professionalism in the event industry: a practitioner's perspective', *Event Management*, 18. doi:10.3727/152599514X13883555341760

Brown, S. and Hutton, A. (2013) 'Developments in the real-time evaluation of audience behaviour at planned events', *International Journal of Event and Festival Management*, 4(1): 43–55.

Brown, S. and James, J. (2004) 'Event design and management: ritual sacrifice?', in I. Yeoman, M. Robertson, J. Ali-Knight, S. Drummond and U. McMahon-Beattie (eds.), *Festival and Events Management: an international arts and culture perspective*. Oxford: Butterworth-Heinemann, pp. 53–64.

Byrne, C.L. and Shipman, A.S. (2010) 'Leader vision formation and forecasting: the effects of forecasting extent, resources, and timeframe', *The Leadership Quarterly*, 21(3): 439–56.

Cher (1998) 'Believe' on *Believe* (CD), WEA Warner.

Cheron, E.J. and Ritchie, J.B. (1982) 'Leisure activities and perceived risk', *Journal of Leisure Research*, 14(2): 139–54.

Crespi-Vallbona, M. and Richards, G. (2007) 'The meaning of cultural festivals', *International Journal of Cultural Policy*, 13(1): 103–22.

Ensor, J., Robertson, M. and Ali-Knight, J. (2007) 'The dynamics of successful events: the experts' perspective', *Managing Leisure*, 12(2/3): 223–35.

Ensor, J., Robertson, M. and Ali-Knight, J. (2011) 'Eliciting the dynamics of leading a sustainable event: key informant responses', *Event Management*, 15(4): 315–27.

Getz, D. (1997) *Event Management & Event Tourism*. New York: Cognizant Communication Corp.

Getz, D. (2002) 'Why festivals fail', *Event Management*, 7(4), 209–19.

Getz, D. (2012) *Event studies: Theory, research and policy for planned events*. London: Routledge.

Goffman, E. (1959) *The Presentation of Self in Everyday Life*. Garden City, New York: Doubleday.

Hagen, U. (1991) *A Challenge for the Actor*. New York: Scribner's.

Hall, C.M. (1992) *Hallmark Tourist Events: impacts, management, and planning*. London: Belhaven.

Hawkins, C.J. and Ryan, L.-A.J. (2013) 'Festival spaces as third places', *Journal of Place Management and Development*, 6(3): 192–202.

Hay, B. (2013) *From Leisure to Pleasure: societal trends and their impact on possible future scenarios for UK rural tourism in 2050*. European Commission. Online. Available <http://ec.europa.eu/digital-agenda/futurium/> (accessed 29 January 2014).

Howell, R. and Hill, G. (2009) 'The mediators of experiential purchases: determining the impact of psychological needs satisfaction and social comparison', *The Journal of Positive Psychology*, 4(6): 511–22.

Jean, S. (2006) 'Beyond the fourth wall', *Back Stage East*, 47(5): 6.

Kotler, P. (1973) 'Atmospherics as a marketing tool', *Journal of Retailing*, 49(4): 48–64.

MySkiStar (2012) 'We're making skiing more fun!' Online. Available <www.skistar.com/en/MySkistar/> (accessed 21 January 2014).

Nelson, K.B. (2009) 'Enhancing the attendee's experience through creative design of the event environment: applying Goffman's dramaturgical perspective', *Journal of Convention & Event Tourism*, 10(2): 120–33.

Packer, J. and Ballantyne, J. (2011) 'The impact of music festival attendance on young people's psychological and social well-being', *Psychology of Music*, 39(2): 164–81.

Pettersson, R. and Getz, D. (2009) 'Event experiences in time and space: a study of visitors to the 2007 World Alpine Ski Championships in Åre, Sweden', *Scandinavian Journal of Hospitality and Tourism*, 9(2/3); 308–26.

Pettersson, R. and Zillinger, M. (2011) 'Time and space in event behaviour: tracking visitors by GPS', *Tourism Geographies*, 13(1): 1–20.

Pine, B.J. and Gilmore, J.H. (1998) 'Welcome to the experience economy', *Harvard Business Review*, 76, 97–105.

Pine, B.J. and Gilmore, J.H. (2011) *The Experience Economy* (updated version). Boston, Massachusetts: Harvard Business Review Press.

Ramaswamy, V. and Gouillart, F. (2010) 'Building the co-creative enterprise', *Harvard Business Review*, 88(10): 100–09.

Richards, G. (2007) 'Culture and authenticity in a traditional event: the views of producers, residents and visitors in Barcelona', *Event Management*, 11(1/2): 33–44.

Robertson, M. (2004) 'Sport and leisure narrative', in U. McMahon-Beattie and I. Yeoman (eds.) *Sport and Leisure Operations Management*. London: Thomson Learning, pp. 16–27.

Robertson, M. (2012a) 'Festivals, governance and sustainability: the director at the research crossroad', in *International Conference on Tourism and Events: Opportunities, Impacts & Change*. Belfast: The University of Ulster, pp. 295–303.

Robertson, M. (2012b) 'Expert opinion: trends and the future of events', in Getz, D., *Event Studies: Theory, Research and Policy for Planned Events* (2nd ed.) Oxford, UK: Routledge, pp. 32–4.

Robertson, M. and Wardrop, K. (2012) 'Festival and events, government and spatial governance', in S. Page and J. Connell (eds.) *The Handbook of Events,* London: Routledge, pp. 489–506.

Robertson, M. and Yeoman, I. (2014) 'Signals and signposts of the future: literary festival consumption in 2050', *Tourism Recreation Research*, 39(3).

Ryan, C. (2012) 'The experience of events', in S.J. Page and J. Connel (eds.) *The Routledge Handbook of Events*. Oxon: Routledge, pp. 248–59.

Simendinger, E., Puia, G., Kraft, K. and Jasperson, M. (2000) 'The career transition from practitioner to academic', *Career Development International*, 5(2): 106–11.

Slovic, P. (2013) *Risk, Media and Stigma: understanding public challenges to modern science and technology*. London: Routledge.

Smith, H. and Dean, R. (eds.) (2009) *Practice-Led Research, Research-Led Practice in the Creative Arts*. Edinburgh: University of Edinburgh Press.

Steinbrink, M., Haferburg, C. and Ley, A. (2011) 'Festivalisation and urban renewal in the Global South: socio-spatial consequences of the 2010 FIFA World Cup', *South African Geographical Journal*, 93(1): 15–28.

Stevenson, T. (2006) 'From vision into action', *Futures*, 38(6): 667–72.

Stokes, M. (2014) 'Dream Catcher: the neuroscience behind decoding dreams'. Online. Available <www.nature.com/scitable/blog/student-voices/dream_catcher_the_neuroscience_behind> (acccessed 21 January 2014).

Tarssanen, S. and Kylänen, M. (2009) 'What is an experience', in S. Tarssanen (ed.) *Handbook for Experience Stagers* (5th ed.). LEO, Lapland Center of Expertise for the Experience Economy (OSKE). Rovaniemi: Oy Sevenprint Ltd, pp. 8–23.

Torkildsen, G. (2002) *Leisure and Recreation Management*. London: Routledge.

Turner, V. (1977) 'Variations on a theme of liminality', in S.F. Moore and B.G. Myerhoff (eds.) *Secular Ritual*. Assen: Van Gorcum Ltd, pp. 36–52.

Van Boven, L. and Gilovich, T. (2003) 'To do or to have? That is the question', *The Journal of Personality and Social Psychology*, 4(6): 511–22.

van der Heijden, K.A. (2002) *Sixth Sense: accelerating organizational learning with scenarios*. Chichester: Wiley.

van der Helm, R. (2009) 'The vision phenomenon: towards a theoretical underpinning of visions of the future and the process of envisioning', *Futures*, 41(2): 96–104.

Walmsley, B. (2013) 'Co-creating theatre: authentic engagement or inter-legitimation?', *Cultural Trends*, 22(2): 108–18.

Yeoman, I. (2013) 'A futurist's thoughts on consumer trends shaping future festivals and events', *International Journal of Event and Festival Management*, 4(3): 249–60.

Yeoman, I., Robertson, M. and Smith, K. (2012) 'A futurist's view on the future of events', in S.J. Page and J. Connel (eds.) *The Routledge Handbook of Events*. Oxon: Routledge, pp. 507–25.

18 The future of event design and experience

Andrew McLoughlin

Future points

- Futuristic approaches within the realms of event design and experience.
- The future event design process – an operational and experiential perspective.
- Co-creational consideration in 'mutuality' event design orientation.
- The emergence of the 'event experientialist practitioner'.

Introduction

This chapter provides an overview of how event design is a fundamental part of the event management process and will be a determinant factor to future event success over the next 25 years. It examines the role of event design in the delivery of contemporary event experiences and influenced by the demands of the audience and audience expectation for technological integration as part of the overall end user event experience. The core theme of this chapter establishes the interrelationship between event design and experience and specifically examines the future of event design approaches and how some of the emerging themes will dominate in event management thinking, policy and research.

The future role of event design

Globalization, technological innovations and a changing consumer and business focus have served to dramatically change the way event managers manage and operate in today's turbulent business environment. It has become very evident, for example, that businesses must continuously adopt new and innovative strategies to improve or maintain their competitiveness in the marketplace (Rumelt 2008). Event managers, therefore, have been increasingly forced to develop a range of different strategies that will optimize their competitive advantages, while at the same time, minimizing their operation's vulnerability to external threats and emulation.

Because of these changing trends in the marketplace, festivals and events need to innovate and differentiate themselves to remain relevant and distinctive, and as a result, event managers must be willing to provide better value (as perceived by the consumer) than their competitors. Corporate clients and external event and creative agencies are pushing the boundaries in creativity and production to go beyond the brief and deliver the wow factor and the desired outcomes.

The future of event design is aligned to ensuring these changes and influences are interpreted and integrated into the planning of the event concept at the early stage and to deliver an event or festival that is contemporary, relevant, value driven and delivers the desired outcomes as well as offering a multi-layering of experiences for all participating stakeholders. Design features as a key activity component in the planning, development and management of events (Berridge 2007: 82), and critically a core principal of competitive advantage in the future.

Mega trends affecting the future role of event design

Competition in the global marketplace and the competitiveness of events means the future is uncertain and risky. Especially in Europe and North America, there is a strong culture of popular music festivals. But music festivals worldwide and especially in the United Kingdom are at saturation point, and the differentiation between festivals is negligible – it's usually the pulling power of the headliner act and style of music festival that determines if the festival sells out and makes a profit or loss.

One of the aspects that separate music festivals from other music events is the provision of nonmusic attractions, such as catering, accommodation, secondary events and retailing, all of which must be present in order to generate an 'authentic' festival experience (Bowen and Daniels 2005).

Music events and festivals, both in closed venues and outdoors, are amongst the biggest exponents of light, sound and stage equipment, since these are the core elements that create a powerful, dominating and memorable atmosphere. The size and capacity of the music festival actuate the design formatting and complexity of event production and many combinations generally are determined by the budget, performers and creative production team. Increasingly, a range of multimedia technology is used by the event production team to engage and focus the attention on the audience and augment participation in the festival.

The typical 'festival goer' is aged between 18–35 years of age, which is lucrative from a commercial perspective, as brands want to engage with participants emotionally in a leisure environment and develop experiential content to persuade and nurture relationships with the music festival audience. Music festivals promote a hedonistic lifestyle. They are, indeed, a purely intrinsic and hedonistic activity for most people, offering relaxation, freedom and an opportunity to socialize with friends. On the other hand, the lifestyle promoted by festivals is for beer brands to sell their products and launch new products and sampling campaigns. In fact,

> beer might be the most widely sold drink at open-air music festivals, where excessive consumption and inappropriate behaviour seem to be good manners. That way, a beer brand can attach itself to a certain image while selling a lot of their products. (Preston 2012: 10)

Large sponsorship programmes exist, as brands like Orange and Carling (in the United Kingdom) headliner sponsor music festivals such as Glastonbury and Leeds and Reading Carling Weekends. But new festival formats over the past few years are attracting different nontraditional music festival demographics including families, as festival organizers look for new market opportunities. Changes in staging of music festivals are attracting a wide range of consumers but devaluing commercial sponsorship rights (Bowen and Daniels 2005).

Music festivals are changing. File-trading and file-sharing technologies have made it very easy for music to be shared and traded across the globe, particularly illegally, but this has led to unprecedented growth in live music events throughout the last decade, as artist are now keener to tour because incomes from recorded music have drastically fallen (Keynote 2010). In fact, live music in the last decade has come to be regarded as the saviour for music companies and artists alike (Mintel 2004). Meanwhile, this has expedited the oversaturation of the music festival market and contributed to festival failures.

Another mega trend affecting the future of event design is consumption and consumerism, which has changed dramatically because of advances in the digital environment and smart phone technology. This has influenced how event audiences (in the corporate and consumer sectors) have become informed and interacted with event brands at the actual event and in doing so augmented the end user experience and participation.

The corporate sector of event management has remained at the cutting edge of technological advancement through its use of groundbreaking multimedia technology; especially where a corporate speaker or performer demonstrating a product or service to an invited audience over a given time span, multimedia is used to engage and focus the attention of the audience and enlarge the physical presence of the presentation. A large video wall, satellite links with live feedback or pre-programme information accompanied by laser, amplified sound and lights combine to achieve a memorable and powerful experience. Integrating corporate event production and smart phone technology accord the end user the opportunity to participate innumerably and to engage, inform and further enhance participation through 'gamification', using mobile phone apps and selected social media. Other technological formats that exist using virtual technology include an expanding range of virtual events such as trade fairs, webinars and digital/video conferencing.

Smart phone technology is indirectly prescribing the future direction of event design and interaction with audiences and furthermore stakeholders in a wider context. The global popularity and use of smart phones and burgeoning innovative technologies are expediting ingenious ways of engaging audiences worldwide. Every event has the opportunity of becoming an international event because of advancements in a multiplicity of digital formats.

The handheld device is the ultimate representation of technological convergence. It has a profusion of uses; it's a telephone, videophone, it can download content such as films, it's a still and video camera, a computer, television, access to the Internet. It offers about any communication application that can be imagined.

For all intents and purposes, it is an extension not only of technology, but of the human brain (Preston 2012). Other laptop and touch screen devices exist, which are being slimmed down and powered to give even more technological capability on the move. This revolution is taking place and undoubtedly will continue to develop. Wireless communication is fast becoming the norm. The limitless communication potential with information-hungry consumers who live their lives through technology include 400 million smart phone users and growing; over 200 million active users of Facebook; 70 percent of the world population owns a mobile and over 60 billion iPhones have been sold (Preston 2012).

Communications is everywhere and the virtual and real have become so intermeshed that it is not easy to tell which is which. The convergence of technology and communication into the handheld device has profound implications for events and the future of event design and experience.

The events industry is exploiting this phenomenon with an integrated event solution – the hybrid event that incorporates both physical and virtual live content. And some events and festivals are also early adopters in the use of smart phone technology in a variety of ways. Bluetooth and SMS technologies make it possible to send messages to individual mobile phones in which consumers can be called to action such as completing a survey or using a forward link to online information or remind them of possible ticket sales promotions.

Consumers are increasingly using specific event-related social media platforms such as Facebook, as the site offers event information and enables dyadic communication between visitors and the opportunity to interact with each other to create value and relevance of context of that event. This not only leads to a more valued consumer experience but also stronger brand, consumer loyalty and retention. Many event brands are adopting this strategy as part of a bigger push to build a strong customer base.

Consumers are also attracted to mobile apps because of the event brand identity and content or options included within it (relevance, context, social interaction, orientation) and the potential shared experience with friends and other visitors at the same event. These applications lead to stronger brand recognition but require an active action to opt in (that is, to download it from an app store). Uptake of new event mobile phone apps can be slow, as the event industry is just starting to adapt to new ways of developing digital strategies within and for events.

Sundbo and Hagedorn-Ramussen (2008) define three stages in the development of new experience productions and innovative systems:

- the backstage (the focus is on all e-business and e-commerce processes);
- the stage (where the created experience is being offered and communicated from the perspective of the producer); and
- the front stage (where the consumer is sharing an experience with others but also actively influencing the participation in and creation of that experience).

Event organizers gravitate towards website and social media services as 'digital development', but it's the front stage that is all about interacting, socializing, sharing and communication that can be enabled and augmented with the use of smart phones/mobiles and social media.

Smart phone technology enables the consumer to acquire knowledge, be entertained, socialize, purchase and function in everyday life, and the advantages of mobile devices are immediacy, simplicity and context. Within the event product lifecycle, the mobile device can be engaged in a variety of ways from pre-promotion, in a multiplicity of interactive ways within the periodicity of the 'live event' to post-event evaluation.

The first event-specific mobile phone apps appeared in 2010 (V-Festival and Glastonbury). Within the apps V-Festival introduced a friend-finding functionality using the Facebook powered friend-finder tool. Meanwhile Glastonbury Festival launched an augmented reality feature: by scanning the phone at the stage, the customer can receive specific date on performers linked to the stage in question. Early adopters online commented favourably about the Glastonbury Festival mobile phone app.

Event organizers within the United Kingdom are late adopters in comparison to European counterparts in music festivals (Raj, Walters and Rashid 2013: 243). Current trends indicate more festivals are developing mobile phone apps. Manchester Pride launched a festival mobile phone app in 2012, one month before the actual festival began, and as such, end user uptake was slow.

Current trends indicate that mobile phone marketing is increasing and is expected to grow in the next five years (Comscore 2011). The early success from this increase in uptake will be with event entrepreneurs who grasp this social and digital revolution through the handheld device and exploit every opportunity to develop intimate and interactive experiences and relationships with consumers at every stage of the event product lifecycle.

Futuristic approaches within the realms of event design and experience

Event managers and entrepreneurs need to approach the future of event design and experience management in an entirely different way. The rapid expansion of smart phone consumption worldwide and the progressiveness of new digital technology mean that technological integration into event design is inevitable, as end users expect and demand it as part of the overall experience. The physical live event will not coexist without some form of technological input in the future.

Corporate clients and audiences demand more from the experience at the events they attend. Event managers' and agencies are pushing the boundaries in creativity and production to fulfil the brief and deliver the desired outcomes.

Audience expectation to interact, participate and change event format mean event professionals face uncertainty and many challenges to deliver memorable event experiences in the future. This will become critical and more complex as audiences travel less but want to engage through a computer screen in the comfort of their own environment. The computer terminal in the future will need to be considered as an extended events space to interact and participate.

The language of events is also changing. No longer can you refer to an event as a 'live event'. Events management discourse amongst event professionals acknowledges and discusses events as either 'live physical event', 'live virtual event' or 'live hybrid'.

Emerging events that focus not just on the aesthetic value of the event environment but design event concepts that combine societal influences such as integrating smart phone technology into the event itself make them relevant and interactive and make audiences emotionally connected and engaged.

The future event design process – an operational and experiential perspective

Event design precedes practice as a creative and conceptual aspect within event management. It's about visualizing how everything 'fits' within the event concept before the event production process begins. Very little event design academic literature and no universal definition exist. Different approaches to event design exist based on bias. According to Bladen *et al.* (2012: 56), 'event design involves the conception of an intended event experience with the intention of delivering it through event production'. Meanwhile O'Toole (2011: 183) defines event design as 'a purposeful arrangement of elements of an event to maximize the positive impression on the attendees and other key stakeholders'. Ferdinand and Kitchin (2012) suggest that:

> Event design as a stimulus activates the five senses of hearing, sight, smell, touch and taste embedded in the event experience. The design of an event is both an experience-maker and experience enhancer, which provides ample opportunity for the attendee to engage in sensory and emotional interaction with the event. Thus event design is not simply a matter of production but participation to create memorable and unique happenings. (2012: 52)

According to Brown and James (2004: 53), the design of an event is 'the very heart and soul, the raison d'etre of any great event'.

Event design is a combination of different dimensions at the initial conceptualization stage. It's the linkage between creativity, practicality and foresight. It cannot be defined within the realms of a management or production process but as a stage of realization and opportunity.

The future of event design can be understood as a creative and conceptual approach that takes into consideration the aims and objectives, stakeholders – in particular event audience – and societal, technological and experiential dimensions needed to engage and deliver a participatory, emotional and memorable experience at the initial stage.

It is the initial stage of the event management process before the event planning and production begins. The wide diversity of event choice and outcomes, technological advancements beyond social media, the sophisticated palate of 'new experiences' demanded by audiences worldwide and the competitive leisure environment dominate the future of event design.

Ferdinand and Kitchin (2012) suggest the critical trend identified to have an impact upon event design is environmental sustainability, but another study amongst senior event managers cites audience exchange and emotional engagement and digital integration into events as important (Adema and Roehl 2010). A pattern is emerging that clearly identifies that designing an event or festival at the initial concept stage needs a lot of skill and attention to detail.

Event formats

'There have been considerable changes in the nature of festivals over the last decade' (Raj, Walters and Rashid 2013: 7). Contemporary events, their size, scope and magnitude and sheer complexity have changed due to a range of factors and over the next two decades, with climatic change and the realization that natural resources are in short supply, many organizations are investing in going green and finding different ways to reduce their carbon footprint. These changes, coupled with cultural shifts, the search for unique experiences, developments in sophisticated technology such as mobiles and virtual applications, represent some of the many challenges practitioners are required to factor into future design decision making, especially in choosing an event platform to meet organizational outcomes.

Virtual and hybrid events

One of the major changes facing the event industry and dividing opinion is the design and development of virtual and hybrid events. The use of virtual and hybrid events is popular especially in the meetings, convention and business events sectors. Virtual events are events represented on the Internet. The growth of virtual and hybrid events is attributed to several factors, including audiences' increasing familiarity with online platforms; the maturation of virtual technology; the availability of higher bandwidth (and hence real-time experience); a potential decline in event attendance related to the impact of reduced travel budgets; the green movement; and virtual media's ability to not only capture would-be event and exhibition attendees but extend audiences' experience of an exhibition (Centre for Exhibition Industry Research 2009).

Meanwhile, very little hybrid event academic literature exists despite the growing popularity of this event platform. Event Industry commentators describe 'a hybrid event offers participants the option to attend physically or virtually' and many companies that have traditionally produced physical events – such as trade shows, conferences and corporate meetings are 'taking a new approach, merging the physical and virtual to create a hybrid event'. And another commentator describes a hybrid event in different terms, as a physical event or conference, accompanied by an online event, whilst another confirms virtual and hybrid events are becoming more popular with the advent of new technology.

The events industry has been 'slow to adapt to its changing environment, including the adoption of IT solutions' (Pearlman and Gates 2010: 261). Several forward-thinking companies have adopted virtual reality applications that meet business needs or have implemented hybrid event formats. Findings from recent research suggest that 'virtual meetings and hybrid events are innovative and viable methods to effectively and efficiently meet organization needs' (Pearlman and Gates 2010: 261). They are environmentally friendly, less expensive and provide alternatives to physical face-to-face meetings. But the biggest challenge from an event design perspective is to understand the opportunities that these formats can bring and the lucrative potential.

Barriers exist to the adoption of new event design formats such as hybrid events. These include the lack of client demand, cultural difference, the emergence of new digital and broadcast technologies, the reluctance to change amongst event practitioners to engage with technologies because of preference towards the physical 'live' event formats, and technophobia amongst practitioners is creating a major dichotomy.

Hybrid events can bring many event design challenges and a range of opportunities in a global and competitive market. The biggest challenge facing event practitioners is decreasing budgets and corporate time constraints, as well as the reluctance to travel. But the positive aspects of hybrids, once understood, can bring a range of benefits: increased revenue potential through leveraging sponsorship and a range of ticketing options such as pay-per-view and accessibility to specific content; audience capacity increases because of the virtual aspect of the event, but event managers need to recognize in design terms they have two audiences to engage in the physical and virtual environment and engage them in different ways. Content kept online for a long period of time can generate endless revenue potential. Another genre of event having to change is the music festival.

Music festivals

In recent times, there has been a growth in the popularity of music and cultural festivals (Bladen *et al.* 2012), but these types of events have changed and evolved based on wider societal influences and aspirational audience demands. Music festivals offer shared experiences, fun with friends and in particular 'promote a sense of belonging to the crowd [. . .] and they can also be about fashion and culture' (Raj, Walters and Rashid 2013: 13). The multiplicity and multi-staging format of music festivals is an opportunity in terms of design creativity, as most festivals take place in outdoor open spaces, but in seeking new audiences, the composition in staging formats and capacity is having to include different types of accommodation catering to a diverse audience including family, and to incorporate other lifestyle aspects such as food and art, to differentiate and innovate the music festival in a saturated marketplace.

But innovations in music festivals worldwide are changing as the power of consumers and engagement in social media empowers and enables audiences to make informed and collective choices regarding which event they attend. The participatory aspect of social media is revolutionizing the way festival goers interact with artists and each other. The 'interactive' music festival enables festival goers to choose the music and playlist for the artist to sing. Ultimately the power of the audience and availability and presentation of artists will dominate the music festival in the future and newly interactive formats will dominate the future event design of the music festival. An example of this took place at the 2013 SXSW music festival in Texas between sponsor Doritos and music artists LL Cool J, Ice Cube, Public Enemy and Doug E. Fresh. Doritos ran a social media competition asking fans to decide the artist lineup on stage and the songs they would perform to the audience attending. Social media (Facebook and Twitter) empowered the audience to control the lineup and performance. A spokesperson for Doritos described it as a 'totally unique and interactive' experience; in reality, it's the advent of a new phenomenon, the interactive music festival.

The world's first holographic music concert

The use of innovative technology, experiential and gaming techniques

The 'Hologram Christmas Surprise' was a multicity, multimedia spectacular featuring Mariah Carey in hologram form using the latest holographic technology. On November 18, 2011, events in public spaces in Germany, Croatia, Macedonia, Montenegro and Poland were witnessed by more than 12,000 people in person, and streamed live globally through lifeisforsharing TV channel, giving Deutsche Telekom customers and Mariah's fans around the world the chance to share in the experience of the concert. There were more than 27,000 visitors to the live stream channel. Each city was satellite linked to the other, to enable interaction. Mariah Carey appeared before audiences in Germany, Croatia, Macedonia, Montenegro and Poland simultaneously in the form of a hologram interacting with real dancers and live audiences in each location, creating a unique *life is for sharing moment*. At first Mariah Carey appeared to the audience as if she was live in concert. After 10 minutes Mariah's hologram form exploded into the sky, revealing the surprise. Mariah then re-formed to lead all five countries in a moving rendition of the traditional carol 'Silent Night', then finishing with the all-time favourite 'All I Want for Christmas Is You'.

The use of holographic broadcast technology, the use of technology to broadcast to five different countries and being the world's first international holographic concert made this a unique and memorable experience. Raj, Walters and Rashid (2013: 362) suggest that 'event goers are continually searching for original and new experiences rather than the traditional event. There is an increasing need to seek out experiences and products which are authentic'.

Fusion events

In the future, event fusion concepts will dominate event product development design and the way events are conceptualized. The fusion event should not be confused with hybrid formatting. Hybrid is about physical and virtual integration to deliver an event experience to two separate audiences, whilst fusion is a combinatorial interactive experience, with two or more subject elements that complement each other to offer an audience experience in a physical venue or space.

The United States offers many examples of fusion concepts, predominantly in the food and drink event and music festival sectors. As audiences become more informed due to accessibility of information via the Internet, a progressive and culturally aware society will desire more sophisticated and aspirational combinations. This trend will continue and event managers have to comprehend the need to change fusion concepts based on wider consumer demand. Event fusion combinations include food and jazz festivals, wine and art and literature festivals and one of the newest combinations in the UK marketplace is CarFest: motoring, music and food attracting a nontraditional music festival family audience.

CarFest North 2013

With 20,000 attendees, CarFest was an amazing sellout in 2012. This motoring, music and food family festival was hosted originally in the north of England, and due to audience demand the event has now been divided into CarFest North and CarFest South.

The event brings together the world's greatest cars, three nights of live music, festival food and a whole remit of fun and games for the whole family. Organized and managed by Brand Events, this innovative festival offers families a great range of experiences under one festival title and a range of residential options from camping to glamping! But is a differentiated and highly consuming experiential event with lots of entertainment and emotional engagement.

The future of event design and end user experiences

The future of event design must also focus away from the traditional approach of simply planning events using logistics and must focus on clearly defining the target audience and end user experience demand in relation to the planned outcomes and objectives set for the event.

It's also important to ensure, within organizational event objectivity at a tactical and strategic level, that an audience experience/engagement and level of participation is one of the expected outcomes.

The basis of event attendee experience formation is sensory stimulation, but authors such as Goldblatt (2005), Monroe (2005) and Getz (2007) acknowledge the necessity of appealing to attendants' sense of sight, hearing, taste, touch, speech and emotions within the experience environment of the event. However, they tend to take an operationalized-only approach and don't offer much explanation of how they stimulate to form experiences. Similarly, The EMBOK model (http://embok.org) categorizes design in the events industry as follows: content design theme design; programme design; environment design; production design; entertainment design and catering design.

Whilst the EMBOK model is useful to cite the event management and logistical approach to design, the categorization indicatively isolates the integrative and creative approach and excludes important design considerations from an audience experience perspective including technological and interactive/participation design aspects.

Technology is an important aspect of contemporary living, and audiences should expect technological integration into an event or festival. Technology should be considered at the initial event design stage to enhance audience level of engagement. To maximize the emotional and participatory engagement of an audience, the event professional must understand the concept of experientialism – the philosophy that experience is the foundation of all knowledge (Voss and Zomerdijk 2007) and the popularity of experiential thinking within the events industry and the growth of experiential event agencies and spend has increased (Event Marketing Institute 2013).

Experiential events can generate short-term impact but also build longer-term changes in attitude and belief (Sneath, Finney and Close 2005); therefore, the challenge for event managers is to understand experiential as a process within an event that can engage and emotionally affect audiences. The measurement of the outcomes of experiential events may be difficult to ascertain, and their effectiveness is related to individual emotional response, but is effective in developing long-term audience retention.

Event design, experiential theory and practical event management

'Events are in reality experiential – interactive, targeted and relational, and as such these characteristics are highly appropriate and desirable given the modern marketing environment' (Raj, Walters and Rashid 2013: 229). For this to become experiential in action the result must be 'something extremely significant and unforgettable for the consumer immersed into the experience' (Caru and Cova 2003: 273). Lanier and Hampton (2009: 9) suggest experiential marketing is 'the strategy of creating and staging offerings for the purpose of facilitating memorable customer experiences'. Raj, Walters and Rashid (2013: 146) indicate 'with the right kind of experiential marketing strategy, event organizations should be able to demand a higher premium'. The event literature emphasizes a need to focus on experiential dimensions of them (Holloway, Brown, and Shipway 2010). You need to involve the audience in all aspects of the sensory (McCole 2004).

The event practitioner has to design and create an event that provides the right level of challenge or stimulation to the skill set of the target audience. Different consumers will therefore experience the event differently, and this has to be accepted as the norm. Some may be bored, others worried, others aroused, but in the main, the practitioner has to plan every phase of the interaction and experiential context to ensure the audience is immersed in the 'totality of the experience' itself, if he or she wants to make the event memorable and worth returning to in the future. However, Raj, Walters and Rashid (2013: 230) argue that 'regrettably, the poor planning as to what needs to be achieved through experiential marketing as part of the overall marketing strategy, these event organizations often have ended up dissatisfying rather than delighting event goers'.

Every experience has to be extraordinary to have an effect and impact on the audience itself. Wood and Masterman (2008) suggest that every event must strive to create a 'flow state experience' for the majority attending. This may involve surprise, novelty or challenge. But these authors miss a vital component of 'experiential activity' in their approach to explaining the level of engagement and participation experienced by attendees. In previous research, they highlight seven event attributes (the 7 I's) that indicatively enhance the event experience: involvement; interaction; immersion; intensity; individuality; innovation and integrity.

This gives a useful insight to aspects that may enhance the actual attendee experience but don't explain how they need to be integrated into future event design and developed by the practitioner in an experiential format. No structure or sequence in structure is evident. To maximize future experiential engagement with an event audience, the practitioner needs to understand the 'sequence of interaction from start to finish' to maximize audience engagement (emotionally and participatory) and therefore, event producers need to clearly articulate, for their own purpose and other stakeholders involved (suppliers, sponsors, etc.) a 'blueprint' of intended stakeholder experiences throughout the event. The experiential event blueprint must include the physical and emotional attributes that contribute and must be clearly referenced to the 'activities' of the various sensory stimuli in the design, such as the programme, staging and timing elements, as well as their intended outcome, such as attendees' memory formations, emotional flow, participation and levels of engagement.

Such blueprinting takes time and focus on planning the audience experience and should be carried out for the whole event cycle, which cannot be limited to the time lines required for operational delivery, but needs to be centred on the multiplicity of experience exchange between the audience (stakeholders) and the event itself at every stage. The future of event design and experience management is centred on a phased approach to planning the experience and event producers and practitioners predicting and designing the totality of audience attendance and participation.

Participation can be active or passive, depending on whether the event attendees directly influence the experience that has been produced. But it's difficult to understand the true passive and active nature of audience experience participation.

For example, an audience at a classical music concert may be perceived to be 'passive participants' but may emotionally actively participate listening intently to the music played. Runners at a charity fun run actively participate because without their running, the event would not be able to take place, but spectators may also actively participate because they are watching for their loved ones running, and the potential 'emotional subjectivity' of a charitable event may evoke memories of loved ones who may have passed away.

Co-creational consideration in 'mutuality' event design orientation

Vargo and Lusch (2008) regard consumers as co-creators of value. Value is created in events when the event product is utilized, and in order to determine aspects of value, the elements of experience and perception are essential (Payne, Storbacka and Frow 2008). The customer value-creation process should be viewed as dynamic, interactive, participatory and in line with the event context and other stakeholder involvement. Payne, Storbacka and Frow (2008) discusses co-design, and argue that events enable guests to participate and co-design activities. In building a long-term 'experience relationship' with an audience, an alignment to audience feedback systems such as questionnaires and post-event surveys is important. Not just in trying to determine aspects of actual experience satisfaction, but to engage in the future mutually agreed upon aspects of 'experience need' within the strategic development of the event.

Theme, dramaturgy and creative considerations in the future of event design

The future of event design will need to continue to utilize all the elements encapsulated in thematical, dramaturgical and creative context. But the event practitioner who focuses at the event design and conceptualization stage in the 'totality of emotional need' of the audience will deliver a long-term memorable and lasting event experience, which in terms of revisionism, will resonate for years to come. The future of event design is in attention to detail, knowing your audience and that every decision made at its core is from an experiential and emotional perspective.

For example, the venue is not just an event space – it's an integral part of the participatory level of audience engagement. It may have heritage, a vista, a uniqueness in character and ceremony, which can enhance the overall 'emotional and participatory experience' of the audience that evolves whilst the audience is in attendance. The practitioner needs to integrate the choice of venue and its 'unique and emotional collateral' in the event design experiential blueprint and develop a 'cohesive fit' practically, participatory and interactively.

Events have been employing the theme space strategy with constant success. Dramaturgy lives in all things theatrical and themed. Elements that should be considered in the event design blueprint include the setting: furnishings, decoration, physical layout, special context and props. According to Pine and Gilmore (1999), plain space must become a distinctive space – a place to stage an experience. The space is layered with amenities (props) that give nonverbal cues to the audience about the organization. Successful treatment of props should enhance the audience's perspective, not detract from it.

The emergence of the 'event experientialist practitioner'

The event manager of the future will need to understand the complexity of event design in relation to the burgeoning need to offer not just a differentiated level of event experience, but a logical and structured and evidentially multi-layered, immersed, participatory, interactive and emotionally engaging sequence of experiences that 'fits' the target audience and event occasion. It involves a complex sequential and creative project management approach to decision making that takes skill, past experience, knowledge and foresight beyond the realms of operational understanding and delivery. The need today to understand audience complexity, cognitive and behavioural aspects of the audience is crucial in contemporary event management. Event managers need to perceive themselves as 'experiential practitioners'. The era of the event experientialist is here.

This chapter has presented an overview of the future of event design as a fundamental part of the event planning process as something that cannot be ignored. It's the primary point of conceptualizing event innovation and differentiation at the initial idea stage. Event design is all about 360-degree event management and interpreting societal changes such as technological innovation and consumption trends and integrating aspects into the actual event or festival offering, to keep it fresh and relevant. But it is also about understanding the experiential demands of audiences and clients alike and developing events that offer the end user the opportunity to interact and participate at a much deeper level. Event design is all about anticipating and interpreting change and 'the experiential event practitioner' must offer technological and interactive events that will capture the emotionality of the audience in order to be successful in an ever changing and complex global environment.

References

Adema, K.L and Roehl, W.S. (2010) 'Environmental scanning the future of event design', *International Journal of Hospitality Management*, 29: 199–207.

Berridge, G. (2007) *Event Design and Experience*. Abingdon: Butterworth-Heinemann.

Bladen, C., Kennell, J., Abson, E. and Wilde, N. (2012) *Events Management: an introduction*. London: Routledge.

Bowen, H.E. and Daniels, M.J. (2005) 'Does the music matter? Motivations for attending a music festival', *Events Management*, 9(3): 155–64.

Brown, S. and James, J. (2004) 'Event design and management: ritual or sacrifice?', in I. Yeoman, M. Robertson, J. Ali-Knight, S. Drummond and U. McMahon-Beattie (eds.) *Festival and Events Management: an international arts and cultural perspective*. Oxford: Elsevier Butterworth-Heinemann, pp. 53–64.

Caru, A. and Cova, B. (2003) 'Revisiting consumption experience: a more humble but complete view of the concept', *Marketing Theory*, 3(2): 267–86.

Centre for Exhibition Industry Research (2009) *Digital and Exhibiting Marketing Insights*. Chicago: Centre for Exhibition Industry Insight Research.

Comscore (2011) *Mobile*. Online. Available <www.comscore.com/Industry_Solutions/Mobile> (accessed 20 August 2013).

Event Marketing Institute (2013) *Event Track 2013*. Online. Available <www.prweb.com/prfiles/2013/03/25/10568065/EventTrack%202013.pdf> (accessed 15 February 2014).

Ferdinand, N. and Kitchin, P.J. (2012) *Events Management: an international approach*. London: Sage

Getz, D. (2007) *Event Studies: theory, research and policy for planned events*. Oxford: Butterworth-Heinemann.

Goldblatt, J. (2005) *Special Events: event leadership for a new world*. Chichester: John Wiley & Sons.

Holloway, I., Brown, L. and Shipway, R. (2010) 'Meaning not measurement: using ethnography to bring deeper understanding to the participant experience of festivals and events', *International Journal of Event and Festival Management*, 1(1): 74–85.

Keynote (2010) *Leisure Outside the Home Market Review 2010*. Online. Available <www.keynote.co.uk/market-intelligence> accessed 18 January 2014.

Lanier, C.D. and Hampton, R.D. (2009) 'Experiential marketing: understanding the logic of memorable customer experiences', in A. Lindgreen, J. Vanhamme, and M.B. Beverland (eds.) *Memorable Customer Experiences: a research anthology*. Farnham: Gower Publishing, pp. 9–24.

McCole, P. (2004) 'Refocusing marketing to reflect practice: the changing role of marketing for business', *Marketing Intelligence & Planning*, 22(5): 531–39.

Mintel (2004, August) 'Music concerts and festivals', *Mintel Report*. Online. Available <www.academicjournal.mintel.com>

Monroe, J.C. (2005) *Art of the Event: complete guide to designing and decorating special events*. New York: Wiley.

O'Toole, W. (2011) *Events Feasibility and Development: from strategy to operations*. Oxford: Butterworth-Heinemann

Payne, A., Storbacka, K. and Frow, P. (2008) 'Managing the co-creation of value', *Journal of the Academic Marketing of Science*, 36(1): 83–96.

Pearlman, D.M. and Gates, N.A. (2010) 'Hosting business meetings and special events in virtual worlds: a fad of the future?', *Journal of Convention and Event Tourism*, 11(4): 247–65.

Pine, B.J. and Gilmore, J.H. (1999) *The Experience Economy*. Cambridge, MA: Harvard Business Review.

Preston, C.A. (2012) *Event Marketing*. Hoboken, New Jersey: John Wiley & Sons.

Raj, R., Walters, P. and Rashid, T. (2013) *Events Management: principles and practice*. London: Sage.

Rumelt, R. (2008) 'Strategy in a "structural break"', *The McKinsey Quarterly*, December: 10–18.

Sneath, J.Z., Finney, R.Z. and Close, A.G. (2005) 'An IMC approach to event marketing: the effects of sponsorship and experience on consumer attitudes', *Journal of Advertising Research*, 45(4): 373–81.

Sundbo, J. and Hagedorn-Ramussen, P. (2008) 'The backstaging of experience production', in J. Sundbo and P. Darmer (eds.) *Creating Experiences in the Experience Economy*. Cheltenham: Edward Elgar, pp. 83–110.

Vargo, S. and Lusch, R. (2008) 'Service dominant logic: continuing the evolution', *Journal of the Academy of Marketing Services*, 36: 1–10.

Voss, C. and Zomerdijk, L. (2007). 'Innovation in experiential services: an empirical view' in DTI (ed.) *Innovation in Services*. London: DTI, pp. 97–134.

Wood, E. and Masterman, G. (2008) 'Event marketing: measuring an experience?' Paper presented at 7th International Marketing Trends Congress, Venice. Online. Available <www.escp-eap.eu/conferences/marketing/2008_cp/Materiali/Paper/Fr/Wood_Masterman.pdf>

19 eScaping in the city
Retailvents in socio-spatially managed futures

Martin Robertson and Gavin Lees

Future points

- Retail is a significant factor in the resilience of city development for the future and requires integration with experiential events to prosper.
- Retail, organized events and festivals are likely to form a narrative function in socio-spatial management of the megacity of the future.
- As gaps in age groups appear in the population of Australia of the future, retail events will rely on an older staff profile.
- Exploratory trend impact analysis may utilize normative trend narrative to expedite sustainable or social improvements in the future.

Introduction: shopping and events

Retail

From a mercantile past, of the travelling merchant and adventures and travels around the world, to proliferation of market towns, to the growth of individual – specialist – shops and then to the emergence of retail giants (supermarkets to superstores), retail has gone through many changes. With the emergence of hyper-markets, of self-service retail, global retail chains, and the emergence of luxuriant city centre shopping (Park, Reisinger and Noh 2010), so too the world has witnessed a radical change in the expectations of consumers. This has been discussed as a transition of shopping as activity based on functionality to one based on leisure values (Carr 1990; Timothy 2005). The integration of retail with an online digital platform has seen these values altered again.

Events and shopping

Retail has then often been a component of the event experience, and most often an addition. This can take also the form of souvenirs, foods, clothing and art ware. Often it is the largest income generator (Timothy 2005). Significantly, retail consumer behaviour has been a pivotal component in developing analysis of the behaviour of event attendees.

Doyle (2004) explains how merchandise can be used within an event for a number of outcomes. These include income generation, as a reward, to enhance brand awareness, as an integral component (such as in Ideal Home and Motor shows), and experience enhancement or experience memory. From a list of definition of special events, Goldblatt (2005) defines retail events as being live events with advertising, publicity and sales promotions. Professional event organizers and managers are often employed by the retailers and producers of products to organize events. For companies like Sony, Xbox and Disney these events can be epic activities tightly knit in their communication strategy. For the producers of smaller products they may be simple selling activities. For mega-stores and large city centre stores they may be large pageants or displays – often at times of seasonal activity or significance, e.g. Chinese New Year.

Shopping is also seen in the context of an experience economy in which 'fun' is a pervasive theme (Metz, Schrijver and Snoek 2002; Yeoman 2012, 2013), and 'fun shopping' prevails in urban development projects (Bauman 2003; Marling, Jensen and Kiib 2009). A relatively modern phenomenon derived from theming of restaurants and the way in which shopping malls host shows, events, or expositions provides 'shoppertainment' (Lorentzen 2009: 14).

The city context: retail struggle and experience and the need for an adaptive retail future

Cities have changed. The community of a city, its social and business functions, all ebb and flow (and change) as the forces of the rest of world change. All retail has, within this, been influenced by constant and ongoing changes of consumer wants and needs. As a largely urban experience, shopping has been controlled historically by the attributes of convenience and accessibility. Cachinho (2014) reflects that the cities of the developed world have observed a 'retail revolution' over the last fifty years. As the growth of the cities throughout the world increases, and as the countries of Asia grow commensurately (United Nations 2012), as does their wealth, it is reasonable to considerate that this retail revolution is worldwide – and is affected by both Asian and more traditionally western cultures and consumer mores.

As part of this retail revolution, with convenience and accessibility having far less significance, retail has been designed, marketed and designed to arouse particular emotions and feelings (Cachinho 2014). This is to say it has been understood for some time that shopping is a leisure experience and that the shopping itself is not necessarily a central element of that experience. As Barr and Broudy (1986: 2) suggest, 'people act out their innermost hopes, dreams and aspirations . . .' and that as an activity shopping is a 'personal mini-drama', sharing, then, many of the attributes of an organized event. For the city, this has meant retailers (individual or as part of a chain) have sought to create mini experiences. Many retail providers (and much retail literature) have acknowledged the importance of understanding customer experiences and maximizing the experience based on that knowledge and, further, the customer's need to have an active and creative part in the experience

(Verhoef *et al.* 2009). Furthermore, that experience has increasingly fewer and fewer links with the location, e.g. city centre, in which it is placed and may have more connection to some other liminal state, i.e. a state of otherness (Turner 1977).

Yet in considering a city as a destination, it has also been suggested as unimaginable that a visitor would not make reference to shopping; where to go, and what to buy (Doyle and Robertson 2004; Yüksel 2007). Further, it has been suggested that shopping has for the visitor an abiding importance to the overall visitor experience (Hui, Wan and Ho 2007; McIntyre 2010; Murphy *et al.* 2011; Tosun *et al.* 2007). The shopping offered by a city is described as a significant element in mediating sense of risk, learning and socialization and – importantly – a component of experience and 'otherness' that allows identification with place and attributes of a visiting experience (Marling, Jensen and Kiib 2009; McIntyre 2007). The shopping experience is also included as a factor in the sustainable development of a destination (Tosun *et al.* 2007).

It is in this gap between the concept of shopping tourism (as related to destination or resident location) and the retail experience (as an emotional concept, one devoid of physical location) that cities find themselves today. Add to this a growth of alternative experiences, and both convenient and exciting online shopping experiences (Chen and Cheng 2013; Wann-Yih *et al.* 2014), and then it is clear the future of bricks and mortar shopping in city centre locations may not be certain.

Conceptual base and methodology

Trend impact analysis and trends

Trend impact analysis (TIA) has been used since the 1970s (Gordon 2009), and its application has been wide ranging, for both commercial information services and in the public sector. It has been the tradition that quantitative forecasting based solely on historical data has formed TIA projections (Agami *et al.* 2008; Gordon 2009). This has meant the extrapolated data has formed conclusions without reference to 'unprecedented future events' (Agami *et al.* 2008: 1439). Thus, TIA has previously required only one algorithm, in acceptance that while the future may have other influences, these will not have a dramatic effect on forecast. However, in times of rapid change, with an increasing number of influences and affecting contingencies the chance of a single frame seems unlikely. Further, in an increasing global (sometimes volatile) culture (in Australia as elsewhere), and with a greater range of sophisticated projective and foresight analysis available, it is not a surprise that its legitimacy has been queried. The tradition of utilizing one algorithm model has been questioned, and a hybrid model of TIA has emerged. It integrates qualitative analysis with the quantitative. By adding qualitative analysis and by allowing for the unprecedented, a different (more advanced) algorithm emerges. Further, as Agami *et al.* (2008) indicate, one can offer degrees of probability or severity of outcome in the analysis.

In this, the first stage of this process, this work undertakes a trend analysis. This is to say that a search for patterns of trends has been sought, to provide 'insight as to how the world is performing now, and to illicit foresight as to what is coming next' (Yeoman 2013: 250). The work shows *drivers* of change (as an aggregate of trends), *trends* (which contribute to the driver of change) and a discussion of *impacts* around the 'unprecedented future events' (Agami *et al.* 2008: 1439), which may contribute to an advanced algorithm (as discussed above). One short scenario is constructed in the form of a story as both an exploration and analysis of the effect of the drivers (van der Heijden 2000). In so doing it illustrates the purpose of the future study (Yeoman 2012) and, it is proposed, gives the opportunity for discussion. As such, it increases the utility value of the trend analysis.

Scenario

A single scenario is constructed here from the three drivers of change that are indicated below: socio-spatial management of the inner city, an increasingly ageing population and the convergence of technology. These are constructed in the form of a story. The character, Jeanne Yip, and her employment activity serve to explore and animate how events and retail could merge in the capital city of the future. In the first part of the scenario, the introduction, the story draws principally on the first and second drivers.

Jeanne Yip

Jeanne (aged sixty-eight) works on a freelance basis as a Retailvent Experience Flow Consultant. Her initial training and her ongoing certification accreditation are facilitated by City Centre Spatial Partnerships (CCSP). This is her third year of employment as an Experience Flow Consultant, and her fifth month working for Retailvent. Jeanne genuinely loves her work. She had never thought of herself as an actor but enjoys working with her colleagues, bringing to life each new experience event project. As a long-standing employee in this area, she plays a key part in developing the performance skills of her colleagues – inserting product awareness with spatial theme recognition.

Jeanne normally works three days a week. While Jeanne on her arrival to Australia, twenty-five years ago, had certainly not anticipated that she would still be working in her late sixties, the CCSP work package and the extra remuneration awarded by the retail and product franchises she is involved with on a day-to-day basis are extremely attractive. Besides, with the great likelihood of living well and actively into her nineties and having (as with most of her friends) a lot of energy, it keeps her mind and body active. Jeanne updates her accreditation (certificate) for experience flow management monthly. She builds up the accreditation through a mixture of peer review (by colleagues and spatial experience visitors) and the accumulation of points through virtual training enactments.

Drivers, trends and impacts

Driver 1: The urban space – now and socio-spatial context of the future

While retail and events do come together in small towns and rural outlets, this article concentrates on the inner city, city centre location – the urban space. An estimation and projection of world urban population indicates that the world's urban population is expected to increase by 72 percent by 2050, from 3.6 billion in the year 2011 to 6.3 billion in the year 2050 – the same size as the total world population (urban and rural) in the year 2002. Further, the proportion of the world that will have 10 million or more citizens living within one city will increase dramatically (United Nations 2012).

In 1975, there were only three cities in the world with a population of 10 million citizens or over (i.e. megacities). In 2002, there were seventeen cities in this category. By 2025, the United Nations projection is for thirty-seven megacities to have populations of 10 million or more. Over the same period, as a percentage of the world's urban population, there is a change from 3 percent (in 1975) to 8 percent (in 2000) to 14 percent in 2025 (United Nations 2012). While cities in Australia will not reach the 10 million population mark, the country will nonetheless become ever more urban. Figure 19.1 is a summary of the population growth between 1950 and 2025 of the cities Adelaide, Brisbane, Melbourne, Perth and Sydney. The Australian Bureau of Statistics (2013) projects Melbourne to have a

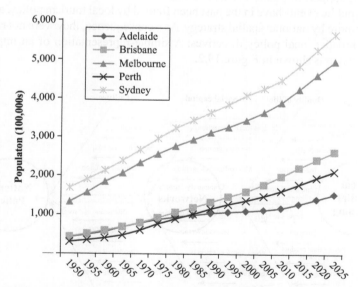

Figure 19.1 Projected population (Adelaide, Brisbane, Melbourne, Perth and Sydney) 1950 to 2025

Source: Adapted from United Nations (2012)

population of 8.6 million and Sydney one of 8.5 million by 2061 in two of their three scenarios. Accordingly they are likely to become megacities.

The entrepreneurial style and the competitive driver for the planning required for cities of the early twentieth century has faced numerous changes. Organized events have often played a significant part of the developing place narrative (Robertson and Guerrier 1998; Robertson and Wardrop 2004), i.e. as part of the fabric of change that creates a sense of place, rather than something that equivocally manages its image (Prentice and Andersen 2003). This narrative can also be seen in the themes that emerge in transient stages of place development and in affirmation of place brand (equity).

Spatial themes such as knowledge communities, industrial districts, compact cities, livable cities, creative cities, etc., form part of a narrative of transformation and integration (Albrechts 2010). Led by the public sector, but dependent on networks, the purpose is to create special places where there are interrelations between activities and other arising networks (Albrechts 2010; Healey 2004). Spatial policy thus aligns itself to the creation or the reimaging and brand construction of *place*. Festivals, sport events and cultural activities are very crucial elements in that process (Paiola 2008), as are business events (Jago and Deery 2010). Festivals, sports, events and culture are, therefore, not only adding to the social capital index of a location – working at a *bonding* and *bridging* capacity – but also as part of spatial development.

Taking the perspective of the public sector of the future, Robertson and Wardrop (2012) comment that for strategic reasons and for pragmatic purpose (principally cost), the support of public events must fit into a local spatial strategy. This is to say that public events have in the past been framed by local tourism policy, and yet defined more by national spatial strategy. As a consequence, they were not responsive to broader local policy directives. A simple representation of an improved spatial vision is shown in Figure 19.2.

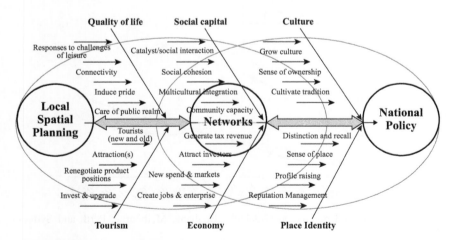

Figure 19.2 The emerging local (city) spatial domain
Source: Adapted from Robertson and Wardrop (2012)

Trend 1: The holistic experience (Driver 1)

Increasingly, then, it is noted that, for the visitor, the shopping experience is not necessarily considered separate from the rest of the experience. For example, in evaluating the success of a museum visit experience retail space may be best when integral to the whole experience. This may indeed expedite a co-creative element that is complimentary and a 'synergistic balance of holistic, sociocultural-economic experience' (McIntyre 2010).

Trend 2: A spatial experience future (Driver 1)

The researchers propose here that shopping in the city will increasingly be part of a socio-spatially defined development. Importantly and increasingly its link to other elements of the urban experience will be recognized for its spatial significance. Set in a framework of national and international competition, the capacity of cities to ensure a competitive social-spatial environment will be all the more important. Figure 19.3 shows how the relationship of shopping and the consumer has moved from being one of defined leisure activity to one that is integrated as a component of spatial experience. Further, this indicates that there is (currently) a transition stage in which shopping is converging with other urban activities, as part of socio-spatial consumption. Organized events are an indispensable part of this convergent process.

Impact: Urban retail resilience

'Urban retail resilience has been defined as the ability of stores and shopping districts to tolerate and adapt to changing environments that challenge the retail system's equilibrium, and failing to perform its functions in a sustainable way' (Cachinho 2014: 131). Accordingly it makes sense that all city retail becomes more active and open to new experiential notions. Yet there is, it is suggested, a current duality of retail space – one in which some individual providers have architecture based on theatrical design, and those with a more traditional basic exchange model, i.e. money for goods. Those people that come from the dramaturgical (Nelson 2009)

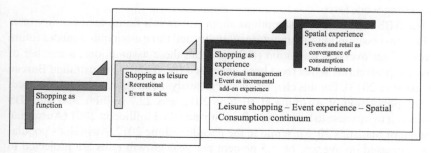

Figure 19.3 Progression of retail

and utilize the hyper-real sense, where the symbolism of the architecture and design comes together in 'the new retail spaces cast into the city show where consumers are both the spectators and the actors', are referred to as *consumactors* (Cachincho 2014: 133). This consumactor relation (based on co-creative activity similar to that on a theatrical stage) offers potential for liminal experience for both consumer and staff.

The linkage between stage and liminal space is a powerful one. The concept of retail space as being a stage is equally noteworthy. It has been the tradition in stage performance that the performance is dominantly one-way activity, from performance (or performer) to audience, i.e. there is defined distance between the actors and what they create and the audience (and what they receive). In theatre literature, this distance from the actor and the performer has been known as the fourth wall, a theatrical device outside the physical dimensions, which creates belief in the fictional (Jean 2006; Katherine 2007). In the current era, the fourth wall is broken frequently when the actor converses with the audience (or appears to converse), and to a greater or lesser extent the two are co-creating the experience.

Driver 2: The Australian population – projection for an ageing population

Utilizing the statistics from the Australian Bureau of Statistics (ABS) (www.abs.gov.au), it is possible to observe that the population of Australia is getting older. The baby boomers (those born between 1946 and 1964) are either retiring or approaching retirement age. The net effect of this is that there could be more people leaving the workforce than entering it. What are the indicators for Australia's future population over the next fifty to one hundred years?

From 2011 the baby boomers have (and have had) the potential to exit the workforce en masse. That is, the baby boomers born in 1946 will be sixty-five and be eligible for a pension. Accordingly they could stop work. The number of boomers who reach sixty-five increases each year and will peak around the year 2021. This is diagrammatically represented in the *pig in the python* (Figure 19.4) where baby boomers are shown moving through the population demographics. Accordingly, over the next twenty plus years we have an ageing population and a decreasing work force.

The ABS makes three assumptions about Australia's future total fertility rates (TFR), two assumptions about future mortality and three assumptions about future levels of net overseas migration (NOM). From these assumptions, a number of possible projections series have been generated (A, B and C) (Australian Bureau of Statistics 2013). For this chapter, as a trend analysis, an aggregate figure is used.

The population of Australia at 30 June 2012 was 22.7 million, and the ABS projects it to increase to between 36.8 million and 48.3 million in 2061 (Australian Bureau of Statistics 2013). While in the decade to June 2012, Australia's population increased on average by 1.5 percent per year growth rates are projected to decline over the long term.

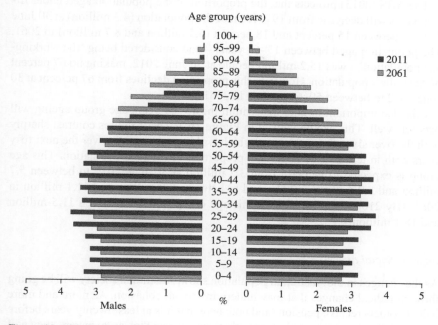

Figure 19.4 Pig in the python
Source: Australian Bureau of Statistics (2013)

Trend 1: Net overseas migration becomes increasingly vital

The other main contributor to Australia's population growth is net overseas migration (NOM). For example in 2011–12 net overseas migration contributed 223,100 people to Australia's population. Net overseas migration also impacts on population growth through not only the actual levels of migration but also by children born to migrants to Australia.

Cultural and social activity in Australia will become increasingly more diverse. In large state capital cities, a multitude of interpretative materials and applications (streamlining, virtual and enacted in events) will be required both inside and outside of employment.

Trend 2: Ageing of the population for the next fifty years

One of the most dramatic changes projected to occur to Australia's population is the ageing of the population especially over the next half century. This ageing is reflected in the median age, which the ABS projects to increase from 37.3 years in 2012 to between 38.6 years and 40.5 years in 2031, and between 41.0 years and 44.5 years in 2061.

The ABS (2013) projects that the proportion of the population aged under fifteen years will decrease from 19 percent of the population (4.3 million) at 30 June 2012 to between 15 percent and 18 percent (5.5 million and 8.7 million) in 2061. The population aged between 15–64 years – and considered being 'the working-age population' – was 15.2 million people at 30 June 2012, making up 67 percent of Australia's population. However, this proportion declines from 67 percent at 30 June 2012 to between 59–61 percent in 2061.

It is also important to note that within the 15–64 years age group ageing will occur as well. This can be viewed in Figure 19.4. These figures contrast sharply with the over sixty-five age group, which will increase rapidly over the next fifty years both in terms of numbers and proportion of the total population. This age group is expected to increase from 3.2 million at 30 June 2012 to between 5.7 million and 5.8 million in 2031, and to between 9.0 million and 11.1 million in 2061. (By 2101, the ABS expects this age group to reach between 11.5 million and 18.1 million.)

Impact: Social query

As the changes in the Australian population show, Australian society will be going through radical changes that may undermine social cohesion. As more and more baby boomers receive pension (and note here that it is at least twenty years before self-funded retirees enter retirement), they may expect that, as taxpayers, they will be looked after in their retirement years, i.e. receive adequate health care and a reasonable pension based on their previous income. These expectations may well clash with the focus of the current generations X and Y who as part of a diminishing 'taxpaying' work force might otherwise be expected to be paying taxes to fund these expectations. These short-falls in expectations – and a decrease in spending power by the now newly retired baby boomers – mean they may reenter the retail events work force. Retail may thus need to develop a new motivational employment scheme, appropriate to the expectations of younger and older members of the community.

Driver 3: Technology and the retail industry

In their profile of the event goers of the future, Yeoman, Robertson and Smith (2012) suggest that the relationship between physical and social-networking experiences, respectively, has become an ever more significant one. This is also true for retail.

The combination of social-network and physical function that technology can perform will become ever more extensive. Handheld technologies – (such as the ubiquitous iPhone or smartphone) and the increasing number of wearable technologies, e.g. Samsung's Smartwatches (emulating the smartphone concept); smart bracelets – will make way for new technology, which be less obtrusive and more synchronous, either in skinlike membranes or using transparent nano-technology, and will subsume much of the handheld technology we know and expect. So too the range of lifestyle combinations offered to the trend conscious will expand. Included in this combination are retail communication and communities, and real-time and augmented retail event attendance and experience. These technologies and the changing requirements of city visitors will become synonymous with the needs of urban spatial consumption, and the response of cities to that demand to remain both 'livable' cities and 'competitive cities'.

Yet it is important to start from the driver of technological development (Yeoman 2012) and the sense in which retail is said to be under attack. Or particularly, as a physical place location retail is often cited as living on borrowed time (Niemeier, Zocchi and Catena 2013). Further, Niemer, Zocchi and Catena (2013) talk of how the technology that had previously given great power to larger retailers is now 'beginning to leech power from them' (24). However, this fails to observe the power that technology may also give to retail.

Trend 1: Mobility and big data

In the current time environment mobile technology has given the consumer huge amounts of decision-making power. As well as ensuring immense choice and liberty for consumers, technology has also allowed retailers prodigious amounts of knowledge. Central to both consumer experience and retail power to satisfy this in a strategic way is the phenomena 'big data', i.e. the collation of information from a number of different streams – architecture of data. Niemeier, Zocchi and Catena (2013) indicate that for access to data to be termed 'big data' it must have at least two of the following characteristics: scale, massive distribution, diversity, timeliness and analysis. This is to say that big data is related to the large *scale of data*, i.e. data sets will be immense and relatively easy to access, they will be from *diverse* sources and will be convergent in their digital format. Importantly these sources can be *distributed* inside and outside the organization, and be easily analyzed. Indeed the analysis will be learning based, and increasingly adaptable.

An increasingly vital vessel for the big data is of course the Internet. In recognition of the way both information and objects are increasingly digitally interconnected or networked the term 'Internet of things' or 'Internet of objects' has been coined (Xia *et al.* 2012: 1011). Importantly, what marks this development as distinct from simply being part of the Internet per se is that these networked objects are often equipped with omnipresent (ubiquitous) intelligence. For retail, Niemeier, Zocchi and Catena (2013) indicate the two broad areas of application, which are significant. These are the capacity to inform and analyze and, second, automate and control (see Table 19.1). Geo-visualization has the capacity to bridge both of these.

Trend 2: Geo-visualization (Driver 3)

People expect to have spatial information extremely quickly. Global positioning systems (GPS) in cars and in digital cameras are simple examples of how this is used by a great many people each day. So geo-visualization has roots in

Table 19.1. The Internet of things

Information and analysis	Tracking behaviour; monitoring behaviour of persons (or things) or data through space and time	Enhanced situational awareness; real-time awareness of physical environment	Sensor-driven decision analytics assisting human decision making through deep analysis, data visualization
Automation and control	Process optimization	Optimized resource consumption	Complex autonomous systems

Source: Adapted from Niemeier, Zocchi and Catena (2013)

cartography in the same way as the GPS system but now integrates information and knowledge from various scientific fields, including scientific information, information visualization and the virtual environment (Jiang and Li 2005). Geo-visualization has been used within retail outlets to determine the best market consumption patterns and, thus, the best locations for stock and associated promotion (Arentze, Borgers and Timmermans 2000). It has also been used by multiple shop chains to determine the best geographical locations for their retail outlets (Benoit and Clarke 1997; Hernandez 2007). Their purpose has been to utilize best available data to predict the capacity and value of networks of their shops.

Geo-visualization does use an increasing number of sources to inform propriety decisions, and these relate to customer perception, traffic flow, access, distance, differentiation of offer (from others) and, it is suggested, may operate with CSR issues in mind (Karamychev and van Reeven 2009; Martinuzzi *et al.* 2011).

Impact: Consumactors in livable cities

What the researchers feel pressing is the way in which technology can in the future bring together data in an asynchronous way for both visitors and the domestic urban populations, which is attractive, pleasing and supportive of urban-spatial strategies. In the retail spaces provided, consumers will be both the spectators and the actors, i.e. '*consumactors*' (Cachincho 2014: 133). Governing bodies and policy will be actioned appropriately. Core to this is the development of geo-visual management capacity and convergence with other systems.

In the future there will be a need for more dynamically interactive GIS retail location technology, which interact with social media, including Google Maps, as well as with theming event communication and the latest in shopping technology. As well as offering a retail plan, it will offer a reactive response in relation to this – and will converge with other data sources, from event organizers to other entertainment resources. Big data and its capacity to be spliced for the needs of organizations and single retailers, as well as public and private sector spatial-experience managers, will remain challenging in the next ten to twenty years, but will develop quickly. Vitally, spatial governance bodies (and related policy) will be able facilitate this.

It is not the purpose of this work to review all technology. Technology will continue to change. Medicine is one convergent element of this. Engineering, teaching, psychology and sport are others. Thus, technology will become asynchronous to the needs of life in an increasing number of ways. We have seen these as physical manifestations (from the massive to infinitely small). In the mid- to long-term future – as indicated by current development by neuroscientists on brain wave control of keyboards (and other communication and technology platforms) for those with either speech or physical impairment (Dangelis 2013) – we will also see them in mental and psychological forms.

Scenario

Jeanne at work

This second part of the single scenario construct story draws principally on the second and third driver.

In the scenario, Jeanne has had three years of ongoing training in people collaboration skills. With the exception of meeting her team of Retailvent performers and promoters at the start of each of the three days of the inner city spatial experience events, most her activity is actioned through her *Gogirl* contact lenses (provided and pre-orientated by CCSP). In addition to this, Jeanne has generic pass keys (voice and fingerprint activated) for all the sensors and trackers that exist in the five spatial zones in the city centre in which she has jurisdiction. The pass key allows her to work with the design team to alter ambient controls (sounds, vision – projections and 3D holograms), smell and heat in each of the zones based on the schedule that the event design expert will have produced for her. Clearly a response to the growth of the city, and the busy streets, natural uncluttered landscapes, woodland, seascapes and cloud scenes (and colour scapes) are often the most popular environments integrated with performance activity, live theatre, product launches and fashion shows.

Importantly, all activity is screened by the geo-visual system. This can notify Jeanne of any changes occurring that day, or simply as a reminder of the schedule for the day. When Jeanne's eyes are dry or if there are problems with her contact lenses, she can use her 'thin-as-paper' backup controller version of the data system (in Jeanne's case she has been provided with Asis's new *PapeLet*).

Using either the contact lenses (with retina and voice control) or *Papelet* she can speak to suppliers, performers, designers and security. To ensure clarity, each spatial control area has a unique colour that appears in her lenses (and screen) so that she knows to whom she is talking. Again, the geo-visual system keeps her on the correct path, learning from her actions and supporting her when required.

It's important that the Jeanne and her team work in ways in which they all feel they contribute. Jeanne is given frequent reminders to check up on team members. Messages will appear on their screens (or contact lenses). Short messages of encouragement, reward or concern can be sent as colour senses (appearing on the inside of their palm – and/or warm, cold, tickly or patting sensations on the skin (depending on the emotional purpose of message). As well as a regular 'chat' facility, facial and voice changes are monitored to check for stress or unhappiness of the team player. This is particularly important for some of the younger members of the team. As part of a learning process, Jeanne is able to update the database and the geo-system if there are matters that need to be addressed or if people need support. Everyone – from suppliers to visitors – is encouraged to have their feelings regularly assessed.

Retailvent team members have human relation and performance work-shops each week. Often these include prospective customers – either as real attendees or projected holograms. It is important that staff members are also able to release their desire for artistic (creative) experience with a capacity to entertain, share ideas (with and from guest experiences) and also bring for-ward commercial acumen. Making products and product brands come alive and memorable in these events is important.

The security team is rarely called upon, as stealing is very rare in an age where no one carries cash and up-market experience acquisition is automatic. Most people are able to indicate when they want to buy something through their own voice or retina-activated hardware. This can either be delivered to your requested location (home, holiday accommodation or office) or – when available – the product can be picked up from one of a number of central retail outlets. If you move fifty meters or more from the point in which you picked up a product, you have confirmed that you wish to buy the product and pay-ment is drawn automatically.

Conclusions

The implications of this work for the future of the event industry based on the present is that events have becoming increasingly interconnected with society and are supported for a number of social and economic outcomes. In the future, the integration of organized events into the networks of social urban living can become more profound.

This chapter looked at the future of events as a component of retail for Aus-tralia. The drivers of change are increased urbanization as it affects Australia and global positioning of its cities as livable and attractive cities; an ageing population influenced by changed pressures on local and national economies and technology and its effect on the retail sector and consumption, respectively.

The researchers here do not foresee a dystopia in which technology will deter-mine where life (for mankind) goes. It is clear, however, that technology will certainly assist it in its path. Moreover, the researchers conclude that here has been only limited review of how technology will influence visitors to (and residents of) a city. Thus, many of the trend projections that exist are incomplete.

In a predominantly urban world in which social and economic governance will need to be correlated sensitively to ensure success for the population and visitors, the spatial experience will bring together activities previously seen as separate (or as distant relatives). Arts, culture and other city activity will need better unity (while not threatening uniqueness). Events will be a part of this unification – offering an almost invisible social and experiential glue. The use of big data and a necessarily more active and contributory input by the older members of the population are likely: bridging both a skills gap and a retirement funding gap is a very significant component of the unified environment.

An initial look at impacts indicates that in order to proceed with a trend impact analysis, it is necessary to discover (from a wide range of resources, news, trends and social indicators) possible unprecedented events. Determining the severity of their impact is a challenge but would be needed to add more functionality to trend impact analysis.

References

Agami, N.M.E., Omran, A.M.A., Saleh, M.M. and El-Shishiny, H.E.E.-D. (2008) 'An enhanced approach for Trend Impact Analysis', *Technological Forecasting and Social Change*, 75(9): 1439–50.

Albrechts, L. (2010) 'Strategic planning and regional governance in Europe: recent trends and policy responses', in J. Xu and A.G.O. Yeh (eds.) *Governance and Planning of Mega-City Regions: An international comparative perspective*. Hoboken: Routledge, pp. 75–97.

Arentze, T., Borgers, A. and Timmermans, H. (2000) 'A knowledge-based system for developing retail location strategies', *Computers, Environment and Urban Systems*, 24(6): 489–508.

Australian Bureau of Statistics (2013) *Population Projections, Australia, 2012 (Base) to 2101*. Online. Available: <http://www.abs.gov.au/ausstats/abs@.nsf/Lookup/3222.0main+features52012%20%28base%29%20to%202101> (accessed 12 December 2013).

Barr, V. and Broudy, C.E. (1986) *Designing to Sell: a complete guide to retail store planning and design*. New York: McGraw-Hill.

Bauman, Z. (2003) 'City of fears, city of hopes', in H. Thomsen (ed.) *Future Cities: the Copenhagen lectures*. Copenhagen: Fonden Realdania, pp. 59–90.

Benoit, D. and Clarke, G.P. (1997) 'Assessing GIS for retail location planning', *Journal of Retailing and Consumer Services*, 4(4): 239–58.

Cachinho, H. (2014) 'Consumerscapes and the resilience assessment of urban retail systems', *Cities*, 36: 131–44.

Carr, J. (1990) 'The social aspects of shopping: pleasure or chore?', *Royal Society of Arts Journal*, 138: 189–97.

Chen, S. and Cheng, F.F. (2013) 'The influence of online atmosphere on perceived quality, satisfaction and purchase intention', Paper presented at 2013 Fifth International Conference on Service Science and Innovation (ICSSI), Kaohsiung, Taiwan.

Dangelis, A. (2013) 'Mind Meld! Top Brain-Controlled Techs', *Discovery News*, 6 June, viewed 20 October 2013, <http://news.discovery.com/tech/robotics/mind-meld-top-brain-controlled-techs-130606.htm>.

Doyle, S.A. (2004) 'Merchandising and retail', in I. Yeoman, M. Robertson, J. Ali-Knight, S. Drummond and U. McMahon-Beattie (eds.), *Festival and Events Management: an international arts and culture perspective*. Oxford: Butterworth Heinemann, pp. 158–70.

Doyle, S.A. and Robertson, M. (2004) 'The intergrated tourist city: shopping expectations and destination image in Edinburgh and Birmingham', Paper presented at the *Conference CIRM: Retailing in Town and City Centres: current issues, future prospects*, Manchester Metropolitan University.

Goldblatt, J.J. (2005) *Special Events: event leadership for a new world*. Hoboken, NJ: Wiley.

Gordon, T.J. (2009) 'Trend impact analysis', in J.C. Glenn and T.J. Gordon (eds.) *Futures Research Methodology V.3.0*. Washington: The Millenium Project, pp. 1–19.

Healey, P. (2004) 'The treatment of space and place in the new strategic spatial planning in Europe', *International Journal of Urban and Regional Research*, 28(1): 45–67.

Hernandez, T. (2007) 'Enhancing retail location decision support: the development and application of geovisualization', *Journal of Retailing and Consumer Services*, 14(4): 249–58.

Hui, T.K., Wan, D. and Ho, A. (2007) 'Tourists' satisfaction, recommendation and revisiting Singapore', *Tourism Management*, 28(4): 965–75.

Jago, L. and Deery, M. (2010). *Delivering Innovation, Knowledge and Performance: The role of business events*. Melbourne: BECA. Online. Available: <http://businesseventscouncil. org.au/files/BE_Innov_Report_Mar10.pdf> (accessed 7 February 2014).

Jean, S. (2006) 'Beyond the fourth wall', *Back Stage East*, 47(5): 6.

Jiang, B. and Li, Z. (2005) 'Geovisualization: design, enhanced visual tools and applications', *The Cartographic Journal*, 42(1): 3–4.

Karamychev, V. and van Reeven, P. (2009) 'Retail sprawl and multi-store firms: an analysis of location choice by retail chains', *Regional Science and Urban Economics*, 39(3): 277–86.

Katherine, T.-J. (2007) 'The literary origins of the cinematic narrator', *British Journal of Aesthetics*, 47(1): 76–94.

Lorentzen, A. (2009) 'Cities in the Experience Economy', *European Planning Studies*, 17(6): 829–45.

McIntyre, C. (2007) 'Survival theory: tourist consumption as a beneficial experiential process in a limited risk setting', *International Journal of Tourism Research*, 9(2): 115–30.

McIntyre, C. (2010) 'Designing museum and gallery shops as integral, co-creative retail spaces within the overall visitor experience', *Museum Management and Curatorship*, 25(2): 181–98.

Marling, G., Jensen, O.B. and Kiib, H. (2009) 'The experience city: planning of hybrid cultural projects', *European Planning Studies*, 17(6): 863–85.

Martinuzzi, A., Kudlak, R., Faber, C. and Wiman, A. (2011) *CSR Activities and Impacts of the Retail Sector*. Vienna: RIMAS Working Papers. Online. Available: <www. sustainability.eu> (accessed 12 December 2013)

Metz, T., Schrijver, J. and Snoek, O. (2002) *Fun! Leisure and landscape*. Rotterdam: NAi.

Murphy, L., Moscardo, G., Benckendorff, P. and Pearce, P. (2011) 'Evaluating tourist satisfaction with the retail experience in a typical tourist shopping village', *Journal of Retailing and Consumer Services*, 18(4): 302–10.

Nelson, K.B. (2009) 'Enhancing the attendee's experience through creative design of the event environment: applying Goffman's dramaturgical perspective', *Journal of Convention & Event Tourism*, 10(2): 120–33.

Niemeier, S., Zocchi, A. and Catena, M. (2013) *Reshaping Retail: why technology is transforming the industry and how to win in the new consumer driven world*. Hoboken: Wiley.

Paiola, M. (2008) 'Cultural events as potential drivers of urban regeneration: an empirical illustration', *Industry and Innovation*, 15(5): 513–29.

Park, K.S., Reisinger, Y. and Noh, E.H. (2010) 'Luxury shopping in tourism', *International Journal of Tourism Research*, 12(2): 164–78.

Prentice, R. and Andersen, V. (2003) 'Festival as creative destination', *Annals of Tourism Research*, 30(1): 7–30.

Robertson, M. and Guerrier, Y. (1998) 'Events as entrepreneurial displays: Seville, Barcelona and Madrid', in D. Tyler, Y. Guerrier and M. Robertson (eds.) *Managing Tourism in Cities: policy, process, and practice*. Chichester: John Wiley & Sons, pp. 215–28.

Robertson, M. and Wardrop, K. (2004) 'Events and the destination dynamic: Edinburgh festivals, entrepreneurship and strategic marketing', in I. Yeoman, M. Robertson, J. Ali-Knight, S. Drummond and U. McMahon-Beattie (eds.) *Festival and Events Management: an international arts and culture perspective*. Oxford: Butterworth-Heinemann, pp. 115–29.

Robertson, M. and Wardrop, K. (2012) 'Festival and events, government and spatial governance', in S. Page and J. Connell (eds.) *The Handbook of Events*. London: Routledge, pp. 489–506.

Timothy, D.J. (2005) *Shopping Tourism, Retailing, and Leisure*. Clevedon: Channel View Publications.

Tosun, C., Temizkan, S.P., Timothy, D.J. and Fyall, A. (2007) 'Tourist shopping experiences and satisfaction', *International Journal of Tourism Research*, 9(2): 87–102.

Turner, V. (1977) 'Variations on a theme of liminality', in S.F. Moore and B.G. Myerhoff (eds.) *Secular Ritual*. Assen: Van Gorcum Ltd, pp. 36–52.

United Nations, Department of Economic and Social Affairs, Population Division (2012) *World Urbanization Prospects: The 2011 Revision*. CD-ROM Edition – Data in digital form (POP/DB/WUP/Rev.2011).

van der Heijden, K. (2000) 'Scenarios and forecasting: two perspectives', *Technological Forecasting and Social Change*, 65(1): 31–6.

Verhoef, P.C., Lemon, K.N., Parasuraman, A., Roggeveen, A., Tsiros, M. and Schlesinger, L.A. (2009) 'Customer experience creation: determinants, dynamics and management strategies', *Journal of Retailing*, 85(1): 31–41.

Wann-Yih, W., Chia-Ling, L., Chen-Su, F. and Hong-Chun, W. (2014) 'How can online store layout design and atmosphere influence consumer shopping intention on a website?', *International Journal of Retail & Distribution Management*, 42(1): 4–24.

Xia, F., Yang, L.T., Wang, L. and Vinel, A. (2012) 'Internet of Things', *International Journal of Communication Systems*, 25(9): 1101–02.

Yeoman, I. (2012) *2050: Tomorrow's Tourism*. Bristol: Channel View Publications.

Yeoman, I. (2013) 'A futurist's thoughts on consumer trends shaping future festivals and events', *International Journal of Event and Festival Management*, 4(3): 249–60.

Yeoman, I., Robertson, M. and Smith, K. (2012) 'A futurist's view on the future of events', in S.J. Page and J. Connell (eds.) *The Routledge Handbook of Events*. Oxon: Routledge, pp. 507–25.

Yüksel, A. (2007) 'Tourist shopping habitat: effects on emotions, shopping value and behaviours', *Tourism Management*, 28(1): 58–69.

Part 3

What does this all mean?

20 Cognitive map(s) of event and festival futures

Ian Yeoman, Martin Robertson and Carol Wheatley

Future points

- A series of illustrative cognitive maps capturing the core concepts from preceding chapters' authors' thoughts about the future of events and festivals.
- An aggregate cognitive map that represents the collective thoughts of leading academics and researcher about the future.
- The field of events and festivals is clustered around three future views: new consumer values and identity, political reasons and power and the future role of technology.

Introduction

The future cannot be forecasted with a high degree of certainty and precision (Eden and Ackermann 1998); however, understanding the environment and context as explanation is a purposeful way to examine the future. In the future studies literature (Yeoman 2012; Bergman, Karlsson and Axelsson 2010) there has been a movement from singularity and prediction to understanding multiplicity and context, and thus the purpose of the future as explanation. One emphasis of explanation is in examination of the layers, links and spaces to make sense of the future and thus to inform decisions and directions. So, what then are the underlying layers, phenomena and spaces associated with the future of events and festivals? In order to address this question a cognitive mapping approach has been used. This has been applied previously in tourism research (Yeoman, Munro and McMahon-Beattie 2006; Yeoman and Watson 2011).

Each chapter of this publication has been interpreted through a cognitive map from which an aggregate map has been produced. This aggregate map represents the contribution of this book to future of events and festivals knowledge, and research is clustered around three views: namely, new consumer values and identity, political reasons and power and the future role of technology. These views draw attention to where the authors conclude future discourses will lie.

Conceptual frameworks: a cognitive mapping approach

According to Pearce (2012), conceptual frameworks are used in various ways and in different forms but are, nonetheless, purposeful in addressing emerging, fragmented or broad themes. They identify and bind knowledge and form a framework to help researchers understand a particular phenomenon and thus make explanatory claims (Bergman, Karlsson and Axelsson 2010). Essentially, conceptual frameworks are concepts explained in diagrammatical form and indicating relationships through connections. Further, conceptual frameworks (as cited in Pearce 2012: 13) are '. . . not intended to be theories, but devices to map, categorize and communicate the diverse efforts of family researchers, practitioners and would be theorists' (Nye and Berado 1981: xxvi). And:

> Essentially, the conceptual framework is a structure that seeks to identify and present in a logical structure format, the key factors relating to the phenomena under investigation. Depending on the nature and purpose(s) of the research project, the conceptual framework may correlational or causal in form. (Brotherton 2008: 78)

One way to represent conceptual frameworks is through the use of cognitive maps. Cognitive maps are mental representations of an individual's understanding of a series of psychological transformations. Applied as a research methodology, cognitive maps are used to represent the cognition of researched thoughts utilizing a series of links in the form of a map or picture. Jones (1993: 11) states that a cognitive map:

> Is a collection of ideas (concepts) and relationships in the form of a map. Ideas are expressed by short phrases which encapsulate a single notion and, where appropriate, an opposite notion. The relationships between ideas are described by linking them together in either a causal or connotative manner.

The method used by the authors is drawn from Eden and Ackermann's (1998) process of cognitive mapping, which they apply in the area of strategic management. Cognitive mapping is derived from the methodological framework Personal Construct Theory (PCP) (Kelly 1955). PCP theory of personality was developed by the psychologist George Kelly in the 1950s and was used to help patients discover their own 'constructs' through a depth repertory grid conversation process (Ensor, Robertson and Ali-Knight 2007; Fransella and Bannister 1977). The repertory grid process – as an eliciting process, entirely dependent on the respondent – has the advantage of minimal intervention or interpretation. The repertory grid has been adapted for various uses within organizations (Jankowicz 1995), including decision-making and interpretation of other people's world-views – and more recently in the analysis of the perceptions of festival leaders (Ensor, Robertson and Ali-Knight 2007, 2011).

Eden and Ackermann's (1998) approach to cognitive mapping is focussed on the idea of concepts. Concepts are short phrases or words that represent a verb in which ideas are linked as cause/effect, or as means/end or as how/why. A cognitive map, then, is a representation of a respondent's perceptions about a situation. It relies on bipolar constructs, where the terms are seen as a contrast with each other. For example, 'event leadership . . . ' may lead to 'conservative leadership . . . radical leadership'. The result is not unlike an influence diagram or causal loop diagram, but is different in that it is explicitly subjective and uses constructs rather than variables (Mingers 2003). Cognitive mapping can also be used to record transcripts of interviews in a way that promotes analysis, questioning and understanding (Eden and Ackermann 1998). However, the literature on the application of cognitive mapping is often compromised, as researchers adapt the theory based upon their own skills and research philosophies (Yeoman 2004).

Decision explorer

A Computer Assisted Qualitative Data Analysis (CAQDAS) assists the researcher through the capturing and processing of concepts and data (Barry 1998), thus helping a modeller see the relationships, order and complexity of that researched. In addition, a CAQDAS approach allows the modeller to track changes and makes notes, which embodies the principles of grounded theory (Strauss and Corbin 1994). Decision Explorer (DE) (Jenkins 1998) is a CAQDAS tool in the form of cognitive mapping developed by the team at Strathclyde University (Eden and Ackermann 1998). DE allows a modeller to search for 'multiple viewpoints', 'the holding of concepts', 'tracing of concepts' and 'causal relationship management'. The tool allows the modeller to come to conclusions, connect thoughts and construct a purposeful interpretation of the phenomena researched that make sense (Levi-Strauss 1966; Weick 1979). What is critical to the success of DE is the ability to categorize concepts, values and emergent themes (Eden and Ackermann 1998), thus allowing the modeller to elicit data and code concepts. This approach to modelling and map building in tourism research is documented by Yeoman and Schänzel (2012); Yeoman and Watson (2011) and Yeoman, Munro and McMahon-Beattie (2006) using DE.

The contribution of each chapter

Chapter 2: Back to the future: analysing history to plan for tomorrow

According to Devine and Carruthers (2014), the twenty-first century will be a very competitive period for the events industry, as towns, cities and countries clamber to attract events and satisfy an increasingly discerning audience. Accordingly politics is one of the central features of this cognitive map (Figure 20.1) with the key concepts of 'political reasons . . . ', 'level of acceptable violence . . . ' and 'present day and technological revolution'. To succeed, event organizers must be strategic, i.e., manage politics and plan for the future. However, the future is unpredictable. There are no archives of the future through which we can trawl, nor can we interview participants in events that have yet to occur. However, event organizers

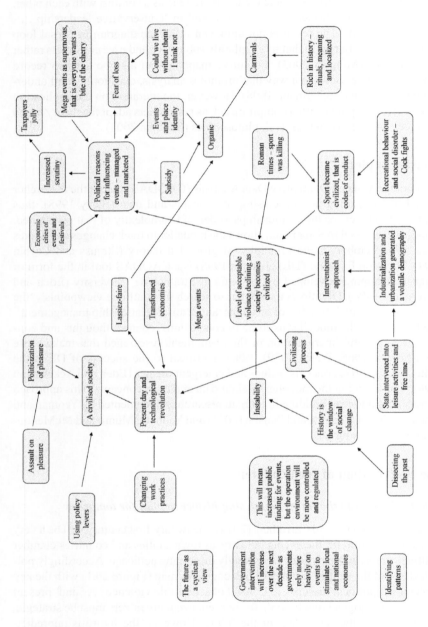

Figure 20.1 1: Back to the future: analysing history to plan for tomorrow

should not despair because history is an excellent way to think about and plan for the future. So futurists should and can use history to create a scenario that will help event organizers prepare for, and respond to, change. This was the approach the authors used in this chapter. Based on the scenario portrayed in this chapter, it is possible to ask whether event managers consider the following four areas in their planning for the future: increased regulation will require event organizers to strike a balance between risk and creativity; to influence policy makers and to achieve this, industry must speak with a united voice; treat the media as potential partners and supply it with good news stories that highlight the positive impacts of events; and evaluation should be a high priority for all event managers, and the findings should be disseminated to all stakeholders including government agencies.

Chapter 3: The forms of functions of planned events: past and present

Getz (2014) brings us back to the assumption that all kinds of events are important in the functioning of a human society. Events provide social, symbolic and economic exchange, and act as vehicles for personal development (see Figure 20.2). The key concepts identified in Getz's writings include 'social exchange', 'symbolic exchange', 'prediction – an ontological perspective', 'meaning', 'personal development', 'convergence' and 'divergence'. Getz starts by saying the forces of globalization, economic development and the increased legitimation of events as tools for public policy and industry strategy are propelling the growth of the events industry. Within this context, Getz (2014) identifies two important interrelated trends: that of *convergence* and *divergence* in the forms and functions of events. Larger, public events exhibit increasing convergence because they are being planned so as to meet multiple goals and attract wide audiences. Simultaneously, numerous events are being created within social worlds and for special-interest tourist segments. Taking these forces and trends into account, predictions are made in the form of a set of propositions that hold important implications for the future of planned events, their design and their management.

The contribution of Getz's chapter lies in the fact that convergence of forms and functions will be an increasingly important proposition in the near future. This is shaped by the forces of reality in which hallmark events have become part of the political landscape in which cities and destinations are co-branded. Accordingly events facilitate capital (social and cultural) for all parts of society.

Chapter 4: Scenarios for the future of events and festivals: Mick Jagger at 107 and Edinburgh Fringe

The contribution of Yeoman and colleagues (2014) is in the context of the need to understand what is coming, and to understand the underlying causes of change and how these changes interact with each other. The authors propose two scenarios, both set in 2050, as stories for discussion. The cognitive map (Figure 20.3) is

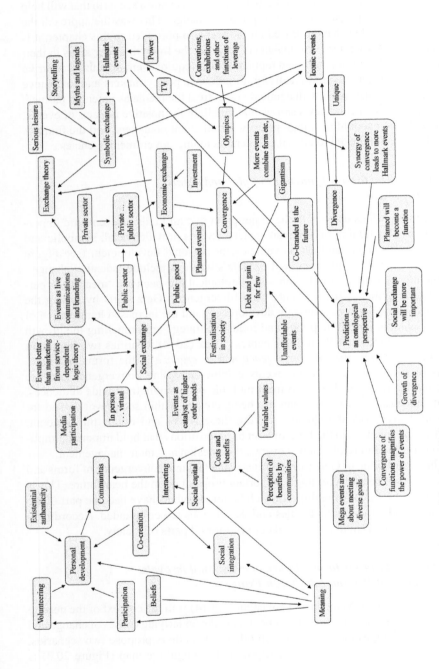

Figure 20.2 The forms and functions of planmed events

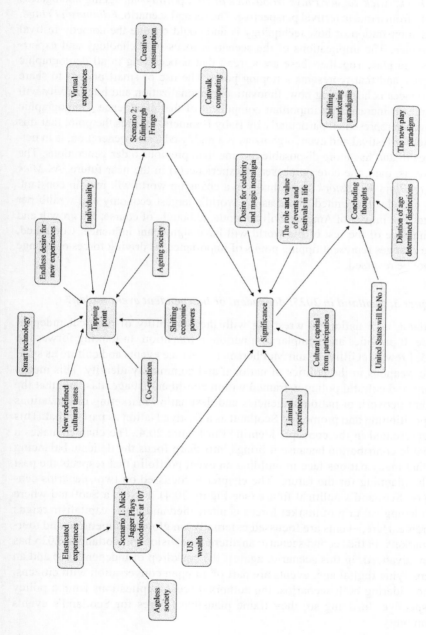

Figure 20.3 Scenarios for the future: Mick Jagger at 107 and the Edinburgh Festival Fringe

clustered around the drivers and scenarios portrayed in the chapter. First, *Heritage Rock: Mick Jagger Plays Woodstock at 107*, portrays an ageing and ageless society from a music festival perspective. The second scenario, *Edinburgh Fringe*, is a demonstration of how technology is and could change the comedy festival experience. The implications of the scenarios focus on technology and experiences and play. Together these are a trend that is occurring in all demographic groups – and that represents a tipping point. The use of smart phones to share experiences is happening now. Innovation, personalization and interactivity will become an increasingly important component of that experience. Demographic change, as represented particularly by Baby Boomers, extends the point that this market for festival and event organizers is a highly educated generation, is in better health and has more disposable income than previous older generations. The market is, then, the core purchaser of experience(s) in the near future. As *Mick Jagger Plays Woodstock* some things in a changing world will remain constant. This includes the United States as the world's largest economy and wealth per capita. The impact of America will continue; although, of course, the growth and significance of the rest of the world will have significant influence. Combined, these changes represent tipping points of importance, as driving forces of change cannot be reversed.

Chapter 5: Scotland in 2025: dependent or independent event nation?

Scotland, as a nation, is wrestling with the possibility of political independence. It provides an exemplar of a nation in transition. In looking forward to 2025, Frew, McGillivray and McPherson (2014) see events and culture as symbolic weapons in the politics of national and community identity. This means events and cultural policy is framed within neo-liberalist agendas, and that the current network of national agencies and destination marketing organizations are positioning and promoting Scotland as a Festive Nation as part of that. This is represented in the concepts identified in Figure 20.4. The chapter makes a valuable contribution because it brings into sharp focus the delicate balancing act that many nations face in building an event portfolio that respects the past whilst planning for the future. The chapter is focussed on two scenarios centred on Scotland's political future (see Figure 20.4). First is a Scotland where the ideological grip of market forces is intensified and hyper capitalism reigns supreme. Here, events are focussed externally, on global competition and tourist markets. In the second scenario an alternative vision of Scotland in 2025 has been advanced. In this scenario, against the backdrop of independence and an intensifying digital age, events are part of an open conversation with citizens. In considering both scenarios, the authors discuss implications from a policy perspective. In doing so, they frame plausible futures for Scotland's events community.

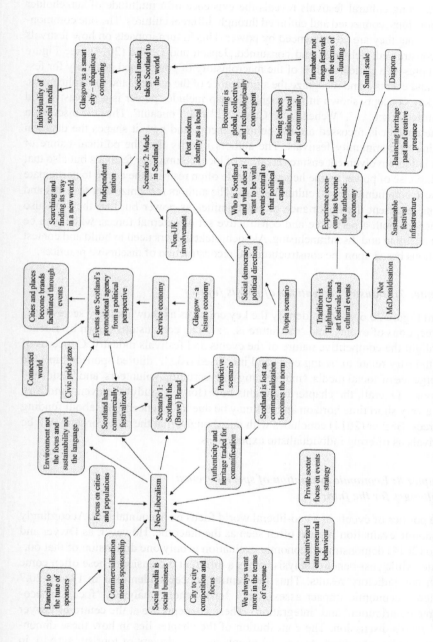

Figure 20.4 Scotland in 2025: dependent or independent event nation?

Chapter 6: The future power of decision making in community festivals

Researching cultural festivals reveals the existence of a multitude of stakeholder relationships, connected and enforced through different cultures. The one commonality is that they are all influenced by power. This in turn impacts on how festivals are constructed, delivered and consumed. Jepson and Clarke (2014) (see Figure 20.5) present a critical review of the macrohistory of power used generally for festival and events – and recognize the significance of the concept and its applications. The key concepts shown in the cognitive map include 'power is a pervasive and constructive set . . . ', 'Weber . . . ', 'Clegg . . . ' and 'Foucault'. Thus the discussion in the chapter is focussed around political theory and how it shapes the decision making of community festivals. The authors identify that the political nature of stakeholder involvement ensures creation of local community festivals but also that the exercise of power by the hegemonic state often restricts the desire to participate in these community-based cultural events. The authors recognize that festivals and events represent the importance of communities as power but that they are also influenced both a pervasive and constructive set of external forces, which can be both enabling and disenfranchising. As such, stakeholders need to build and contest positions based upon the construction and reconstruction of discursive practices.

Chapter 7: Industry perceptions of events futures

From Figure 20.6, we can identify the key concepts as 'how industry see events', 'perceptions of events' and 'the future is. . . '. The conclusions drawn by Backer highlight the competitive nature of the events and festivals industry. Concerns of the industry relate to 'rising costs and increased risks', 'diluted sponsorship', the emergence of social media, 'maintaining and recruiting volunteers' and 'residents' support'. Overall, the chapter highlights how (for this study) the events industry has a very short time horizon and this may be due to the uncertainty about funding sources. Backer (2014) concludes with one thought, that the only constant will be festivals as offering individualistic experiences.

Chapter 8: Economic evaluation of special events: challenges for the future

The politics of events in a neo-liberal world focus on accountability. Accordingly economic evaluation is most often seen as the outcome. However, as Dwyer and Jago (2014) demonstrate, economic evaluation is only one dimension of that outcome, while cost-benefit analysis brings a different dimension. These often come with contradictory results. Thus the central concepts identified in Figure 20.7 include 'economic impact assessment', 'cost-benefit analysis', 'focus on economic contribution' and 'integration'. These concepts are at the centre of Dwyer and Jago's discussion. The contribution of the chapter lies in how these dimensions can be integrated. As special events are key drivers of tourism activity in many destinations around the world and the staging of special events is often dependent on the financial or in-kind support of the public sector support, it is critical for the long-term viability of special events that it is possible to demonstrate

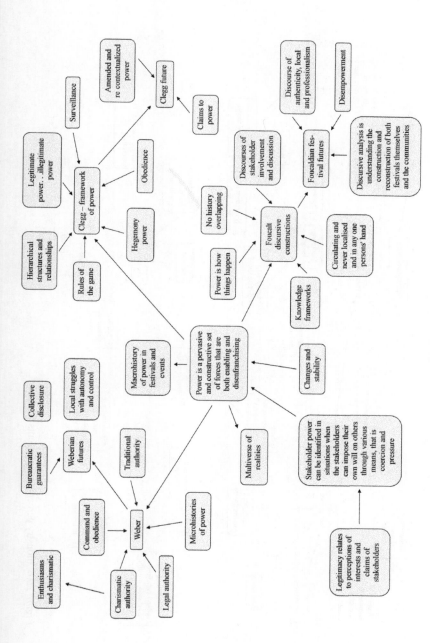

Figure 20.5 The future power of decision making in community festivals

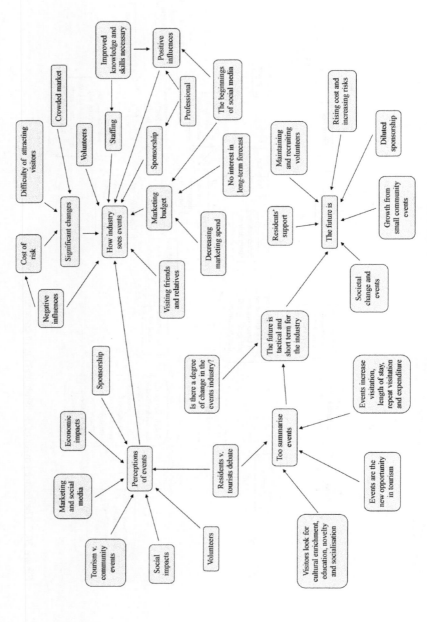

Figure 20.6 Industry perceptions of events futures

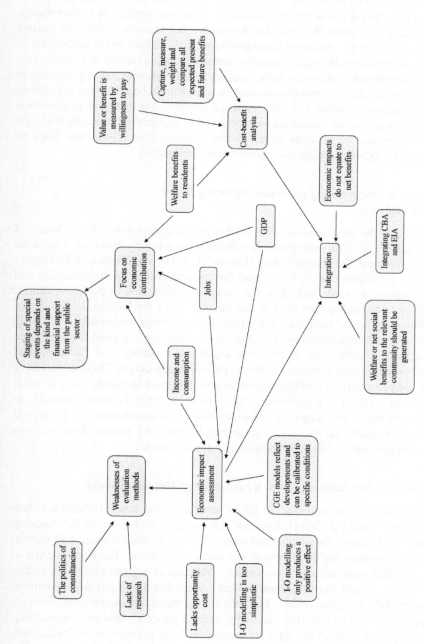

Figure 20.7 Economic evaluation of special events: challenges for the future

their contribution to the host community in credible ways. Although special events have broad-based impacts involving economic, social and environmental dimensions, it is often the case that decisions – for reasons of political interest and accountability – focus on economic aspects. So where event assessment is focussed on economic impact alone the assessment is too narrow in scope to provide sufficient information for policy makers and government funding agencies to use effectively. More comprehensive approaches should be employed to embrace the importance of social and environmental impacts – as additions to economic impacts. In particular, estimation tools required to measure welfare effects associated with special events need more detailed attention from researchers. Thus, as Figure 20.7 indicates, integration is the central philosophy.

Chapter 9: The greening of events: exploring future trends and issues

Considering the importance of climate change and sustainability, Frost, Mair and Laing (2014) use a drivers approach to explain the greening of events. This is the central feature of the cognitive map (Figure 20.8). The significance of the chapter is that it highlights current trends and drivers with respect to sustainability and the greening of events and, thus, the creation of scenarios as potential futures. Eight key drivers are identified in this chapter. They are 'economic and demographic inequities', 'increasing urbanization', 'existential authenticity', a 'rise in environmental consciousness', 'the regulatory paradigm', 'a trend towards green communities', a 'growth in corporate social responsibility' and 'technological developments' (such as social media and mobile phone usage). These drivers have been used to create four different scenarios with respect to events. They involve, firstly, the creation of a coalition of cities to bid for mega events; secondly, an imperative that events play their part in addressing climate change; thirdly, the use of events as platforms for social change and, fourthly, the demise of mega events and the consequential focus on smaller community events.

Chapter 10: The future is green: a case study of Malmoe, Sweden

Using Malmoe as a metaphor for future benchmarking, where the driver is sustainability, Wessblad (2014) describes the concepts and some of the roadmap of making Malmoe, Sweden's third largest city, a sustainable event and festival place. It considers the environment and social dimensions. The key concepts of the cognitive map include 'movements', 'Malmoe as a green place', 'Greening Malmoe . . . ' and 'for the future present'. Wessblad draws out four prominent features of the greening project. First of all, inspiration is about personal commitment, striving for an enduring society by taking a personal stand on sustainability. Secondly, it is voicing the topic of sustainability in the context of institutions. Thirdly, it is about promoting sustainability 'evangelism' inside the municipality in which engagement creates progress. Finally, progress takes time. These are part of a roadmap (see Figure 20.9), and events are part of the journey to a green future in which communities themselves are the driving forces of change.

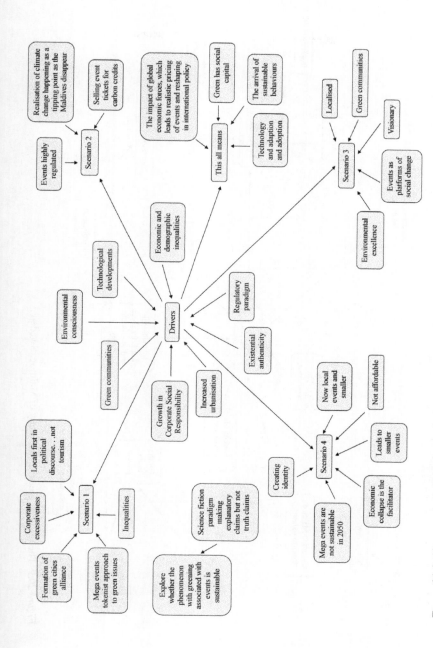

Figure 20.8 The greening of events: exploring future trends and issues

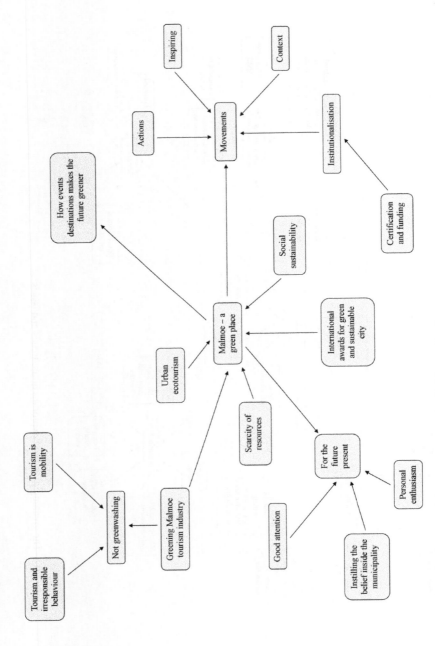

Figure 20.9 The future is green: a case study of Malmoe, Sweden

Chapter 11: The future of local community festivals and meanings of place in an increasingly mobile world

What makes a festival special given the homogeneity and sameness of many urban and mobile event environments? McClinichey and Carmichael (2014) draw relevance from community constructs through the lens of the Kitchener-Waterloo Multicultural Festival. Using a model of a space of flow, the authors cleverly show that festivals need to be grounded in order to create a sense of place. From Figure 20.10, we can see that festivals allow culture to flow by maintaining cultural ties through ethnic group organizations communication, through performance, through practice, through music, through costumes, through ethnic food and crafts and by encouraging travel to the country of origin. Thus, despite the globalization process that surrounds them, festivals can combat feelings of placelessness. Festivals allow cultures to be showcased and also connect participants with the next generation, and act as connection between communities. Finally, festivals allow a flow and connection geographically to the rest of the world, in which food products like spices, chocolate or sweets, clothing, fabrics or music are displayed. The chapter thus demonstrates festivals as fluid rather than static embryos in a local but global world.

Chapter 12: Developing brand relationship theory for festivals: a study of the Edinburgh Festival Fringe

Todd (2014) illustrates the relevance of the brand relationship paradigm to future festivals through the present setting of the Edinburgh Festival Fringe. It provides a predictive forecast of significance, festival-consumer brand relationships and highlights consumers' symbolic engagement with festival brands. As a foundation, the author recognizes the shifts occurring in festival marketing, production and consumption. In an increasingly competitive environment, Todd proposes that brand equity is becoming the distinguishing factor determining engagement. As increased consumerism is taking power from brand owners, festival goers are becoming increasingly individualized. Festival brands are correspondingly co-created with festival goers and other stakeholders rather than managed by their owner. This is also influenced by accessibility, by the growing ease of digital communications and because social networking has allowed society to become increasingly interconnected (Figure 20.11). The contribution this chapter makes is represented most clearly in a number of its conclusions. This includes the observation that brands are no longer made by organizations but are, rather, constructed in a space in which organizations are influencers and listeners. This, it is concluded, will lead to a greater festival market in virtual, physical and combined worlds. Further, in developing future festival brand concepts managers must build profitable, mutually beneficial and reciprocal relationships with consumers through effectively leveraging functional, symbolic and experiential conceptual brand dimensions. The present Fringe-consumer brand relationship typology provides evidence of such brand relationships within the setting of a festival-consumer setting and this is of relevance to successful future festival brand managers. In

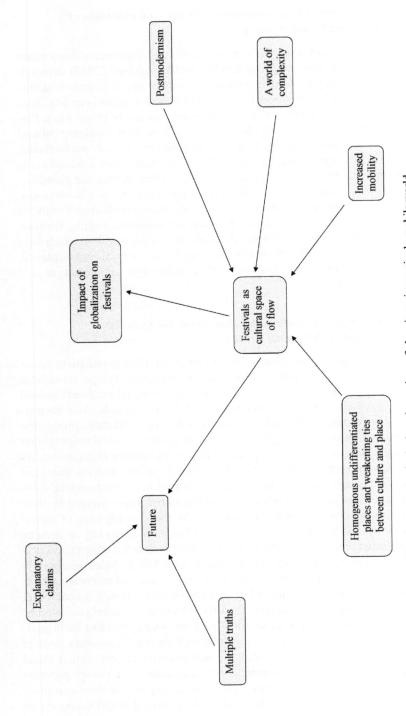

Figure 20.10 The future of local community festivals and meanings of place in an increasingly mobile world

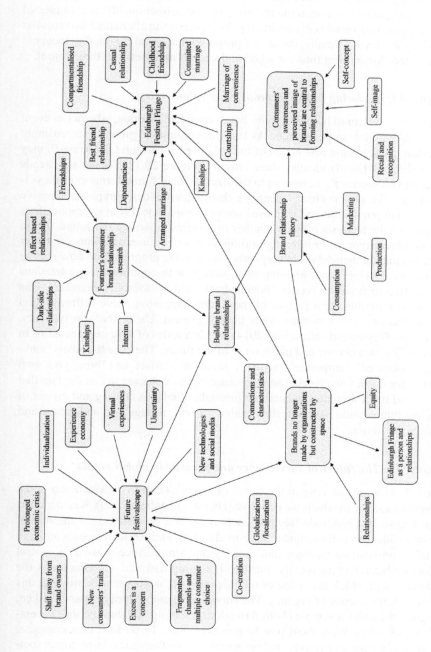

Figure 20.11 Developing brand relationship theory for festivals

considering Fournier's (2009) measures of love and passion; self-concept connection; interdependence; commitment; intimacy and partner quality, it is suggested there are potential benefits in considering this matrix as an alternative to consumer brand loyalty levels. Finally, the author proposed that brand personality theory is a useful tool for shaping future marketing decisions as a means to future proof.

Chapter 13: Exploring future forms of event volunteering

Events are a system of human activity based upon participation, whether as event goers, stakeholders or performers. As festivals continue to grow, an increasingly important participation role is that of the volunteer, for which Lockstone-Binney and colleagues (2014) identify three clusters (Figure 20.12). These are 'trends affecting volunteering', 'according to the size . . . ' and 'future forms of event volunteering'. The authors clearly identify a changing set of demographics, inclusive of an ageing population and increased use of leisure time. From an implications perspective the analysis offers a number of insights regarding the future. These include observation as to how high-profile and well-resourced events are better placed to market themselves to corporate volunteering programs and how regular events can develop good, ongoing relationships with community organizations and local companies to recruit 'bounce-back' and outsourced volunteers. The volunteer scenarios are a picture of the future, suggesting more differentiation and segmentation of volunteer types than at present. Using scenario typology, Lockstone-Binney and colleagues (2014) profile a series of volunteer scenarios in order to illustrate change and make sense of the future. They use the labels 'junkies', 'outsourced', 'corporate', 'virtual', 'invisible', 'offset' and 'bring your own (BYO)' for event volunteers. The significance of this chapter lies in the fact that it is one of the few studies to combine foresight of what is coming and insight of how the future could play out, thus enabling event managers to understand and manage the future.

Chapter 14: The future of surveillance and security in global events

Bajc (2014) brings security to the centre of events debate in consideration of the Orwellian society in which we now live (Hier & Greenberg 2009). Key concepts from Figure 20.13 include 'security meta-ritual is a process . . . ', 'the role of planned collective activity under controlled events' and 'security events order. . . '. Bajc's proposition is, thus, that security and surveillance is used to control collective behaviour in society. Further, it is proposed that surveillance is the means through which the vision of order is imposed, while security provides this ambition with a sense of urgency. The surveillance and security apparatus, then, imagines the order it imposes both through data mining and through the processing of this information about past human behaviour. To do so it uses computer modelling, statistical analysis, and computational mathematics. In so doing, society and its apparatus impose and create a vision of a new social relation, which the author calls a security meta-ritual. This transforms social and physical spaces

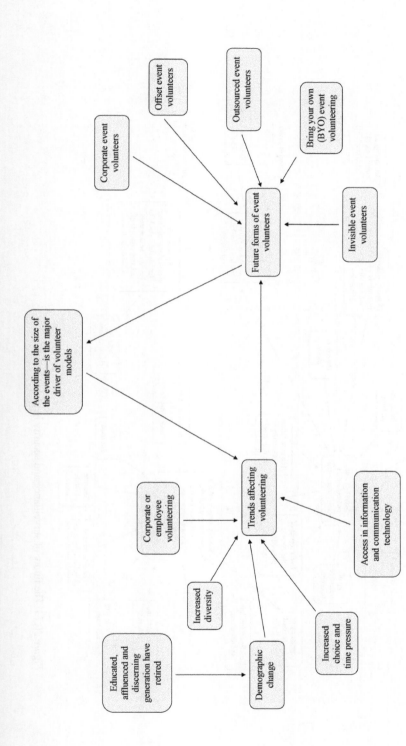

Figure 20.12 Exploring future forms of event volunteering

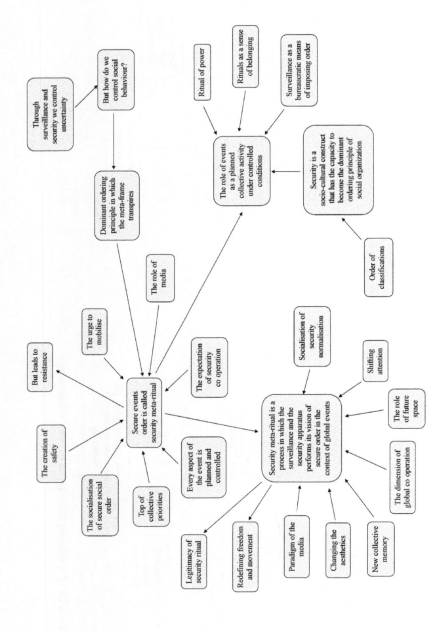

Figure 20.13 The future of surveillance and security in global events

into a sterile zone of safety within every citizen's movement and in which communication is controlled. Post–9/11 the security and surveillance discourse has changed and has created a legitimacy that has compromised the Founding Fathers' principles. In a security-sanctioned order of the future, people will be divided into insiders and outsiders, those who will be allowed to participate at the event and all others who will be barred from attending. From an events perspective, order is now the culture that shapes and changes the events experience – bringing us closer to Orwell's Big Brother society.

Chapter 15: A perspective on the near future: mobilizing events and social media

Focussing on mobile applications (apps) and social media, Bolan (2014) examines how the use of digital media technology will not just impact on the future of events but will fundamentally change their nature and structure. The key concepts identified from Figure 20.14 include the 'virtual experiences', 'marketing and promoting an event', 'digital media technology' and 'enhancing the event experience'. As the key word is technology, the significance of the chapter is in the identification that the implications of such technology are an underresearched area in the field of events and event management despite the significance of the subject. Research in this area can provide a crucial and necessary developmental benefit to the planning and promotion of events, as well as contributing to the enhancement of the event experience itself. The future of events is, then, inextricably tied with mobile digital technology and a desire of the public for constant and immediate use of social media platforms. As such this chapter discusses how and why such technology needs to be utilized more and the potential benefits it can bring. The chapter also sets the scene for future research in the vital area.

Chapter 16: The future is virtual

From Figure 20.15, the key concepts are 'justification', 'AR . . . ', 'concerns about the replacement of real experiences' and 'the future'. Sadd (2014) provides an insight into the world of Italian futurism with a focussed on technology – and its likely impact on events and society. This draws on the evidence that the consumption of events has become (or is becoming) one in which people are immersed in an experience. Already, it is possible to enter a world of computer games in 3D and, through unique headsets, a virtual world of entertainment where one is part of the experience. There are silent discos, holograms and animation available. But will events of the future utilize these new developments? Sadd doesn't present a dystopian future but an explanation of what is coming next and why – something that is virtual, immersed and complementary. Technology is now transforming every aspect of our lives, and in particular generation 'C' (Solis 2012) thrives on its evolution. As our lives are becoming more dependent upon advances in technology, the question is asked, what will events of the future be able to offer in relation to experience and transformation? Ever more remarkable, technological

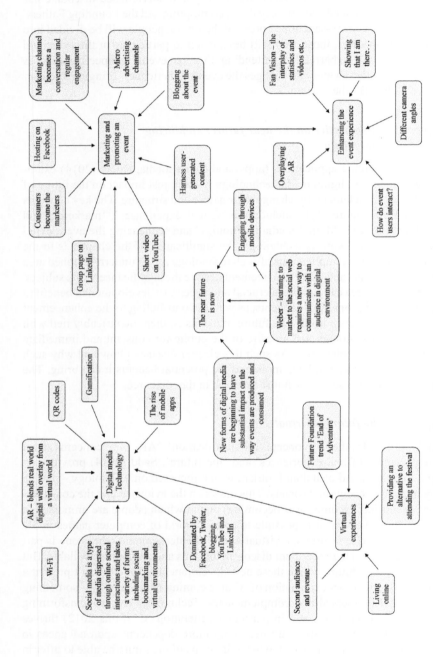

Figure 20.14 A perspective of the near future: mobilizing events and social media

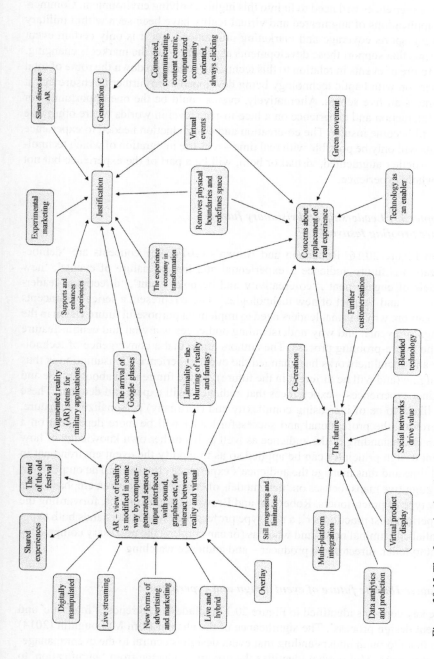

Figure 20.15 The future is virtual

developments are being delivered on a daily basis. Accordingly the design of event experiences will need to fit into this highly evolving environment. Commercial applications of augmented and virtual reality have been seen within military training, sports coverage and marketing promotions, yet it is only certain event concepts that support those developments at present – but the market is changing. The future of events in relation to this technology could go down the route of total immersion with haptic technology being developed even further to ensure that it embraces all five senses. Alternatively, events could be the one opportunity for real interaction and experience on a face-to-face level in worlds where otherwise we will become insular. The co-creation and co-production needed to experience events will only be possible with real time – real-life integration of which technology, whether augmented, virtual or both, will be a part of the experience but not the whole experience.

Chapter 17: Leadership and visionary futures: future proofing festivals

From Figure 20.16, Robertson and Brown's (2014) key concepts are 'democratization', 'future audience', 'experiential and liminal nature of events', 'new models of engagement', 'co-creativity and bespoke event', 'directional leadership . . . ' and 'impact of new technologies'. These represent a series of concepts that capture why it is that leaders need to implement purposeful future vision in the design of events, and why understanding audiences is a vital and central feature of the future-proofing process. The authors argue that a convergence of technology and social networks has changed the event experience. Consumption is thus changing (and will be different in the future). So the future is all about unique and distinct experiences – experiences that audiences will expect and demand. These are likely to be of increasing complexity and (for many) personalized in nature. Therefore, the professional and successful leader will be more dependent on a deep understanding of the audience as well as his or her own knowledge of how event design principles can be applied so as to modify the event environment in real time and thus manage the audience's experience effectively. The output from the cognitive maps focuses on 'new models of engagement' with an emphasis on a new type of practitioners. Robertson and Brown elaborate on this, forwarding the 'experientialist practitioner', a new type professional who understands both experiential and liminal needs and who has (or can employ) the necessary competency of storyteller, director and producer – and audience watching.

Chapter 18: The future of event design and experience

The key concepts identified in Figure 20.17 include 'megatrends', 'futuristic' and 'event design process'. The significance of the chapter from McLoughlin (2014) lies in a thorough understanding that event design is central to the event management process. McLoughin identifies the drivers of change from 'gamification' to 'social media', which drive a futurism paradigm of technological change. The

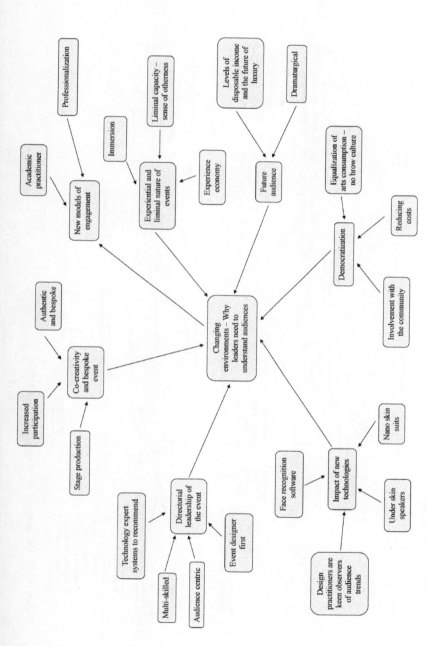

Figure 20.16 Leadership and visionary futures: future proofing festivals

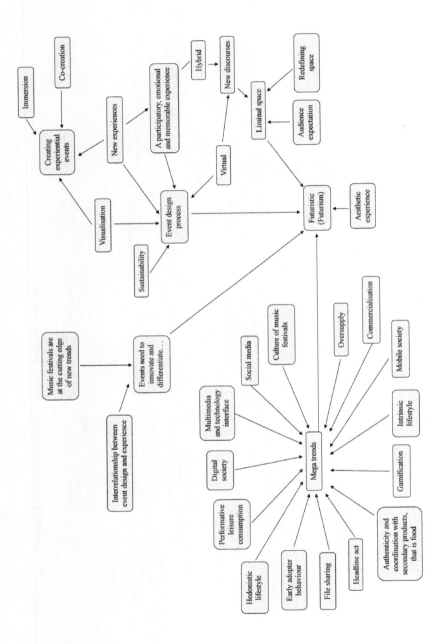

Figure 20.17 The future of event design and experience

role of technology is clearly changing the experience for the event goer with a more participatory, visual and experienctial event concept emerging. The chapter discusses a number of emerging concepts focussed on the event practitioner as a experientialist and the mutuality of co-creation. Fundamentally, McLoughlin reemphasizes continually that the relationship between event design and experience is evolutionary, as the external environmental forces change consumer behaviours and events are at the forefront of these changes in society.

Chapter 19: eScaping in the city: retailvents in socio-spatial managed futures

From Figure 20.18, the chapter focusses on the future relationship between events and retail, focussing on an explanation of the drivers of change. These are 'urban socio-spatial management', 'the ageing population' and 'technology and the retail industry'. The chapter uses a single scenario to propose a particular future as a demonstration of change. Robertson and Lees (2014) drive a series of proposals that the resilience of city development in Australia will be a creative culture driver of events in that country, stating that organized events and festivals with integration into city socio-spatial activity, inclusive of retail, will be the prominent discourse of events in the future. The authors are not stating that technology does not offer a dystopian future for events but that is a key shaper as both a supplement and core avenue of consumption in society. The author's trend analysis concludes with a range of social changes that will occur given the cities become creative hubs for populations and future wealth.

Developing an aggregate map of the future of events and festivals

The purpose of this section in the chapter is to demonstrate how a construction of the aggregate cognitive map took shape. Because of the complexity and subjectivity of the construction, the section is only an illustration of the process in order to guide readers' understanding of how the process happened. At this stage, all the chapters had an individual cognitive map. The merger of the individual cognitive maps into an aggregation is a process in which the researcher immerses into the maps and searches for concept connections – driven by semantic similarity. These allow the drawing out of key concepts from each individual map and remapping the concept Decision Explorer (DE). Once this is complete and after several iterations, an aggregate cognitive map is formed (see Figure 20.19).

As this aggregate map is complex, and given that are a great number of connections, DE has a number of features that allow the breaking up of the aggregate map into viewpoints. From this the researcher can build, explore and reflect on these maps as component parts of the total aggregate map. The 'central' command looks at specified band levels, which are connected to the concepts. This allows the researcher to view the importance of the length of linkage between concepts. Each concept is weighted according to how many concepts are traversed in each

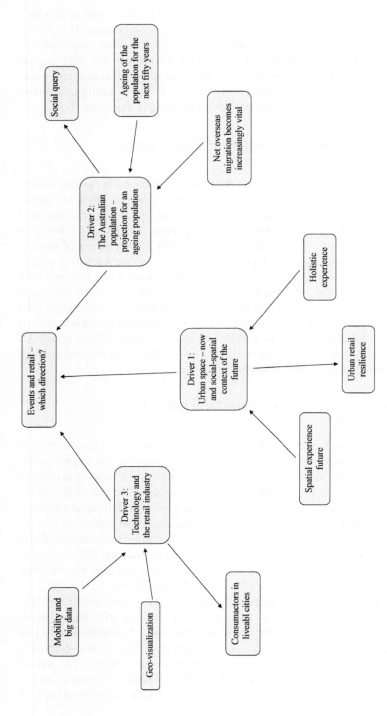

Figure 20.18 eScaping in city: Retailvents in socio-spatial managed futures

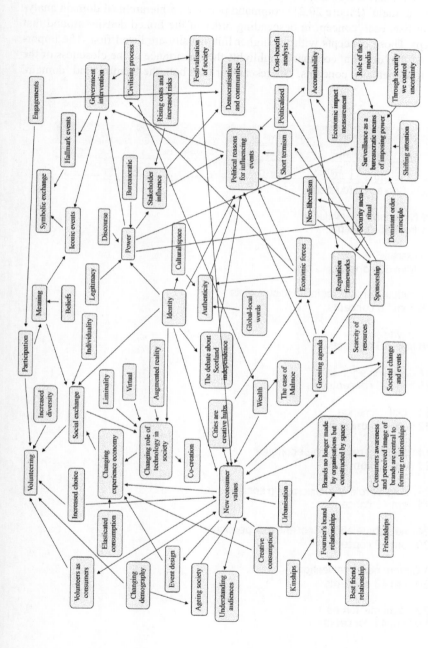

Figure 20.19 Aggregate map of events and festivals futures

band level. Fundamentally, the central command shows how many concepts are dependent upon one concept. Figure 20.20 demonstrates this view.

The 'domain' (Figure 20.21) command performs a hierarchical domain analysis that lists each concept in descending order of the linked density around that concept. Those concepts with the higher link density are listed first. The importance of the 'domain' command highlights the importance of the closeness of the local links between concepts. The researcher uses both the 'central' and 'domain'

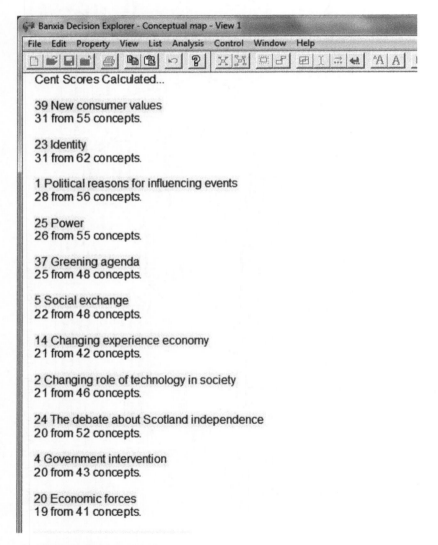

Figure 20.20 Central analysis

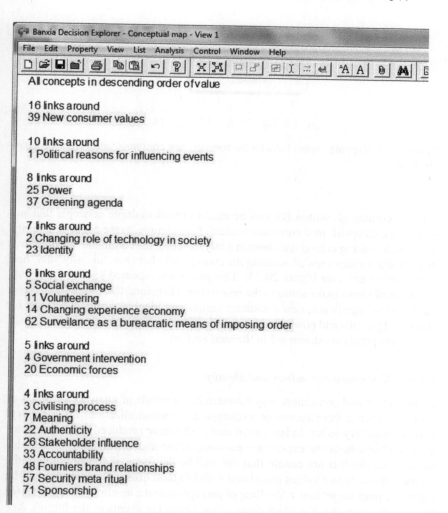

Figure 20.21 Domain analysis

commands as a means to identify the most important concepts in order to explore and construct maps. Further, both the 'central' and 'domain' commands identify a number of concepts to map in which the modeller makes a judgement to construct and explore these concepts while holding them as a central view.

Figure 20.22 shows a DE screen with the concept 'new consumer values'. By using the command 'show unseen links', the modeller is able to find the connection between the concepts and thus start to build and feel a cognitive map. From here the researcher can start to build a map, explore links and reflect upon them.

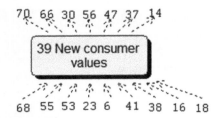

Figure 20.22 Mapping unseen links for the concept 'new consumer value' from the aggregate map

Other commands within DE can be used to recall multiple concepts that surround the concept of 'new consumer values'. For example, as the concept 'identity' was a high ranking central and domain analysis score, the command 'explore' was then used to build a view illustrating the connectivity between 'identity' and 'new consumer values' (see Figure 20.23). This process is repeated several times until a number of views make sense to the researcher. Therefore, three viewpoints were identified as significant, new consumer values and identity, political reasons for influencing events and power and future role of technology in events and festivals. These viewpoints are discussed in the next section.

View 1: New consumer values and identity

Consumption and consumers may resonate in the minds of many as attributes or skill sets arising from economic exchange and industrialization, i.e. a concept born of monetary value. Indeed, even many who have produced work that introduces and discusses the experience economy (Pine and Gilmore 2011) will also talk of this. But it is not certain that this will be the focus of consumption in the future. Creativity and values associated with life (and lifestyle) are changing. The aggregate map shows how a levelling of perception and a levelling of authority (or power) are exercising the researchers of the future (or events of the future). Age and other demographic shifts – alongside volunteerism and the use of technology – are seen to facilitate much of this change.

Consumption, both in respect to how people experience and how society consumes day to day is converging (Deuze 2007; Han, Chung and Sohn 2009; Hur, Yoo and Chung 2012). In melting the sharp and distinctive ways people have lived life in the past, forward to a more fluid set of activities in the future (where work and nonwork time divisions dissipate), the gluing effect of events offers a myriad of research perspectives. In looking at consumer values identities of consumers (and nonconsumers) may emerge. Events are both testing ground and barometer of that identity. As the contributing authors have shown, both consumption and identity cluster around the areas of managing and designing events, social and cultural influence and effect and psychological and technical, respectively. But these

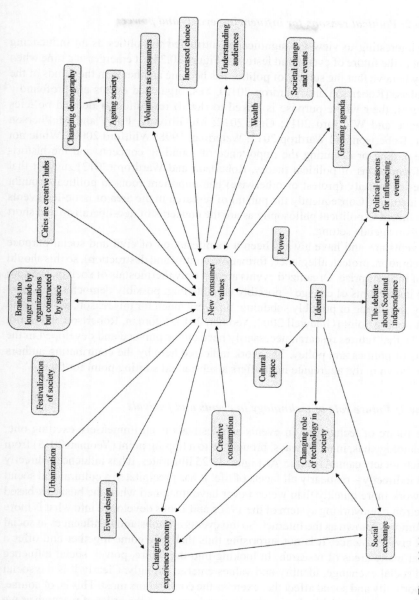

Figure 20.23 New consumer values and identity

The boxes in the figure read:

Changing demography

Ageing society

Volunteers as consumers

Increased choice

Understanding audiences

Wealth

Societal change and events

Greening agenda

Cities are creative hubs

Political reasons for influencing events

Brands no longer made by organizations but constructed by space

New consumer values

Power

Identity

The debate about Scotland independence

Festivalization of society

Cultural space

Urbanization

Creative consumption

Changing role of technology in society

Event design

Changing experience economy

Social exchange

are also linked (as the aggregate map Figure 20.19 shows) and evolving rapidly as an area of research. The future of events research in this area is a rich one indeed.

View 2: Political reasons for influencing events and power

It is interesting to view the significance attributed to politics as an influencing agent in the future of events and festivals (Figure 20.25). It emerges at a time when many believe that the subject of politics has become anathema in the minds of the populace (Robertson and Wardrop 2012). Yes, organized events are profoundly political; their whole purpose is linked to (local) resolution or defined policies (Dredge and Whitford 2011; Getz 2012; McGillivray, Foley and McPherson 2011; Robertson and Wardrop 2012; Waterman 1998; Whitford 2009). While not disregarding or disputing the importance of founding concepts and the historical foundations of political theory, Robertson and Wardrop (2012) suggest that issue-led activity (protest or otherwise) has important roots in political thought and ideology. Consequently the pursuit of research in the area of issue-led events is as linked to political philosophy as are the concerns of neo-liberalism and short termism agenda setting.

Events are and have always been a manifestation of civil and social purpose (celebration, protest, allegiance, formation, control and destruction), so this should be of little surprise. Organized events are not only thermostats of society; they are also instruments of change – possibly enlightening, possibly democratizing, possibly stupefying or possibly subduing. It is very much for this reason, as the world is at tipping point (Gladwell 2002; Yeoman 2013; Yeoman, Robertson and Smith 2012), that futures research necessarily needs to be pursued and developed in the areas of politics and policy. The work indicated here by the contributing authors and shown in the aggregate map offers a substantial starting point for that.

View 3: Future role of technology in events and festivals

The future of technology in events and festivals is an immensely exciting one. Technology has, in many ways, brought us to a tipping point (Yeoman 2013) from which society cannot reverse. As Figure 20.25 illustrates, it has influence – directly and indirectly – on nearly all facets of life. It has precipitated a cultural and social network more quickly than we can ever have imagined when the business-based electronic networking system of the 1950s and 1960s developed into what is more commonly known as the Internet. So too events are substantial influences in social and civil existence. It is not surprising thus that they come together and offer a great many areas of research. In looking into the future, power, social influence and social exchange, identity and values emerge strongly. Clearly it is the social opportunity and social affect that exercise the contributors most. This is, of course, entirely understandable. Rationalization and control is the order of research as we know it.

In looking at the 'the Internet of things', in which data and the capacity to manage that data has grown at a rate that would never have been envisioned

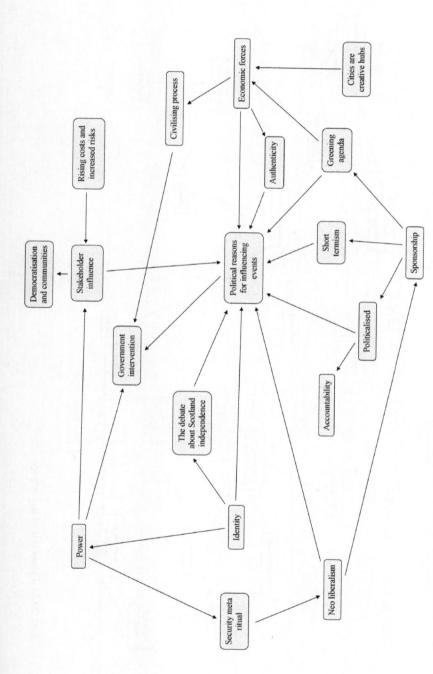

Figure 20.24 Political reasons for influencing events and power

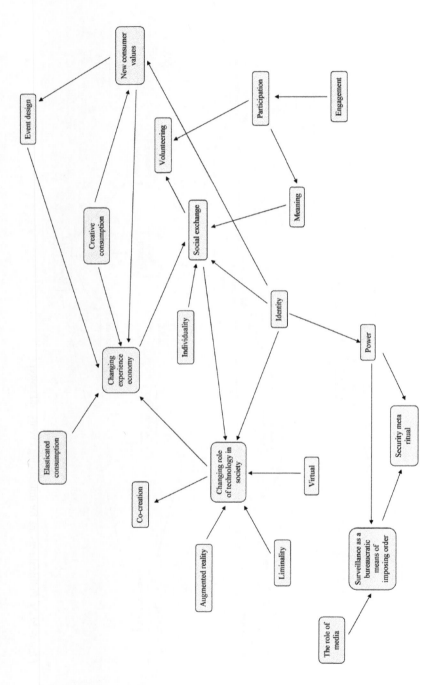

Figure 20.25 Future role of technology

when it first emerged, security and identity threat, theft and manipulation continues to be the axis of research and concern (Sarma and Girão 2009). While indeed some of those concerns may be apocryphal, this remains a very important area of research, and clearly spans many subject disciplines as well as research paradigms. Similarly though, social and consumption experience opportunity and how they influence identity and relationships is an area that continues to provide subjects to be researched. Technology, events and research clearly have a symbiotic relationship in the future. The contributions in this book and the aggregation of the research indicated in the maps should offer an important launching pad for that.

Concluding thoughts

This chapter is a pointer to where the future directions and discourse about the event industry will be and is a critical representation of experts' thoughts about future issues. The growth of events and festivals has been significant over the last decade, but they are not new. Events and festivals have a strong history, whether it is the first recorded Olympic Games in 776 BC or the beginnings of Edinburgh International Festival in 1948.

As Dator and Bezold (1981: 1) said:

> No one can predict the future (meaning the next 30 to 50 years). But policy-makers are forced to attempt to do so very frequently. From my experience, most decisions which affect development policies, for example, are based on wholly inadequate forecasts.

Thus, as Dator and Bezold illustrate, there is a need for policy makers not to view the future as an extension of the past and present but to look long term and understand how change is occurring, providing insight of patterns of change in order to predict, vision and shape the future as foresight. The contribution of this chapter lies in identifying the underlying principles, connections and spaces for the future in a comprehensive manner, thus bringing a robustness to the explanation process. The chapter identifies that future discourses will evolve around the concepts of 'new consumer values and identity', 'political reasons for influencing events and power' and 'future role of technology in events and festivals', thus addressing the chapter's question of 'what are the underlying layers, phenomena and spaces associated with the future of events and festivals'.

The phenomenal future of events and festivals is similar to futures in general and is complex, connected to the presented, blurred by viewpoints and history. It is of a heterogeneous nature, multidisciplinary with many ontologies and paradigms (Postma 2014). They are difficult to control and manage given the diversity of stakeholders, and no one person is in charge. In fact events and festivals are fundamentally shared visions, cooperatives and community partnerships. They are networks of people who have different reasons for acting out in their sphere. Governments cannot alone in the management of mega or

Hallmark events – community support is essential. And at the same time many events couldn't work without the support of government and agency, as the neo-liberal capitalist model usually doesn't work. Events and festivals are not like airlines or hotels, where revenue managers can forecast demand (Yeoman and Ingold 1997) – the industry is still embryonic in the terms of professionalization (Getz 2014; Robertson and Brown 2014) and diverse. The events and festivals industry is part of the wider experience economy and competes with many other forms of entertainment, both in the home and out of the home. As consumers are more knowledgeable, better informed and astute, these factors combine to increase uncertainty. However, events and festivals do have a future. This chapter and book is part of the development of the topic and subject – giving events and festivals a future studies paradigm.

References

Backer, E. (2014) 'Industry perceptions of events futures', in I. Yeoman, M. Robertson, U. McMahon-Beattie, E. Backer and K. Smith (eds.) *The Future of Events and Festivals*. Oxford: Routledge.

Bajc, V. (2014) 'The future of surveillance and security in global events', in I. Yeoman, M. Robertson, U. McMahon-Beattie, E. Backer and K. Smith (eds.) *The Future of Events and Festivals*. Oxford: Routledge.

Barry, C.A. (1998) 'Choosing qualitative data analysis software: Atlas/ti and Nudist compared', *Sociological Research Online*, 3(3). Online. Available: <http://socresonline.org.uk/3/3/4.html>

Bolan, P. (2014) 'A perspective on the near future: mobilizing events and social media" in I. Yeoman, M. Robertson, U. McMahon-Beattie, E. Backer and K. Smith (eds.) *The Future of Events and Festivals*. Oxford: Routledge.

Bergman, A., Karlsson, J. and Axelsson, J. (2010) 'Truth claims and explanatory claims: an ontology of future studies', *Futures*, 42(6): 857–65.

Brotherton, B. (2008) *Researching Hospitality and Tourism: a student guide*. London: Sage.

Devine, A. and Carruthers, C. (2014) 'Back to the future: analysing history to plan for tomorrow', in I. Yeoman, M. Robertson, U. McMahon-Beattie, E. Backer and K. Smith (eds.) *The Future of Events and Festivals*. Oxford: Routledge.

Dator, J. and Bezold, C. (1981) *Judging the Future*. Honolulu: University of Hawaii Press.

Dredge, D. and Whitford, M. (2011) 'Event tourism governance and the public sphere', *Journal of Sustainable Tourism*, 19(4–5): 479–99.

Deuze, M. (2007) 'Convergence culture in the creative industries', *International Journal of Cultural Studies*, 10(2): 243.

Dwyer, L. and Jago, L. (2014) 'Economic evaluation of special events: challenges for the future', in I. Yeoman, M. Robertson, U. McMahon-Beattie, E. Backer and K. Smith (eds.) *The Future of Events and Festivals*. Oxford: Routledge.

Eden, C. and Ackermann, F. (1998) *Journey Making*. London: Sage.

Ensor, J., Robertson, M. and Ali-Knight, J. (2007) 'The dynamics of successful events: the experts' perspective', *Managing Leisure*, 12(2/3), 223–35.

Ensor, J., Robertson, M. and Ali-Knight, J. (2011) 'Eliciting the dynamics of leading a sustainable event: key informant responses', *Event Management*, 15(4): 315–27.

Fournier, S. (2009) 'Lessons learned about consumers' relationships with their brands', in D. MacInnis, C. Park and J. Priester (eds.) *Handbook of Brand Relationships*. New York: ME Sharpe Incorporated, pp. 5–23.

Fransella, F. and Bannister, D. (1977) *A Manual for Repertory Grid Technique*. London: Academic Press.

Frew, M. McGillivray, D. and McPherson, G. (2014) 'Scotland in 2025: dependent or independent event nation?', in I. Yeoman, M. Robertson, U. McMahon-Beattie, E. Backer and K. Smith (eds.) *The Future of Events and Festivals*. Oxford: Routledge.

Frost, W. Mair, J. and Laing, J. (2014) 'The greening of events: exploring future trends and issues', in I. Yeoman, M. Robertson, U. McMahon-Beattie, E. Backer and K. Smith (eds.) *The Future of Events and Festivals*. Oxford: Routledge.

Han, J.K., Chung, S.W. and Sohn, Y.S. (2009) 'Technology convergence: when do consumers prefer converged products to dedicated products?', *Journal of Marketing*, 73(4), 97–108.

Hier, S. and Greenberg, J. (2009) *Surveillance: power, problems and politics*. London: UBC Press.

Hur, W.-M., Yoo, J.-J. and Chung, T.-L. (2012) 'The consumption values and consumer innovativeness on convergence products', *Industrial Management & Data Systems*, 112(5): 688–706.

Getz, D. (2012) 'Event studies: discourses and future directions', *Event Management*, 16(2), 171–87.

Getz, D. (2014) 'The forms and functions of planned events: past and future', in I. Yeoman, M. Robertson, U. McMahon-Beattie, E. Backer and K. Smith (eds.) *The Future of Events and Festivals*. Oxford: Routledge.

Gladwell, M. (2002) *The Tipping Point: how little things can make a big difference*. Boston: Little Brown and Company.

Jankowicz, A.D. (1995) *Business Research Projects*. (2nd ed.) London: Chapman and Hall.

Jepson, A. and Clarke, A. (2014) 'The future power of decision making in community festivals', in I. Yeoman, M. Robertson, U. McMahon-Beattie, E. Backer and K. Smith (eds.) *The Future of Events and Festivals*. Oxford: Routledge.

Jenkins, M. (1998) 'The theory and practice of comparing casual maps', in C. Eden and J.C. Spender (eds.) *Managerial and Organizational Cognition*. London: Sage, pp. 231–250.

Jones, M. (1993) *Decision Explorer: reference manual version 3.1*. Glasgow: Banxia Software Limited.

Kelly, G.A. (1955) *The Psychology of Personal Constructs*. London: Weidenfeld and Nicholson.

Levi-Strauss, C. (1966) *The Savage Mind*. Chicago: University of Chicago Press.

Lockstone-Binney, L., Baum, T., Smith, K. and Holmes, K. (2014) 'Exploring future forms of event volunteering', in I. Yeoman, M. Robertson, U. McMahon-Beattie, E. Backer and K. Smith (eds.) *The Future of Events and Festivals*. Oxford: Routledge.

McClinchey, K. and Carmichael, B. (2014) 'The future of local community festivals and meanings of place in an increasingly mobile world', in I. Yeoman, M. Robertson, U. McMahon-Beattie, E. Backer and K. Smith (eds.) *The Future of Events and Festivals*. Oxford: Routledge.

McGillivray, D., Foley, M. and McPherson, G. (2011) *Event policy: from theory to strategy*. Oxford: Routledge, Taylor & Francis.

McLoughlin, A. (2014) 'The future of event design and experience', in I. Yeoman, M. Robertson, U. McMahon-Beattie, E. Backer and K. Smith (eds.) *The Future of Events and Festivals*. Oxford: Routledge.

Mingers, J. (2003) 'A classification of the philosophical assumptions of management science', *Journal of the Operational Research Society*, 54(6): 559–70.

Nye, F. and Berado, F. (1981) *Emerging Conceptual Frameworks for Family Analysis*. New York: Praeger.

Pearce, D. (2012) *Frameworks for Tourism Research*. Wallingford: Cabi.

Pine, B.J. and Gilmore, J.H. (2011) *The Experience Economy* (updated version). Boston, Massachusetts: Harvard Business Review Press.

Postma, A. (2014) 'Anticipating the future of European tourism', in A. Postma, I. Yeoman and J. Oskam (eds.) *The Future of European Tourism*. Leeuwarden: Stenden University, pp. 290–305.

Robertson, M. and Brown, S. (2014) 'Leadership and visionary futures: future proofing festivals', in I. Yeoman, M. Robertson, U. McMahon-Beattie, E. Backer and K. Smith (eds.) *The Future of Events and Festivals*. Oxford: Routledge.

Robertson, M. and Lees, G. (2014) 'eScaping in the city: retail events in socio-spatial managed futures', in I. Yeoman, M. Robertson, U. McMahon-Beattie, E. Backer and K. Smith (eds.) *The Future of Events and Festivals*. Oxford: Routledge.

Robertson, M. and Wardrop, K. (2012) 'Festival and events, government and spatial governance', in S. Page and J. Connell (eds.) *The Handbook of Events*. London: Routledge, pp. 489–506.

Sadd, D. (2014) 'The future is virtual', in I. Yeoman, M. Robertson, U. McMahon-Beattie, E. Backer and K. Smith (eds.) *The Future of Events and Festivals*. Oxford: Routledge.

Sarma, A. and Girão, J. (2009) 'Identities in the future Internet of things', *Wireless Personal Communications*, 49(3): 353–63.

Solis, B. (2012) *Meet Generation C: the connected customer*. Online. Available: <www.briansolis.com/2012/04/meet-generation-c-the-connected-customer/> (accessed 24 August 2013).

Strauss, A. and Corbin, J. (1994) 'Grounded methodology: an overview', in N. Denzin and Y. Lincoln (eds.) *Handbook of Qualitative Research*. London: Sage, pp. 262–72.

Todd, L. (2014) 'Developing brand relationship theory for festivals: a study of the Edinburgh Festival Fringe', in I. Yeoman, M. Robertson, U. McMahon-Beattie, E. Backer and K. Smith (eds.) *The Future of Events and Festivals*. Oxford: Routledge.

Waterman, S. (1998) 'Carnivals for elites? The cultural politics of arts festivals', *Progress in Human Geography*, 22(1): 54–74.

Weick, K.E. (1979) *The Social Psychology of Organizing*. New York: Random House.

Wessblad, H. (2014) 'The future is green: a case study of Malmoe, Sweden', in I. Yeoman, M. Robertson, U. McMahon-Beattie, E. Backer and K. Smith (eds.) *The Future of Events and Festivals*. Oxford: Routledge.

Whitford, M. (2009) 'A framework for the development of event public policy: facilitating regional development', *Tourism Management*, 30(5), 674–82.

Yeoman, I. (2004) *The Development of a Soft Operations Conceptual Framework*. PhD Thesis. Edinburgh Napier University.

Yeoman, I. (2012) *2050: Tomorrow's Tourist*. Bristol: Channelview.

Yeoman, I. (2013) 'A futurist's thoughts on consumer trends shaping future festivals and events', *International Journal of Event and Festival Management*, 4(3), 249–60.

Yeoman, I. and Ingold, A. (1997) *Yield Management: strategies for the service industries*. New York: Continuum Press

Yeoman, I., Munro, C. and McMahon-Beattie, U. (2006) 'Tomorrow's: world, consumer and tourist', *Journal of Vacation Marketing*, 12(2), 174–90.

Yeoman, I., Robertson, M., McMahon-Beattie, U. and Mysarurwa, N. (2014) 'Scenarios for the future of events and festivals: Mick Jagger at 107 and the Edinburgh Fringe', in I. Yeoman, M. Robertson, U. McMahon-Beattie, E. Backer and K. Smith (eds.) *The Future of Events and Festivals*. Oxford: Routledge.

Yeoman, I., Robertson, M. and Smith, K. (2012) 'A futurist's view on the future of events', in S.J. Page. and J. Connel (eds.) *The Routledge Handbook of Events*. Oxon: Routledge, pp. 507–25.

Yeoman, I. and Schanzel, H. (2012) 'The future of family tourism: a cognitive mapping approach', in H. Schanzel, I. Yeoman and E. Backer (eds.) *Family Tourism: multidisciplinary perspective*. Bristol: Channelview, pp. 171–93.

Yeoman, I. and Watson, S. (2011) 'Cognitive maps of tourism and demography: contributions, themes and further research', in I. Yeoman, C. Hsu, K. Smith and S. Watson (eds.) *Tourism and Demography*. Oxford: Goodfellows, pp. 209–36.

Endnote

Delivering for Scotland post-2014

Paul Bush, OBE
Chief Operating Officer, EventScotland

EventScotland, the lead public body for events in Scotland, celebrated ten years of work in the industry in 2013. A decade of development and growth has positioned Scotland on the world-stage, and with the hosting of the Commonwealth Games and The Ryder Cup in 2014, Scotland will benefit from increased profile and significant economic impacts through event tourism.

Looking back on EventScotland's ten-year history we can be proud of how far we have come, and also excited about the future direction and landscape. However, what is clear is that we cannot afford to stand still. We must continue to innovate; we must not be complacent; and we must continue to raise the bar across our portfolio to ensure Scotland retains its position on the international stage. Hence the importance of this book by Dr Ian Yeoman and colleagues in providing foresight of what is coming next and insight of how this will happen.

Post-2014 Scotland's reputation as a global events destination will be greater than ever before. New and improved infrastructure following the Commonwealth Games presents Scotland with the opportunity to host events that would not previously have been possible, including track cycling and diving. The new Hydro Arena in Glasgow is up there with the world's best indoor venues and will host the 2014 MTV EMA.

However, the next few years will not be without their challenges. As we have seen a number of times, countries, which have hosted major multi-sport games, have struggled to maintain momentum. There are a number of contributing factors to why that might happen, including time, budget and resource issues; sustained capacity and capability for delivery; relationships and reputation with rights holders; lack of appetite or vision; and increased competition. From the outset Scotland wanted to make sure this wouldn't happen in 2015 and beyond.

With three world (gymnastics, IPC swimming, orienteering) and two European (eventing, judo) championships, alongside the return of the Open Championship and the Women's British Open, a strong sports programme has already been secured. We are also proud to be presenting the Turner Prize in Glasgow for the very first time, which will be a wonderful addition to Scotland's cultural portfolio for the year.

In 2015 Scotland will also launch a refreshed national events strategy, which will set the agenda for events through 2020. Maintaining momentum, focus, and sustainable growth will be everyone's business, and EventScotland will continue to lead in attracting, bidding for, and securing major events.

Domestically, Scotland must continue to make the most of key assets such as Edinburgh's festivals and our position as The Home of Golf, which are incredibly important in driving our industry. Our focus now is on 2016 onwards, where events must work harder than ever to stay ahead of the field.

The current economic climate will certainly play a part, coupled with increased competition – including the BRIC nations (Brazil, Russia, India, China) and other emerging nations and regions such as the Middle East, Soviet Bloc, Africa, and South America – which will make the marketplace tougher.

There are a number of uncertainties looking into the future, but what is important is how we prepare for that future. *The Future of Events and Festivals* plays a significant part in opening up the debate about the future (including Scotland's), we hope you have enjoyed the journey.

Index